Winston Churchill

A
Life
in
the
News

Winston
Churchill

RICHARD TOYE

OXFORD
UNIVERSITY PRESS

OXFORD
UNIVERSITY PRESS

Great Clarendon Street, Oxford, OX2 6DP,
United Kingdom

Oxford University Press is a department of the University of Oxford.
It furthers the University's objective of excellence in research, scholarship,
and education by publishing worldwide. Oxford is a registered trade mark of
Oxford University Press in the UK and in certain other countries

First Edition published in 2020

Impression: 1

Published in the United States of America by Oxford University Press
198 Madison Avenue, New York, NY 10016, United States of America

British Library Cataloguing in Publication Data
Data available

Library of Congress Control Number: 2019947977

ISBN 978–0–19–880398–0

Printed and bound in Great Britain by
Clays Ltd, Elcograf S.p.A.

Acknowledgements

No book is an island. It would not have been possible for me to complete this one had it not been for the help and support of a large number of individuals and organizations. I would like to thank all my colleagues at the University of Exeter. Gajendra Singh gave me helpful information about the Indian press. Nick Terry was an excellent source of advice on the German media. Andrew David generously helped me by tracking down material at the Howard Gotlieb Center. Many other people—too many to record in detail—gave me useful hints and suggestions. Arddun Hedydd Arwyn kindly provided a translation from Welsh.

I conceived and wrote the book in parallel with teaching a new third-year module on News, Media, and Communication. I initially taught it with Sara Barker, who has since moved to the University of Leeds, and latterly with Freyja Cox-Jensen and Helen Birkett. All three have helped me learn much about news in the centuries prior to Churchill's birth and this has encouraged me to think more deeply about issues such as rumour and celebrity. The students who have taken the course have also been a source of inspiration.

For valuable discussions on issues related to the book I would like to thank Warren Dockter, Gary Love, Julie Gottlieb, Steven Fielding, Daniel Hucker, and Bill Schwarz. Allen Packwood and his staff at the Churchill Archives Centre were amazingly helpful too.

My literary agent, Natasha Fairweather, has been as wonderful as ever. At Oxford University Press, Matthew Cotton believed in the project from the beginning and helped guide it through to completion. Kizzy Taylor-Richelieu also provided invaluable help, coordinating on issues such as cover design and permissions. Rosanna van den Bogaerde helped with permissions too. Howard Emmens was a superb copy-editor. Sathiyavani Krishnamoorthy did an equally excellent job at the proof stage.

Richard Batten, with his customary meticulousness, made the index.

Quotations reproduced from the speeches, works and writings of Winston S. Churchill are reproduced with permission of Curtis Brown, London on behalf of The Estate of Winston S. Churchill © The Estate of Winston S. Churchill. Mass-Observation material is reproduced with permission of the Curtis Brown Group Ltd, London on behalf of The Trustees of the Mass Observation Archive © The Trustees of the Mass Observation Archive.

My parents, John and Janet Toye, always take a great interest in my work and I always benefit from their comments and suggestions.

Kristine Vaaler has been unfailingly kind and supportive, as with every other book I have written. It is to her and our sons Sven and Tristan that I dedicate this book.

Witikon, Zürich,
October 2019

Contents

Introduction

On 4 June 1929, a photograph of Winston Churchill appeared on the back page of the *Daily Herald*. It showed him outside 11 Downing Street, the Chancellor of the Exchequer's residence which he had not yet vacated following the defeat of the Conservative government at a general election a few days earlier. The picture showed Churchill carrying a book with the one-word title—'WAR'—clearly visible. The caption to the photograph suggested that war was 'one of his favourite subjects'. But was the photograph genuine? Churchill angrily concluded that it was not, after a member of the public wrote to him comparing the *Herald*'s shot with a similar one that appeared in another paper; in this version the word 'WAR' could not be seen. On Churchill's instructions, Edward Marsh, his friend and private secretary, wrote to the *Herald*'s editor, William Mellor, in outraged terms. 'Obviously your photographer, or someone at your office, has deliberately faked or forged a copy of the photograph which was published in the "Daily Herald" for the purpose of sustaining a prejudicial caption', he claimed.[1]

To understand why Churchill jumped to this conclusion, it helps to know of the bad blood that had long existed between him and the radical left-wing *Herald*. Ten years before, when he was Secretary of State for War and Air, it had passionately opposed his support for the 'White' anti-Bolshevik forces in the Russian civil war. He, in turn, had issued orders that the War Office was no longer to facilitate the circulation of the paper to British troops in France and Germany, because it contained 'propaganda of an essentially disloyal and subversive character'. Some copies that had already reached their destination may have been destroyed.[2] The anti-war poet and former soldier Osbert Sitwell had been moved by this to pen the following lines:

> The DAILY HERALD
> Is unkind.
> It has been horrid
> About my nice new war.
> I shall burn the DAILY HERALD.[3]

Now, perhaps embittered by the Labour Party's success at the polls and his own loss of office, Churchill was seen by his enemies to be lashing out once more. The *Herald*, for its part, was absolutely sure of its ground, to the point of appealing as a referee to the organ that was its ideological polar opposite. This was the *Morning Post*, sometime defender of General Reginald Dyer (the 'Butcher of Amritsar') and former employer of Churchill himself as a young correspondent three decades earlier. The *Post*'s experts examined the materials submitted to them and were 'unanimously agreed that they can find nothing in the negative to suggest that it is not perfectly genuine'. The contact print from the negative and the enlargement from which the reproduction in the paper was made were also genuine and bore no trace of having been touched. Whereas in the printed version the word 'WAR' had been made blacker and more distinct, this was 'merely an emphasis of definition such as is employed in every process room to make clear some point of special interest in a picture'.[4]

The book, it turned out, was recently a published anti-war novel by Ludwig Renn. Clearly, Churchill had casually picked a copy up, carried it with him in the street, and then had forgotten having done so. Other papers' photographers had taken their pictures from slightly different angles, and although the lettering was not quite as legible as in the *Herald*, the title, on close inspection, was visible enough.[5] Checkmate, it seemed. But Churchill declined to say sorry for his wrongful allegation, instead offering bland thanks to the *Herald* for its 'assurance' that the photograph had not been tampered with.[6] Mellor demanded a complete and categorical withdrawal and apology, but Churchill took the view that the *Herald's* 'abusive campaign' against him absolved him 'from the need of making any further amends'.[7] It was the *Herald*, though, that had the last word, with its cartoonist's suggestion of the book Churchill should read next: *The Manners of Gentlemen*.[8]

At one level, the *Morning Post* was right to describe this episode as a storm in a teacup.[9] There were no lasting consequences and the story appears to have been forgotten down to the present day. Yet Churchill's cry of 'fake or forgery', and his refusal to back down when proven wrong, are in many ways instructive. Today, in the era of Trump, authoritarian populism, and social media, cries of 'Fake news!' are ubiquitous. Whereas Churchill did, until the end of his career, periodically praise the press as a healthy factor in politics because it drew attention to governments' shortcomings, his attack on the *Herald* was no one-off lapse.[10] As an instinctive showman, and one of the first politicians to be a true global celebrity, he exploited the media (including the new technologies of radio and film) to spectacular effect. But—except when an off-the-record indiscretion happened to suit his purposes—his first instinct was for concealment, by no means always on legitimate national security grounds. As someone who did not merely read newspapers but rather devoured them, he was often nettled by criticism to the point where, during World War II, he wanted to censor opinion and not merely sensitive facts.

In fairness, just as Donald Trump is no Winston Churchill, Winston Churchill was no Donald Trump. He may have refused to apologize to the *Daily Herald*, but he did not actually continue to assert, in the face of the evidence, that he had been right all along. Churchill's legendary capacity for magnanimity was generally not much in evidence when it came to the press, but during the 1930s, he and the (now politically tamer) *Herald* even found some common ground over the threat posed by German rearmament.[11] It could well be argued, moreover, that Churchill's contribution to the defeat of Hitler was a great gift to the cause of press freedom, by comparison with which his recurrent outbursts of anti-press venom pale into insignificance. Churchill's wartime government did, after all, provide a fairly decent semblance of press freedom. 'Hardly anyone will print an attack on Stalin,' suggested George Orwell in his unpublished preface to *Animal Farm*, 'but it is quite safe to attack Churchill, at any rate in books and periodicals.'[12] Even so, the maintenance of that freedom was arguably more the result of systematic limitations upon the Prime Minister's power, and the moderating influence of his colleagues, than of Churchill's own sound judgement. His reflexes, impulses, and gut reactions were generally to crush criticism rather than to take it on the chin.

This may seem strange, given he himself had first made his name as a journalist of small wars, one who was known, furthermore, for colourful expressions of opinion that irritated military high-ups. Actually, though, these early experiences form part of the key to his later attitude when in power. Pontificate as he might, the young Churchill still adhered to a code which admitted the right of the authorities to shape coverage in their own favour and which covered up the most brutal aspects of the British army's conduct. He expected something similar from the British press in 1939–45. Equally, his attitude to political journalism owed much to pre-World War I scepticism about the mass press. In that period, quality of opinion was thought more important than quantity, that is to say it was considered better to persuade a smaller number of highbrow, influential readers than a larger number of rough and ignorant plebeians.[13] At a dinner with the staff of the *New York Times* in the late 1940s Churchill suggested, one of those present remembered, 'that we would increase our influence by concentrating on thoughtful readers, and decreasing our circulation by about a million'. As the circulation of *The Times* was nowhere near a million, 'this proposal was received with an envious sigh'.[14]

One might be tempted to agree with a remark by FDR. 'The trouble with Winston', Eleanor Roosevelt quoted him as saying, 'is that he enjoyed the old world too much to understand the new.'[15] (There was a geographical as well a chronological dimension to this criticism, Europe being associated with the old, and America with the new.) Churchill can be seen more fairly, though, as a genuinely transitional figure, who embraced the dynamic press culture of the Victorian era, continued to welcome innovation through late middle-age, and was only finally overtaken in his senescence by the new media mores and technology of the 1950s. Moreover, as a 'half-breed American' (as one Tory critic unkindly labelled him in May 1940), he was by no means wholly imprisoned by his aristocratic background.[16] His style gave plenty of nods to antiquity, but also reflected a certain brashness, a style that played well with the media on both sides of the Atlantic. A kinder verdict on Churchill than that given by Roosevelt, and perhaps a fairer one, was offered during the interwar years by the Conservative MP Major John Colville (not to be confused with Churchill's private secretary of the same name). 'Literature has been his constant attendant,' Colville wrote, 'and though some hypercritics may say that he has never appreciated the distinction between literature and journalism, yet it is truer to say that he has been a pioneer to a new type of letters forged by calling in the literature of the old world to redress the journalism of the new.'[17]

The purpose of this book, then, is to trace Churchill's life in the news as he moved from the one world to the other, and to show how the tensions between old and new played into his constantly evolving media image. It is a tale of tight deadlines, off-the-record briefings and smoke-filled newsrooms, of wartime summits that were turned into stage-managed global media events, and of often tense interactions with journalists and proprietors, such as Lords Northcliffe, Rothermere, and Beaverbrook. It is also a story of rapidly changing technology, in which the telegraph, the telephone, radio, newsreel, and (to a lesser extent) television all played their parts. Yet in spite of dramatic improvements in communications during the course of Churchill's life, the ways in which the media covered his career were powerfully affected not only by what was technically possible but by news culture. News culture can be defined as the meeting point between technology, economics, and the preferences of both news producers and news consumers. In other words, apparently similar conditions in different locales could produce quite diverse outcomes in terms of the style and content of news output. For example, British and American newspapers shared similar technology across the period but were in many ways very different productions; and it is striking that Churchill himself treated pressmen in the USA much more generously and politely than he did journalists at home.[18]

Churchill was not merely the passive subject of British and global news culture. Rather, he himself did a great deal to help shape that culture. He did so in a variety of ways, not least through his own prolific journalism and through his attempts to influence editors and reporters. He was by no means always successful, however, and even when official control was enforced he was frequently the subject of gossip and rumour—the 'improvised news' that people generate among themselves to help them understand their worlds in the absence of concrete information.[19] The chapters that follow show how the development of Churchill's public life was influenced by the demands of the media, and how press, film, and radio contributed to the many ups and downs of his career. They explore the symbiotic relationship between his political life and his media life and the ways in which these were connected to and were affected by his personal life. The book draws on an extensive range of personal, governmental, and organizational papers, published diaries, and memoirs, but media sources from Churchill's own lifetime are of particular importance. '[A]rchives often tell us things that we should have known anyway, if only we had read through old newspapers', the historian Peter Clarke once noted.[20] The corollary is that old newspapers can often tell us things that archives have failed to preserve.

The journalist Frederic Mullaly argued as far back as December 1945 that any conscientious future Churchill biographer would be obliged to engage with this material:

> No matter how intimate his relationship with the subject, no matter
> how free the flow of confidences and reminiscences between them,
> there is no substitute for diligent, methodical note-taking from the
> press cuttings dated 1900 onwards. Here will be found the raw,
> unadorned substance of Churchill's vacillating career: political cam-
> paigns that the world has forgotten, speeches that have been excluded,
> as if by conspiracy, from every hack panegyric masquerading in the
> form of biography.[21]

Mullaly, of the socialist paper *Tribune*, was a harsh Churchill critic, but
his point stands. Reading the newspapers—as well as engaging with
film, radio, and TV sources—helps us see more clearly the sheer variety of ways in which Churchill was perceived and presented within
his own lifetime.[22] To read every scrap of Churchill's global coverage
throughout his career would, of course, be an impossible task. If one
seeks, more realistically, a very large, representative sample, today's
digitized newspaper archives are invaluable. However, they have their
pitfalls.[23] In particular, it is not necessarily the case that the titles which
happen to have been digitized were those that were most interesting
and important during the period at hand. Therefore, it is essential also
to consult original printed copies. Conveniently, there exist extensive
(though not fully comprehensive) collections of Churchill press cuttings.[24] In recent years, several historians have made good use of them,
but this material is still far from fully exploited.[25] The research for this
book turned up a number of articles by Churchill in these files which
are seemingly unknown to scholars.[26]

Moreover, within limits, it is possible to analyse how ordinary
people reacted to news about Churchill. The sources on this are rich-
est for the World War II years, when both the Ministry of Information
(MoI) and the sociological research organization Mass Observation
(MO) collected a huge amount of evidence of popular opinion. For
example, MO went as far as recording the number of seconds of
applause when public figures, including Churchill, appeared in cinema newsreels. On a more sporadic basis, individual MO diarists
recorded their impressions through to the end of his final premiership in 1955. This type of material presents its own well-known

methodological problems.[27] But to some degree it is possible not merely to work out what people's views of Churchill were, but how such views were affected by the specific ways they obtained information about him through the media.

This book, then, investigates the theme of 'Churchill and the news' in three dimensions: Churchill's own writings, his image as a news subject, and his efforts to influence and control the media. In so doing it builds on a substantial body of previous scholarship, which has explored how Churchill deliberately and consciously constructed his own myth.[28] There is also much other relevant literature. The innumerable biographies all deal with Churchill's early journalistic exploits, his involvement with the *British Gazette* during the General Strike, his relations with the Press Lords, and so forth. There are helpful compilations of his articles and his press coverage.[29] There are also valuable books, articles, and essays that deal with aspects of his journalism and his wider involvement with the media; the role that writing played in sustaining Churchill's troubled finances has received thorough treatment too.[30] Until now, though, there has been no thorough and comprehensive assessment of how Churchill's own media life intersected with the wider issues of press freedom and political iconography.

If such an account is to succeed, it must not only deal with Churchill's own personal proclivities as an individual but relate them to broader themes such as media manipulation and the globalization of news. Churchill was a master of publicity who cultivated a new form of political celebrity. There were precursors: Palmerston, Gladstone, and Disraeli had all had their personal cults. What was new was the sheer scale of Churchill's coverage and its transmission across the world. Churchill's longevity as an object of public discussion (including posthumously) is one of the things that make him special if not absolutely unique. Moreover, although the media did become more intrusive and in some ways more challenging of politicians over the course of his life, Churchill (in the various stages of his career) had many routes to informal influence over what was printed. He was a public political personality, who brought elements of his private life into the public sphere but in a way that he was generally able to control.

Churchill, then, was a politician who courted the media, albeit during his final period in office he seemed to be losing his touch. At the same time, as will be seen throughout these pages, he often showed bitter resentment of the press, and also of the BBC. Of course, some of the treatment he received was deeply unfair. In the search for circulation some newspapers often played fast and loose with the facts and made spurious allegations. Others displayed blatant ideological bias. But even making all due allowance for the frustrations that politicians typically meet, and indeed for the extreme stress that he experienced during both world wars, Churchill's profound sensitivity is notable. Throughout this book we will see both how he nonetheless thrived in the heat of the media battle and how, in part because of robust institutional constraints, his autocratic and repressive instincts against journalistic freedom were successfully contained.

I

A Pushing Age

The arrival of Winston Churchill into the world at Blenheim Palace in 1874 made the front of *The Times*—but not as a news item. Rather, it featured as a paid announcement at the head of the 'Births' column:

> On the 30th Nov., at Blenheim Palace, the Lady RANDOLPH CHURCHILL, prematurely, of a son.

The item shared the page not only with reports of deaths and marriages but also with advertisements for goods and services, concerts and events, and enigmatic personal messages such as 'Psidium! You will find me at the old address.'[1] News did not appear on the *Times* front page, in fact, until 1966—although an exception was made for Churchill's death the year before. Other British papers had been providing eye-catching banner headlines for decades. The decision of 'The Thunderer', as it was known, to maintain its nineteenth-century look for so long represented a conscious effort to distinguish itself from vulgar competitor titles. In the words of one of its former editors, 'There was *The Times*, and there were other newspapers.'[2] Churchill, as a young MP, shared this assessment: 'The London *Times* satisfies my ideal of a newspaper—a paper that gives a great deal of space to news from foreign countries.' Other papers had larger circulations, but the people 'who run the country, who take an interest in politics, read the London *Times*'.[3] Yet the youthful Churchill relied on less staid and more sensational organs to achieve the fame that acted as a springboard for his parliamentary career.

The old-style *Times* represents the side of the Victorian era that holds sway in the popular imagination: crusty, conventional, and conservative. But although these were genuine dimensions of the age, they sat side-by-side with a much more colourful popular and journalistic culture that thrived on melodrama, scandal, and invective. One of the most remarkable things about Churchill is that—with varying degrees of effectiveness—he succeeded in straddling these two worlds, the tensions between which continued to play out throughout the whole length of his career. He was both a rebel and a conformist and used the battering ram of the press to break his way into a political establishment that justly regarded him with suspicion. It helped, of course, that he was an aristocrat. It also helped that he wasn't too concerned about acting the gentleman. In all this, he had a model: his father, the mercurial Lord Randolph Churchill. 'I took my politics almost unquestioningly from him', Winston recalled.[4] In respect of actual policies, that is more than debatable, but the claim is accurate when looked at in terms of the two men's styles of political conduct and, in particular, the cultivation of the Fourth Estate. The nature of the approach is best summed up in a letter Winston wrote to his mother in 1898, three years after Lord Randolph's death: 'It is a pushing age and we must shove with the best.'[5]

Technology, politics, economics, and ideology combined to give the age its shoving aspect. Britain was getting wealthier and more urban; from the 1880s its Empire expanded dramatically. The birth of the mass press, mass education, and mass voting went hand in hand with new developments in news-gathering and dissemination. The telegraph, invented in 1833, was crucial, but so too were other factors such as the spread of railways and improvements in the postal service. This was also a time of 'poverty in the midst of plenty', and of ongoing class, racial, and gender discrimination, including the continued exclusion of women (and many men, by no means all of them working-class) from the parliamentary franchise. It may have been the Age of Progress, but what 'progress' meant was bitterly contested. Technology did not sweep everything before it. The steam-powered printing press, developed in the early nineteenth century, had revolutionary possibilities. However, these were for some time held back by persistence of the state's efforts at control of published news and opinion, which were strengthened after 1819 as part of a crackdown on demands for parliamentary reform. The so-called 'taxes on knowledge'—the best known of which was the stamp duty, a penny charge levied on newspapers published more than once a month—were a brake on the growth of the popular press. Their repeal was a long-drawn-out process that took place across two decades, starting around mid-century, and it occurred only in response to popular campaigning pressure. Charles Dickens, who foresaw 'a flood of piratical, ignorant and blackguard papers', was not the only person who feared the consequences of a cheap, unregulated press.[6]

Another was Lord Palmerston, one of the major founders of the modern Liberal Party, who himself has aptly been described as 'the first media-manipulating prime minister'; he boasted that he could get papers to insert any item he wanted.[7] A celebrated controversy in 1860 brought him into conflict with his Chancellor of the Exchequer, W. E. Gladstone. Gladstone wanted to abolish duties on paper, the last of the 'taxes on knowledge', but the very idea of a mass popular press struck many as potentially subversive, and Palmerston and many other ministers were opposed. Gladstone recorded in his diary that in one Cabinet meeting 'Lord P spoke ¾ hour . . . agt. [against] Paper Duties Bill!' The legislation went ahead anyway and passed through the Commons, but Palmerston wrote to Queen Victoria that the House of Lords 'would perform a good public service' if it rejected the Bill. The Lords did in fact do so, and Lady Palmerston was ostentatiously pleased. It was Gladstone who had the last laugh, though. The follow-ing year he made abolition of the duties part of his Budget, thereby forcing his colleagues and the Lords to swallow it. One consequence of the reform was that *The Times* permanently lost its position as the biggest-circulation daily.[8] Another was the boost to Gladstone's own position as the darling of Radical opinion. He subsequently served four times as prime minister, and was to be the dominating political figure of the childhood of Winston Churchill, who recalled him, with irony, as 'a very dangerous man who went about rousing people up, lashing them into fury so that they voted against the Conservatives'.[9]

The press was a vital part of this process of 'rousing people up'. The Grand Old Man was not only the master of the mass public meeting; he turned these occasions into media events. It helped that extra-parliamentary speech by major political figures was a comparative novelty; also that legislation passed in 1868 gave the press a privileged position with respect to the use of the telegraph. When Gladstone spoke to an audience of 25,000 in a building with poor acoustics, as he did when the National Liberal Federation was launched in 1877, not all of his immediate audience could necessarily hear what he was saying, but this did not matter too much when even hostile papers were guaranteed to provide very full reports of what he said the next day. One Press Association journalist, who had the particular task of copying down the speeches, was known as 'Mr. Gladstone's Fat Reporter'.[10] From the late 1870s, the press increasingly turned away from backing Gladstone, creating a potential opportunity for the Conservatives, who nonetheless had problems in turning newspaper support into votes.[11] These conditions set the stage for the remarkable rise and swift fall of Lord Randolph Churchill, a creature too fascin-ating for the press to ignore. As a consequence of his brilliance and notoriety, the Tory Party's leaders could not ignore him either.

Born in 1849, Lord Randolph was the third son of the seventh Duke of Marlborough. As an Oxford undergraduate he had an early brush with the press when he was convicted by the university Vice-Chancellor's Court of assaulting a policeman after a drunken student dinner and fined 10 shillings.[12] 'Lord Randolph Churchill, of Merton College, Oxford, having no brains of his own, took a policeman's hel-met, to see if he could find any there', observed the radical *Reynolds's Newspaper*.[13] Lord Randolph was accused of having secured the dis-missal of a waiter who had testified against him, but he buttered up the *Oxford Chronicle*, which had criticized him, by inviting one of its journalists to a dinner given in his honour by his hunting friends.[14] For the next few years he did little, but in 1874 he wed the beautiful American heiress Jennie Jerome, whose father Leonard settled a £50,000 fortune upon the couple. As a quid pro quo for the Duke of Marlborough's consent to this controversial match, Lord Randolph agreed to contest the local Woodstock constituency at the forthcoming general election.[15] He was duly elected, not long before the wedding took place. Most papers contented themselves with reporting the bare facts of the ceremony, at the British embassy in Paris, although the *Newcastle Courant* sarcastically observed that 'The Churchill family do not seek or find alliances in any quarter where money is not abundant.'[16] Lord and Lady Randolph's names often appeared in long lists of people who had attended particular 'fashionable entertainments', but Winston's (doubtfully premature) birth later that year does not appear to have been considered newsworthy.[17]

As a young MP, Lord Randolph came to the attention of Henry Lucy of the Liberal *Daily News*. (Later, working for *Punch* in the guise of 'Toby, MP', Lucy was to become the greatest parliamentary sketchwriter of the age.) Recalling a speech of May 1875, Lucy wrote that 'the young Member was so nervous, his voice so badly pitched, his delivery so faulty, that there was difficulty in following his argument'. Yet now and then 'there flashed forth a scathing sentence that made it worthwhile to attempt to catch the rest. When he sat down Lord Randolph had made his mark, had established himself as an interesting personality, in an Assembly in which within ten years he was predominant.'[18] Before he came to the front rank of politics, though, Lord Randolph placed another obstacle in his own path. In an attempt to prevent his brother, the Marquess of Blandford, being named as co-respondent in a divorce case, he threatened to expose the fact that the Prince of Wales (the future Edward VII) had himself written compromising letters to the lady concerned. The Prince intervened to halt the divorce proceedings and protect Blandford from scandal, but was naturally outraged at being blackmailed. As a consequence,

Lord Randolph was sent into a form of social exile; his father was appointed by Disraeli as Lord Lieutenant of Ireland and Randolph accompanied him as his private secretary. The Duke's ceremonial entry into Dublin in January 1877 brought the infant Winston his first media coverage (birth announcement aside). *The Standard*, a British Conservative paper, glowingly described the warmth of the Duke's reception, and noted: 'There came over with his grace's family his grand-son, master Winston Spencer Churchill, who was held up in the nurse's arms and cheered by the people.'[19] Winston's 'first coherent memory' was of a later occasion, when his grandfather unveiled a statue in Phoenix Park: 'A great black crowd, scarlet soldiers on horseback, strings pulling away a brown shiny sheet, the old Duke, the formidable grandpapa, talking loudly to the crowd.'[20] Newspaper evidence allows us to date this recollection very precisely to 21 February 1880, shortly before the family returned to London, although this time little Winston did not feature in the story.[21]

That same year, the Tories were thrown out of office when Gladstone won a landslide general election victory. The social ostracism of Lord Randolph was not yet at an end. The episode involving the Prince of Wales was common knowledge, and there were even occasional dark hints in the press.[22] His return to Westminster politics brought him new prominence, though, as he gained notoriety as one of a small number of rebellious or unconventional Tories known as 'The Fourth Party'. Lord Randolph was particularly critical of Sir Stafford Northcote, the Conservatives' stuffy Commons leader. Relations deteriorated further when Northcote blamed his young rival for press stories that the Fourth Party might in future run its own election candidates. Lord Randolph wrote back that he refused to be held responsible for Westminster gossip, blamed Northcote's colleagues for inspiring press attacks on the Fourth Party, and ridiculed 'respectable' Tories for sacrificing the party's true interests in the hope of 'gaining a passing cheer from *The Times* Newspaper for their judicial impartiality'.[23]

In terms of how fully the newspapers covered his speeches—an important contemporary measure of political success—the MP for

Woodstock was doing well, but he still had plenty of critics. The weekly *Spectator* denounced him hotly, but by no means wholly unfairly, for his 'total absence of coherent political thought'. It judged, moreover, that 'There may lurk in him, though he is no longer in his first manhood, some unsuspected sobering force; but he has seemed to the world as yet a political Puck, with a strain in him which admirers might misinterpret into genius, but also a strain of waywardness, deepening occasionally until his foes have half-doubted his perfect sanity.' Yet even this paper could not entirely deny that Lord Randolph had succeeded in securing the 'sometimes enthusiastic' support of an important section of the Conservative Party.[24] He was certainly not insensitive to criticism, but he did have ways of dealing with it. 'Never revise your speeches', one acquaintance recalled him saying. 'If you are ever reproached with an inconvenient expression, you can always say that you have been badly reported.' When, years later, the friend retailed the comment to Winston, who by that point was a successful politician in his own right, the boyish would-be statesman observed: 'A public speaker provides the raw material for the reporter, who then manufactures it according to his ability. [...] You are no more responsible for a published report than you are for the success of an artist or a photographer, to whom you may have given a sitting.'[25]

Winston may also have learned from his father that a wife could be a political (and media) asset. In May 1885, Gladstone's government fell, and the new Prime Minister, Lord Salisbury, reluctantly appointed Lord Randolph as Secretary of State for India. Under the rules then current, the new minister then had to fight a by-election, and Lady Randolph campaigned on her husband's behalf in his constituency, as he insisted that it was impossible for him to leave London. Her activities provided excellent journalistic copy: 'Lady Randolph Churchill, accompanied by Lady Curzon, was out at an early hour driving to and fro in a smart tandem, the horses of which were decorated with his lordship's colour—pink. [...] After interviewing a considerable number of agricultural electors, reputedly Liberal, she had no hesitation in affirming her belief that her husband's majority would not undergo the least reduction at the poll on Friday.'[26] She was right; his majority increased.

Winston was now at school in Brighton where one of the pleasures was that he was permitted to study volumes of *Punch* on Sundays.[27] According to a press account of his childhood published during the Great War, he created his own magazine called *The Critic*, although it failed to reach a second issue.[28] It was around this time that Winston began to feature from time to time in the gossip national columns. In April 1886, an item appeared in near-identical terms in several newspapers: 'Master Winston Churchill, Lord Randolph's eldest son has, under the care of Dr. Robson Roose, almost entirely recovered from the sharp attack of pneumonia with which he was recently seized at his Brighton school (Miss Thompson's), and which at one time looked serious.'[29] Roose, a well-known 'Society doctor', seems to have been something of a publicity hound; the story may have come from him.[30] Later that same year, one Northern paper's 'London Letter' reported that young Winston was 'one of the most curious infant phenomena of his time'. The Conservative politician Sir Henry Drummond Wolff, 'who has a keen sense of the ridiculous', was said to have screamed with laughter over some of the boy's sayings. 'His [Winston's] humour, like that of his father, inclines to the sardonic.'[31]

Lord Randolph's career now met its crisis. Gladstone returned briefly to office in 1886, but his attempts to enact Home Rule for Ireland split the Liberal Party, which was crushed at the ensuing general election. Lord Randolph was the rabble-rousing delight of the Conservative grassroots—he described Gladstone's policies as 'the programme of a maniac'—and Salisbury appointed him as Chancellor of the Exchequer and Leader of the House of Commons in his new administration.[32] Yet although on the face of it his star was rising, he proved himself all but impossible to work with; his health was worsening and his marriage was in trouble too. The tensions in the ministry were openly discussed in the press, and Lord Randolph soon overplayed his hand. After only a few months in office, he threatened resignation over what he saw as excessive spending on the armed forces. Salisbury called his bluff and accepted. As Winston told the story in his 1906 biography of his father, Lord Randolph paid a late-night visit to *The Times* office, authorized the paper's editor to disclose that he had resigned, 'and so to bed. [...] With the first light of the morning the announcement appeared'.[33] What Winston did not mention was that it was only by reading the paper that his mother learnt the news herself.[34]

This was the end of Lord Randolph's Cabinet career. He had miscalculated, but his nocturnal visit to Printing House Square demonstrated that, at least, he understood the growing power of the press. The era of 'government by journalism' seemed to beckon.[35] And even out of office, Lord Randolph's doings kept him in the public eye. Winston's relationship with his father was never intimate, and that with his mother only became close once he was an adult. Whether or not his parents were truly neglectful is debatable, but it is fair to say that Winston craved attention and affection that was rarely forthcoming. Yet he was a 'vehement partisan' of Lord Randolph and followed his career avidly. 'For years I had read every word he spoke and what the newspapers said about him', Winston recalled of the post-resignation period. 'Although he was only a private member and quite isolated, everything he said even at the tiniest bazaar was reported verbatim in all the newspapers, and every phrase was scrutinized and weighed.'[36]

In 1887, Winston moved up to the elite Harrow School. In general his performance was indifferent, but he learned to write effective prose, winning a prize for an essay about an imaginary battle; his skills would later serve him well as a war correspondent.[37] In 1891, he avidly watched the progress of his father when he made a journey to South Africa. Lord Randolph gave *The Daily Graphic* 'the exclusive right to publish a Series of Letters signed by himself, giving a detailed account of his experiences' in return for the astounding sum of two thousand guineas.[38] (He and Jennie were wildly profligate—a habit Winston would also contract—so he needed the money.) The articles seemed almost designed to stir controversy, from his complaints about the food on board his ship to his insults directed at women and at the

Boer inhabitants of the Transvaal. 'I have just been reading your description of the Kimberley and De Beer diamond mines', Winston wrote to him. 'I think your letters very interesting. The papers are exceedingly spiteful & vicious.'[39] Lord Randolph considered that some of the stories that were printed about his behaviour were 'malicious lies'.[40] One paper suggested that he had been as great a failure as an amateur journalist as Don Quixote had been an amateur knight, but if anything the sheer outrageousness of his articles made them ahead of their time.[41] On his return, Lord Randolph turned the articles into a book.[42] Later, Winston directly emulated his father's example, from his choice of *The Graphic* as his first journalistic employer to the way in which he often reused his articles for other purposes. It is also significant that he believed that Lord Randolph regarded being a reporter as a respectable calling.[43]

Yet this is not to say that Winston imitated his father in all respects. Throughout his active life, many observers found him to be unreliable, erratic, irresponsible, and imprudent, by turns. But by comparison with Lord Randolph, both his personal behaviour and his journalistic writings appear as models of restraint. It is hard to judge how far Lord Randolph's unreasonableness was innate and how far it was exacerbated by the disease that eventually killed him. In the spring of 1894 his family became aware that he was seriously ill. Although a range of diagnoses is possible, Winston believed—not necessarily correctly—that his father died of 'locomotoraxia, the child of syphilis'.[44] Whatever the cause, Lord Randolph's decline could not go unnoticed. 'Almost every week he delivered a speech at some important centre', Winston recalled. 'No one could fail to see that these efforts were increasingly unsuccessful. The verbatim reports dropped from three to two columns and then to one and a half. On one occasion *The Times* mentioned that the hall was not filled.'[45] Lord Randolph's friend Lord Rosebery later wrote that 'He died by inches in public'.[46] He might equally well have written 'column-inches'.

A round-the-world tour failed to restore Lord Randolph's health and had to be cut short. Winston took a hand in briefing the press on his condition, and on the comings and goings of the egregious Robson Roose.[47] In January 1895 the end finally came. For some years, Winston would remain, as far as the newspapers were concerned, 'Lord Randolph Churchill's Brilliant Son'.[48] This was, to say the least, a double-edged compliment, because it carried with it the hint that he might have inherited his father's mental instability along with his brilliance. 'A Churchill is sure to do something erratic', was a typical comment on one of his early adventures.[49]

At the time of Lord Randolph's death, Winston, who had just turned twenty, was a cadet at the Royal Military Academy at Sandhurst; his father had not thought him intelligent enough to go into the Law. The younger Churchill was, however, determined to make a name for himself, and it would be hard to do that through soldiering alone, especially at a time when—as it appeared at the time—there was a general shortage of wars. Once he had passed out of Sandhurst, and with a substantial amount of leave due him before his regiment was deployed overseas, Churchill devised a plan, together with his fellow subaltern Reginald Barnes, to visit Cuba, where Spanish forces were fighting against indigenous rebels. With the help of Sir Henry Drummond Wolff, who was now ambassador to Madrid, Barnes and Churchill secured the necessary introductions and permissions. It seems clear that the Spanish authorities spotted a potential propaganda advantage. When the two young men embarked at Liverpool, the *Diario de la Marina*, an official paper published in Cuba, claimed that they were travelling 'with the idea of adding themselves to the Spanish Army on the island', which seemed to carry the false implication that they would be combatants.[50] The pair arrived in Havana in November 1895 and spent a fortnight in the field, where Churchill received his baptism of fire as a journalist. He soon found out that one of the chief pitfalls of the war reporter's trade is that when there is a lot going on there is little time to put it on paper: 'where material is plentiful opportunity is scarce', and vice versa.[51] In addition to his articles, Churchill provided *The Graphic* with sketches of scenes he had witnessed, which were then redrawn for publication by a professional artist.[52]

On Churchill's twenty-first birthday he and Barnes accompanied a military column commanded by General Suarez Valdez. Churchill came under fire for the first time in his life: 'The bullets whistled over our heads.' His articles were for the most part competent rather than brilliant, but they had some vivid touches. He noted how the 'deep note' of the guerrillas' guns 'contrasted strangely with the shrill rattle of the magazine rifles of the Spaniards'.[53] His final article, which reflected on the rebellion's prospects, is recognizably Churchillian, demonstrating an authoritative-cum-portentous tone and a taste for paradox. He sympathized with the rebellion, he wrote, but not with the rebels—for while the Cubans were monstrously overtaxed by a corrupt administration, their ill-disciplined fighters used only the tactics of 'incendiaries and brigands'.[54] It should be noted, moreover, that if his style was shaped by his personal proclivities and by the literary conventions of the age, it was also influenced by the means he had at his disposal to convey his writings home. Technology, though, did not determine everything: it intersected with geography and economics. Churchill had access to the telegraph, at least when he was in Havana, and used it for personal and financial communications, including asking his mother to lend him some money. He did telegraph to New York a denial that he had taken part in the fighting against the Cubans.[55] Yet he did not send his lengthier *Graphic* articles in this way: he was not yet a celebrated correspondent and the expense would have been prohibitive. By 6 December, by which time he was back in the capital, he had written four of his five articles; he completed the last in Tampa Bay, Florida. They must have been sent to England by sea, and the first was published on 13 December, two days before Churchill boarded his boat home from New York. However, the last did not appear until 13 January 1896.[56] What this tells us is that these 'letters', as they were described—and for which he earned five guineas each—were not intended either by author or editor to be seen as up-to-the-minute news, but rather as more reflective, feature-style journalism, to be spread out across a series of weeks.

Even before Churchill's *Graphic* articles appeared, other papers started to cover his doings, albeit on a relatively small scale. There was a certain amount of sarcastic comment: the *Newcastle Leader* wrote that 'Spending a holiday in fighting other people's battles is rather an extraordinary proceeding, even for a Churchill.'[57] He also received coverage in Cuba itself. One acquaintance wrote to him: 'After your departure [from the island] the local newspapers all had notices and every mother's son of them knighted you'. At the same time, the rebels put about the story that Churchill had developed sympathies for their side and had fallen out with General Valdez for that reason.[58] Yet Churchill's actual view was that, bad as the current government was, an indigenous Cuban government would be significantly worse— a view he expressed in a further article in the *Saturday Review*.[59] Drummond Wolff, who was concerned that Churchill might have put him in a difficult position by making criticisms of the authorities, was delighted when it was widely translated and warmly received in the Spanish press.[60] The authority of Lieutenant Churchill's opinions was boosted by presenting him as 'a distinguished officer' in the army of a great colonial power.[61] This exaggeration was small beer in the annals of press deception, of course. Interviewed by the press pack at the New York dockside before departing for England, Churchill accused one American newspaper—which, unfortunately for the historian, he did not name—of faking a cablegram over his forged signature and then using its editorial columns to attack him for the views it expressed![62] In Britain, the concept of the press interview was a relative novelty, which to some extent reflected the 'Americanization' of the country's press.[63] By today's standards, Churchill gave rather few published interviews over the course of his career.

Churchill was, however, interviewed again at Liverpool when he touched land, this time emphasizing that 'I took no part in the fighting, and the statement published in some of the English papers as to "our valorous conduct" was absurdly untrue.'[64] The fact that this interview was conducted by the Central News flags up an important point about the role of news agencies in general. Disseminated world-wide by telegraph, this particular article appeared not only in Britain but as far away as New Zealand.[65] And newspapers tended simply to copy one another, so a reader in Perth, Australia might well be confronted with exactly the same short profile of Churchill that had appeared in London some weeks earlier.[66] The volume of coverage was significant, insofar as it was greater than most of us receive in a lifetime, but its importance should not be exaggerated: it was typical disposable Victorian newspaper content, which was doubtless instantly forgettable to most readers. Nevertheless, it is fair to say that the Cuban affair marked the small beginnings of Churchill's global fame; and the same model of adventure plus controversy would help him feed a hungry press and his own desire for celebrity over the remaining years of the century.

Once back in the UK, Churchill came on the receiving end of sustained hostile coverage for the first time. This was at the hands of the radical weekly *Truth*, owned and run by the brilliant but idiosyncratic Liberal MP Henry Labouchere. The paper alleged that a group of officers, including Churchill, had bullied one of their fellows out of the army because he was not rich enough to maintain the expected cavalry lifestyle. There appears to have been some truth in the claims, although it does not seem that Churchill was the ringleader. However, the bullied officer's father undermined his son's own case by alleging that at Sandhurst Churchill had taken part in 'acts of gross immorality of the Oscar Wilde type'. Churchill sued and quickly obtained an apology and £500 damages—the first of a series of successful libel actions that he would pursue across the length of his career.[67] In September 1896 he shipped out with his regiment to Bangalore, but even there he was stung by an article from Labouchere's pen, this time implicating him in a betting scandal. 'He is a scoundrel and one of these days I will make him smart for his impudence', Churchill told his mother. He urged her to 'muzzle him if you can', but it seems that this time no legal action was taken.[68]

Churchill was concerned that the accusations might destroy his chances of a future in public life, an ambition that was no secret. As early as 1895 it had been reported that he had 'determined to give up the army and go into politics at once.'[69] In practice, it was expedient for him to enhance his reputation by accruing a decent amount of service before he did so. Unfortunately, though, military life in India was dull, especially for someone who wanted to keep up to the minute with events at home. 'The newspapers when they arrive are out of date and one gobbles up a week's *Times* in a single morning', he complained. Showing his customary disdain for all things Indian, he added that the country's press was 'despicable—being chiefly advertisements and hardly a telegram. The articles are written in Pigeon English, by Eurasians or natives—the paper is bad & the printing slovenly.'[70] Churchill now threw himself into a phase of vigorous self-education, reading seriously, widely, and eclectically, from Plato to Darwin and much in between. He digested old copies of the *Annual Register* and wrote down his thoughts on the issues that they raised, which included questions related to the press. One of his comments dismissed as 'ridiculous' the idea that newspapers fanned the flames of international crises in their own interests: 'Exciting times cost the newspapers much more in telegrams, correspondents etc. than they gained in increased circulation.' And whilst he strongly approved of capital punishment—and even of public executions—he wrote that he would 'not allow the press to pander to the morbid tastes of a certain section of the nation by retailing highly coloured versions of the scene'.[71] But, in addition to his heavyweight reading matter, copies of *Strand Magazine* sent by his younger brother Jack (in which a Conan Doyle serial might rub shoulders with an article on Gladstone's visitor's book) were also welcome.[72] Moreover, Churchill again tried his own hand at journalism, with an article on Sandhurst appearing in the *Pall Mall Magazine* under the pseudonym 'A Cornet of Horse'.[73]

In 1897, Churchill made use of a period of leave in Britain to try to kick-start his political career. He gave a speech in Bath to a fete held by the Primrose League. This was a mass-membership organization,

with a strong emphasis on social activity. It was designed to help
support the Conservative Party: Lord Randolph had been one of
the founders. This first example of Winstonian political oratory was
a capable effort, which poked fun at the 'croakers' who predicted
the decline of the British Empire. It was extensively covered in the
Bath Daily Chronicle, which reported plenty of laughter, cheers, and
applause.[74] Few other papers gave it more than a paragraph. (An interesting indication of how globalized news had already become is that
the speech attracted a few lines in *The Times of India*, albeit not until a
few weeks after it had been given.[75]) The exception was the *Morning
Post*.[76] The *Post* was controlled by his close contemporary Oliver
Borthwick, son of the paper's owner, Lord Glenesk, who had been a
political ally of Lord Randolph.[77] Borthwick and Churchill were on
first name terms, and the generous coverage presaged Churchill's own
subsequent employment by the *Post*.

Before that, however, Churchill was to work for the *Daily Telegraph*.[78]
It was events on the Indian North-West Frontier that brought this
about. The previous year Churchill had met General Sir Bindon
Blood, an experienced commander, and extracted a promise from
him 'that if ever he commanded another expedition on the Indian
frontier, he would let me come with him'. Now, during his leave in
England, Churchill read the news of a revolt by Pathan tribesmen, and
that Blood had been put in charge of a Field Force that was to be sent
to suppress it. 'Forthwith I telegraphed reminding him of his promise,
and took the train for Brindisi to catch the Indian Mail.'[79] Churchill
remained on tenterhooks until he reached Bombay: would Blood live
up to his pledge? The message he eventually got was encouraging.
The general's personal staff was full up. But: 'I should advise your
coming to me as a press correspondent, and when you are here I shall
put you on the strength at the first opportunity.'[80] Churchill succeeded in obtaining the necessary permission from his own regiment,
and then set off on the 2,000 mile train journey to the scene of the
fighting. He still needed a newspaper to work for, though. He got a
commission as a correspondent for the Allahabad-based *Pioneer Mail*,

to which he was required to telegraph three hundred words a day.[81] But it was possible that this paper would not be judged of sufficient importance to secure him the journalist's pass he required. Accordingly, he lobbied his mother to make an arrangement with the *Daily Telegraph*. Edward Levy Lawson, the proprietor, replied to Lady Randolph's approach to him with a telegram which read: 'Tell him to post pictur-esque forcible letters.'[82] Churchill took him at his word.

On the face of it, it might seem surprising that a serving soldier should also act as a journalist; and perhaps even more so that Churchill continued to do so even after General Blood appointed him as his orderly officer. Yet this type of arrangement was quite common. Viscount Fincastle, another soldier-correspondent who served in this Malakand campaign, was seen by Churchill as something of a rival. The military authorities naturally felt ambivalent about the repre-sentatives of the press, recognizing their usefulness for the purposes of publicity, but of course also wanting to control them—which was obviously easier if they were on the army's own payroll.[83] Churchill cannot be dismissed as a mere stooge. He was a much more interesting writer than Fincastle, for example, in part because he engaged in much more detailed and thoughtful analysis of the strategic purposes for which the war was being fought. Yet, although Churchill's articles were never bland, he was careful to stay on the right side of his superiors.

This can be seen through his campaign writings, which reveal him as an advocate of the so-called Forward Policy—the idea that the Empire should expand into contested regions of the frontier.[84] One of his *Telegraph* letters—which he was forwarding to the paper via his mother—promoted this idea, and Lady Randolph held it up because she felt that he was straying into dangerous territory. Churchill wired her to insist that it was published and then reproved her in a letter. Far from being too controversial, he said, the article in fact expressed 'what is essentially the military view'. He suggested, rather flippantly, that her hesitancy was the product of the limitations of her social circle: 'Of course if you will always be ruled by a syndicate of colonels—who though gallant and charming men—have a detestation of print—it is probable that you will see danger and impropriety in everything.'[85] Although the youthful Winston is often presented almost as an anti-establishment figure, these remarks of his are suggestive of the true position. Yes, there were plenty of crusty military types who were annoyed by this young officer having the temerity to express any opinions at all, but the opinions themselves were far from radical. He was, in fact, quite prepared to censor himself. 'I wonder if people in England have any idea of the warfare that is being carried on here', he wrote to his grandmother, telling her of the appalling methods used by both sides, including the 'shattering effects' of the British dumdum bullets that were designed to produce massive exit wounds. 'The picture is a terrible one,' he added, 'and naturally it has a side to which one does not allude in print.'[86]

Depending on whether he was writing for the Indian *Pioneer* or the London-based *Telegraph*, Churchill adopted somewhat different methods. For the first of those papers, he supplied a series of telegrams and letters, and the resultant articles generally appeared within a few days, although there was sometimes a delay of over a week. The *Telegraph* letters, by contrast, took much longer to appear in print. The first of them was written on 3 September but was not published until 6 October, nearly a month after his first *Pioneer* piece saw the light of day.[87] (The fact that he routed the letters to London via his mother suggests that he did not regard them as particularly time-sensitive.) To his intense annoyance, the *Telegraph* articles were printed without his name attached, something which had not bothered him in the case of the *Pioneer*. This was because of the nature of his intended or imagined audience: 'the everyday reader, at his breakfast table in "comfortable England"'.[88] He had specifically planned to use the *Telegraph* pieces as means 'of bringing my personality before the electorate [...] This hope encouraged me to take the very greatest pains with the style and composition and also to avoid alluding to any of my own experiences.'[89] His thinking here, presumably, was that he wanted to portray himself as a detached and authoritative commentator rather than as a mere glory hunter. He adopted, then, a thoughtful and ironical tone, in which he reflected, for instance, on the influence of the climate upon the character of the enemy 'savages', and offered little homilies on the nature of British power.[90] Much of it was portentous, even a little pompous, but it was intellectually richer than the offerings of many of Churchill's journalistic contemporaries, and there was a leavening of humour. By the third letter in the series, he was joking: 'I am indeed becoming painfully conscious that this correspondence is now so far advanced that a battle or some other exciting affair is necessary, or at least desirable, in order to make it acceptable to your readers.'[91]

Writing from Inayat Kila on 18 September, Churchill was able, at last, to provide the kind of dramatic account that he believed his readers craved. He described an action in the Momand Valley in which the British forces sought to punish the recalcitrant tribesmen by destroying their villages, but encountered heavy resistance and suffered substantial casualties. Churchill himself took part in the fighting and earned a mention in dispatches. He later described in *My Early Life* a vivid scene in which he came face to face with one of the enemy:

> I pulled out my revolver, took, as I thought, most careful aim, and fired. No result. I fired again. No result. I fired again. Whether I hit him or not I cannot tell. At any rate he ran back two or three yards and plumped down behind a rock. The fusillade was continuous. I looked around. I was all alone with the enemy. Not a friend was to be seen. I ran as fast as I could. There were bullets, everywhere. I got to the first knoll. Hurrah, there were the [British-supporting] Sikhs holding the lower one! They made vehement gestures, and in a few moments I was among them.[92]

Yet in his original article—in line with his decision not to describe his personal experiences—none of this appeared. Instead, he merely commented that when he and his comrades came under attack 'It became impossible to remain an impassive spectator.'[93] Thus, in the apparent interest of crafting his public persona in a way that he thought would best help him with the voters, Churchill actually held back much of his best material. This was self-effacement as a paradoxical form of self-promotion.

Although in later years Churchill was doubtful of whether the 'punitive devastation' inflicted during the Malakand campaign had really achieved anything, at the time he was an ideologue of British expansion.[94] Therefore he closed his series of articles by drawing attention to their didactic, imperialist purpose. He hoped that they would 'stimulate the growing interest which the proud democracy of England is beginning to take in those great estates beyond the sea of which they are proprietors'.[95] This dimension can also be seen in his book *The Story of the Malakand Field Force*, which he dashed out in order to capitalize on the interest that press articles had generated. Naturally, he made use of his existing material, but he resisted the temptation to simply cannibalize it wholesale.[96] *The Graphic* noted 'The book is, to a certain extent, made up of letters from the front to those papers [the *Telegraph* and the *Pioneer*], but worked up into a complete and detailed account of the operations, with numerous digressions, which are, perhaps, the most interesting part of the whole.'[97] This was just one of a wide range of generally very positive reviews that attended the book's publication in March 1898. The *Times of India* was sufficiently struck with it to devote a leader column to discussing its conclusions—the first but by no means the last time that Churchill would receive this type of editorial treatment.[98] This reminds us that Churchill's literary career did not just earn him money but helped generate the type of press attention and discussion that he so clearly craved.

Having returned to his regimental routine, and even before his book came out, Churchill immediately began to seek out another adventure. He managed to get himself attached to another frontier campaign, the Tirah expedition, and he impressed Aylmer Haldane, aide-de-camp to the general in charge, as 'remarkably clever'.[99] To Churchill's chagrin, though, peace soon broke out, and the expedition wound up its activities. Thus he looked further afield, to Sudan, where Sir Herbert Kitchener was commander or 'Sirdar' of the Egyptian army.

Kitchener was about to lead a combined British–Egyptian force to complete the reconquest of the country from the indigenous 'Dervish' forces that had triumphed there thirteen years earlier. Churchill returned to London on leave, and set about pulling as many strings as he could. (He also made some political speeches and even gave an interview to the *Morning Post* on the subject of Cuba, where the United States had now intervened against the Spanish.[100]) The obstacle was Kitchener himself, who was not fond of war correspondents at the best of times, but Churchill's connections helped him get round this. He succeeded in getting himself attached to the 21st Lancers, and agreed with his 'great friend' Oliver Borthwick that he should write 'as opportunity served a series of letters to the *Morning Post*' outlining his experiences.[101] Churchill departed at the end of July; being on board ship put him out of the reach of news, because although radio (or 'wireless telegraphy') had recently been invented it was not yet in widespread use. He wrote to his mother: 'The fact that I have seen no telegrams about the war or the events of the world—reminds me that I am again slipping away from the centre of civilization.'[102]

It might be tempting to portray Churchill's early writing career as part of a narrative whereby journalism became progressively faster, brasher, and more 'modern'. Yet, in the Sudanese case, we can see how Churchill intended to write in a manner which seems quite unlike today's journalism—and which indeed pretended not even to *be* journalism. His idea was to publish the articles anonymously in the first instance, presenting them as though they were letters to a friend, which the friend had then decided to publish without the author's knowledge. This was an effort to emulate the eighteenth-century writer and politician Joseph Addison; the *Morning Post* was to be complicit and all was to be revealed when the series finished. As Churchill explained to Borthwick:

> The style is essentially literary and the farcical manner in which they are presented to the public will add I think to the interest and amusement with which they will be read. I shall keep up the illusion to the

vy end—and in about 3 weeks I will write and bitterly reproach my
'friend' for his indiscretion. [...]

I shall arrange for my mother to let the 'secret' out gradually through
the other newspapers...You must continue to wink your eye.[103]

In fact, the *Post* edited the letters, which were written according to
this plan, in order to dispense with the ruse; although Churchill's
authorship was only revealed at the end of the final article, the pretence that he was not writing for publication was discarded. Churchill
was annoyed, telling his mother:'This was a most amusing conceit and
from a literary point of view added to the elegance of the letters. [...]
You should have insisted on my idea being used or the letters destroyed.
As it is the whole series will lose its peculiar idea and become mere
banal penny a line journalism.'[104] This episode may look slightly strange
to modern eyes, and presumably Borthwick rejected Churchill's idea
because he too found it odd, inappropriate, or just old-fashioned. But
it does show that Churchill was attempting to be playful and innovative in his writing. In some ways this marked him out as unusual
among his war correspondent peers.

When one knows Churchill's original plan, the format of the published articles and their arch tone starts to make sense.[105] 'You would
rightly call me faithless, my dear', he began his first letter,'if I were to
make no effort to carry out my promise to give you some account of
the features and the fortunes of the war on the Nile.'[106] This was from
Korosko, on the Nile. The next several letters recounted his progress
with Kitchener's forces towards Khartoum. As there was as yet no
fighting his accounts were filled with vivid descriptions of the scen-
ery, together with reflections on the impact of Western technology.
For him, the telegraph wire that ran along the bank of the Nile was
the sign of civilization.

Looking at the slender poles and white insulators [...] it is impossible
not to experience a glow of confidence in the power of science which
can thus link the most desolate regions of the earth with its greatest
city and keep the modern pioneer ever within hail of home. We may

also wonder as we look what news that wire will presently carry back
to Great Britain, whether of success or failure, of peace or war, or
whose names it will flash homeward as being of no more account to
living men.[107]

Towards the end of August he reached Wad Hebeshi, and let his
mother know that from that point on there would be no more mail
until such time as Khartoum—still sixty miles away—had been
taken.[108]

The capture of the capital was preceded by the Battle of Omdurman,
which saw the catastrophic defeat of the spear-carrying Dervishes
who were destroyed by the huge firepower of the Anglo-Egyptians.
It was a bloodbath, a massacre—although the industrialized killing
was leavened by the famous old-style cavalry charge of the Lancers, in
which Churchill was caught up. Until this point, as in India, Churchill
had eschewed much in the way of personal narrative in his articles,
with the exception of a dramatic story about getting lost in the desert
when separated from the column he was travelling with. Now, though,
his journalism went up a gear, as he related his own experiences to an
elucidation of the battle as a whole, spread over two articles. He wrote,
for example, of one British sergeant whose face was cut to pieces
during the cavalry charge rallying his men as 'the whole of his nose,
cheeks, and lips flapped amid red bubbles'. Churchill himself was one
of the few officers who came through the charge entirely unscathed.
'The whole event seemed to pass in absolute silence', he wrote. 'The
yells of the enemy, the shouts of the soldiers, the firing of many
shots, the clashing of sword and spear were unnoticed by the senses,
unregistered by the brain.'[109] A few days later he followed up with a
remarkable piece of reportage describing the horror of the aftermath
of battle as the dead rotted and the wounded suffered agonizing tor-
ments of thirst and pain: 'there was nothing *dulce et decorum* about the
Dervish dead. Nothing of the dignity of unconquerable manhood. All
was filthy corruption. Yet these were as brave men as ever walked the
earth.'[110] There were plenty of war correspondents at Omdurman

('They treat 'em all like dirt here', Churchill noted) but the young amateur gave the professionals more than a run for their money.[111]

According to Margot Asquith, Churchill was still convinced years later 'that Kitchener tried to "do him in" after the Sudan campaign' by ordering him 'to attach himself to a convoy of camels which was to make a long, slow and dangerous trek'. Instead, according to this story, Churchill 'hurried home in defiance of the Army'.[112] Even if Churchill did tell her something like this, the story should be taken with a pinch of salt, as it does not seem to be supported by other evidence. But the job of a correspondent was undoubtedly dangerous, as had been demonstrated when *Times* correspondent Hubert Howard, whom Churchill had known since Cuban days, was killed by a British shell during the occupation of the city of Omdurman, having earlier survived the cavalry charge unhurt. Another doomed journalist whom Churchill came to know was G. W. Steevens, who got through the Nile campaign unharmed only to perish during the Boer War.[113]

After Omdurman, Steevens and Churchill took the same ship back to Britain and became firm friends. 'Mr. G. W. Steevens was the "star" writer of a certain Mr. Harmsworth's new paper called the *Daily Mail* which had just broken upon the world', Churchill recollected. 'Harmsworth relied enormously upon Steevens in these early critical days, and being well disposed to me, told him later on to write me up, which he did in his glowing fashion.'[114] Steevens's profile appeared just as Churchill, who had decided to leave the army, returned to his regiment for his final spell in India. The article dubbed him 'the youngest man in Europe'. It boosted Churchill, without being blind to his faults:

> He is ambitious and he is calculating; yet he is not cold—and that saves him. His ambition is sanguine, runs in a torrent, and the calculation is hardly more than the rocks or the stump which the torrent strikes for a second, yet which suffices to direct its course. It is not so much that he calculates how he is to make a career a success—how frankly, he is to boom—but that he has a queer, shrewd poser of introspection,

which tells him his gifts and character are such as will make him boom.
He has not studied to make himself a demagogue, and he happens
to know it.[115]

This passage is worth quoting at length for a number of reasons. First,
it was genuinely insightful. Second, it shows that the complexities of
Churchill's character, including his mercurial nature and his naked
ambition, were part of his public image from a very early stage. Third,
it helps illustrate the type of writing that helped make the young
Daily Mail such a success—'jaunty, breezy, slap-dash', as Churchill not
unfairly described Steevens's contributions to it.[116]

But to understand the *Mail* fully—and thus to appreciate the part
it played in Churchill's career—requires an understating of the 'certain
Mr. Harmsworth' to whom he referred with such ironic casualness
in his memoirs. This was Alfred Harmsworth, who later, as Lord
Northcliffe, would become the prototypical 'press baron' and perhaps,
in all his finally unhinged glory, the greatest of them all. (His saving
grace was that he always preferred good copy to ideological conformity, which meant that the *Mail*, although generally reactionary, could
be surprisingly idiosyncratic too.) Brought up in genteel poverty as
the eldest son of a large family, he saved enough capital as a budding
journalist to found his own press empire. His brother Harold (later
Lord Rothermere) was crucial on the business side and other family
members helped out too. Harmsworth was already brilliantly successful in the sphere of magazines by the time that the brothers moved
into newspapers; not long before he set off for Sudan, Churchill sent
off a short story, 'Man Overboard!', that in due course appeared in one
of their publications.[117] The *Mail*, launched in 1896, prided itself on
being different, unstuffy, and accessible. A pre-launch advert boasted
that 'Four leading articles, a page of Parliament, and columns of
speeches will NOT be found in the *Daily Mail* on 4 May, a halfpenny.'
It was immediately successful, selling 397,215 copies on its first day.[118]
Within a few weeks Churchill received his first, brief mention in the
paper when a groom was charged with stealing some riding equipment from him.[119]

The *Mail* was self-consciously modern, aspirational, plain-speaking and unintellectual, and was replete with titbits and human interest stories. Brash, populist, and exciting, it was a key exemplar of the personality-focused 'New Journalism' that had been developing since the 1880s, and with which Churchill himself has been linked.[120] Churchill has aptly been described as 'the Quintessential Sensation Seeker'; the *Daily Mail* was, in his own words, 'what we call a sensational paper'.[121] It was also decidedly 'common', at least according to Conservative Prime Minister Lord Salisbury, who said that it was 'written by office-boys, for office-boys' (but read it himself all the same).[122] And though Churchill's politics at this time fitted with those of the *Mail*—imperialistic and staunchly Conservative—he shared this snobbish approach, even while he benefited from the type of publicity that the paper offered. When Lady Randolph was planning her (short-lived) periodical *The Anglo-Saxon Review* he told her that her ideas were too downmarket, like 'Harmsworth's cheap Imperialist productions. I don't say that these have not done good and paid but they are produced for thousands of vulgar people at a popular price.'[123] As individuals, Churchill and Harmsworth were in some ways very similar: both could be charming, both could be bullies, both were prone to enthusiasms (they had a shared interest in aviation). They had a mutual fascination but the relationship between them would eventually turn sour; for the time being, it was professionally useful to them both, and Churchill kept Harmsworth informed of his political plans.[124]

When he returned to England, having given up his army commission, in the spring of 1899, Churchill had already done a great deal of work on *The River War*, his book on the Sudan campaign. Rather than simply recycle his articles, he opted to produce a weighty, two-volume history, which put recent events in long-term perspective. That summer Churchill's political career kicked into gear when he was invited to contest a by-election in Oldham. The *Mail* praised the soundness of his political views and the 'refreshingly frank and unhesitating manner' in which he put them across.[125] It also poked gentle fun at him when he and James Mawdsley (Churchill's elderly running-mate in what was a two-member constituency) encountered two pretty young suffragist campaigners at the local Conservative Club. Mawdsley supported female enfranchisement. Churchill did not, but according to the *Mail* this did not prevent him from flirting with the women:

> He did not say so in so many words, but his smiles conveyed that he was an unmarried, chivalrous gentleman, and that he had far too exalted and devoted an opinion of the sex into which he proposed eventually to marry, ever to think of putting upon them the ignoble duty of the vote.
>
> I never (telegraphs the 'Daily Mail' representative) saw a more delighted deputation. Though Mr. Churchill declared himself dead against them, they beamed upon him as delightedly as they had frowned severely upon his married colleague who had declared himself in their favour. It is safe to say that the women suffragists of Oldham will go solidly for Mr. Churchill, though it is unfortunate that
>
> THEY HAVE NO VOTES.[126]

Yet though such national attention—for which Churchill thanked Harmsworth personally—was doubtless welcome it was surely less important than the attitude of the Northern press.[127] On the one hand, there was the fiercely Tory *Oldham Daily Standard*, which dressed up its articles on Churchill's and Mawdsley's meeting with fawning accounts of how the two men had asked to be allowed 'to devote the talent which heaven has given them for the benefit of humanity'.[128] On the other, there was the staunchly Liberal *Oldham Evening Chronicle*, which ridiculed him as a tyro.[129] The *Manchester Guardian*, an important regional paper of growing national significance under its Liberal editor C. P. Scott, found Churchill 'perfectly ingenuous' but gave a balanced critique of his strengths and weaknesses.[130] The processes of Victorian globalization had by no means eliminated local and regional diversity, or the proud political partisanship that came with it—albeit within a couple of further decades the position would be considerably less healthy. It is hard to say what effect the press coverage had on the actual result, but in the event Churchill and Mawdsley lost narrowly to their Liberal rivals.

As the summer progressed, the crisis in Britain's relations with the independent Boer Republics in South Africa—the Transvaal and the Orange Free State—was coming to a head. Ostensibly, the dispute was about the rights of British settlers—the so-called Uitlanders—but the broader reality was that the British were determined to bring the troublesome Dutch-descended Boers to heel in order to secure their own strategic supremacy in the region. In September, with the situation teetering on the brink, Harmsworth asked Churchill to go to the Cape as a correspondent. Borthwick counter-offered.[131] As Churchill later recalled: '£250 a month, all expenses paid, entire discretion as to movements and opinions, four months' minimum guarantee of employment—such were the terms; higher, I think, than any previously paid in British journalism to War Correspondents, and certainly attractive to a young man of twenty-four with no responsibilities but to earn his own living.'[132] At the time, Churchill wrote to Lord Curzon, the Viceroy of India, enclosing a copy of *The River War*. 'I hope to be on the frontiers of the Orange Free State before you receive this,' he informed him, 'as I sail on the 14th of October as correspondent of the Morning Post.'[133] At last, the Transvaal government issued an ultimatum to the British, triggering war. Churchill's extraordinary adventures during the conflict were to be the making of him. It is well known, of course, that his remarkable courage played a major part in this. Less understood, though, is the part that the media played in representing his heroism to the public in Britain and around the world, and shaping how he was perceived.[134]

The Boer War was a pivotal moment, not only in terms of the history of warfare and of the British Empire, but also—and this was not mere coincidence—of the history of the media. On the one hand, it seems to fit in to a similar pattern to the small colonial wars in which Churchill had already participated, with a style of journalism to match. On the other, its long-drawn-out aspect seems to prefigure the 'total' conflict of World War I, and the huge body of journalists on the ground in South Africa seemed to suggest an increasingly industrialized approach to news-gathering. Moreover, the roll-call of Churchill's fellow correspondents was remarkable, suggesting a growing link between celebrity and journalism. In addition to G. W. Steevens, there were the novelists Edgar Wallace and Sir Arthur Conan Doyle, Churchill's future Cabinet colleague Leo Amery, and J. A. Hobson of the *Manchester Guardian*, whose powerful critique of imperialism was later to influence Lenin. Furthermore, this is the point from which it begins to make sense to talk about 'the media', plural, rather than simply about the press. The Spanish–American war had been the first to be captured on newsreel; Churchill toyed with the idea of taking a Cinematograph 'machine & expert' with him to South Africa.[135] The scheme came to nothing, but he did travel to the Cape on the same ship as W. K. L. Dickson, a cinematic pioneer who became 'the man who filmed the Boer War'.[136] Deprived of news, those on board were reduced to signalling to a steamer coming in the opposite direction to ask for information about the war's progress. Churchill and his fellows then observed a blackboard held up from the deck of the other ship:

BOERS DEFEATED.
THREE BATTLES.
PENN SYMONDS KILLED.

(William Penn Symons was a British general.) From this, the passengers concluded that the British had practically won already. In fact, the early trend of the war was quite the other way. As soon as the ship landed at Table Bay, Churchill grabbed a stack of newspapers and learned of the Boer invasion of Natal and the retreat of the British to Ladysmith where they were soon to be cut off and besieged.[137]

Still lacking a full picture of what was going, and facing many obstacles to progress, Churchill headed towards the front in the company of J. B. Atkins of the *Manchester Guardian*. Churchill's articles were again cast in the form of 'letters'—the first of these, describing his voyage, did not appear in the *Morning Post* until about three weeks after it was written, by which time he had been taken into captivity.[138] His name was appearing in the papers in Britain in the meantime—but on account of reviews of *The River War*, not of his activities in South Africa.[139] One might ask, why didn't he just send telegrams, not least given that the telegraph system was certainly better than on the North-West Frontier or in Sudan? In fact he did, but they were also subject to delays; probably because of wartime conditions, one of Churchill's took three days to arrive, and another was not published until a week after it was sent.[140] There was also the question of expense. Every message telegraphed from the Cape cost at least eighteen pence per word, and sometimes six or even twelve shillings per word, if sent at the 'urgency rate'. A normal newspaper column would cost—counting only the cost of the telegram, at the lowest rate—about £185.[141] Later in the war, when his celebrity was assured and his employer perhaps accordingly more indulgent, Churchill did send some much longer telegrams in addition to letters; one of them was said to have cost £350.[142] This all reminds us that there was more to the story of news globalization than the telegraph plus news agencies. Complementary use of telegrams and articles illustrates how the journalism of the period was 'two-speed'—or rather multi-speed. The interplay between technology, economics, and happenstance determined how and when content appeared.

Churchill and Atkins made it as far as the small township of Estcourt, where they encountered Leo Amery (working for *The Times*) and also Aylmer Haldane (the officer who had befriended Churchill during the Tirah expedition). Churchill wanted to find a guide to take him through the Boer lines but in the end adopted another method of finding some action.[143] As Atkins recounted the events of 15 November: 'At about 4.30 a.m. Mr. Winston Churchill, who was sleeping in my tent, woke me up to say that he was going in that death-trap, the armoured train, with Haldane. I said that he would either see too little or too much.'[144] The train made it safely as far as Frere, but on the return journey came under fire and then collided with rocks that the Boers had used to block the line. As the bombardment continued Churchill kept a cool head, urging on the British soldiers and helping get the engine past the obstruction. As it moved off with the wounded on board he went back to fetch Haldane and his company who had been left behind. Yet they had already been taken prisoner: and Churchill was now taken prisoner too. Decades later, the *Natal Daily News* ran an interview with Frans Changuion, who claimed to have been one of his captors.[145] When Churchill objected that 'as a war correspondent he should not be held captive [...] it was made clear to him that it was just this sort of people who caused wars'.[146]

The news that Churchill might have been captured travelled swiftly back to Britain by telegram and was reported in the papers on 17 November. (This was only possible because a damaged cable had just been repaired; there had previously been a time lag of a week.)[147] There was strong agreement that Churchill had acted heroically in the defence of the armoured train, of which there were lengthy accounts.[148] The following day, several reports suggested, inaccurately, that he had been carrying a rifle when he headed back to try to round up the stragglers. This led to some juicy speculation that, under a strict interpretation of the laws of war 'this intrepid young gentleman might be hanged!'[149] There is no evidence that the Boer authorities ever did consider executing Churchill—he was too valuable a prize—although he failed to persuade them that he was a non-combatant and that therefore he ought to be released.

A lively recent account of the affair labels Churchill as a *Hero of the Empire*.[150] The notion of him as a hero was certainly the dominant press narrative, even in the Natal newspapers, which had fallen into Boer hands; these 'glowing accounts' persuaded his captors that he had hurt their cause by freeing the engine and therefore that he should be treated as a prisoner of war.[151] His heroism was not wholly uncontested, though, even within the United Kingdom. This is hardly surprising given that, although the war had strong popular support, there was also a powerful minority current of anti-war 'Pro-Boer' opinion, not least in Ireland. Also, a degree of scepticism towards colourful tales was perfectly natural. The *Dublin Herald* suggested that Churchill's 'friends in the Press are overdoing it. [...] Now, nobody would like to see this promising young fellow shot or hanged, but really these push-ing young men will have to be careful.'[152] Another Irish paper, the *Freeman's Journal*, complained about the paucity of meaningful war coverage, in spite of the presence of large numbers of British press-men in South Africa. However: 'We do not mention Mr. Winston Churchill, for he at once, in the most brilliant manner, solved the difficulty of his position by fighting himself into the Boer lines and getting transformed into a Boer prisoner with nothing to do but twirl his thumbs.'[153] The *Cheltenham Examiner* felt that his role in the affair had been exaggerated by journalists 'chorusing his valiant deeds'.[154] *The Globe* observed that 'we do not desire to see the establishment of a mutual admiration society among the War Correspondents'.[155]

Churchill was keen to point out in his memoirs that he had been 'in no way responsible for the tales which the railway men and the wounded from the armoured train had told, nor for the form in which these statements had been transmitted to England; and still less for the wide publicity accorded to them there. I was a prisoner and perforce silent.'[156] He had been taken to Pretoria and held at the State Model Schools, the building of which was serving as a makeshift prison for British officers; but he was by no means wholly silent. Remarkably, the Boers permitted him to send lengthy accounts of the armoured train incident and of his experiences since his capture to the *Morning Post*; it must of course be assumed that they vetted the contents.[157] His cap-tors also permitted him to be interviewed by a representative of the Reuters news agency; he expressed the view that the war would be 'bloody and protracted'.[158]

In mid-December, readers around the world learned that Churchill had escaped. He had broken out of the State Model Schools via the latrine window; he then made his way towards Portuguese East Africa, at one stage hiding in a mine operated by sympathetic Britishers. Of course, none of these details were known to the public at the time. Papers were filled with fanciful speculation. For example, the *Novoe*

Vremya (St Petersburg), published a telegram from its London correspondent:'Winston Churchill, the Correspondent of the *Morning Post*, who was a prisoner a[t] Pretoria, escaped, but has again been captured. It is feared that his life is in danger. It is said that he decided to escape because his paper continues to pay him £1,000 per month, and he considers it obligatory to fulfil his duties as correspondent.'[159] This was not so much the globalization of news as the globalization of rumour and gossip.

Far from being recaptured, Churchill succeeded in smuggling himself aboard a goods train headed for Portuguese territory. Arriving, dishevelled, in Lorenço Marques, he presented himself to the British Consul. As soon as he had bathed and eaten he 'devoured the file of newspapers' that had been placed before him.[160] At 10 p.m. on 21 December he despatched a telegram describing his escape at some length; but this was not published until the 27th.[161] However, the bare fact that he had made it to safety had been reported in the British press on the 23rd, courtesy of a Colonial Office telegram.[162] Churchill had got the fame that he had always wanted, and on a global scale— but now he had to come to terms with the 'undercurrent of disparagement' that had begun to 'mingle with the gushing tributes'. It is clear that he resented the aspersions some parts of the press cast upon his honour, especially the false allegation that he had broken a promise to the Boers not to abscond; a long passage in *My Early Life* is dedicated to quoting and then rebutting criticisms made of him in *Truth*, the *Phoenix*, the *Daily Nation*, and the *Westminster Gazette*.[163]

Churchill swiftly returned to British territory, receiving a rousing welcome when he landed at Durban. But his own behaviour, and his highly opinionated despatches, ensured that he could never be an *uncontroversial* hero. He persuaded General Sir Redvers Buller, the Commander-in-Chief in South Africa, to allow him to once again take up an officer's commission while continuing to write for the *Morning Post*, even though, in the aftermath of the Sudan campaign, the War Office had forbidden soldiers to act as correspondents. Buller was rewarded, for although Churchill took a dim view of his generalship he backed him up in his articles. He privately admitted: 'If there were any one to take Buller's place I would cut and slash— but there is no well known General who is as big a man as he is and *faute de mieux* we must back him for all he is worth—which at this moment is very little.'[164] Accordingly, Churchill's telegraphed accounts of the Battle of Spion Kop, which took place at the end of January 1900, were resolutely upbeat, even as it became evident that a serious defeat was unfolding. 23 January 1900: 'There is every prospect that a deliberate and careful, but surprising advance, conducted with General Buller's great skill, and supported by his terrible artillery, will lead to a magnificent victory.'[165] 24 January: 'our troops showed a stubborn defence in spite of severe loss.'[166] 27 January, 1.10 p.m.: 'the British troops evacuated Spion Kop last night, withdrawing in perfect order in the general line.' 27 January 5.55 p.m.: 'Spion Kop was not a disaster, for we lost neither guns nor unwounded prisoners.' 28 January: 'The Army is exasperated, not defeated. [. . .] General Buller will persevere. All will come right in the end.'[167] In a perceptive reading of Churchill's lengthier despatches, his granddaughter Celia Sandys notes that taken collectively they 'reflect dismay at Buller's plodding leadership; but when they are read singly, as they were written, the faults are excused'.[168]

Churchill's attitude towards Buller and Spion Kop reminds us once again that he viewed things through a nationalist-imperialist lens; he sought not merely to report events but to spin them in the best interests of the British cause. This was consistent, though, with considerable independence of mind, because he was determined to judge for himself what those interests were. Hence his willingness to court controversy by advocating a conciliatory attitude towards the Boers once they had been defeated, as in his view this would help secure Britain's supremacy in the region.[169] In the spring, Churchill attached himself to the force led by his friend General Sir Ian Hamilton, on the flank of the main army of Lord Roberts, the new Commander-in-Chief, as it progressed from Bloemfontein. Here was a journalistic opportunity, for this column 'was, owing to the difficulties of telegraphing, scarcely attended by a single newspaper correspondent'. He was present at the relief of Ladysmith and at the conquest of Pretoria. At last, scenting the prospect of a general election, and with the war giving the misleading appearance of entering its final phase, he returned to Britain.

His final despatch, sent from Cape Town on 28 June, appeared in print nearly a month later. By this point, the first volume of his letters had already been published as *London to Ladysmith, Via Pretoria*; the second soon came out with the title *Ian Hamilton's March*. These were very much 'instant books', not attempts at more thoroughgoing history, like *The River War*; the copy had been set up by the publishers as each despatch arrived from the war.[170] They were superior examples of the genre, although they were gratingly pompous at times. 'He is never a mere chronicler of events', noted one reviewer of *London to Ladysmith*. 'The temptation to stop aside for the purposes of directing the concerns of the Empire is always a little too much for this very capable and complacent young man.'[171] Another, the writer Richard Le Gallienne, made a comparison between Churchill and G. W. Steevens, who had died of fever during the siege of Ladysmith:

> Mr. Steevens was one of the cleverest reporters of war as a 'picnic,' but he was not really a great war correspondent for that very reason.
>
> [. . .] behind a pen no less precisely graphic than Steevens', he [Churchill] makes one conscious of a richness of temperament, or warmth and depth of feeling, of which Steevens in his writing gave no hint. Mr. Churchill is gay and 'modern' enough, but he is 'au fond' deeply serious, and has the gift, rare just now among our young writers, of being Moved by Moving Things.[172]

This latter comment is an appropriate point at which to conclude discussion of Churchill's pre-parliamentary career. We have seen how late Victorian news culture allowed Churchill the space to conduct his literary experiments, even though editors did not simply give him carte blanche. His journalism during this period shows remarkable skill and thoughtfulness, mixed with an extraordinary self-confidence that often crossed into bumptiousness. Perhaps it was the very combination that made it so appealing.

As the *Navy and Army Illustrated* observed, Churchill's vivid articles were 'excellent illustrations of the methods of the new journalism'.[173] More broadly, his early journalism is illustrative of the links between the rise of the mass press, imperial expansion, and globalization more generally.[174] For him, the availability of news was one of the key features of 'civilization', of which the telegraph line was a symbol and which it helped to spread. In this brave new world, Churchill's own articles became globalized products, as papers in Britain and around the world reprinted his contributions to the *Morning Post*, showing little concern for copyright.[175] (This reflected the contemporaneous 'culture of transatlantic reprinting' that has been identified by the news historian Bob Nicholson.[176]) Churchill himself was an exponent of the New Journalism, yet he was no slavish imitator of established styles. His writings were peppered with moralizing 'philosophic reflections', as Steevens termed them, which justified and sought to strengthen the British Empire.[177] If anything, it was the *explicitness* with which he did this that marked him out: he was, the *Daily Express* noted, 'an Englishman first and a war correspondent afterwards'.[178] Glenn R. Wilkinson has argued that the newspapers of the era presented war 'as a positive event' and that 'images of sport, games, hunting, theatre and spectacle created a distance between reader and war', disguising the harsh realities of conflict.[179] Indisputably, Churchill failed to present war in its full brutality, and it is certainly possible to claim that he viewed it as a game, although it should be noted he did not disguise from his readers the fact that he was writing under censorship, which he argued was not unnecessarily restrictive and was justified on military grounds.[180] As will be seen in a later chapter, this habit of self-bowdlerization conditioned his view, as Prime Minister during World War II, of what constituted appropriate journalistic behaviour.

At the same time, it should be emphasized that the press was not monolithic and that tales of heroism were not always taken at face value. Discerning readers would have been well aware that war news was not to be trusted unquestioningly.[181] Much as Churchill's courage was praised, he was actually cut remarkably little slack in the aftermath of the armoured train incident. As soon as one set of journalists built him up, another set started looking for ways to cut him down to size. As the twentieth century dawned, then, Churchill's media persona was already cast in terms that were to become familiar: larger than life, brilliant and brave, but highly self-opinionated and far from fully trustworthy. As he prepared to make the transition from celebrity journalist to celebrity politician, this pushing young man had already secured what he wanted from the press: its undying fascination with himself.

2

Stage Thunder

The evening of 9 January 1901 found Winston Churchill MP being heckled in the auditorium of the University of Michigan. Fresh from his South African triumphs, he had faced no problem being elected as member for Oldham during the so-called 'khaki election', at which Lord Salisbury's Conservatives had crushed their Liberal opponents. But, at this time, MPs did not receive salaries. Therefore, a highly paid North American lecture tour was just what Churchill needed to replenish his coffers in order to sustain his Commons career over the next few years. Yet, as the USA's own recent acquisition of former Spanish territories had made 'imperialism' highly controversial there, Churchill's boosting of the British Empire sometimes went down badly. But although his peroration on this winter's evening was met with jeers and hisses, he was sufficiently cool-tempered and generous to grant one of the students present, Gustavus Ohlinger, an interview for the college paper—on condition that nothing was published that would reflect on his parliamentary position. Ohlinger was true to his word, and the full text was not published until over sixty years later.[1]

As the two men settled down over drinks in an Ann Arbor hotel room, Churchill outlined his career to date and offered an oblique comment on the causes of his own success. 'I think the press affords the ladder which is available to everyone in a way afforded by no other profession', he remarked; 'put out good stuff and in time people will say, "We must have this" '. He also discoursed on the differences between the British and American press. He saw the former as superior, albeit for reasons which might today seem somewhat surprising. Rather than viewing American newspapers as having too much influence over the political process, he believed that they did not have enough. 'In England, the newspaper has great power; you cannot say that here', he argued. 'No strong paper, if it starts out to do a thing, fails of accomplishing it in England.' Part of the problem, he thought, was that Americans had no national newspaper, in part, of course, because of the sheer size of the country. He then slipped into visionary mode:

> To overcome the difficulty you must call in the aid of the telegraph. There should be centers in different sections of the country where the national paper could be published for the section. Your millionaires could do a great deal better than founding hospitals, endowing universities, and building libraries by starting some good national paper that would give correct news that would aid in forming national sentiment, and in giving expression to national aspirations.

He also dispensed some highly practical counsel. 'You ask my advice to the young correspondent? It is: verify your quotations and avoid split infinitives.'[2]

Churchill's midnight musings are striking, and not only because they reveal the attention to detail which he brought to his own journalistic writings. His belief that the press could be a positive force for national cohesion reflected contemporary attitudes. James Thompson has explored the concept of 'public opinion' in the pre-1914 period, showing how it was intertwined with ideas about the platform, parliament, and the press. The Edwardians and Victorians did not see public opinion as simply the sum of the citizenry's private opinions; rather, what concerned them was opinion expressed *in* public. How sincerely and persistently a given view was expressed was at least as important as the number of people who happened to hold it. Opinions were to be '*weighed* rather than *counted*'. Moreover, it was often assumed that newspapers mirrored their readers' opinions—as if they did not, sales would dry up—and therefore genuinely expressed what the public cared about.[3]

Considered in this light, Churchill's assumption that a powerful press was a good thing, and his seemingly naive belief that millionaire proprietors would act as benign philanthropists, appears less surprising. The fact that the Conservative Party benefited from heavy press support probably contributed to his sanguine approach, as too, no doubt, did the fact that he had not as yet been on the receiving end of serious or sustained newspaper hostility. Within a few years he would be taking a rather different line, but in retrospect he looked back on the time of his first election to Parliament as something of a golden age of public discussion, aided by the press. 'Speeches of well-known and experienced statesmen were fully reported in all the newspapers and studied by wide political classes', he recalled. 'Thus by a process of rugged argument the national decision was reached in measured steps.'[4]

It is easy to see how nostalgia for a lost time could have influenced him here; and it could be said that the politics of the Boer War period were not so much 'rugged' as rancorous and bitter. Still, it is quite true that the House of Commons which he entered upon his return from his lecture tour was significantly better reported than it is today, or even than it was during the interwar years.[5] Of course, even in those days, the more obscure MPs would struggle to get coverage for their remarks—and Churchill himself complained around this time that his speeches made outside Parliament did not get reported in the London papers.[6] But when he stood up to make his Commons debut in February 1901—in defence of the government's actions in South Africa—he could be sure that his existing fame would be sufficient to guarantee him plenty of column inches. He was still aware, too, that recollections of his father were strong. He alluded to this at the end of his speech, attributing the patience with which he had been heard to the 'splendid memory' of Lord Randolph which many MPs still retained.[7] Few of the journalists who reported the speech—generally very favourably, although Churchill's nerves had been evident—could resist drawing comparisons. 'In him a good deal of his father survives', noted *The Scotsman*.[8]

Far from feeling overshadowed, Winston played up the personal and political resemblance. With a few parliamentary friends, including Lord Hugh Cecil (son of Lord Salisbury), Churchill established a small group known as 'The Hooligans' or 'Hughligans', a move which recalled the days of the Fourth Party. The group benefited from the encouragement of Leo Maxse, editor of the right-wing *National Review*.[9] Churchill developed a reputation, which even crossed the Atlantic, as an irresponsible 'free-lance' Commons performer.[10] Early on, he launched a bold attack on his own government's scheme for army reform, decrying it as wasteful. In the Commons he quoted Lord Randolph's resignation letter and claimed to be raising once more 'the tattered flag of retrenchment and economy' that his father had once brandished.[11] Churchill had colluded with the press in order to improve the speech's coverage. 'I had sent it off to the *Morning Post* beforehand, and it was already in print', he remembered. 'What would have happened if I had not been called, or had not got through with it, I cannot imagine.'[12] Churchill also recruited the military correspondent Charles à Court Repington to advise him and his fellow dissidents; Repington led the assault on the army reform plans in the press, promising Churchill that he would 'keep on shooting until the enemy retires'. He was thus able to exploit the fact that Repington, like many other journalists, wanted to shape events as well as report them. Eventually, when it became clear that the reforms had failed, Prime Minister A. J. Balfour shunted the war Secretary St John Brodrick sideways to the India Office.[13]

Churchill wrote for the *Daily Mail* as part of his army reform campaign, but, notwithstanding a number of contributions to periodicals, mainly on military themes, he did not undertake much paid journalism at this time.[14] He and some associates, including Repington, had a plan for a journal called *The Gauntlet*, which was to 'throw down the gauntlet to all and sundry abuses which afflicted the realm'; but due to lack of funds it never got off the ground.[15] Churchill was at

this time a fairly prolific contributor to newspaper letters pages, especially to that of *The Times*. For example, after the Liberal leader Sir
Henry Campbell-Bannerman denounced the government's use of
'methods of barbarism', Churchill defended the use of concentration
camps to house Boer women and children.[16] He was also drawn in to
a lengthy and somewhat bizarre controversy with a correspondent,
'J.C.B.', who had attacked the conditions under which Harris Tweed
was produced; Churchill portrayed this as a malicious anonymous
attack on an industry upon which many poor people depended for
their livelihoods.[17] It seems he had little genuine interest in the topic
but was simply looking for an opportunity to be mischievous, and
clearly enjoyed his attempts to out 'J.C.B.' as the psychiatrist Sir James
Crichton-Browne. Although Churchill generally wrote for money,
political advantage, or for some combination of the two, sometimes
he did it simply for enjoyment.

Churchill was constantly in need of mental stimulus, and his close
reading of the press helped provide this. In a light-hearted speech to
the annual dinner of the London Press Club in 1903, he commented
that he was 'a confirmed and systematic newspaper reader' who 'took
a pile of papers every morning'. He joked:

> He read 'The Times' because it gave one a feeling of the seriousness
> and responsibilities of life. He read the 'Morning Post' because it made
> one feel so respectable.
>
> He glanced at the 'Daily Mail' in order that he might catch the mood
> of the moment. He looked at the 'Daily News' because he liked to put
> his hand upon the throbbing heart of the people, and he liked to finish
> with the 'Daily Telegraph' because that paper left one in such a con-
> tented frame of mind.

The *Daily News* was a Liberal paper, so this was a reasonably catholic
range of reading. Churchill also twitted Lord Burnham, proprietor of
the *Telegraph*, who was chairing the dinner, for the slavishness of his
paper's devotion to the government: 'According to that loyal critic
[i.e. the paper itself], the transference of Mr. Brodrick to the India
Office was a proof that his great work of reforming the Army was

complete, while a few days later the removal of Mr. Arnold-Forster to the War Office was accepted as a proof that the great work of Army Reform had begun. (Laughter.)'[18]

Churchill's speech also alluded to the split in the government's ranks that had opened up a few months earlier, when Colonial Secretary Joseph Chamberlain blew apart the longstanding consensus in favour of free trade with a speech in Birmingham announcing his conversion to a scheme of imperial tariff preference.[19] As early as October 1902—already out of sympathy with his party's leaders— Churchill had foreseen that the tariff issue might force a reshaping of British politics. He did not, however, at this stage imagine that this would lead to him crossing the floor. Rather, he hoped for a Tory–Liberal 'central coalition', perhaps with former Liberal Prime Minister Lord Rosebery at its head.[20] Moreover, although his first reaction to the Birmingham bombshell was one of strong opposition, the situation was in many ways still unclear. As Churchill observed a few months later, Chamberlain gained from keeping his precise pro- posals vague.[21] The water was muddied further by Balfour's decision to commit himself to a policy of 'retaliation', whereby tariffs would be used by Britain in order to get other countries to lower their own trade barriers. Meanwhile, Churchill was much more eager than his Conservative and Unionist pro-free trade allies to reach out to the Liberals, who for their part feared that his impetuous public state- ments risked alienating some of the more cautious Tories. 'I thought your interview with the *Westminster* [*Gazette*] rather unwise', Hugh Cecil told him as the tariff controversy heated up. 'I am sure it w[oul] d offend the trembling sheep.'[22] Churchill, who had warned that the Conservatives were courting 'political annihilation', apologized, but did not reform his behaviour.[23] Cecil thought his Press Club remarks unwise as 'jokes about party loyalty are a mistake just now'. He also begged Churchill to watch his words in his speeches: 'remember that the newspaper reader of tomorrow is much more important than the audience of tonight'.[24]

Churchill, of course, was well aware of the power of the press, even if he differed with Cecil on tactics for using it. He briefed St Loe Strachey, editor-proprietor of Unionist weekly *The Spectator*, with confidential information on plans to form a Free Trade League to counter Chamberlain's activities.[25] Strachey was a convinced free trader and Churchill suggested to him editorial lines to take. 'I could tell you several things if we were talking that I hesitate to put upon paper', Churchill wrote, and invited Strachey to dinner.[26] Churchill even had plans for a bold scheme 'to coordinate the entire Free Trade Press of the country' by creating a press bureau that would circulate articles, 'gossipy newsletters', and speeches in print-ready form.[27]

Churchill tried to interest Alfred Harmsworth in this plan, but to no effect.[28] This was part of his broader effort to keep the *Daily Mail*'s owner on the side of the free trade angels. Harmsworth was ambivalent about the Colonial Secretary's plans, and was opposed in particular to food imports (in contrast to manufactures) being subjected to tariffs; he did, however, negotiate with him behind the scenes. At the same time, Harmsworth was a great admirer of Lord Rosebery, who seemed eternally and tantalizingly on the verge of returning to the head of affairs, and Churchill used the former Prime Minister as a lure: 'I think this is the time for a central Government and if Lord R lets the opportunity pass, it may never return.'[29] However, Rosebery firmly rebuffed Harmsworth's (characteristically tactless) approach. When Chamberlain soon afterwards resigned from the government to pursue his campaign in the country the *Mail* shifted towards backing him, although it continued to be sceptical of 'food taxes'.[30] Churchill and Harmsworth remained friendly, but their political paths were now diverging. H. W. Wilson, the *Mail*'s chief leader writer, told the latter: 'It is excellent that you have held aloof from Winston, and are not in the camp of the stand-stills.'[31]

By the end of 1903, Churchill had decidedly burnt his boats with the Conservative Party. He annoyed Cecil, and, crucially, alienated his own constituency party in Oldham, by sending a supportive message to a Liberal by-election candidate.[32] (He then rubbed salt into the wound by praising the Liberal Party in a speech at Halifax.)[33] The letter in question was not a personal communication but was rather an expression of Churchill's views intended for publication, a then-common technique that was not dissimilar to politicians' use of press releases today.[34] A few weeks later, Churchill read in the *Daily Telegraph* that he was to be deprived of the Tory whip.[35] It was not, however, until the end of May 1904 that he formally crossed the floor of the House of Commons and joined the Liberals. It was a good moment to do so, as the free trade issue had helped reunite the party, whereas the government was by now in serious difficulties. J. A. Spender, editor of the *Westminster Gazette*—a Liberal paper whose influence outstripped its small circulation—recalled that Churchill succeeded in catching 'the changing tides of opinion which the more scientific calculators seemed to miss'. Spender judged that this instinctive approach to politics made Churchill more like Harmsworth than like his new colleague, the rising Radical statesman David Lloyd George.[36]

Although it may seem clear with the benefit of hindsight that the free traders were bound to sweep all before them, Churchill felt at the time that there was a serious risk that Chamberlain and his fellow tariff reformers would triumph.[37] He complained about the skewed coverage offered by the protectionist press, and in a speech at Coatbridge he launched a strong attack: 'The establishment of a mammoth newspaper trust, which works through five, ten, or a dozen newspapers at a time, very often with one management, yet animated by totally different opinions in politics, but which can turn on its writers on this side or that at the caprice of some individual who is out of touch with the politics or the interests of the population affected, is to be deplored.'[38] Churchill's attacks on the 'trustification' of the news market—i.e. the attempt by large companies to secure monopolistic control—reflected a familiar Liberal complaint of the period.[39]

Harmsworth thought the speech was aimed at *him* and Churchill hastened to assure him otherwise.[40] Rather, the comments were targeted at C. Arthur Pearson, founder of the *Daily Express* and 'the champion "hustler" of the Tariff Reform League', who had acquired the Conservative *Standard* and converted it away from free trade.[41] Pearson and Churchill fought it out in the letters pages of *The Times* and *The Spectator*, with the latter alleging that the former had 'been able to pervert' the *Standard*'s writers.[42] The growth of newspaper combinations and the resulting decline in editorial independence would, Churchill argued, 'inevitably degrade journalism [...] to a sordid and irresponsible traffic in words and phrases'.[43] A few months later he expressed the rather different view that, on the whole, newspapers reflected public opinion more than they influenced it—but on that occasion he was speaking to the Newspaper Society annual dinner and was probably trying to soft-soap his audience.[44]

At the end of 1905, the Conservative government resigned and was replaced by a Liberal administration under Campbell-Bannerman. Churchill was given a junior ministerial role—that of Undersecretary of State at the Colonial Office. A general election was called at once. Churchill had some time since decided to give up Oldham and fight instead the Manchester North-West seat: the *Manchester Daily Dispatch* mockingly portrayed him as 'contemplating the publication of another story of adventure, "How I escaped from Oldham," as a sequel to "How I escaped from Pretoria"'.[45] During the election campaign, Churchill commented on the fact that press proprietors sympathetic to the Conservatives had been given peerages; he specifically referred to Harmsworth, who was ennobled in the resignation honours list and became Lord Northcliffe.[46] Although Churchill was now a member of a party that the Northcliffe press despised, this did not prevent him as an individual from receiving sympathetic coverage in them.[47] In the world of personality-driven journalism, he was to be prized as a good source of copy. As the *Mail* could not resist pointing out, Mancunians found 'Winston' more interesting than free trade. The paper's Special Correspondent, Charles E. Hands, dwelt on Churchill's sex appeal and his 'new old-fashioned hat, a flat-topped sort of felt hat' which had provoked a flood of orders to local hatters for similar items.[48] As was then customary, polling took place across the country over a number of weeks. Churchill's victory came fairly early on and signalled a wider Liberal landslide. A spread in the *Illustrated London News* depicted 'THE EXTRAORDINARY TURN OF THE TIDE AT MANCHES-TER', contrasting Churchill's triumph with Balfour's humiliating defeat in his own nearby constituency.[49]

The *ILN*'s pictures were not photographs, but rather hand-drawn illustrations by the French-born artist Amédée Forestier, who worked regularly for the magazine. This raises interesting questions about Churchill's media image at this time as well as about visual news culture more generally. By the turn of the century, the advent of cheap portable cameras increased the possibilities of exciting documentary photography. There are several good candid photos of Churchill at this period, including some of the aftermath of the armoured train episode and of Churchill in captivity.[50] Nevertheless, many of the most dramatic episodes of the Boer War were presented to the British people in the form of sketches. Some of these were by genuine war artists.[51] Some of them were done from photographs.[52] Others, we have to assume, were done in Britain by people who had never been anywhere near the places they were drawing.[53] This was understandable, given that there was as yet no means for pictures to be conveyed telegraphically. In 1904, Harmsworth's newly-launched *Daily Mirror* was pioneering in its more widespread use of photographs.[54] However, the culture of hand illustration persisted in other publications, even for domestic events such as elections.[55] The *ILN* published its first 'action' shot of Churchill (which shows him having just descended from an aeroplane) as late as 1914, although the technology that allowed it do so had existed well before.[56]

As Churchill's ministerial career started, though, there was no shortage of visual representations of him in the press. He was increasingly depicted in editorial cartoons. This was a genre in which he himself took much interest. 'I always loved cartoons', he wrote in an interwar essay on the subject. 'At my private school at Brighton there were three or four volumes of cartoons from Punch, and on Sundays we were allowed to study them.' But, he asked his readers, how would they like to be cartooned themselves? 'Fancy having that process going on every week, often every day, over the whole of your life; and all your fellow-countrymen and friends and family seeing you thus held up to mockery and shame!' However, he confessed, 'it is not so bad as you would expect. Just as eels are supposed to get used to skinning, so politicians get used to being caricatured. In fact, by a strange trait in human nature they even get to like it.' They even had a tendency, he wrote, to get 'offended and downcast' when the treatment stopped.[57]

The 'treatment' of Churchill was pretty robust during his initial time in government. During this period he made a series of perceived gaffes or provocations. Most notorious was his comment on the position of Chinese indentured labourers in South Africa, a system established under the previous government which many Liberals had denounced as 'Chinese slavery' during the election campaign. Churchill now admitted that it could not 'in the opinion of His Majesty's Government be classified as slavery in the extreme acceptance of the word without some risk of terminological inexactitude'.[58] The cartoonists leapt on such missteps with alacrity. One of the cleverest offerings, by the justly celebrated Bernard Partridge, showed a bas-relief in the style of the Parthenon frieze (or 'Elgin marbles'). Churchill was a horse-born warrior, while his boss, the Secretary of State for the Colonies, attended on him in the guise of a servant. As the Secretary of State was Lord Elgin, grandson of the Seventh Earl (of Parthenon fame), this was particularly neat, but neater still was its comment on ministerial relationships within the Colonial Office.[59]

The suggestion that Churchill was really in charge was misleading, though; Elgin, who had previously served as Viceroy to India, had much to teach his subordinate, and the two men rubbed along fairly well in spite of some fractiousness. Yet Elgin was shy and undemonstrative, and it was natural that the idea should develop that his flamboyant junior colleague was running rings round him. Certainly, Churchill became the media face of the Colonial Office, and took the heat accordingly. This was not merely a matter of domestic politics. The original reaction to his appointment from the Empire press had been cool, to say the least: the *Ottawa Citizen* commented that 'The appointment of Winston Churchill would suggest that the new Liberal Government has reverted to the old Liberal belief that anything is good enough for the Colonies.'[60] What lay behind this type of remark? Strange as it now may seem, given Churchill's longstanding reputation as an imperial diehard, he was often seen at this time as as someone who played up to the Radical critics of Empire on the Liberal back-benches, and as out of touch with the needs and realities of white British settlers. This, of course, made the implementation of policy all the more difficult. As Churchill complained in a 1907 memorandum, the news agencies played a part in this. They operated under the guise of political neutrality but were inevitably selective in their reporting, including the reporting of opinion. As Churchill put it:

> It ought not to be forgotten that a Liberal Government has to encoun-
> ter in Colonial affairs the steady and malignant detraction of a most
> powerful press service. Every action or inaction is presented in the
> Colonies—and, I think, particularly in Australia—in the most odious
> light by the press telegrams. The worst excesses of partisan opponents
> at home are cabled to the newspapers of every Colony as the opinion
> of patriotic newspapers in England upon this or that particular event.
> By these agencies a great volume of prejudice has been excited in the
> past, and is still being aggravated.[61]

Even allowing for the possibility that Churchill was exaggerating the agencies' bias, his complaint reminds us that they played a role not just in 'the globalization of news' but also in 'the globalization of views'. And, undeniably, he and his fellow Liberals faced an uphill struggle to win over colonial opinion; a few years later, after he had moved on from the Colonial Office, the government decided to give Reuters a secret subsidy to ensure that the details of ministers' speeches were relayed to the colonies.[62]

In the meantime, the 1907 Colonial Conference, which took place in London, created the opportunity to build bridges with the Empire's

Prime Ministers and to create good publicity all round. But the visitors had to push the British hosts to ensure that a daily summary of the discussions would be prepared for the press. 'We live in the light of a publicity which you gentlemen are hardly accustomed to', said Alfred Deakin of Australia, in a comment that casts a sidelight on the differing media environments of colonial and metropolitan politics.[63] Although Churchill and his colleagues disappointed their guests by the strength of their continued commitment to free trade, the conference was reasonably successful. The day after it closed, though, the *Daily Mail* reported that Sir Robert Bond, Premier of Newfoundland, had in the final session begged for Britain's assistance in her dispute with the USA over fishing rights. When Elgin blankly refused his 'pathetic appeal', the paper alleged, Bond leapt to his feet and denounced this 'great humiliation', and then gathered up his papers and left.[64]

Questioned in the Commons about the story, Churchill took a *de haut en bas* attitude towards the *Mail*: 'I cannot undertake, as a general rule, to correct misstatements appearing in journals of that class and character; but as I learn that this particular report has been cabled fully to the Colonies, it has become necessary for me to say that it is from beginning to end a baseless and impudent fabrication'. He then took a swipe at Northcliffe: 'it is a matter of surprise to me that a person who has lately been created a Peer of the realm should be willing to allow newspapers under his control to employ, for political objects, methods of such transparent mendacity.'[65] The *Mail* sent a telegram to Bond, who was at a banquet in Bristol, asking whether Churchill's denial was accurate. He replied equivocally: 'Cannot admit that anything so dramatic as alleged took place.'[66] On this basis the paper claimed Bond had confirmed that its account was 'substantially correct', and attacked Churchill for his denials: 'This is "not cricket," and it is something new and unpleasant in British public life.'[67] Churchill doubled down, using a speech in Edinburgh to accuse the Northcliffe press of perverting the truth on a daily basis.[68]

Neither the paper nor Churchill came out of the episode with much credit. Although the story was not actually fabricated, the *Mail* seems to have published first and checked its facts afterwards. Northcliffe himself disapproved, and made his displeasure known to the paper's editor, Thomas Marlowe.[69] For its part, the Colonial Office's handling of the press was also revealed as cack-handed. The official precis of the proceedings was bowdlerized in order to disguise Bond's grievances, yet it was hardly surprising that this attempt to suppress controversy turned out to be ineffective. Moreover, Churchill's tactic of attacking the press bore mixed results. On the one hand, his blatant contradiction of the report seems to have been taken at face value in the South African press.[70] On the other hand, in Canada, the notion that Bond had been humiliated seems to have struck a nerve.[71] It is also worth asking how seriously Churchill's criticisms of the Northcliffe press were meant. It seems that Churchill did get genuinely upset when his personal honour was called into question. Yet, at the same time, he seems to have regarded attacks on his *political* honour—such as over the Newfoundland incident—as simply part of the game. Northcliffe's papers gained readers; Churchill stoked up his political base. In his Edinburgh speech, Churchill told his cheering audience that the power of the Radical and Liberal platform would defeat the Tory and protectionist press: 'We have done it before; we can do it again.'[72]

Churchill was not quite the typical Liberal politician, of course. He proved this again at the end of the 1907 parliamentary session when—pausing only to attempt to settle a cap-makers' strike in his constituency, and then to observe some French military manoeuvres while en route—he set off on an extended journey to East Africa, via Malta and Cyprus.[73] This, Elgin grumbled later, was originally intended as private trip but had in time developed into 'an official progress'—if the term had then been current, he might have added 'and media circus'.[74] In fairness to Churchill, he succeeded in generating colour and spectacle while largely avoiding giving hostages to fortune. The *Bystander* commented that his 'discreet and statesmanlike' replies to

Maltese and Cypriot delegations made 'the once wayward and wilful Winston' seem unrecognizable.[75]

Lady Gwendeline Bertie, Churchill's future sister-in-law, wrote to him with an account of the coverage he was getting: 'The English Press gives the English Public a full account of your doings, & it was this morning in a half penny illustrated [paper] that I saw you land at Mombassa, in a big white helmet [...] you are always in the lime light.'[76] There was a fair amount of satire, too: *Punch* showed Churchill denouncing the *Daily Mail* to a small African child.[77] The trip also offered a bonanza to the local settler press, which praised Churchill as an individual although its scepticism about the government that he represented continued unabated; there was a sense of excitement with an undercurrent of grumbling. The *Star of East Africa* complained at the exclusion of the press from Churchill's meetings with deputations: 'There could not have been any international questions involved which might have rendered secrecy desirable, therefore we regard this as a deliberate slur on every white man in the country.'[78]

Churchill's friend and private secretary Edward Marsh, who accompanied him, had been commissioned to provide a series of articles about the adventure for the *Manchester Guardian*.[79] Churchill himself had apparently not originally intended to write up the expedition for public consumption.[80] However, as H. Hesketh Bell, the Governor of Uganda, recorded in his diary:

> Last night he kept me awake for some time by what appeared to be a solilioquy in his bath. But I found, this morning, that while performing his ablutions he was dictating to a clerk a description of some of the country we had passed through. He evidently believes in making the most of time. It seems that he has agreed to supply to The Strand Magazine a series of articles on his tour through this part of Africa, and I understood him to say that he is to get £150 a piece for them.[81]

In due course, the articles were published in volume form as *My African Journey* (1908). Reviewing it, the *Observer* commented: 'If there were such a thing as the public journalist of the Empire, there could only be one nomination. Mr. Churchill would be chosen with unanimity.'[82]

It seems that powerful people were watching and learning. Not long after he left the White House in 1909, former president Theodore Roosevelt followed almost literally in Churchill's African footsteps, and like him produced magazine articles and a book.[83]

Paul Addison's pioneering work has established that, by the time Churchill arrived back in Britain, his mind was turning increasingly to the questions of social reform that would dominate his thinking for the next few years. Addison quotes at length from a letter by Churchill to this effect, outlining the need for some kind of welfare safety net.[84] It is worth asking, though, why Churchill decided to send his musings to a newspaper editor—J. A. Spender—rather than to a political colleague. It is not that he offered his opinions completely out of the blue—he was responding to a letter from Spender about the political situation—but a section not quoted by Addison makes his motivation clearer: 'this is the sort of tune I think will sing at Birmingham on 23rd Jany. "Social Bulwarks" "Security" "Standardisation".'[85] In other words, Churchill was flagging up the contents of a speech to a friendly newspaper in the hope of getting good coverage.[86]

Churchill also made use of *The Nation*, an influential but loss-making weekly, which had a 'New Liberal' social reform agenda but which was by no means uncritical in its approach to the Liberal Party itself. In March 1908 he published an article in its columns called 'The Untrodden Field in Politics'. In it he argued that political liberty was incomplete unless matched by a measure of social and economic security and advocated the notion of a 'Minimum Standard'.[87] *The Spectator* was scornful, portraying Churchill's 'hubbub of words' as marking an ominous departure from the true principles of free trade Liberalism.[88] Although it did receive praise in the *Daily Chronicle*, a Liberal paper, the article did not otherwise generate much attention.[89] This may explain why Churchill did not take up the solicitations of *The Nation*'s editor, H. W. Massingham, for further contributions.[90] He did, however, continue to meet and chat with him in order to make sure that his speeches got the right editorial treatment.[91]

Churchill, then, did not merely express his views in public and wait for them to be reported. Instead, he cultivated the press actively, and was very much his own spin-doctor. We can see this in his interactions with two other key figures in the pre-1914 period and beyond, C. P. Scott (editor of the *Manchester Guardian*) and George Riddell (owner of the *News of the World*). Scott and Riddell were on intimate terms with a host of other leading politicians too, as part of a political-journalistic nexus of a kind that might seem familiar today. It is plain that Churchill was eager to be at the heart of this network.

Others, however, remained sceptical and suspicious of the press. In April 1908, the severely ailing Campbell-Bannerman was replaced by H. H. Asquith. Asquith was in many ways more progressive and dynamic than his exceptionally stolid predecessor, but he retained a 'rooted dislike of anything like currying favour with the Press'.[92] Thus he was likely far from pleased when his key Cabinet appointments were published in the *Daily Chronicle*, before the names had been sub-mitted to the King. Asquith's private secretary told him that the *Chronicle*'s editor 'had telephoned and asked him in all innocence whether he would add to the information about Cabinet changes which had already been given to him by Mr. Lloyd George'. Other senior ministers were furious, but as Asquith's daughter Violet recalled: 'Winston came in after dinner and made a passionate defence of Lloyd George, assuring my father that he had indignantly denied having given the names to the press.'[93] Churchill seems to have been the only person who believed in the new Chancellor's innocence; at the same time, he probably did not feel that the offence itself was particularly grave.

Churchill himself replaced Lloyd George as President of the Board of Trade. As was then required of newly appointed Cabinet ministers, he stood for re-election to the Commons. The government had recently lost three by-elections, and this one was bound to be a high-profile affair, as the Tories sought a famous scalp: 'all eyes will be on it, every paper will report on it', noted one of their MPs.[94] Free trade, women's suffrage, Home Rule—these were all issues that helped stir the contest into a ferment, with Churchill himself suffering what some saw as 'rabid abuse' from parts of the press.[95] Unsurprisingly, Northcliffe's *Manchester Courier* was in the forefront. 'The fact that Mr. Churchill makes no pretence at verbal consistency makes it exceedingly difficult for the electors of North-West Manchester to place any reliance on anything which he says', one article declared.[96] Churchill hit back hard. At a meeting chaired by C. P. Scott, who praised his 'powerful and attractive personality', Churchill decried the efforts of 'a vast and wealthy syndicated press' to promote tariff reform.[97] Later in the campaign, the *Courier* repeated the libel that Churchill had broken his parole when escaping from Boer captivity. In response he lambasted Northcliffe publicly, and also sued, with eventual success.[98] While the legal action was still ongoing, Northcliffe wrote to him professing amazement 'that you considered our criticisms a personal matter. There was a well understood agreement between us that we should use our stage thunder in the furtherance of our mutual interests.'[99] Churchill replied accepting Northcliffe's assurance that he was not motivated by personal resentment and that the *Courier*'s statements were not his fault.[100] Still, he may well have taken satisfaction when, several years later, Northcliffe cut his losses and closed the paper down, having failed in his ambition to make it the leading Conservative organ in the North.[101]

The effects of the negative coverage are of course impossible to quantify, but it may have played some part in Churchill's defeat by the Conservative William Joynson-Hicks by 5,417 votes to 4,988. The 'howls of triumph from the Tory Press' added insult to injury.[102] However, he quickly fought another by-election in Dundee: cue a series of cartoons in differents papers portraying him as a quick-change artist slipping into a kilt and putting on a phony Scottish accent.[103] This time he won, and with the electoral contest out of the way, he plunged into a Whitehall battle over military spending. In alliance with Lloyd George, he pursued cuts in Army spending, which brought the two men into conflict with R. B. Haldane, the Secretary of State for War. Charles Repington, now working for *The Times*, was strongly opposed to this bid for economy, notwithstanding his earlier support for Churchill in his campaign against St John Brodrick. He published an article which denounced the 'self-advertising tiros' who, he argued, were interfering in matters of which they knew nothing.[104]

Repington did not mention Lloyd George and Churchill by name, but it was obvious that he was referring to them; it was also clear that he had inside information. Where did it come from? On the day the piece was published, Haldane wrote privately: 'They [*The Times*] have got no information from me anyhow. I do not think it will do harm.'[105] Churchill accepted his assurance that he had had nothing to do with the leak.[106] Yet Haldane also admitted, in another private letter, that 'Repington had come to me a week before', although he claimed he had discouraged the correspondent from making a direct attack on his fellow ministers.[107] If you spoke to Repington it was unwise to say anything you weren't happy to see in print.[108] But whether he was naive or disingenuous, the War Secretary quickly came to see Repington's article as counterproductive. A few days after it appeared, Haldane wrote: 'The avalanche is crashing about me—the Liberal papers have opened this morning with demands for the cutting down of the Army.'[109] But he remained unmoved by the press storm, and successfully saw off his Radical colleagues' manoeuvres. Within a few years, Churchill himself would be using the press to defend naval expenditure from a challenge by Lloyd George.

In the late summer of that year, Churchill's press coverage focused less on affairs of state than on affairs of the heart. In mid-August, the *New York Times* gushed that the announcement of his engagement to Clementine Hozier 'will bring confusion to phalanxes of conspiring mammas who for several years have considered the gallant but dom-ineering young writer, soldier and statesman as the most brilliant "catch" in London'.[110] Clementine, who was only twenty-three, had not been impressed the first time she had met Churchill a few years before, but when he met her again at a dinner party in March 1908 he swept her off her feet. She was a talented young woman, as the newspapers were quick to note. Violet Asquith received a letter from her friend Venetia Stanley: 'My darling Aren't you thrilled about Winston [...] what do you think about Clementine's accomplishments as set forth in the Manchester Guardian—six languages, a good musician, a brilliant conversationalist.'[111] (In fact, the Prime Minister's daughter was probably less than thrilled, as she may have entertained hopes of snaring Churchill for herself.[112]) When the couple married in September, the *Daily Mirror* ran a front page photographic spread.[113] It did the same a few weeks later when Clementine gave her 'first speech at public function'; she had opened a bazaar.[114] Throughout their married life, Clementine was to be a media asset to her husband. She was not always an easy person, but she was certainly long-suffering. She once related the story of her honeymoon in Venice. 'It was all new to her, and as they walked down some famous street of palaces she looked about her with wonder and delight. Suddenly she missed Winston. He had dived into a newspaper shop and presently emerged with a bundle of copies of the *Times* under his arm. He sat down on a stone and buried his head in the paper, oblivious to all the beauties of Venice.'[115] However, a joint interest in current affairs would turn out to be an element of strength in the marriage.[116]

We may imagine that, upon the couple's return to England, Churchill relished getting back into harness at the Board of Trade. During his time in that office, he pursued his social reform agenda, implementing minimum wages in low-paid (or 'sweated') industries and introducing Labour Exchanges, the purpose of which was to help the unemployed find work. One of the bright young men whom he recruited to help him fulfil his agenda was William Beveridge. Beveridge was an Oxford graduate who had dedicated himself to the cause of social reform rather than pursue the scholarly or legal career that his parents wished for him. Latterly, he had been employed as a leader-writer for the *Morning Post*, and had been given a free hand to express his progressive views, even though the paper's general line was Conservative. Under the editorship of Fabian Ware—Churchill's friend Oliver Borthwick having died in 1905—it 'threw itself wholeheartedly into the campaign of the National Anti-Sweating League'.[117] In 1908, however, the paper passed under the control of Lady Bathurst, who was much more partisan in her opinions, and within a few years the *Morning Post* would become a relentlessly anti-Churchill organ. Churchill succeeded in getting some decent coverage for his handling of the Board of Trade by careful briefing of what he called the 'Keynote' press.[118] In public, though, he continued to insist that the Liberal Party faced 'a hostile press', which was 'ranged against it.'[119]

Actually, the picture was more complicated than that comment suggested. The press was deeply divided and both the main parties reached out their tentacles in efforts to control, influence, and manipulate it; the Tories were particularly adept at providing covert subsidies to favoured papers.[120] One of the most dramatic developments at this period was Northcliffe's surprise acquisition of *The Times*, but if he hoped that ownership of this prestige organ would bring him into intimacy with Asquith he was to be disappointed; the Prime Minister appears to have despised him.[121] The veteran editor G. E. Buckle survived the advent of the Northcliffe regime, although he would be forced out within a few years. Churchill was not always happy with his own coverage in the paper, but he continued to receive more than a semblance of fair treatment. A speech by him would be allocated plenty of space if he sent notice that he was planning a major statement—and also an advance copy of his notes.[122] Buckle assured him that when he struck a statesmanlike rather than a partisan tone 'you will never find any reluctance to praise you on the part of *The Times*' in spite of its many differences of opinion with the government on many issues.[123] Indeed, Balfour's private secretary J. S. Sandars complained on one occasion about the excessive prominence Churchill received. Sandars did not blame Buckle but rather Northcliffe himself, who supposedly fell prey to 'the embraces of Winston who flatters and toadies him in a sickening way, and then laughs at him behind his back'.[124]

Throughout his tenure at the Board of Trade, Churchill worked closely with Lloyd George at the Treasury to create a state system of

National Insurance against unemployment and ill-health. It is hard to exaggerate the degree to which the two men were twinned with one another in the minds of the press and the public at this time, and indeed for many years afterwards.[125] They were seen as the 'principal engineers' of a new form of Radicalism, attractive to many, anathema to the Establishment.[126] The most obvious symbol of that Establishment was the House of Lords, which still retained its capacity to veto Commons decisions; the government's Licensing Bill had been a conspicuous victim. In early 1909, the Cabinet was treading cautiously. Churchill gave a speech in Birmingham in which he attempted to be simultaneously 'suggestive and discreet'.[127] He does not appear to have been very successful, as he was widely interpreted as throwing down the gauntlet to the Lords, daring it to reject the forthcoming Budget; he also hit out at the press.[128] The *Liverpool Daily Post* alleged that although ministers appeared united in public, two of them wanted an early general election: 'One is Mr. Winston Churchill, who detests his present office, and did his best to precipitate an appeal to the country by his speech telling the House of Lords how to bowl out the Government. The other is Mr. Lloyd-George, who is far too shrewd to fail to see that the taxation he must impose in the next Budget will react on his own popularity.'[129]

Yet if Churchill was viewed by the right-wing press as acting in a deliberately provocative fashion, there were also critics on the left who viewed him as pusillanimous. Massingham of *The Nation* felt that the government was pussyfooting around by failing to press ahead with traditional Liberal causes such as disestablishment of the Welsh Church. He told Churchill that, unless he, Churchill, intended a genuinely radical, socialistic type of social reform, 'you will find, after small experiments like labour exchanges, that you have an empty wallet'. This, Massingham thought, meant 'abolishing Liberalism as a fighting force & falling back on moderation, with a little Tory democracy thrown in'.[130] Churchill, however, dismissed this line of argument, claiming that the rejection of the Licensing Bill had gained popular support for the Upper Chamber. It followed, in his view, that to launch a fight purely on the question of the Lords' formal powers was to court defeat: 'the constitutional attack, however vigorous, must be backed up by some substantial political or social demand which the majority of the nation mean to have and which the Lords cannot or will not give.'[131]

It is notable that, although Churchill could easily have treated Massingham merely as an irritant, he actually continued to make efforts to stay in his good books. In April, Lloyd George unveiled his famous, tax-raising 'People's Budget', a dramatic symbolic assault on wealth, aristocracy, and privilege. In July, while it was still uncertain whether the Lords would swallow it or not, Churchill met Massingham to give him guidance on how *The Nation* should treat one of his big speeches, to be given in Edinburgh, in defence of the Budget. He also tried to assuage him on another important matter. Churchill and Lloyd George had recently made a joint bid to persuade the Cabinet to restrain spending on the navy, in the face of growing public concern about the threat posed by Germany. They had failed even though, as Asquith noted, they had 'by their combined machinations [...] got the bulk of the Liberal press—such as it is—into the same camp.'[132] Now Churchill tried to reassure Massingham, who was uneasy about the clamour for military expenditure, which many Radicals thought was based on hysteria whipped up by the press. Any forthcoming government announcement, he said, 'would not cause offence to him [Massingham] and those who thought with him'. At the same time Churchill stressed the need to be ready in case the Germans stepped up their naval building programme.[133] The following month, Massingham wrote to Churchill advising against a dissolution of Parliament if the Lords threw out the Budget. Instead, he urged, the House of Commons should itself take steps to deal with the Lords' powers in the face of such a 'constitutional offence' against it.[134] All this suggests that Massingham believed that he was in Churchill's confidence, and that Churchill felt that *The Nation* represented a strand of Liberal opinion that it was worth his while to cultivate.

Meanwhile, Churchill had become President of the Budget League, a body aimed at building popular support for Lloyd George's proposals. Sir Henry Norman, an MP and former journalist who had worked under W. T. Stead, was the League's honorary secretary. At the outset, Norman advised Churchill of the best way for him and his colleagues to secure coverage and comment. What editors wanted, he said, was 'a digest of the speeches beforehand, upon which their leader-writers could work.' He explained: 'a verbatim report of a speech by telegraph arrives in a perfect jumble, on excessively thin paper, without punctuation or paragraphs, and is almost useless for an hour or so for editorial purposes.' This was less problematic for speeches delivered on Saturdays which were reported on Mondays. But in general it would be useful, Norman said, for 'a few selected papers' to receive a 'strictly confidential' summary in advance. Moreover, the League sent out a weekly column of 'Budget Points' to two hundred papers via the National Press Agency.[135] In other words, the secret of getting a good press was to make the newspapermen's jobs as easy as possible.

Yet smoothing the path in this way could only achieve so much. Lloyd George and Churchill were at the forefront of the campaign of mass meetings, and both used knockabout humour at the expense of their opponents. In his famous 30 July speech at Limehouse, the Chancellor laid into the aristocracy without mercy: 'Oh! these dukes, (loud laughter) how they harass us. (More laughter.)'[136] Even to some on the Liberal side, the language and approach seemed crude. When the Tory press denounced the speech, Churchill mocked the critics in turn:

> Why, *The Times* blushed as pink as the *Sporting Times* (laughter)—that other great organ of Tory refinement (more laughter)—and the *Daily Telegraph* became purple with purple patches, all over, of repressed emotion (laughter), and as for the *Daily Mail*, it assumed the sort of air of sorrow and deportment that one would associate with the head-mistress of a seminary for young ladies (more laughter), and they set the office boy to work to write a leading article on how to elevate the tone of public controversy. (Cheers.)[137]

Not long after this, a cartoon in the *Pall Mall Gazette* depicted Lloyd George and Churchill congratulating themselves on their quips at the expense of the upper classes and of tariff reform (which was still a live issue). An unemployed workmen responds: 'Ah, gentlemen, I daresay you're very funny; but whilst you are cracking your jokes I'm *starving*.'[138]

In November, the House of Lords showed its hand and vetoed the Budget. This precipitated a protracted constitutional crisis, which was not resolved until the 1911 Parliament Act trimmed the Lords' powers. In the meantime there were two general elections, each of which was a virtual draw between Liberals and Conservatives; but as Asquith could expect support from Labour and Irish Nationalist MPs he was able to stay in office. Churchill retained his status as a darling of the press, even while many papers continued to hammer him for his political conduct and views. His image was still evolving. We now associate him with cigars, yet at this stage in his career, the 'trademark' which cartoonists started to use to identify him was a very small hat. According to Churchill, 'the legend of my hats' dated from an occasion around this time when he went for a walk with Clementine on the sands at Southport, and unthinkingly put on 'a very tiny felt hat' that had been packed with his luggage. 'As we came back from our walk, there was the photographer, and he took a picture. Ever since, the cartoonists and paragraphists have dwelt on my hats; how many there are; how strange and queer; and how I am always changing them, and what importance I attach to them, and so on. It is all rubbish, and it is all founded upon a single photograph.'[139]

He was probably being slightly disingenuous—as we have seen, the press had taken an interest in his hats during the 1906 election, and we may doubt that he had failed to see the advantages. As the cartoonist David Low recalled: 'Winston Churchill [...] deliberately advertised himself in his early political days by wearing a succession of unusual hats, and in later years, by always carrying an outsize cigar, foibles which were eagerly used and improved upon by the cartoonists, with his open encouragement.'[140] Indeed, in his recollections, Churchill offered a knowing wink to the reader, hinting that the legend of the hats was helpful to his image: 'Well, if it is a help to these worthy gentlemen in their hard work, why should I complain?' he asked. 'Indeed, I think I will convert the legend into reality by buying myself a new hat on purpose!'[141]

After the first of the 1910 general elections, Asquith promoted Churchill to the position of Home Secretary. Although Churchill was a firm believer in both corporal and capital punishment, he had some modestly reforming instincts with respect to penal policy. (His predecessor, Herbert Gladstone, felt that he was too quick to take credit for rule-changes that had already been in train; Churchill blamed the newspapers for creating this impression.[142]) His power to remit sentences created opportunities for good publicity, for example when he ordered the release of a twelve-year-old boy who had been sentenced to birching and to several years' detention for stealing a piece of coal.[143] However, such humanitarian gestures could also backfire, as in the case of the 'Dartmoor Shepherd', an habitual thief whose severe sentence Churchill modified, only for the man to abscond from the job that he had been found and to reoffend.[144] Lloyd George—who had been the first to highlight the case—complained that the Tory press had 'behaved like cads' over the affair.[145] Yet the criticism was hardly surprising, given that Lloyd George himself had originally tried to make capital out of the shepherd's plight, in the context of the battle over the Budget; he had used it in a speech as an example of society's harsh treatment of the poor. In some eyes, then, the release of the convict looked less like mere misplaced kindness and more like a deliberate political stunt. As *The Times* put it, the matter had been used 'to emphasize the bitter lesson of class hatred [...] and to exalt the superior humanity of Mr. Lloyd George himself and of the Home Secretary'.[146]

Churchill's responsibility for law and order issues was bound to involve him in controversy, given the growing social unrest of the period. For quite some time by now, stories had been cropping up in the papers about him being accosted by suffragettes or having his meetings interrupted.[147] He was, nominally, a supporter of votes for women, but really only on the most lukewarm and qualified basis. Basically, he was a sceptic, and shortly after he moved to the Home Office he voted against the so-called 'Conciliation Bill', brainchild of the Radical journalist H. N. Brailsford, which would have brought about limited female enfranchisement. In November 1910, on the day that became known as 'Black Friday', a mass of women protesters descended on the House of Commons. The police treated them brutally and arrested 115 of them (and four men). Churchill ordered most of them released. A few days before, in response to a miners' strike in the Rhondda Valley, which had led to riots, Churchill had despatched the army to restore order, albeit at one point he commanded a temporary halt to their journey.[148] In later years, he was met with Labour charges that he had 'sent troops to shoot down Welsh miners' (even though no one was actually shot). At the time, though, he was attacked from the right for his supposed leniency. The *Daily Mail* made a connection between his approach to the suffragettes and to the miners. On the one hand, because of Churchill's halting of the prosecutions after Black Friday, 'the police were prevented from justifying their action, and the prisoners were deprived of all opportunity of proving their innocence. Yesterday a fresh riot broke out in the same place'. On the other hand, his decision to (briefly) hold back the troops on their way to the Rhondda had caused 'a fierce riot [...] Tonypandy has continued in the hands of the mob.' Churchill, the paper alleged, vacillated and showed timidity in the face of violence.[149]

One wonders how far the perceived need to appear tough influenced Churchill's behaviour during the notorious 'Siege of Sidney Street' early the following year. In the context of widespread fears about immigration, and about Jewish migrants in particular, the news that a gang of foreign anarchists had murdered three policemen when disturbed raiding a London jewellers' shop was bound to be a hot potato. When the men's East End hideout was discovered they fired on the police, who asked for help from the army. Churchill, with typical disregard for convention, rushed to the scene. In later life, when he recounted the story in a newspaper article, he conceded that he really ought not to have put himself in the danger zone, and admitted that his curiosity had got the better of him. He arrived in time to see the house go up in flames. He ordered that it be allowed to burn down with the anarchists still inside.[150] The dramatic events were caught by newsreel cameras, although only the British Pathé crew got footage of Churchill himself. In a sequence lasting about twenty seconds, he can be seen gesticulating, while around him are officials and policemen, some carrying guns.[151] Edward Marsh, who was part of the retinue, afterwards saw himself on screen at the cinema: 'I make a most gratifying appearance as almost the central figure of "Mr Churchill directing the operations" at the Palace, which is nightly received with unanimous boos and shouts of "shoot him" from the gallery'.[152]

The press, too, was hostile. Even the courtier Almeric Fitzroy, no friend to Churchill, felt that he had been treated harshly: 'Much exaggeration was used by the Press in describing Winston Churchill's movements & such nonsense was easily swallowed by public credulity.'[153] Of course, not all, the coverage was negative, and Churchill wrote to Spender of the *Westminster Gazette* to thank him for his backing:

> The Times blamed me for stopping the soldiers going to Tonypandy and now blames me for allowing them to go to Stepney, where I was appealed to by the authorities on the spot. Their doctrine is therefore apparently that soldiers should always be sent to shoot down British miners in Trade Disputes, but never to apprehend alien murderers engaged in Crime. This is on a par with Tory thought in other directions.[154]

Fascinatingly, Northcliffe himself protested to Thomas Marlowe of the *Mail* that the paper had gone over the top. He told his own editor:

> Now that you have had your annual outburst against Churchill, I trust that you will leave him alone for a time. As a result of the 'Daily Mail's' action, the 'Evening News', without any orders, joined in. The 'Daily Mirror' also began but was stopped, and the 'Times' people took up the cry.

As I have to bear the responsibility for this sort of thing, and do not like it, I wish you would not do it unless I suggest it, because it has far-reaching effects in my other Newspapers. They naturally think the 'Daily Mail' represents my views, and they immediately start to 'please the governor'.[155]

This casts intriguing light on the inner functioning of the Northcliffe press. The journalists, it seems, 'worked towards the governor' by trying to anticipate his wishes, sometimes with an excess of zeal, and then had to be reined in. The lesson applies more generally: if newspapers tended to reflect their owners' political views in general terms they did not always do so in detail.

Later in 1911, Asquith moved Churchill to the Admiralty where his capacity to generate controversy remained undiminished. Yet throughout his Edwardian Liberal phase, although he had plenty of enemies in the press, he also had many supporters. And even though he was often treated harshly by Northcliffe's papers, Northcliffe himself, as we have seen, sometimes urged his minions to tone things down. On occasion, moreover, Churchill's star status could trump politics. When he married, the *Daily Mirror* gushed: 'whatever opinion may be held of him as a politician, [he] is universally popular as a man and as a bridegroom.'[156] His continuing fame was, of course, very much a product of his willingness to court the press, both through personal networking and through his instinctive (if often politically dangerous) capacity to provide good copy. As we have seen in this chapter, Churchill's view of the press—as expressed publicly—became more negative after he left the Conservative Party. He made frequent attacks on the newspaper trusts, which, he argued, were trying to distort the political process in their own interests. Using the kind of language that went down well with Radicals, he counterpointed these comments with Liberal optimism about the influence of political speech on public opinion: 'Boldly and earnestly occupied, the platform will always beat the press.'[157] When he said this, at the beginnings of the Budget fight, *The Times* noted drily: 'we are well aware that there is a vast amount of platform speaking which derives most of its efficacy from the Press.'[158] In reality, Churchill knew this well. Essential though the platform still was, it was the press that took his platform message to the nation as a whole; and he knew how to make the best of it. He did of course get much bad coverage and it undoubtedly hurt. But at the broadest level, his denunciations of the press were simply good platform fare—stage thunder—that could not disguise his essential fascination with and involvement in the developing practice of celebrity politics.

3

Any Home News?

'Winston is very fond of discussing military subjects', noted Sir George Riddell, proprietor of the *News of the World*, in late 1911. 'He is evidently a soldier at heart. [...] He said that a great war should be carried on by a joint ministry, and that if such an event took place during the present Liberal administration, Balfour and several more prominent Conservatives should be invited to join the Government.'[1] This diary entry succinctly captures Churchill's taste for war, which had been rekindled by the heightening of tensions in Europe that summer. He had enthusiastically embraced Asquith's decision to move him to the Admiralty, and had definitively abandoned his previous commitment to naval economy. His Radical phase was at an end. Moreover, the entry is simultaneously revealing of his consistent taste for centrist politics and coalition, and of his capacity for self-deception. As time would show, the Tories would certainly be prepared to join the Liberals in a wartime government, but only on conditions; and, with Balfour having recently been displaced as leader by the harder-line Andrew Bonar Law, those conditions were likely to mean the exclusion of Churchill himself. He might now be tacking to the right but that did not make him better loved or trusted by those Conservatives who regarded him as a traitor. Finally, the simple fact that Churchill shared his views with Riddell is telling in itself. It was both a sign of a developing relationship between the two men and a symbol more generally of his willingness to take pressmen into his confidence, a habit he shared with many of his colleagues. 'It is curious how much

attention the members of this Government pay to the Press', Riddell
had recorded a few years earlier. 'I doubt whether such frequent and
intimate relations have ever existed between so many Ministers and so
many newspaper editors.'[2]

It was this type of intimacy that Riddell craved. From humble
beginnings, he first made a career as a solicitor before moving into
newspapers by acquiring a shareholding in the *Western Mail*. By the
time that he started keeping a diary in 1908, his stake in the once-
ailing *News of the World* had made him wealthy man, although, craving
respectability, he was not especially comfortable with that paper's sal-
acious tone. Asquith gave him a knighthood, hoping that in return he
would 'help a hospital' and give the Liberals a friendly press.[3] The
Prime Minister, however, had other recipients for his confidences, and
Riddell seems, above all, to have craved access and information. This
he got, in particular, from Lloyd George, who regularly spilled the
beans to him about the inner workings of the government, but also
from Churchill and others. The conversations often took place on
Walton Heath golf course in Surrey. At one stage, Churchill and
Riddell were playing together once or twice a week.[4] Churchill was
really there for the talk rather than the sport, which was one more
aspect of the wider social-journalistic-political network of which he
was a member, and which to some extent transcended party. Northcliffe
was involved as well, as his brother Cecil Harmsworth (a Liberal MP)
described in his diary: 'Alfred arrives full of victory over Winston
Churchill at golf on Princes Links. He is to play Bonar Law in a day
or two.'[5] Churchill spoke remarkably frankly on such occasions, and
perhaps to some extent unselfconsciously, yet at times, it seems clear,
with an agenda of his own. He could rely on Riddell's discretion but
sometimes gave him information that he knew was likely to be of
direct use. We are lucky to have such detailed accounts of what he
said, yet we need to bear in mind that behind his gossip there often
lay some deeper purpose.

It was the Agadir Crisis that presaged Churchill's transition from
the Home Office to take charge of the navy, and Riddell was privy to

many of the key developments. In the summer of 1911, by sending a gunboat to the port of Agadir the Germans made clear that they would not accept French control of Morocco as a fait accompli. They intended to extract concessions from France elsewhere in Africa. 'The French Press is unanimous in relying on the support of Great Britain to remove the danger threatened by this surprising move on the part of Germany', reported the Paris correspondent of the *Daily Mail*.[6] Sir Edward Grey, the Foreign Secretary, told the German ambassador that Britain must be consulted with respect to any new Moroccan settlement.[7] When Berlin failed to respond, and with the full agreement of his senior colleagues, Lloyd George made a dramatic intervention, in a speech at London's Mansion House on 21 July. He stated that were 'Britain to be treated where her interests were vitally affected as if she were of no account in the Cabinet of nations', then 'peace at that price would be a humiliation intolerable for a great country like ours to endure'.[8]

The significance of this lay in the fact that Lloyd George was associated with the Radical pacific wing of the Liberal Party. Sentiments that would have been unexceptional coming from the mouths of Grey or Asquith were—in Churchill's words—a 'thunderclap' when they came from the former pro-Boer inhabitant of 11 Downing Street.[9] Churchill knew, a few hours in advance, what was coming. Riddell recalled: 'I was playing golf with Winston on the day when Lloyd George made his celebrated speech at the Mansion House. He told me that the Chancellor of the Exchequer was to make a big declaration. I had an invitation to the dinner so hurried back.' Having been tipped off by his golfing partner, Riddell was well placed to see the significance of remarks that went over the heads of many of the immediate audience.[10]

The following morning, Lloyd George and Churchill had a meeting with C. P. Scott, who had been called urgently to London after he had written to Asquith about his concern over the prospect of war. The summons was an indication of how seriously the government took Scott's paper, which saw itself as the custodian of the conscience of the Liberals. The two colleagues did their best to flatter the editor, trying to persuade him that the party would be smashed up if the government and the *Manchester Guardian* were at odds.

> Churchill said to Lloyd George that I ought to be kept constantly informed as to all important matters. Lloyd George said that was just what he had tried to do and rather reproached me for not coming to him sooner now. [. . .]
>
> Churchill's only contributions to the discussion, beyond his remarks about me, were highly rhetorical denunciations repeated at intervals of the insolence of Germany and the need of asserting ourselves and teaching her a lesson.[11]

This succeeded as a short-term technique for making sure that the paper did not become too critical at a vital moment, but once the threat of war had faded, the *Guardian* felt free to express its scepticism. An editorial in October chastised the government for assuming that if a European conflict had broken out then Britain would have taken part in it, and took one of Churchill's recent speeches as an example: 'He need not have mentioned the strength of our navy at all in connection with the negotiations about Morocco unless he believed that failure in them would have brought England as well as France to the brink of war with Germany.'[12] Overall, however, the speech was an effort to build bridges with Germany and was recognized as such even in the conservative *Kreuz Zeitung*, which said that Churchill had 'done much to make amends for the harm done by his colleagues'. Still, as the Berlin correspondent of *The Times* noted, there was in general little inclination there to meet British overtures halfway. The moderate *Börsen Courier* opined that 'all such declarations, though well meant and meriting recognition, will remain void of result till English diplomacy ceases to spin threads and lay mines which are calculated to prepare unpleasant situations for Germany'.[13]

Churchill's appointment as First Lord, made public a few weeks later, also received a cautious reception in the German press. Asquith's motives for making the switch are not wholly clear, but the Agadir crisis had caused (arguably exaggerated) concern about the performance of the Admiralty.[14] Churchill—who had been taking an increasingly belligerent line towards industrial unrest at home—seemed like an energetic figure and he was undoubtedly enthusiastic for his new role. He was not, as yet, perceived as an implacable foe of Germany. The *Berliner Tageblatt* observed that he was known to be a friend of Kaiser Wilhelm II, that he had previously attended German military manoeuvres, and that 'he passes for a supporter of a moderate naval policy'. However, with world politics in its current state, it was hard to say whether or not it would now be easier to reach agreement on limiting Anglo-German naval competition. The *Berliner Neueste Nachrichten* argued that the German government had recently demonstrated a lack of firmness which would lead to British pressure for joint arms limitation, which it thought would be to Germany's disadvantage. The paper suggested: 'Weakness invites interference, and as Mr Churchill is a great friend of economy in naval matters, and on the other hand has the present sea power of Great Britain behind him, it would not be surprising if he sought with friendly but energetic persuasion to induce us to comply with his wishes, as Great Britain successfully did in the Agadir affair.' Although it had a reputation for ultra-patriotic chauvinism, *Die Post* commented simply that Churchill had 'the reputation of a great power for achievement and a great power of work. We shall follow his activity with great interest.'[15]

Not long after this, the German naval attaché in London informed Berlin of an episode which had allegedly taken place at the end of August at the house of a London banker:

> After dinner the invited ladies and gentlemen reconvened [in another room], but Mr. Churchill, who was one of the guests, abstained and read the evening news instead. A lady known for her quick-wittedness was evidently annoyed by this lack of politeness. She asked Mr. Churchill if he found politics in the presence of ladies so interesting that he preferred the newspaper to a conversation with them.—Mr. Churchill answered very sharply that he had indeed no time for chit-chat with ladies at such a serious hour; and pointing to an article which dealt with the approaching naval review at Kiel, he continued: *Let them come, they can have war if they want.*

Reading this, the Kaiser offered the phlegmatic observation that the Germans indulged in similarly violent rhetoric themselves; yet did not in fact intend to go to war.[16] Such efforts to read between the lines may help explain why German newspapers remained divided in their opinions even when Churchill's attitude seemed tactless, even openly provocative. In February 1912, in a speech in Glasgow, he asserted the 'essentially defensive' nature of British naval power, and also described Germany as a 'great and friendly Power'. However: 'The British navy is to us a necessity and, from some points of view, the German Navy is to them more in the nature of a luxury.'[17]

Many German papers assumed that, because Lloyd George's Mansion House speech had turned out to represent the approved government line, standard operating procedure meant that Churchill's pronouncement could be taken as the Cabinet's agreed position.[18] In fact, the British government was divided. Churchill's colleague Lewis Harcourt described his words as 'an inconceivable blunder', although he also suspected it was a deliberate and 'malicious' effort to undermine Haldane, who had been sent by the government to see if compromise was possible with Berlin.[19] Lloyd George told Riddell that the speech was 'most imprudent', although Riddell himself took a more positive view.[20] With the German Foreign Office Press Bureau failing to give an official steer, papers adopted a variety of attitudes. The *Berliner Tageblatt* condemned Churchill's phraseology but actually agreed with him that in Germany the army rather than the navy offered the fundamental guarantee of national security. The socialist *Vorwärts*, condemning the arms race, described Churchill's speech as 'the unmistakable reply to the announcement of German naval expansion'. The *Frankfurter Zeitung*, viewed as the organ of the commercial and financial classes, said by contrast that some passages sounded like 'menace conveyed in affable language'. *Die Post* judged that the speech 'supplies a cogent proof that any attempt at an understanding about armaments would only be an attempt to reach a useless object by useless means'.[21]

It seems doubtful that Churchill had really intended to torpedo the prospect of a concord. At home, he faced a clamour from the right-wing press for more ships, while many in his own party felt that this would only increase the risk of war. (Northcliffe, it should be noted, made some effort to calm the patriotic hysteria, by instructing his papers to hold back news of German naval plans, at the behest of the British Embassy in Berlin.)[22] Faced with this dilemma, Churchill attempted a balancing act. In March, when he presented his annual estimates to Parliament, he simultaneously promised to match any increased German construction and put forward the idea of a 'naval holiday' under which both countries would halt the building of Dreadnoughts for a year.[23] The now increasingly hostile German press reacted with scorn, although the estimates themselves had shown a small decrease.[24] In Britain, the *Daily Chronicle*, while regretting that it had not been possible to make more extensive cuts, accepted Churchill's argument that this particular year happened to require various forms of exceptional spending. It praised his 'quiet, non-bellicose, dignified determination' to mantain Britain's naval supremacy.[25] But as far as the *Daily News* was concerned, the First Lord had revealed his commitment to a bloated budget. 'He is assured of a good Opposition Press, and that will doubtless gratify him; but what has Liberalism or economy to do with such a programme?'[26] Similarly, *The Economist* regretted the burden on taxpayers and scathingly noted that Churchill was 'now the hero of the same newspapers who denounced and vilified him two or three years ago'.[27] A little later, from the opposite political perspective, the *Pall Mall Gazette* noted: 'There is no good word for him from the Radical Press.'[28]

It was quite true that Churchill received the backing of the *Daily Telegraph*, the *Daily Mail*, and *The Times* (although to say that they presented him as a hero was an exaggeration).[29] However, the *Observer*, a right-wing paper contemptuous of 'muddle-headed peace fanatics', was not won over.[30] It had recently been sold by Northcliffe to the Astor family; its naval correspondent judged that 'Mr. Churchill has done his best, but his best is not good enough.'[31] J. L. Garvin, the paper's influential editor (who at this time also edited the *Pall Mall Gazette*), gave Churchill rather cold comfort. Privately he told him:

'I cannot support you, but I can always call for something *more* than you are doing, so that I shall in effect give you support.'[32] Later in the year, after Garvin wrote to him expressing regret at not being 'able to take a more favourable view of your recent policy', Churchill responded with a lengthy exposition of relative British and German strength.[33] 'This letter is for your private eye *alone*,' he said, 'and I write it because you are a patriot and deserve to be reassured.'[34] Churchill was also solicitous towards Liberal journalists, suggesting to Asquith that C. P. Scott, J. A. Spender, H. W. Massingham and others should receive honours.[35] The Prime Minister was dismissive, pointing to a number of press figures who had already received titles from his government. It probably did not help that Churchill had credited the idea to Northcliffe, who in Asquith's view had 'done more than any living man' to bring the journalistic profession into disrepute.[36]

Although Churchill's attitude to Germany helped blunt the hostility of the Tory press, he was still a long way from being its darling. There were other issues with which he was involved, in particular Ireland, which were bound to bring its wrath upon him. The question of Home Rule—that is to say, greater self-government—had been something of a dead letter until 1910; but the general elections of that year had left the nationalist Irish Parliamentary Party holding the balance of power in the Commons. Churchill, in fact, was an early supporter of some form of special treatment for Protestant-dominated Ulster, where there was widespread opposition to what was labelled 'Rome Rule'. He was nonetheless a powerful advocate of Home Rule, on the grounds that it would strengthen the Empire.[37] He approved of a popular pamphlet, *Home Rule in a Nutshell*, by nationalist MP Jeremiah MacVeagh. The booklet was republished in collaboration with the *Daily Chronicle* with a new introduction by Churchill.[38] This preface was circulated via the press agencies and printed in extenso by the *Manchester Guardian* and *The Times*.[39] The *Yorkshire Herald* commented that 'Mr. Churchill's ponderous dissertations on world-politics have before now caused infinite amusement, but his new Mutual Improvement Society essay on the inner meaning of the Home Rule problem is more screamingly funny than any preceding effort from the same pen.'[40] In Churchill's own constituency the *Dundee Advertiser* took a more friendly tone, noting that his contribution was interesting 'for what we may call its news value', as it implied that reform in Ireland would be followed by what was called 'Home Rule All Round', that is to say, devolution for other parts of the United Kingdom too.[41]

Even more newsworthy was Churchill's decision to hold a joint meeting with IPP leader John Redmond in Belfast, a move that many Unionists portrayed as a calculated insult to their community.[42] The *Belfast News-Letter* referred to him as 'a pervert from Unionism', given his earlier hostility to Home Rule.[43] The whole event, heavily trailed in advance, became a huge press extravaganza. It was initially planned that the meeting should take place in the Ulster Hall, where Lord Randolph had spoken in opposition to Home Rule in 1886. In the event, Churchill was forced to switch venue, although the fact that he was able to hold the meeting at all could be claimed as a success. There was no full-scale rioting, but in a dramatic scene drawn in the *Illustrated London News* by the artist Cyrus Cuneo, Churchill's car was mobbed by angry demonstrators; the police prevented it being overturned.[44] His speech also received a good deal of booing. At Larne, while he and Clementine waited for their boat to England to depart, the hostile crowd treated him (the *Irish Times* related) to a chorus of 'We'll hang Winston Churchill on a sour apple tree'.[45]

The anti-Home Rule *Belfast Evening Telegraph* made special arrangements for reporting the speech, feeding its employees on the premises rather than run the risk of them going home to eat and being unable to return because of disturbances. The paper was rewarded with a record sale of 123,286; but, being reliant on old-fashioned messengers for its account of the speech, it was technically outdone by parts of the English press.[46] This was because this was 'the first instance in which newspapers at a distance have reported verbatim an important speech by telephone', as the Postmaster General, Herbert Samuel, informed Churchill.[47] This came about when a Post Office official discovered that the *Liverpool Daily Post* intended to get its report by phone. At the time there were only two phone lines between Ireland and Great Britain; there was therefore a risk that the ordinary service to the public would suffer if one of them was monopolized. 'The suggestion was therefore thrown out that a number of the most important Northern newspapers should combine to get a joint report; and the manager of the *Liverpool Post* quickly persuaded the *Manchester Guardian* and the *Yorkshire Post* to come into the arrangement.' (Because of the route of the submarine cable, which hit land at Stranraer, it was not possible to include London papers.) A third phone circuit was also established so that the other two lines could be kept clear for normal use. An attempt was made to use the Electrophone audio-relay system to transmit Churchill's actual words live, but due to a combination of bad weather, the low pitch of his voice, and the heckling, he could not be heard in Liverpool. Therefore, the speech was instead transmitted down the line by reporters working in relay. 'The transmission under these conditions was exceedingly good, and the whole speech was taken down in the offices of the newspapers in question ten minutes after Mr. Winston Churchill had sat down and considerably before the telegraphic reports of the speech arrived.'[48]

The enterprising role of the Post Office in bringing about these arrangements was an impressive testament to the technological capacity of the British state.[49] The method of the speech's dissemination was also related to the broader story of rapidly quickening global and intra-imperial communications. Coincidentally, the month following Churchill's Belfast visit, the government awarded the Marconi Wireless Telegraph Company a contract to build an empire-wide radio network of eighteen stations. This gave rise to the so-called Marconi affair—an insider trading scandal—and although Churchill himself was not personally implicated he became involved in the fallout. In brief summary, Lloyd George and Rufus Isaacs (the Attorney General) bought shares in the American Marconi Company. This was legally separate from the British Marconi Company which had been granted the Empire tender, and thus the two men could not be said to have tried to profit from their inside knowledge about it. However, in the face of rumours about their dealings, they were needlessly evasive and failed to disclose the facts of what they had done.

It was some months before the truth was finally dragged into the public domain; Churchill did his best to limit the damage. At some stage, he assured Northcliffe that his colleagues had not done anything wrong. Northcliffe accepted this, but he criticized the way Lloyd George and Isaacs were handling the press. In the spring of 1913 he advised Churchill: '*Do* get the PM or Rufus & LG to make some simple plain statement expressing regret for error; everyday it is postponed makes things worse.'[50] Then, in June, there was another revelation. It turned out that, at the point when he was Chief Whip, Alec Murray (known as the Master of Elibank) had bought Marconi shares on the Liberal Party's behalf. This did not really change the picture, but it was embarrassing to Churchill, who quickly assured Northcliffe that 'This newly revealed transaction [...] is a complete surprise to us all.'[51] Northcliffe accepted this too, but, as he pointed out, the fact that Elibank had disappeared on a business trip to South America made things look fishy: 'His absence gives the impression, probably quite erroneous, that there is what newspapers call "a big story" behind the whole of this matter, and I have no intention of letting my journals remain silent on this matter.'[52]

Eventually, the scandal blew over, but Churchill's involvement does highlight how, within limits, even generally hostile papers could sometimes be influenced through informal contacts in directions favourable to the government. There were also more formal methods of control, although these did not always work smoothly. The growing tension with Germany had heightened Churchill's existing interest in spies and spying; and the Agadir Crisis had provided him as Home Secretary with a golden opportunity to tighten security, via the sweeping Official Secrets Act of 1911.[53] Churchill's anxiety did not lessen, though, and he often proved heavy-handed. Soon after he became First Lord, he was visited by Archibald Hurd of the *Daily Telegraph*, who disclosed to him some piece of naval gossip he had picked up at third or fourth hand. Churchill insisted on being told who had originated it, and Hurd refused to comply. Afterwards, Hurd wrote to Churchill: 'I am sorry that my first and last visit to the Admiralty since your accession should have been so unfortunate. I have been interested in naval affairs for over 20 years and this is my first experience of any unpleasantness.' While he still refused to give up his source, he offered the assurance that the person concerned was not at the Admiralty.[54] Churchill was not mollified. Although he softened the first draft of his letter, he nonetheless adopted a somewhat threatening note. 'The lack of secrecy which prevails in this country with regard to Naval matters, and the levity with which disclosures are regarded, appear to me to amount to a very considerable national evil, and unless by cooperation between the newspapers and the Admiralty some protection can be assured for public interests, legislation will undoubtedly become necessary in the near future.'[55]

In the event, however, legislation proved unnecessary (and his relationship with Hurd was soon patched up when Churchill sent him a copy of one of his own memoranda—so much for secrecy!).[56] The following year, the government reached agreement with the press on the creation of the so-called D-Notice (or Defence Notice) system, under which newspapers might from time to time be requested in advance to refrain from publishing certain types of information. The assurance was given that papers would only be asked to so 'in really important cases where national interests were at stake', and they were to be represented on the committee that administered the workings of the scheme.[57] However, the system experienced some early hiccups, partly in consequence of Churchill not recognizing its limits. In 1913, some naval construction work was swapped between public and private builders, and he decided he did not want this reported in such a way as to imply that the programme was being speeded up, for fear of the effect on foreign opinion. But when the Admiralty issued a circular to this effect—without the sanction of the committee—it caused a negative reaction. Churchill seemed to be trying to influence interpretation, not just the reporting of fact, and the Liberal press wanted to be free to maintain its criticism.[58] The right-wing papers were, in general, more pliable on occasions where national security could be invoked. Even before the D-Notice committee was established, Northcliffe confessed himself in favour of 'most drastic censorship before and during war', and agreed with reluctance (at the behest of the British ambassador to Berlin) to suppress news about Germany's naval programme.[59] Yet, if the *Daily Mail* was to help officialdom hush things up, this required the officials themselves to know what they wanted kept quiet, and the requisite competence and communication skills were by no means always in evidence.[60]

One senses that during this immediately pre-war phase—with a vital part of the nation's defences in his hands—Churchill's anger at the press, when it failed to comply with his wishes, was much more intense than it had been during his 'stage thunder' phase of ritualistic platform denunciations. Nevertheless, he continued to court the newspapers, cultivating a flamboyant, daredevil image. Jan Rüger has shown how at this time the naval competition between Britain and Germany was played out partly in terms of the 'public theatre' of fleet reviews and launches of ships, 'where the modern mass market of media and consumerism collided with politics and international relations'.[61] Churchill's taste for the spectacular in many ways made him the ideal front man for this particular form of geopolitical swagger.

But his swashbuckling style was in some respects a double-edged sword. Taking flying lessons was a good way of ensuring copy—Northcliffe, for one, shared his fascination with aviation. But when an officer who had been piloting the First Lord was killed in the very same plane just a few days later, it was bound to raise questions about Churchill's endless search for a thrill. The *Manchester Guardian* chided: 'It has always been Mr. Churchill's way to be in the forefront of adventure, and we need not be surprised at his desire to become a qualified airman, though it ought to be remembered that the duty of the civil, as of the military, head of a fighting force is not to take unnecessary risks.'[62] Churchill claimed, though, that the press greatly exaggerated the dangers.[63] He continued to fly, albeit often only as a passenger. His various trips in army airships and seaplanes created the impression of frenetic activity. A 1913 *Punch* illustration shows Asquith and Churchill on board the Admiralty yacht *Enchantress*, which was greatly beloved of the latter; his trips were widely reported. In the cartoon, the First Lord is smoking languidly (this marks an early appearance of the Churchillian cigar). He enquires of the Prime Minister, who is reading a newspaper: 'Any home news?' Asquith replies drily: 'How can there be with you here?'[64]

Of course, Churchill's obsession with flying was about more than just his taste for publicity and his quest for sensation; it was a question of military preparedness too. (Responsibility for aviation was divided between the Army and the Navy.) He had been forced to confess Britain's weakness in the air relative to France and Germany, and was determined to make good.[65] When it came to such matters, the Tory press was prepared to cut Churchill ('who is at all events a man') a certain amount of slack, compared, at least, to the treatment they dished out his supposedly weak-kneed Radical colleagues.[66] This was partly because they revelled in exposing—and trying to widen—government divisions. Over the winter of 1913–14, Lloyd George and Churchill fell out dramatically over the Naval Estimates; the latter proposed an increase of almost £3 million. When Lloyd George, battling for economy, gave an inflammatory interview to the *Daily Chronicle*, Churchill pointedly declined to give an interview to the *Daily Mail* on the grounds that he would not speak to newspapers on important questions while they were under the consideration of the Cabinet.[67] Behind the scenes, though, Churchill acted to gain favourable coverage for his point of view. At his behest, an Admiralty official briefed a friendly Liberal MP, Leo Chiozza Money, with figures that he could use in press articles to help boost the case for greater naval spending.[68]

Such efforts did not go unnoticed, and attracted some sarcastic comment. 'On Thursday the *Daily Telegraph* told its readers the exact position in the Cabinet, with the names of those Ministers who were for and against Mr. Churchill', noted *The Economist* at the end of January. 'So certain is it about Mr. Churchill's attitude towards the

Cabinet that a novice might suppose this highly respectable journal had actually obtained Mr. Churchill's own statement of the case for the very estimates which he is now trying to force through the Cabinet.'[69] Lloyd George at last gave in—as perhaps he had intended all along—in return for the notional promise of spending cuts in the future. J. A. Spender recalled how this affair fitted into established pattern in Lloyd George and Churchill's behaviour: 'Each in turn used to threaten to get me unshipped from the *Westminster* [*Gazette*] if I wouldn't do what they wanted, but the difference between them was that L.G. really meant it, but Winston was only chaffing.'[70]

Such credit as Churchill extracted from the Conservative press was soon dissipated. The crisis over Ireland was deepening, as the North's resistance to the government's Home Rule plans intensified. In early March 1914, by way of concession—and to the inevitable disgruntlement of the nationalists—the Cabinet agreed to allow each Ulster county the choice of a time-limited exclusion from the authority of the proposed new Irish Parliament. To the government's embarrassment, the story appeared in the *Daily News* the next day: someone had blabbed. Asquith tried to find the culprit, but to no avail. A couple of days later he wrote privately: 'The mystery of the leakage is still unpenetrated: I can see that Ll.G. suspects Winston, who preserves an unbroken silence in regard to the incident.'[71] Later that month, Churchill—who was known to be sympathetic to special treatment for Ulster—made a speech in which he both emphasized the generosity of what was on offer and that the government would not shrink from tough measures to enforce its will. Certainly, his language was lurid, and so was the reaction.[72] 'Mr. Churchill made a bitter and violent speech at Bradford on Saturday', commented the *Daily Express*. 'Under a thin veneer of conciliation he did what was possible to hurry Mr. Asquith and the Government into civil war.'[73]

There followed the so-called 'Curragh mutiny', when a group of army officers, believing that they were about to be asked to coerce Ulster into accepting Home Rule, stated that they would rather resign than do so. The assertions of Churchill and his colleagues that it had all been a misunderstanding failed to allay claims in the press that a dastardly anti-loyalist plot had narrowly been thwarted by the heroic actions of the soldiers.[74] In the wake of the affair, Northcliffe declined a lunch invitation from Churchill, and deplored the latter's 'recent outrageous threatenings'.[75] It was only around this point, in fact, that the London papers, and those of Northcliffe in particular, started to give sustained attention to the Ulster issue.[76] The out-break of war in Europe in the summer put the whole problem on ice—for the time being. The Irish question had, however, served to crank up the Tory press's hostility to Churchill; this would soon find an outlet in other ways. Indeed, the Curragh episode marked the start of a broader crisis in civil–military relations that persisted throughout the Great War and beyond, and in which leading figures from the armed services intrigued with parts of the press to desta-bilize or frustrate the elected politicians whom many of them essentially despised.

For the time being, though, the gloves stayed on. Asquith secured a brilliant short-term coup—and at the same time landed himself with a long-term problem—by appointing Kitchener, the hero of Omdurman, as War Secretary. Even the government's harshest critics could not complain about that; they could only seek to take the credit for having created the necessary pressure. Moreover, in the patriotic atmosphere of August 1914, Conservative papers also held back from attacking Churchill. After all, he had been firmly of the war party within the Cabinet, had flirted with the idea of bringing the Tories into a coalition government, and had acted swiftly to mobilize the fleet.[77] 'We close the differences we have had with Mr. Churchill', commented the *Observer*, which now described him as 'a statesman who well understands the nature of war, and has the nerve to face its immense responsibilities.'[78] Ralph Blumenfeld, editor of the *Daily Express*, perhaps feeling some compunction about his paper's earlier criticisms, wrote to Churchill to convey an admiration that was clearly genuine.[79] However, this wartime press honeymoon was not to last.

Churchill swiftly announced the creation of a Press Bureau, which was to be headed by a good friend of his, the Conservative MP F. E. Smith. The aim was to ensure a 'steady stream of trustworthy information' from the War Office and the Admiralty would be given out, and thus, by providing as much information as possible, to prevent the spread of rumours.[80] The theory was good, but it clashed with Kitchener's determination not to have war correspondents at the front on the grounds that they gave 'great trouble to Commanders'.[81] Furthermore, the execution was poor. For three weeks the press was starved of information about the rapid advance of the German armies. Then, at the end of August, Smith actively encouraged *The Times* to publish an alarming report which portrayed the British as being in headlong retreat, and then lied to the Commons about his role in the affair.[82] Churchill undoubtedly grasped, in the abstract, the importance of good public relations, and used interviews with the American and Italian press to appeal to opinion in neutral countries.[83] Asquith appreciated his ability to serve up 'journalistic condiments' to the hungry journalists.[84] Yet, the censorship regime continued to cause discontent, a problem not helped by Churchill's attempts at meddling.

Impulsive as ever, in October, Churchill travelled to the Belgian port of Antwerp and placed himself in charge of its defence. Although he managed to postpone its fall to the Germans for a short while, the military value of this was open to question. His actions—including his deployment of untrained naval recruits—were heavily criticized by, in particular, the *Morning Post* (although other papers, including the *Observer*, were supportive).[85] The *Post*'s editor, H. A. Gwynne, had a clear agenda against civilian control of the Senior Service, which he wanted to be run by a sailor—just as the War Office, under Kitchener, was run by a soldier.[86] He also had a personal animus against Churchill: 'we want to have the man out'.[87] As he wrote to the *Post*'s owner, Lady Bathurst: 'What has happened is that Winston Churchill has practically taken command of the Board of the Admiralty and the *Navy is being run by a civilian instead of by naval experts.*'[88]

Gwynne's fixation on this issue did not, however, necessarily invalidate his view that the Antwerp affair was a blunder. Churchill, for his part, both sought to suppress criticism and to encourage the publication of material that presented his actions in a good light. Sir Stanley Buckmaster, who had replaced F. E. Smith as chief censor after a matter of weeks, declined to interfere with editorial comment, taking the line that the government could only act to prevent publication of material that was helpful to the enemy: 'I told him [Churchill] that I could not stop matter merely because it was unjust.'[89] Following a conversation with Lloyd George, Riddell recorded: 'Apparently Buckmaster's refusal to suppress criticism has annoyed Winston, who, LG says, wants to abolish the Press Bureau and resort to the former practice of censoring Army news at the war office and naval news at the Admiralty.' Lloyd George argued that this would mean 'the publication of what suited Kitchener and Winston and nothing more.'[90] Churchill's methods of news management did have their advantages. Sir Douglas Brownrigg, the Chief Naval Censor, recalled his command of language and skill at framing communiqués. 'He was also a bit of gambler—i.e., he would hold on to a bit of bad news for a time on the chance of getting a bit of good news to publish as an offset, and I must say that it not infrequently came off! On the other hand, there were days when it did not, and then there was a sort of "Black Monday" atmosphere about.'[91]

The press's frustration grew when Churchill insisted on keeping quiet the sinking (in late October) of HMS *Audacious*, on the grounds that the information was not yet known to the enemy. Apparently, his first instinct was to reveal the news but he was 'cajoled and threatened' by the First Sea Lord, the septuagenarian Lord Fisher, who had been recalled to that post by Churchill at the outbreak of war.[92] Although the loss of the *Audacious* was quite quickly reported in the American and then the German press, Churchill persisted in his refusal to publicly admit what was already worldwide knowledge.[93] In Britain, the papers were reduced to referring to 'persistent reports of a naval misfortune which has been withheld from the public', and the loss was only officially acknowledged in 1918.[94] When the Admiralty issued a circular asking papers to refrain from reporting sinkings until they were announced by the Press Bureau, C. P. Scott wrote to advise Churchill that this was impractical: 'if nothing is to be published for days or for a week all sorts of wild rumours will circulate and be believed'.[95]

Churchill's heavy-handed approach not only risked increasing public disquiet; it was also bound to increase the press's resentment of him personally. It is worth stressing that he still had significant newspaper support. On the last day of 1914, an article in the *Daily Mirror* argued that his reputation had been 'remarkably consolidated' during the war.[96] But there was growing hostility in influential parts of Fleet Street, and the disastrous Dardanelles campaign brought it to a head. The story of the attempt to force the Straits by a naval assault, and thus knock Turkey out of the war, has been told many times, as has the failure of the subsequent amphibious attack. Christopher M. Bell has provided the most lucid and comprehensive account to date. He confirms that although the strategy was deeply flawed and Churchill made many serious mistakes, the failure was a collective one in which many others (including the Prime Minister) were implicated. He also shows how Churchill—in spite of taking personal charge of the censorship of the campaign—was subject to a hostile press which piled the blame for the failures directly on him. Gwynne's *Morning Post* again made the running; soon enough, its allegations were being echoed in the German papers.[97] The *New York Times* wrote of Churchill's 'hour of disgrace'.[98] Speaking to Riddell, Churchill himself complained that he had been misrepresented, which to some degree was true, although his expectation that the government should be believed 'because we are gentlemen' combined naivety with arrogance.[99] Although many of the details of the criticisms were inaccurate—and indeed several papers including the *Daily Sketch* and the *Standard* rushed to Churchill's defence—it was hardly surprising that the First Lord should come under attack for a military catastrophe for which he held significant responsibility.[100] Under his leadership, the Admiralty had become a hive of resentments, which, almost inevitably, found their way into the public prints.

There was also, of course, a broader context: the failure of the Allies to break the stalemate on the Western Front, and press discontent at what many newspapermen saw as government over-optimism. Not long after Asquith gave a public reassurance that there was no basis for claims that the army lacked ammunition, a British attack at Aubers Ridge was driven back. On 14 May, *The Times* printed a devastating despatch by its correspondent Charles Repington, blaming the setback on a shortage of high explosive. Although Repington insisted that he had not colluded with Sir John French, Commander-in-Chief of the British Expeditionary Force, he was undoubtedly reflecting his views. French may have been looking for a scapegoat; at any rate he seemed willing to connive with Asquith's rivals and enemies in order to shake up the government.[101]

Repington was not the only senior military figure sowing trouble. On 15 May, Fisher resigned as First Sea Lord. He had long harboured doubts about the Dardanelles campaign—and had communicated them indiscreetly to all and sundry—but had failed to assert clear opposition when it counted. Now, he threw in the towel over a minor disagreement with Churchill over the reallocation of forces from the North Sea. Combined with the Repington revelations, Fisher's actions were the trigger for Asquith's decision to bring the Conservatives into a new coalition government, in order to forestall open criticism by them of the conduct of the war. Kitchener, although directly blamed by the *Daily Mail* for the shell scandal, proved impregnable to press attacks, but Churchill now faced the political abyss.[102]

Churchill's removal from the Admiralty was a condition of Tory participation in the coalition, but, in denial of this reality, he tried desperately to persuade Asquith to keep him in his post. In his diary for 19 May, the courtier Sir Almeric Fitzroy recorded: 'He [Churchill] showed his sense yesterday of what is due to the PM who had adjured his colleagues to be reticent, by going over to the Pall Mall [*Gazette*] Office & placing Garvin in full knowledge of all that was going on.'[103]

This was rather at odds with the statement Churchill put out to *Reynolds's Newspaper*, which asserted that 'Any public man who at this moment nourishes any thought except that of waging war against the enemy by the most effective means should never be forgiven by his fellow countrymen.'[104] He was certainly not the only person undertaking clandestine briefings of journalists, though, and newspaper speculation raged as to what the make-up of the new Cabinet would be. It was not until 26 May that the final line-up was published, with Churchill in the relatively lowly position of Chancellor of the Duchy of Lancaster.[105] Undoubtedly, he was seriously downcast by this reverse, but it is remarkable how quickly—indeed obsessively—he began his political fightback.

Almost at once, Churchill went on the offensive. In a speech in his constituency in early June, Churchill claimed that history would vindicate his tenure at the Admiralty and that victory at Gallipoli was within reach, as well as hinting at the introduction of some form of compulsory service. The speech included substantial comments about the press. Churchill argued that its proper role in wartime was to boost public confidence and that newspapers ought not to be allowed 'to attack the responsible leaders of the nation'. If there had to be criticism 'it should only be the loyal criticism of earnest intention' and should be voiced only within Parliament, if necessary in secret session.[106] Reading the clippings, it is striking how much support Churchill received for his 'manly' utterances, even those comments directed at the press itself, for many editorialists were happy to admit that *other* papers had been profoundly irresponsible. The *Daily Express* endorsed Churchill's denunciation of 'malicious carping'. The *South Wales Daily News* deplored the 'most vicious personal attacks' to which Churchill had been exposed by 'a section of the Unionist Press' which was ruthlessly determined to destroy his political influence. The *Liverpool Daily Courier* wrote of Churchill's 'justifiable bitterness' at certain sections of the press. However, the *Daily News* cautioned against adopting 'a policy of severity' towards the press, and *The Globe* condemned his 'wild talk': 'To ask the nation for its confidence in one

breath and in the other propose to gag the Press and hold Secret
Sessions of Parliament is to mistake the spirit of the people, and to
destroy the only foundations on which confidence can rest.'[107] Overall,
though, it is clear that Churchill's inspiringly optimistic tone, which
seemed like a breath of fresh air, helped him mobilize significant press
backing. This was not least because his confidence and buoyancy provided many editors with a welcome opportunity to condemn influential rivals as partisan and unpatriotic croakers.

Yet in reality the Allied forces at Gallipoli had become horribly
bogged down. Ellis Ashmead-Bartlett, a war correspondent who had
written a stirring account of the landings by Anzac troops, had become
concerned about the lack of progress, and was chafing under the censorship imposed by Sir Ian Hamilton, a friend of Churchill's who was
the commander on the ground. Ashmead-Bartlett returned to London
to try to alert the government to the seriousness of the situation. On
10 June, he dined at Lady Randolph's house thereby to meet Churchill,
who appeared much aged, pale, and depressed: 'he rounded on me,
and accused me of having come home to run down the Expedition. I
denied this accusation, and declared I was as keen as everybody to see
it through, if only it was handled in the right manner. Having convinced him on this point, he became quite calm.' At midnight, the two
men left together, and walked to Admiralty House, where Churchill
had been permitted to stay until his new house was ready: 'Winston
wandered through the rooms, in which he is now only living on
sufferance, his head bent, his face flushed, his hands behind his back,
picking up a book here, a letter there, glancing at them and throwing
them aside, his mind unable to concentrate on anything but the
Dardanelles.' [108]

Churchill at this point considered Ashmead-Bartlett to be an ally
and hoped that he would press for reinforcements to be sent, and
arranged for him to meet Asquith. Yet, when the government's
Dardanelles Committee met to discuss a memorandum that the journalist provided, Churchill stated 'that in many respects he did not
agree with Mr. Ashmead Bartlett', especially the latter's statement that

the seizure of the Kilid Bahr plateau would not have a decisive impact. 'If we succeeded in reaching the Kilid Bahr plateau it would mean a great disaster to the Turkish army in Gallipoli and the whole position would fall into our hands.' For good measure, Churchill advocated attacking the Turks with gas.[109] But a new offensive in August failed. Even with the true extent of the fiasco now apparent—in part due to the activities of Ashmead-Bartlett, who ended up being deported from Gallipoli for supposedly spreading despondency—Churchill remained obsessed with vindicating his Admiralty record.[110] He buttonholed any journalist who would listen, on one occasion staying up till 2 a.m. to try to prove to an unconvinced Charles Repington that he had been right about Antwerp and the Dardanelles.[111] Churchill showed confidential documents about these and other episodes to C. P. Scott, and even offered to let him take them away to study, before having second thoughts.[112]

Gallipoli was to be successfully evacuated at the end of the year, but before that occurred Churchill became increasingly frustrated at being sidelined from the central direction of the war. In November, having been excluded from the membership of the newly-formed War Council, he decided to resign from the Cabinet and take up a military command in France. He made a valedictory speech in the Commons that was generally seen as dignified, or at least 'clever', if not absolutely convincing on all points.[113] In a sympathetic editorial, the *Daily Mail* described it as 'very fine'.[114] Such comments brought down the wrath of Northcliffe upon editor Thomas Marlowe: 'I wish you would not start "booming" Churchill again. Why do you do it? We got rid of him with difficulty, and he is trying to come back. "Puffing" will bring him back.'[115]

Northcliffe's fear was not misplaced. Churchill, even as he set off for the front, was still thinking of his political future. He advised Clementine to cultivate C. P. Scott, J. L. Garvin, and Northcliffe's brother Lord Rothermere, who had taken over the *Daily Mirror* in 1914 and who owned other papers too. This list of 'loyal friends of quality and power' is instructive, as it suggests that Churchill was still seeking support across the political spectrum but had at this point given up on Northcliffe himself.[116] Although there was apparently not much contact between Rothermere and Churchill during the latter's period in the trenches, Churchill did correspond with both Scott and Garvin. During the May crisis, Garvin had risked his position as editor of the *Observer*—owned by the Conservative MP Waldorf Astor—with an article praising Churchill's 'lion-hearted courage'.[117] Over the next few months both he and Scott demonstrated their sympathy for his cause. While acknowledging their faithfulness and personal integrity, Clementine Churchill doubted that Scott and Garvin were good judges of political effectiveness, but this does not seem to have dampened her husband's enthusiasm for intriguing with them.[118]

Initially treated with scepticism by his fellow soldiers, Churchill soon impressed them with his good humour, his relish for war, and his 'somewhat bitter' attitude towards Asquith, which was widely shared by the men in the trenches.[119] He was, however, out of the headlines. Even an early brush with death, when the dugout he was in was hit by a shell, occasioned only a paragraph. (As was quite common in Great War reporting, the information came from a letter from a junior officer to his parents, who had chosen to share it with the press.)[120] He was given the command of a battalion which was deployed in the frontline at Ploegsteert, Belgium, but he continued to hanker after politics. In March 1916 he returned to London on leave. Scott had reached the (frankly bizarre) conclusion that the war effort would be strengthened if Fisher returned to the Admiralty. He went to visit Churchill to try to persuade him of this, only to find that the two men had already been reconciled. Churchill then spoke in the Commons debate on the naval estimates and urged Fisher's recall. Although the proposal met with widespread incredulity, the setback did not crush Churchill's determination to give up soldiering and go back to politics permanently. Before he stepped aboard the torpedo boat that would carry him again to France, he left Clementine with a statement for the Press Association 'announcing his speedy return to political life'. He quickly rescinded his decision, but this was a question of tactics and timing rather than a fundamental change of heart.[121] 'Newspapers arrived telling of the Army debate', Churchill wrote from the field later in the month. 'How different I c[oul]d have made it!'[122]

Churchill was at this stage intent on making himself the nucleus of the anti-Asquith forces in the Commons, and Scott encouraged this. 'The Opposition—that is the party of energy & of concentration—is leaderless & waits for you to lead it', he wrote.[123] Garvin, whom Churchill was also courting, was enthusiastic but more circumspect, as his proprietor, Waldorf Astor, did not want to use the *Observer* to promote Churchill. However, Garvin did suggest that Churchill might offer Northcliffe a series of articles on the 'needs of the army' for *The Times*.[124] It is unclear whether Churchill considered that idea, but he did write Northcliffe a letter, on the advice of Rothermere. It appears to have remained unsent, and indeed to have been destroyed, on the sagacious advice of Clementine: 'after the way Lord N has flouted you I cannot bear that you should write to him in that vein.'[125] Churchill would at any rate have got nowhere, as Northcliffe had recently telegraphed the editor of *The Times*: 'Stated here that Churchill lead opposition. Dont [sic] give least support.'[126] Not long afterwards Northcliffe made a casual joke suggesting that Churchill was hungry for office. In high dudgeon, Churchill returned to him a small bust of Napoleon that Northcliffe had presented to him as a gift years before, and which had had pride of place on his writing desk.[127] Northcliffe did actually make an apology, which Churchill accepted; and the latter soon reverted to trying to curry favour.[128]

The amalgamation of Churchill's battalion with another provided him with the excuse he needed to return to Westminster politics; he left the army at the beginning of May. He did not, however, launch any dramatic assault on the government; in fact, he lent it his skills when he was commissioned to write a press statement on the Battle of Jutland, after the official account issued by the Admiralty had caused public disquiet.[129] The idea, recalled Sir Douglas Brownrigg, was that, as he had 'become a somewhat keen critic of the Admiralty', his assessment would be considered unbiased. Yet in fact 'the whole Press let off a scream asking why the Admiralty had given the ex-Minister opportunities of examining all the material denied to everybody else, and they attacked him for having the temerity to give his views!'[130]

After 1908, when he joined the Cabinet, Churchill had to all intents and purposes given up journalistic activity. Now he started anew, with a series of articles on the war published in the *Sunday Pictorial*. Asquith's wife Margot considered them 'very poor stuff', but the public seems to have thought otherwise.[131] Churchill told his brother: '"Sunday Pictorial" circulation was 448,000 in a single day. This beats all records in journalism.'[132] After he lunched with Repington, the latter recorded: 'He was very pleased with his journalistic success. He had got £1000 for writing four long articles in a Sunday paper, and felt sure that he could make £5000 a year, and place himself on the right side in matters of finance.'[133]

Yet money, although it was very important to Churchill, was not his sole motivation. The articles—which became a source of satirical comment in *Punch*—also gave him the opportunity to vindicate his own record, notably by giving his side of the Antwerp affair.[134] This paralleled his—broadly successful—efforts to defend himself before the Dardanelles Commission, which helped lay the groundwork for his eventual return to office. For the moment, however, he remained politically frustrated. In late November, Scott found him 'suffering acutely' from being kept on the sidelines:

> I urged him to make a business of Parliament and make himself a figure there, but he said the papers (with the exception of the Manchester Guardian) would not report him and on the contrary ill natured remarks were always made, as that 'There were few members present and no one troubled to come in' or 'what a contrast with the days when his rising was the signal for the House to fill' & so on. Therefore he preferred to find his public in the Press. Then at least every word he wished to say was printed and it took him no longer to write an article for the 'Sunday Pictorial' for which he got £250 than to prepare a speech which was not reported.

Churchill also told Scott, with a typical combination of self-pity and resolve, that 'At present he was the best abused man in the country. He was determined, however, to stick it out. [...] The mistake he had made was in not allowing enough for the power of the press, at a time of suspended party activity, to attack and ruin an individual.'[135]

By now, Asquith's government was crumbling, in the face of the widely held suspicion that the Prime Minister himself lacked the steel to pursue the war with the relentlessness that was required. A leading candidate to succeed him was Lloyd George, who had served with distinction as Minister of Munitions after May 1915, but who (following Kitchener's death by drowning) was proving rather less effective as War Secretary. Although he struggled to impose his will on the generals, he had long been a canny media operator. Reputedly, it was George Riddell who persuaded him to reserve his most important speeches for Saturdays to ensure that they would receive coverage in the Saturday evening papers, the Sunday papers, and the Monday ones too.[136] It was Riddell also who hinted to Frances Stevenson, Lloyd George's secretary and long-term mistress, that the couple needed to tread carefully if they were to avoid exposure.[137] But if Lloyd George's newspaper connections helped protect him from scandal, and if his public pledge that the war would be fought 'to a knockout' made him appear as a more dynamic alternative to Asquith, he was still widely distrusted and could not take the support of the press by any means for granted.[138]

In particular, he had an ambivalent relationship with Northcliffe, who was growing increasingly megalomaniacal. According to *Daily Mail* journalist Tom Clarke, writing in his diary in October: 'The Chief is getting a bit restive about Lloyd George. He thinks L.G. is getting too friendly with Winston Churchill, whom he will not forgive for what he calls the Antwerp and Gallipoli blunders, and he is telling us to drive into the public mind the fact that political interference means increasing the death-roll of our army.'[139] But although Lloyd George was in no way eager to do Northcliffe's bidding, the two men's joint interest in getting rid of Asquith contributed to the December drama that drove the Prime Minister from office.[140] When

Lloyd George and Bonar Law proposed a new committee to run the war that would have sidelined Asquith, he tried to call their bluff by resigning. In fact Lloyd George was able to win over enough cross-party support to enable him to seize the keys of Downing Street. As events reached their climacteric, Cecil Harmsworth went to the Ritz Hotel to see his brother Rothermere: 'I find him with Winston who walks rapidly up and down the room talking at the top of his voice. All the swiftly-changing aspects of the crisis are heatedly discussed.'[141]

That same day, 5 December, Churchill also saw Repington: 'Winston full of talk, and declares that he will not take office in the new Government unless he can take effective part in the war.'[142] But this was bravado, or more likely self-delusion, for he was not to be offered the chance. On the night that Lloyd George formed his Cabinet, Churchill dined with F. E. Smith and the Canadian-born financier and Tory MP Sir Max Aitken. Aitken, shortly to be ennobled as Lord Beaverbrook, was a confidant of Bonar Law and had been deeply involved in the machinations that led to Asquith's fall. Frequently described as 'impish', he was motivated partly by malice, partly by ambition, and not least by his sense of fun. He had a capacity for generosity of a kind which threatened to corrupt its recipients and an equal and astonishing capacity for lies and treachery.

On this occasion Aitken was the man delegated to drop the hint to Churchill that he was not to get a post in Lloyd George's administration. According to Beaverbrook's later account, when the penny dropped, Churchill attacked him with violent words and then dashed into the street carrying his hat and coat without even troubling to put them on. However, the next morning 'Churchill called me bright and early on the telephone. He wanted to apologise for the abuse he had given me the night before.'[143] This was a wise approach to adopt towards a man who was in the process of taking over the *Daily Express*. But it also marked the deepening of what had been a mere acquaintanceship into a connection which, though not untroubled, was at least as significant as that between Churchill and Northcliffe and which was based on greater genuine warmth. Churchill's apologetic phone call could be seen as the beginning of a beautiful friendship; or alternatively as the opening move in negotiations for a pact with the devil.

Lloyd George had left Churchill out of the Cabinet largely because his own position was at this stage still too precarious to withstand him making such an inevitably controversial appointment. Churchill was offered 'the hearty support of the Northcliffe Press' if he would cross the Atlantic and explain the British point of view to neutral America, but in spite of a potentially lucrative approach from the Keedick Lecture Agency he chose to stay put.[144] The new Prime Minister used Riddell to pass on the message that Churchill might expect a job of some kind down the line; but Churchill remained resentful.[145] One obstacle was removed when Lloyd George—to use Churchill's term—'appeased' Northcliffe by sending him on a government mission to the United States.[146] Another was removed by the publication of the Dardanelles Commission report, which, while it did not fully excul-pate Churchill, at least spread the blame around. (As the *Daily Mail* summarized it: 'Mr. Asquith Wobbled. Lord Kitchener Did Not Realise the Facts and Ignored His Staff. Mr. Churchill Misled Everybody. Lord Fisher and Other Experts Sat Mum.'[147]) At the same time, Churchill kept up the pressure by intimating that he might go into opposition to the government, perhaps by joining Asquith's forces, while making sure that he did not actually burn his bridges.

There soon came the chance for Churchill to send Lloyd George a warning signal. In April 1917, *The Nation* was banned from being circulated abroad, on the grounds that comments it had made about the military situation were encouraging to the enemy. Churchill sprang to the paper's defence in the House of Commons, ridiculing the idea that the German General Staff or the German people would be influenced in their views by what had been written in a Liberal weekly. As he pointed out, 'all the newspapers of these belligerent countries have continually throughout the War clipped unfairly extracts apart from their context, and twisted them, and made whatever mutilations they thought convenient, from newspapers of the other belligerent countries.' It was unfair, then, to penalize a publication for the use that the German news agencies chose to make of its articles. Moreover, he claimed that in America—which had just entered the war—the press and the people were better and more critically informed than in Britain. He claimed too that 'my experience in reading the newspapers throughout this War has been that very much more frank and virile admissions are made by German newspapers than are made by our newspapers.'[148] The next week, Churchill further showed his support of *The Nation* by dining with editor H. W. Massingham; the export ban was ended later in the year.[149] Churchill was quite right to oppose it, but, given his own previous behaviour at the Admiralty, his new-found hostility to clumsy censorship looked opportunistic rather than principled.

At last, in the summer, the Prime Minister picked his moment and gave Churchill the post of Minister of Munitions (albeit without a seat in the War Cabinet). Bonar Law found out about the appointment from Beaverbrook; a strange way for Lloyd George to treat his key coalition partner. Churchill told C. P. Scott that he owed his new job to the *Manchester Guardian*: 'You and Garvin were my only friends in the press and Garvin had to be very careful.'[150] There was much complaining on the Unionist side. According to H. A. Gwynne of the *Morning Post*, 'I have never, since the war began, seen such indignation against a Government or man as is raging now against Lloyd George for the appointment of Winston.' Gwynne even considered standing against Churchill in the obligatory by-election.[151] Yet the fuss soon died down and in the event Churchill triumphed at Dundee very comfortably. Having realized the extent of Conservative MPs' hostility, he was a (temporarily) somewhat chastened figure, and his time at Munitions saw less public controversy than during many other stages of his career. He had not lost his impetuous streak, though, and many still found his judgement wanting. Riddell was astonished when Churchill read him cablegrams 'from his *friend* Northcliffe, with whom he was now upon terms of intimate association'.[152]

There was, of course, the usual round of speeches, visits to factories, and—it could be said—rather more trips to the Western Front than were strictly necessary for the purposes of his role. Indeed, he was in France at the time of the great German breakthrough of March 1918 and returned there at the end of the month. Clementine wrote to him: 'The Prime Minister rang me up last night on the telephone to tell me your news—I am so relieved that you are confident as the newspapers tho' repeating again & again that we are "holding them" are rather depressing.'[153] On this occasion, the papers were correct; the Germans had overreached themselves and the scene was set for their subsequent collapse. In April, Churchill reviewed his ministry's performance in the Commons, and was said by *The Times* to have convincingly 'conveyed an impression of the massive strength and inexhaustible resources of this wonderful island'.[154]

Arguably, Churchill's own performance in terms of managing arms production was less impressive than has generally been believed, notably in the case of tanks.[155] His positive press—at the time and since—may have owed something to his own public relations efforts. He put Alexander MacCallum Scott, a Liberal MP who was also his first biographer, in charge of the Department's propaganda.[156] He also liaised with Beaverbrook, who had been made Minister of Information, helping to manage the latter's problematic relationship with Lloyd George.[157] In the wake of the Bolshevik revolution, after which Russia dropped out of the war, Churchill wrote to him addressing him as 'My dear Max'. He urged: 'It seems to me that the papers should be encouraged to give much publicity to all the news which reaches us of the chaos and anarchy in Russia. There is a strong feeling among British workmen that these wretches have "let us down", and without overdoing it I think this absolutely true conception should be sustained by a constant stream of facts.'[158]

Churchill knew, actually, that facts alone did not make for a persuasive message. Complex issues had to be crystallized into simple terms, and editors had to be appealed to behind the scenes.[159] As the war drew to a close, he was asked by a journalist to provide 'any form of geometry or mathematics' that would illustrate the workings of the Ministry of Munitions at a glance. With a flourish, Churchill took a piece of paper and listed four 'Elements of Difficulty' before counterbalancing them with five 'Factors of Success', which included 'The perfect loyalty of the workers' and 'Our sturdy national physique'.[160] He might have added: 'The minister's genius for publicity'.

By the time of the November Armistice, Churchill was itching to get more firmly back into the political fray. In the years since he had been appointed to the Admiralty, he had endured many vicissitudes; his problems had often been exacerbated by his own behaviour but also by the press. Riddell's comment that Churchill was 'a soldier at heart' was debatable—politics was at his core—but his fascination with all things warlike was part of what made some newspapers so hostile to him, on account of his real and imagined interferences with the naval machine. (This was in addition, of course, to earlier resentments over issues such as Ireland.) That is to say, although he was largely the architect of his own downfall in 1915, he was also to some degree a victim of press hostility to civilian control of the military and of many senior military figures' willingness to collude with the press to secure their own ends.

Yet Churchill's private complaints about the newspapers exaggerated the extent of the hostility he faced from them; he was never as friendless as he made out, not least because there was always some part of the Fourth Estate that would find its own reasons for rounding on his attackers. Inconsistent in his attitudes to press freedom, his own efforts at censorship when at the Admiralty rebounded on him, as they merely increased journalists' frustrations and made them more inclined to vent their spleen. On the other hand, he attributed more power to published opinion (when directed at him) than was truly merited. This led him to engage in a sometimes humiliating quest for newspaper approval that was likely to enhance the distrust with which his fellow politicians regarded him. As Clementine sensibly told him: 'I am sure it is no use writing private letters to great journalists—Even if they do, in consequence decide to run you, they feel patronising and protective about it & the support then lacks in genuine ardour.'[161]

In fact, Churchill's own command of the written word and his essential publicity *flair* actually helped prove that political success did not depend upon the whims of the proprietors. The post-war period would require him to develop these survival skills yet further, as both the political system and the media itself entered an era of uncertainty and flux.

4

Hell With The Lid Off

Two days after the Armistice, Churchill addressed a dinner held in honour of visiting American trade-journal editors at Claridge's Hotel in Mayfair. Over 'Hors d'oeuvres Quatorze Points' and 'Salade Lloyd George', he paid tribute to the 'extraordinary' part that the press had played in the war, quipping that although they had been 'excluded from even a peep-show on military operations' at the beginning, 'they afterwards took charge of the whole concern'. To this he added a sentiment that was bound to be acceptable to his audience: 'We owe to the Press of this country a good many harsh criticisms, and a good many rough turns, but, in the main, it has been the great vehicle which has expressed the national will.'[1]

The 'national will', as manifested during the electoral campaign that immediately followed the war's end, actually caused Churchill a fair amount of discomfort. This was the famous 'coupon' election, so-called after the telegram that Lloyd George and Bonar Law, who had decided to continue their coalition into peacetime, despatched to parliamentary candidates they wished to back. In retrospect, it may seem obvious that they would have romped home against the weak opposition of the independent (Asquithian) Liberals and the still-youthful Labour Party. Yet the political situation was more confused than it appeared at first glance, and with Beaverbrook, Rothermere, and Northcliffe all displaying their *prima donna* tendencies, the Prime Minister calculated he could not afford to rest on his laurels. It has been argued that the 'jingo' atmosphere of the campaign has been exaggerated, yet Lloyd George undoubtedly gave a huge hostage to fortune by promising to make Germany pay reparations 'to the limit of her capacity'.[2] In his own constituency, Churchill had to counter the perception that he was soft on the Germans, and faced the hostility of the Dundee *Advertiser* as well as the *Courier*, as both were now owned by the same Conservative proprietor, D. C. Thomson.[3] Against his better judgement, Churchill felt constrained to support bringing the Kaiser to trial, while trying to damp down expectations of how much money could be extracted from the defeated enemy. 'The local papers gibbered with strident claims', he later recalled.[4] However (and somewhat surprisingly), even the *Advertiser* was satisfied with Churchill's declaration in favour of nationalizing the railways; and when the results were announced it turned out he had secured a majority of over 15,000.[5]

Lloyd George made Churchill Secretary of State for War and Air (albeit still outside the five-man War Cabinet, which continued to operate until October 1919). Predictably, the *Morning Post* declared that Churchill was 'even more unsuited to direct the affairs of the Army than any other Department of State.'[6] The *Daily Mail* claimed that his was one of the most unpopular appointments, not simply because Churchill himself was distrusted, but because of doubts about the bringing together of the two different responsibilities: 'The official excuse and explanation that the Air Ministry is not subordinate to the War Office, but that Mr. Churchill is to hold two separate Ministerial appointments, has merely given the already strong condemnation a new direction.'[7] Such carping from the *Mail* was no great surprise; Northcliffe, increasingly deluded as to his own importance, had unsuccessfully tried to 'blackmail' Lloyd George into giving him a seat at the Paris peace conference.[8] Alexander MacCallum Scott recorded: 'Winston remarks that for the past fortnight the newspapers have been declaring that if he were to go to the War Office the Army Council would resign, while on the other hand they have been describing [the shipowner] Andrew Weir as the right man for the Ministry of Munitions. Now that the appointments have been made no one has resigned from the Army Council while there have been a shoal of resignations from the Ministry of Munitions.'[9]

The newspaper grumbling, although to be expected, was nonetheless an early sign that the Coalition would not get an easy ride from the press. (A syndicate controlled by Lloyd George himself had recently taken over the *Daily Chronicle*, but he could not of course tame every paper in the same way.)[10] On the other hand, the threat of unrest within the army and in industry meant that the government could be seen as a bulwark against the fear of revolution. Churchill needed to retain hundreds of thousands of conscripts in order to maintain Britain's forces abroad, a factor with obvious repercussions for morale and discipline. He briefed the Newspaper Proprietors' Association on his plans and also sent Northcliffe a file of papers explaining the policy 'For your secret and personal information'.[11] 'All my newspapers will do exactly what you wish on the subject', Northcliffe replied.[12] Churchill's cousin Frederick Guest, who was the Coalition Liberal Chief Whip, reported to Lloyd George: 'You will be interested to hear that Winston's statement re an Emergency Army has been extremely well received; even the Daily News finds it hard to criticise.'[13]

Indeed the first six months of 1919 were ones in which Churchill received—for him—relatively few press attacks. The Prime Minister, for his part, successfully faced down the now-ailing Northcliffe, who was stirring up accusations that he was weakening on the reparations question. Briefly back from the peace negotiations, Lloyd George, in a Commons speech, accused the press lord of 'diseased vanity'. As he did so he tapped his head to suggest mental illness, thereby confirming Northcliffe as his indisputable foe.[14] Churchill, however, did not feel compelled to break with him too. Indeed, the Conservative minister Walter Long warned Lloyd George that Northcliffe was 'undoubtedly trying to run Winston as your successor'—although he said he did not think that Churchill was directly involved in any plot, and the claim at any rate seems exaggerated.[15] In June—as the world waited to see if the Germans would sign the harsh terms of the Treaty of

Versailles—Churchill published an article on Britain's foreign policy in Northcliffe's *Weekly Dispatch*. He urged the admission, before too long, of Germany to the League of Nations: 'We cannot afford to drive the German nation into the jaws of Russian Bolshevism', he argued.[16]

Thus, after a couple of years of relative quiescence, Churchill chose once again to revive his journalistic career.[17] (His friend Lord Birkenhead, the former F. E. Smith, who was now Lord Chancellor, also raised eyebrows by publishing articles which seemed 'framed to advance the "coalition" between him and Winston.'[18]) A slew of further Churchill pieces followed, although his output slowed again in 1921–2. Churchill knew, however, that Northcliffe was an unreliable confederate, even if his papers were a convenient outlet for well-paid articles. At this time the developing 'anti-waste' movement—based around the demand for public spending cuts, which was also backed by Rothermere and others—posed a threat to Churchill's administration of the War and Air ministries.[19] Churchill lamented to Lloyd George that when cutbacks that the papers had demanded were actually implemented they were then attacked in the self-same organs on the grounds that they had been carried out wrongly. 'Even cutting down the airships has been attacked. You will never satisfy the Northcliffe press. Their object is not national economy but Coalition overthrow.'[20]

During the second half of the year, the pressure on Churchill intensified. In particular, his violent opposition to Bolshevism got him into considerable trouble with the press. Over the past several months, Lloyd George and Churchill had been increasingly at odds over the question of intervention in Russia's civil war. Although Churchill aggressively backed British involvement, it is worth noting that soldiers, supplies, and support had been lent to the anti-Bolshevik (or 'White') forces well before his appointment as War Secretary. Lloyd George, for his part, certainly did not want the Reds to win, but he did not favour an unlimited commitment to their opponents, especially given their various military failures and setbacks. Churchill's strong advocacy of help for the Whites brought him into conflict with old Radical supporters such as H. W. Massingham of *The Nation*.[21] Strikingly and significantly, it also raised the ire of the fiery left-wing *Daily Herald* and its editor George Lansbury (a future leader of the Labour Party). The *Herald*, founded in 1911, had only recently been revived as a daily, having been reduced to weekly publication during the war. Unappealing to advertisers and permanently on the edge of bankruptcy, the paper nonetheless succeeded in embarrassing officialdom, notably with the revelation of a secret War Office circular that attempted to gauge the extent of political militancy in the army.[22] In July 1919 Sir George Riddell (as he now was) called on Churchill at the War Office to discuss a planned newspaper briefing on Russia. It turned out that Churchill 'wanted to exclude the *Daily Herald*, to whom he had already sent an invitation. I told him that this would be a fatal mistake and would raise a storm of indignation throughout the country. [...] He ultimately agreed to their presence.'[23]

It was not only socialists who objected to the ongoing British military adventures in Russia. To Churchill's annoyance, Riddell himself 'told Winston what I thought of his Russian campaign and that the working classes would not stand for it'.[24] Paradoxically, moreover, if Churchill's support for the Whites amounted to a rightwards turn, this did not actually help him with a right-wing press that (for the most part) now favoured retrenchment and a more quiescent foreign policy. Sensing that their readers wished to turn their backs on the turbulence and brutality of the war years, the press barons were sceptical of anything that smacked of feverish energy and foreign adventurism. 'I am not vexed with you personally but I am with your Russian policy', Rothermere told Churchill. 'The latter is the devil.'[25] Photo-opportunities were, of course, still welcome, not least if they involved striking headgear. So on the one hand the *Daily Mirror* put the War Secretary on the front page inspecting the Women's Royal Air Force in a white 'topper'; and on the other it poured scorn upon the contradictions in his public statements on intervention.[26]

Beaverbrook too warned that the public desired peace, but Churchill rebuffed him with the threat that if he could not 'square' the press he would 'squash' it.[27] Beaverbrook was incensed, and the *Daily Express* launched systematic attacks on what it called the 'mad gamble' in Russia.[28] The paper contrasted the government's repeated pledges to withdraw with actual performance, and blamed the discrepancy firmly on the occupant of the War Office: 'Mr. Churchill has never loyally accepted the cabinet's decision to retire, had snatched at an excuse to delay and baulk at it, and never meant to give up the game until Petrograd was captured.'[29] Churchill managed to fend off the paper's allegations, invoking operational secrecy.[30] His cousin Lord Londonderry commiserated with him on 'This man-hunting campaign practised by Beaverbrook and Northcliffe', but in fact the latter was fairly restrained on this issue.[31] It was the Canadian, perhaps more motivated by pique than principle, who truly took the bit between his teeth. When Bonar Law complained about the coverage, Beaverbrook cheekily claimed that he did not control what appeared in the *Express*, and simply forwarded the protest to editor Ralph Blumenfeld.[32]

However, it was not too long before Churchill and Beaverbrook were reconciled. The occasion was a dinner party hosted by Alfred Duff Cooper—a future Conservative MP and Cabinet minister—and his new wife, Diana. Cooper recorded the scene in his diary:

> We had dinner in the bedroom as usual. The table is very narrow which I think promotes conversation. The food was excellent, champagne circulated freely and the conversation never flagged. It started on general topics [...] but gradually veered round to politics and Russia. Winston was at his very best, witty, courteous, eloquent. I never liked him so much. Max showed up badly. He was violent and rather rude. I several times feared disaster but it was always avoided. [...] They ended perfectly good friends and both said they had enjoyed themselves tremendously. I think they had.[33]

A few days later, Lloyd George startled the public—and Churchill— with a speech declaring that Britain could not afford to continue its intervention in the 'interminable' Russian civil war (which did not finally end until 1922).[34] But in spite of the ending of the British—and broader Allied—commitment, Churchill did not moderate his public statements. The most notorious of these was an *Illustrated Sunday Herald* piece in which he distinguished between admirable 'National Jews' (including Zionists) who were loyal to their countries, and the 'sinister confederacy' of 'International Jews' whom he suggested were mainly responsible for the Bolshevik revolution.[35] The *Jewish Chronicle* denounced this article vociferously, arguing that it could have been boiled down into two sentences. 'Mr. Churchill could merely have written: 'You Jews have made the Bolshevist movement. If you do not want to be robbed and massacred, shout your hatred of it from the house-tops.' The *Chronicle* went on to suggest 'that a British Cabinet Minister was lending the weight of his authority to a legend which has martyred the Jews by the thousand; and that a prominent British statesman had adopted the hoary tactics of hooligan anti-Semites, and was inviting his victims to confess to a merely imaginary crime [...] We flatly contradict his assertions regarding the predominant part played by Jews in Bolshevism.'[36] Yet although Churchill's comments have been damaging to his posthumous reputation, it is very striking that there does not appear to have been any other contemporary press criticism of his views.[37] Disturbingly, the opinions he expressed were not far outside the mainstream at the time. A few months later, for example, as two readers of the *Saturday Review* argued on the letters page over Churchill's record on Russia, they debated whether the Bolsheviks were 'Jew anarchists' or instead 'agents of Germany and the German-Jewish internationale'.[38]

Yet the wider controversy over Russia was not over yet. At this time, Churchill was simultaneously maintaining his anti-Soviet agenda, equating Bolshevism with pestilence, and ramping up his domestic rhetoric by declaring that the Labour Party was unfit to govern.[39] For its part, the Labour movement increasingly saw Churchill as its special foe. The Welsh-language newspaper poem which cast him as the 'arch-enemy of the worker' was tapping into a rich vein of sentiment.[40] The *Daily Herald* did not hesitate to label Churchill a war criminal on account of the role that he had played in August 1914.[41] In the summer of 1920, new revelations about Churchill's relations with the Whites appeared to confirm the suspicions of many. The Soviet authorities had discovered an embarrassing document among those abandoned by their enemies at Archangel (in Northern Russia). This was a record by former Lieutenant N. N. Golovin, who had been an emissary in London of the White commander Nikolai Yudenich, of a clandestine conversation he had had with Churchill in May the previous year. This had then been handed to a visiting British Labour delegation and to the *Daily Herald* special correspondent Walter Meakin. It seemed sensational for, as the *Daily News* put it, 'The document reveals the mind of Mr. Churchill in regard to the Russian gamble, and makes it appear that—in view of the opposition of the British workers to armed intervention—the evacuation of Archangel was used as a pretext for sending out troops really intended under this secret arrangement to be employed against the Bolsheviks.' The most damning part of Golovin's account read:

> Mr. Churchill told me the question of giving armed support was for him the most difficult one. The reason for this was the opposition of the British working class to armed intervention. But even in this matter, without promising anything, he would try to help. He had declared in the House of Commons that fresh forces were necessary for the purpose of evacuating the north. He would send under this pretext up to 10,000 volunteers [...] He will postpone the actual evacuation for an indefinite period (but will not speak about this). He agrees upon the help of the newly arrived British troops being actively manifested.

Golovin also reported that Churchill, when speaking about the White leader Alexander Kolchak, said: 'I myself am carrying out Koltchak's orders.'[42]

Approached by the Press Association, Churchill refused to comment.[43] The *Herald* compared him to Brer Fox who 'sez nuffin'.[44] In the Commons, it fell to Bonar Law to answer questions on the affair. 'My right hon. Friend informs me that the report gives a very inaccurate account of the conversation,' he explained blandly, 'especially as regards the actual words and expressions employed.'[45] Whereas it does not seem inconceivable that the Bolsheviks had interfered with the document, Churchill did not go so far as to make that claim himself.[46] Nor was he able to produce any alternative record of the meeting.[47] Ultimately, he rested his defence on the claim that the meeting had had no actual impact on the course of events.[48] Overall, given his habit of 'raving on the subject of the Bolsheviks', it seems plausible that he did indeed talk fast and loose to Golovin.[49] Of course, some of his critics raved too. The veteran Liberal journalist A. G. Gardiner wrote of the Churchill–Golovin encounter that 'There has never been so audacious, so colossal an act of treason against the nation in our annals...There will be no end to this treason until Mr. Churchill is suppressed.'[50]

Whether or not Golovin had seriously misrepresented Churchill, the episode is striking for two reasons. First, as long as Churchill retained the support of senior colleagues such as Bonar Law, he was safe in the face of scandalous allegations. Second, it is remarkable that, in spite of the very public nature of the controversy, it has been overlooked by historians—a token, perhaps, of its lack of contemporary purchase outside Asquithian and left-wing circles.[51] As long as Coalition MPs remained broadly united, the shrill but weak Opposition parties could make little impact, even when backed by angry newspaper campaigns. Not long before the Golovin scandal broke, Churchill had argued that the press's 'jealousy' of Parliament's power and authority was reflected in its subtle, persistent, and perhaps unconscious depreciation of the institution and those who inhabited it. 'The immense organization and development of newspapers, which has reached in our island an unequalled magnificence, was the child of Parliamentary freedom; but an ungrateful child.' The press, in his analysis, had become a danger to the state.[52]

These comments, it should be stressed, were in the nature of sorrowful (or resentful) reflections delivered in passing rather than a concerted attack. His real anger remained concentrated on the

Bolsheviks. The Soviets were advancing rapidly in their war against the Poles. One evening in late July, the streets of London were placarded with the legend:

POLAND
BY
WINSTON
CHURCHILL

In this *Evening News* article, Churchill suggested that the defeated Germans could redeem themselves if they stood up against Bolshevik barbarism.[53] This could be read as a 'hint of an alliance with Germany to fight the Bolshevists', which did not go down well in France.[54] An editorial in *Le Temps* poured scorn on the idea, making an extended comparison with the events of 1794–5, which had resulted in the partition of Poland.[55] In spite of some division of opinion, the notion did not go down too well in Germany either.[56] As the *Morning Post*'s Berlin correspondent summarized: 'No German, the newspapers declare, can respond to the appeal made to him to help the nation [i.e. Britain] which has pursued Germany with hate until she is driven to despair, simply because the material interests of that nation are imperilled.'[57]

Understandably enough, the article was read by some in Britain as a deliberate attempt by Churchill to subvert Lloyd George's more pragmatic policy of engagement with the Soviets, an interpretation which then made its way into the German press.[58] However, the reality was somewhat different. The journalist Tom Clarke told the story in his book *My Northcliffe Diary*:

> We published to-day an announcement that Winston Churchill had promised to write an article for tomorrow's *Evening News*. Churchill rang up on seeing the announcement and said he would not do the article. When the Chief was told this he rang me up and said, 'Churchill must do it. Send a good man to him at once and tell him he cannot make the *Daily Mail* look ridiculous.' There was a bit of coming and going about the matter, but Churchill wrote the article.[59]

Churchill was understandably annoyed, then, when *The Times* (also owned by Northcliffe), said that it was 'constitutionally improper' for him to express his views on such a topic in a newspaper article.[60] To the editor, H. Wickham Steed, Churchill argued that from a constitutional point of view an article in the *Evening News* was no different from a speech expressing the same views delivered in the Commons or in his constituency.[61]

Criticisms of the article did not come only from *The Times* (which in fact agreed with its content if not the method). Naturally, some of the attacks were opportunistic, but a serious question was at stake. MPs were starting to ask whether ministers should be allowed to make money by writing in the press on matters of national import-ance, potentially in breach of Cabinet collective responsibility.[62] But in a thinly attended House of Commons on a Bank Holiday Monday, 'Mr. Lloyd George treated with a contemptuous indifference the searching questions on Mr. Churchill's newspaper article on Russia and Poland.'[63] 'I only read the article this morning', he said, when asked if it conflicted with the government's line. To much laughter, he added: 'I do not think it is so much an expression of policy as a han-kering.'[64] This was typical Lloyd George: airy dismissal of pertinent questions, gentle public mockery of a colleague that doubled as a defence (by implying that Churchill's misbehaviour had not been serious), and a rather relaxed interpretation of constitutional propri-ety. If his ministers were to bolster their earnings by publishing articles that sailed close to the wind—well, that was not such bad precedent for the Prime Minister's own literary future.[65]

In fairness, Lloyd George was prepared to indulge Churchill's flam-boyant excesses partly because of the genuine strengths that he brought to the government. He had shown his worth through his successful handling of the tense Commons debate on the Amritsar massacre, in which forces commanded by General Reginald Dyer had shot dead at least 379 unarmed protesters. (The *Morning Post* assisted Dyer in his enforced retirement by raising a huge sum for him via public subscription, whereas Northcliffe, showing his more progressive side, commended Churchill for denouncing the killings.[66]) Yet although Churchill condemned 'frightfulness' in India, he was an advocate of harsh repression in Ireland, where revolutionary violence was by now in full swing. The renowned early modern historian J. G. A. Pocock has even suggested that the Irish revolution was 'the third of the major civil wars which have convulsed British history'— the first being the English Civil War and the second the American War of Independence.[67]

To a degree, Pocock's wording reflects contemporary understandings of what was occurring, albeit in a way that challenges the ways that historians typically name and periodize the conflict. Thus, what is now called the 'Anglo-Irish War' or the 'War of Independence' is generally understood to have started with the murder of two British soldiers in the Soloheadbeg Ambush of January 1919 (less than two weeks after Churchill took over as War Secretary). Yet it was not until March 1920 that the *Morning Post* concluded that 'civil war is now in progress', a conclusion that became more generally shared as time went on.[68] Terminology was important; the British, although notionally militarily superior to the IRA, were dealing with determined adversaries who were skilled in the arts of guerrilla warfare. In this context, the battle for public opinion in both Britain and Ireland became crucial, and to describe the conflict was to define its legitimacy. In June, Churchill used an article in the *Illustrated Sunday Herald* as a platform to defend the new Government of Ireland Bill, a measure intended to appease Irish national sentiment through the devolution of power. He described the Bill as a 'gift' to the Irish, that is to say, as an act of generosity rather than a concession of weakness, at the same time insisting that the British would defeat the IRA 'murder campaign'.[69] The *Freeman's Journal*, although believed by the British to be inciting terrorism and regarded by Churchill as 'the most violent propagandists', actually accepted the label 'murder campaign' and agreed that IRA killings were deplorable. However, it argued that the terror was 'not one-sided', and prayed that the British would not commit an Amritsar-type massacre.[70]

In Britain, by contrast, Churchill's language does not appear to have to have caused any particular controversy or concern, no doubt because it reflected prevailing understandings of the nature of the conflict. One explanation for the excessive violence perpetrated by the British may simply be that, from the domestic political point of view, they did not expect there to be many repercussions. John M. Regan has argued that, 'By September 1920, Churchill was already thinking as a post-Unionist'; that is to say, he was willing to breach the British constitution for the purpose of restoring order.[71] The 'sacking' that month of the town of Balbriggan by the Royal Irish Constabulary—who at the same time carried out two summary executions—was by no means the first act of indiscriminate reprisal. But it did mark a watershed in the press coverage, in part because the Balbriggan, not far from Dublin, could easily be accessed by British journalists.[72] The activities of the 'Black and Tans', the ill-disciplined RIC reserve force, were now becoming notorious. In November, Cecil L'Estrange Malone, a former Liberal who had recently switched parties to become Britain's first Communist MP, struggled to be heard amid cries of 'Bolshie!' when he rose to ask a question. Eventually, he succeeded in saying: 'Would it not be better—[Interruption]—if the Secretary of State for War paid some attention to these regrettable outrages, in preference to reviewing books for the "Daily Mail"?'[73]

Malone was a marginal figure, as at this time was the young Oswald Mosley (who left the Conservatives in protest at the reprisals), but pressure was also growing from Labour and the Asquithian Liberals. The *Daily Express* made what Lloyd George called 'a most unscrupulous attack' on the government's Irish policy—it probably didn't help that Churchill had told Beaverbrook that the Prime Minister thought that he (Beaverbrook) was a cad.[74] In the USA, Ireland was front-page news, from Chattanooga, Tennessee, to Butte, Montana—and not only in Irish–American papers.[75] Readers of the *Washington Times* could peruse a series of articles on 'The New Terrorism' by George Bernard

Shaw, who argued that Churchill's acts of repression could only be explained by the genuine fear of the consequences of a free Ireland.[76] Wickham Steed wrote to Churchill warning him of the bitterness that the issue was generating in America, condemned the government's recent 'vindictive action' in prosecuting the *Freeman's Journal* on a charge of spreading a false report, and lamented 'official recourse to methods scarcely distinguishable from those of the murder gang'. Most importantly, Steed urged a truce, which he hoped would lead to a broader settlement with the representatives of Sinn Féin.[77] The government did not, as yet, follow this advice—although back-channel talks had in fact already begun.[78]

For the time being, though, much of Churchill's attention was diverted to another trouble spot. At the end of January 1921, under the headline 'An Alarming Rumour', the *Daily News* commented: 'The appointment of Mr. Churchill to the Colonial Office would be an achievement so essentially mischievous that there is every probability it will actually happen.' The rumour was true; as the decision had been made a few weeks earlier, it is surprising it had not become public sooner. As War Secretary, Churchill had been the subject of press attacks on his handling of a major rebellion in Mesopotamia (modern-day Iraq). This helps explain why the *Daily News* was so exercised about the idea that Churchill was to be given responsibility for the Middle East (which he had indeed made a condition of taking the job). 'Any satisfaction that might be derived from the reflection that in leaving the War Office Mr. Churchill would get well away from Mesopotamia is therefore entirely premature. Mesopotamia will, if current expectations are realised, be more his playground than ever.'[79]

Within a matter of weeks, indeed, Churchill presided over a conference of British officials in Cairo, including the Arabist Gertrude Bell and the glamorous figure of T. E. Lawrence (Lawrence of Arabia). The conference did much to determine the future of the Middle East, including that of Mesopotamia/Iraq, although arguably the standard picture of lines drawn arbitrarily on a map has been exaggerated, along with Churchill's own personal culpability.[80] Yet in the British press it was relatively little reported at the time, as official secrecy with respect to the decisions taken was successfully preserved prior to their confirmation by the Cabinet.[81] Substantive press discussion did take place after the proposals were at last made public, but in the meantime journalists had to make do with reporting the minister's movements: 'In his leisure moments Mr. Churchill is painting the pyramids.'[82] *Punch* soon picked up on this with a cartoon that depicted Churchill daubing 'A "Futurist" Landscape' entitled 'Arabia Felix'.[83]

Churchill had taken up painting during World War I, as a way of dealing with his post-Gallipoli gloom. Over time, his artistic efforts became a significant element of his public image. His only journalistic output in 1921–2, in fact, was his essay 'Painting as a Pastime', published in two parts in *Strand Magazine*. It is interesting not least because of its confessional description of his feelings when he was dismissed from the Admiralty: 'Like a sea-beast fished up from the depths, or a diver too suddenly hoisted, my veins threatened to burst from the fall in pressure.'[84] It was somewhat unusual for a politician at this time to offer such a frank admission of vulnerability; but if what Martin Francis has called his 'exotic personality' went against conventional emotional codes, this was also part of what made him exciting and attractive to the press and the voters.[85] His purchase around this time of Chartwell, a 'picturesque ivy-mantled residence' near Westerham in Kent, provided a venue for eccentrically media-friendly hobbies such as bricklaying.[86]

But although Churchill's home life was, to a growing extent, on public display, there were limits to his willingness to bare his soul. The year 1921 was very tough for him, beginning in April when his brother-in-law, Bill Hozier, shot himself in a Paris hotel room. In shock, Clementine's mother's first reaction was to cover up the supposedly shameful act of suicide: 'No one must ever know—Winston will keep it out of the newspapers, won't he?'[87] This, of course, was unrealistic, even if Churchill had been willing to try. Then, in June, Lady Randolph died after a fall, at the age of 67. The *Sunday Pictorial* published a photograph of Churchill taking 'a farewell look at the coffin after the remains of his mother had been lowered into the grave'. It thus earned itself a rebuke from the *Morning Post* for 'prying into the affairs of other people and secretly gloating over their difficulties and distresses'.[88]

Plain English, which was a violently anti-Semitic and anti-Churchill publication, riposted that the picture could not possibly have been published without Churchill's acquiescence: 'he has already scored heavily in the sentimental game by drawing out the *Morning Post* in his "defence".' There is of course no reason to credit the allegation that he was trying to exploit his mother's death to gain public sympathy. There was, however, some truth in the observation that 'Press photographers and reporters in this country only require a hint to keep them from publishing anything to which the individual involved could take exception.'[89] This is supported by what occurred two months later, after the tragic death through illness of Churchill's fourth child, Marigold. The *Daily Graphic* sent a photographer to the funeral, but at Churchill's request agreed not to print the pictures.[90] At the least, it may be said that attitudes to politicians' privacy varied from paper to paper and from case to case; and that there was some scope for politicians to place bounds on press intrusion.

Characteristically, Churchill recovered from the blows he had suffered by continuing to throw himself into politics. He was a key member of the team that negotiated the Anglo-Irish Treaty giving most of Ireland de facto independence, the talks being carried out in the glare of publicity; Churchill denied Lloyd George's imputation that he had leaked information to Beaverbrook and the *Express*.[91] But although the Treaty represented a real achievement, it undermined Conservative support for the Coalition, which increasingly seemed to be living on borrowed time. Lloyd George's quasi-presidential style of government could appear dictatorial and high-handed, not least when important announcements appeared in the newspapers prior to Parliament being informed.[92] When the Tories and their press allies stymied his hopes of an early general election, the Prime Minister turned to the international stage as a last means of restoring his battered reputation. He hoped, at the Genoa conference of April–May 1922, to more firmly restore the peace of Europe, an objective he believed required the recognition of the Soviet regime. With Anglo-French tensions growing, Churchill—egged on by both Rothermere and Northcliffe—privately criticized Lloyd George for 'quarrelling with France for not pandering to the Bolshevists'.[93] Moreover, he connived with the Northcliffe press—not for the first time—in order to undermine him.[94] A memorandum by Douglas Crawford, the *Daily Mail*'s Foreign Editor, provides remarkable evidence of this.

Dated 9 May and apparently intended for Northcliffe's eyes, the memo reported that Churchill—who had recently had a polo accident and who had supposedly been told by his doctor to take a rest outside of London—was merely experiencing a 'diplomatic illness'. On account of this, he declined to see Thomas Marlowe, the *Mail*'s editor: 'Winston felt that he could not see Mr Marlowe because of his feeling that he must remain loyal to the Prime Minister while he [Lloyd George] is abroad; had he seen Mr Marlowe he would have been bound to have unburdened himself.' (This carried the obvious implication that Churchill did not feel any obligation of loyalty to the Prime Minister when he was at home!) Nevertheless, he apparently did not object to his close ally, the Conservative MP Oliver Locker-Lampson, feeding his views to the *Mail* in the person of Crawford. On the basis of this, Crawford explained:

> Winston's rest cure is a blind; he says there will be 'hell' in the Cabinet when Lloyd George returns, and he has gone to the country to study the situation from a distance.
>
> Winston believes that Lloyd George is now convinced that the only horse he can ride home is Labour, backed by a certain section of Liberals. Labour and this section of Liberals dislike France. If that be so, and Lloyd George drags France in the mud, Winston is coming out openly to fight

him. The only doubt Winston has at the moment is that France may invade the Ruhr. Winston is strongly opposed to such militaristic enterprise, and if France does go further into Germany the breach between Winston and Lloyd George may be postponed for a little.

Churchill's opinions were then reflected directly in a *Daily Mail* editorial, which warned: 'There are things far more unlikely than that the Prime Minister may soon return to England, and, risking the loss of Conservative goodwill, may seek to stampede the Liberal–Labour elements in the country on behalf of his Genoa scheme.' As Crawford noted (using a technical term for an article which included a subheading), 'The double head "Losing Support", which appeared this morning, is really Winston's view.'[95] In fact, the summit was a diplomatic failure, so there was no 'Genoa scheme' with which Lloyd George could stampede the country. Moreover, according to Austen Chamberlain (who had replaced Bonar Law as Tory leader), the Northcliffe press's criticisms backfired, creating 'public sympathy for LG amongst people who are strongly opposed to his policy'.[96] Churchill's attempt to exploit Genoa for his own advantage went no further. It could be said that the Crawford episode revealed Churchill at his worst, as a would-be Machiavelli, but a grubbily inefficient one.

As the government staggered on through the summer, Northcliffe, suffering from a severe blood infection, was afflicted with delusions. Rothermere informed Churchill that his brother was unlikely to survive, and Churchill in turn reported the news to his wife: 'I cannot help feeling sorry—altho God knows how cruel he was to me in those evil days of 1916.'[97] As the end neared, Churchill passed on to Clementine 'a most sombre account of Northcliffe's closing scenes' that had been given him by Beaverbrook: 'Violent resistances to treatment, 2 male nurses, gt constitutional strength fighting with a fell poison, few friends, no children, mania depression, frenzies.' Churchill added: 'Poor wretch—his worst enemies cd not but grieve for him.'[98] This reflected a sense of pity on his part (combined with a touch of magnanimity) rather than one of loss.

The two men had some time since ceased to be genuinely useful to one another, and so although Northcliffe's death in mid-August marked the end of an era in terms of press history, it was no great watershed in terms of Churchill's career. As the greatest figure in the powerful Harmsworth clan he had been a figure of seminal importance, but arguably he was more influential in cultural than immediately political terms. With the possible exception of his role in Asquith's downfall in 1916, Northcliffe and his papers had been much more influential on the general electoral climate than on specific moments of Westminster weather. Something similar might be said of press barons in general. Whether or not Churchill ever realized this is a moot point; one almost suspects that, latterly at least, he plotted with Northcliffe and his minions more because he enjoyed the thrill of conspiracy than out of realistic hope of concrete results. Certainly, the demise of 'The Chief' did not put an end to Churchill's taste for newspaper-backed intrigue.

Lloyd George, in spite of having survived Northcliffe's repeated attempts to displace him, knew that he could not continue to defy political gravity much longer. The Chanak Crisis, which took place in the autumn of 1922 and which threw him together with Churchill once again, was his last roll of the dice. Britain now faced a challenge from a resurgent Turkey. Mustafa Kemal's nationalists were carrying all before them, driving back the Greek troops who, with Allied agreement, had occupied Turkish territory in the aftermath of the war. As Kemal advanced he appeared to present a threat to British forces stationed on the Asian side of the Dardanelles, at Chanak. On 15 September the Cabinet resolved to make a stand. The neutral 'Zone of the Straits' (as defined in the 1920 Treaty of Sèvres) was to be defended. Churchill was given the job of writing a message to be sent to each of the Dominion governments telling them this and soliciting their help. After Lloyd George approved the text—which seemed to herald 'the prospect of renewed warfare on a grand scale'—the telegrams were despatched that evening.[99] The following day, Lloyd George and Churchill drafted a belligerently worded press statement, warning of the consequences were 'the victorious Turk' to reappear 'on the European shore'.[100] It looked like an effort to pressure the Dominions into war and it caused resentment. Canadian Prime Minister W. L. Mackenzie King deplored what he regarded as an attempted diktat and immediately cabled Churchill 'making mention of [the] fact that contents of his message had been made public in press despatches from Britain before his message had reached me'.[101]

Churchill's subsequent explanation for this embarrassing state of affairs was that New Zealand's swift and positive response to the request for troops had become known in that country throughout the Empire within a few hours of the original telegram being sent. The press communiqué therefore had to be issued, he argued, in order to explain to the world what was going on.[102] This hardly justified the crassly provocative nature of the text. But it was certainly true that official communications with the Dominions struggled to keep pace with the press. This was in part because Churchill could only find time to dictate the necessary messages late on in the day, and in part because of the time taken to encrypt and decipher them. When New Zealand Prime Minister William Massey appeared in Parliament in Wellington, 'He could say at once that he had very little that was new to put before members. Almost everything that had happened since the preceding Friday had appeared in the newspapers.'[103] The Australian Prime Minister, Billy Hughes, joined him in protesting, and later declared that the situation had been 'inexcusable'.[104] At the end of the month, the British Cabinet devised an ultimatum to the Kemalists, which was meant to be transmitted by the commander of the Allied forces in Turkey. 'Please observe that the most important message sent to General Harington yesterday by Cabinet was communicated to you twenty four hours ago and that as yet no inkling of it has appeared in the press', Churchill wrote to Massey and Hughes. But normally, he confessed, he could do little to prevent major decisions becoming public knowledge hours before the Dominions were formally told of them.[105] Ironically, in this case, swifter news technology actually served to foster resentment between different parts of the Empire rather than strengthening the ties.

As it turned out, Harington wisely declined to deliver the Cabinet's ultimatum, Kemal did not attack, and the crisis was defused. It had, however, confirmed the opinion of those who viewed Lloyd George and Churchill as publicity-hungry adventurers, and the government was now doomed. In October, Bonar Law used a letter to *The Times* to obliquely signal his willingness to come out of retirement; then, at a meeting at the Carlton Club, Tory MPs rebelled against the leadership of Austen Chamberlain, who remained loyal to Lloyd George and the idea of coalition.[106] Lloyd George resigned at once and Bonar Law formed a Conservative government and then called an election. In the midst of these events, Churchill was taken ill with appendicitis. He was thus obliged to fight much of his Dundee campaign from his hospital bed, issuing a series of argumentative statements to the press. The *Daily Express* attacked him as a 'war-whooper'; Churchill riposted with a denunciation of 'the tendentious misrepresentations of Lord Beaverbrook', who, he alleged, was the power behind Bonar Law's throne.[107] 'Lord Beaverbrook has a Transatlantic view of politics & with his influence over the Prime Minister he is at this moment probably the nearest approach to a Tammany Boss this country has ever witnessed.'[108] Churchill's resentment was increased by Beaverbrook's successful efforts to help defeat Freddie Guest, in his East Dorset constituency; after the election Churchill and Beaverbrook did not speak for some months.[109]

Churchill also wrote to the *Manchester Guardian* railing against the paper's coverage of the fact that an independent Liberal was standing against him in Dundee.[110] Having delegated most of his campaigning to Clementine, he arrived in the constituency shortly before polling day, still convalescing. In his final speeches he commented sarcastically on the fact that both Dundee newspapers were owned by D. C. Thomson and run out of the same office.[111] He was particularly enraged because the Chairman of the Conservative and Unionist

Association had not been allowed to put a paid advertisement in the Thomson papers advising voters to support Churchill.

> Here we get in the morning the Liberal Mr. Thomson through the columns of the Liberal 'Dundee Advertiser' advising the Liberals of Dundee to be very careful not to give a vote to Mr Churchill because his Liberalism is not quite orthodox. [...]
>
> At the same time, the same moment, you have the Conservative, the 'Die hard Mr. Thomson, through the columns of the Conservative 'Dundee Courier', advising the Conservative electors of Dundee to be very careful lest in giving a vote to Mr. Churchill they should run the risk of building up opposition to the new Conservative Government [...]

Thomson, he said, was a 'narrow, bitter, unreasonable being eaten with his own conceit'. With this he prompted laughter by turning to the reporters present and saying: 'Now put that down for the "Dundee Advertiser" and the "Dundee Courier".'[112] There was, in fact, no attempt to suppress his comments, but the *Courier* responded with a stinging editorial. 'Whatever may be his chances at the poll to-day, there can be no doubt that Mr Winston Churchill is in a vile temper', it noted, adding: 'So long as the newspapers favoured Mr Churchill not a word was said against them. They were all that was good and lovely. It is a different story when they have ventured to express dis-satisfaction with the Coalition Government of which Mr Churchill was a prominent member.'[113] The day after that, the paper published correspondence between Churchill and Thomson from earlier in the year, which had concluded with the latter warning the former to 'cut out all this threat nonsense'. The headline was 'CHURCHILL'S LIES EXPOSED BY HIS OWN LETTERS'.[114] Twenty-five years later, witnesses before the Royal Commission on the press were still debating the (probably exaggerated) claim that the spat had led the *Courier* to mount a decades-long vendetta against Churchill, even to the point of boycotting the mention of his name.[115]

Churchill's anger probably reflected his sense that he was losing the election. In the event he did so heavily, with an independent

Prohibitionist and a Labour candidate heading the poll. Although his defeat had complex long-term causes, Thomson's opposition cannot have helped.[116] In the aftermath, Churchill retreated from the limelight for a little while, although the publication in the spring of 1923 of the first volume of his memoir-cum-history *The World Crisis* assured him of acres of new coverage. First, it was serialized in *The Times* and in eight Canadian newspapers; then, when published in book form in April, there were reviews and rebuttals.[117] There were press rumours that he would rejoin the Conservatives, or that he would become the leader of a new Centre Party; the former, he denied.[118] The *Sunday Illustrated* detected a change in his image alleging that, after his sensational exit from Parliament, 'Mr. Winston Churchill seems to have lost all his former interest in bizarre headgear. His hats are just like anyone else's now.'[119] But before long he was back on the platform, brandishing his hat ('I talk about hats because I know something about them') and using hat prices as an illustration of the virtues of free trade.[120]

This was because in the autumn Stanley Baldwin, who had replaced the terminally ill Bonar Law as Prime Minister, called a snap general election. His aim was to secure a mandate to introduce tariffs, which he believed were necessary to solve the problem of unemployment. This was the one issue that could be guaranteed to re-energize the battered and demoralized Liberal Party, which now reunited as Asquith and Lloyd George temporarily put their differences to one side. Churchill himself was discussed in the press as a potential Liberal leader, and was selected to fight as the party's candidate in West Leicester.[121] His Labour opponent, F. W. Pethick-Lawrence, recalled that Churchill was disappointed by the attitude of the constituency's two newspapers. The *Leicester Mail* was committed to the Conservative cause, whereas the *Leicester Mercury* had previously been Liberal but was now non-party. 'To counter this, his supporters brought out daily a Liberal sheet, and paid for it to be distributed *gratis* to the electorate. But as this was printed by the *Nottingham Guardian*, it proved something of a boomerang, for Leicester people did not like the idea of receiving political instruction from the "rival" city.'[122] At the national level, Churchill did rather better. From a socialist perspective, Beatrice Webb complained: 'To read the capitalist press, whether Tory or Liberal, the Labour Party barely exists as a political party. [...] Lloyd George and Winston, and less usually Asquith, are given verbatim reports; they are treated as His Majesty's Opposition.'[123] But Churchill nonetheless lost to Pethick-Lawrence, who beat his celebrity opponent by over 4,000 votes.

When all the results were in it turned out that Baldwin's gamble had misfired badly. Although the Conservatives remained the largest party in the House of Commons they had lost their majority, paving the way for Labour's Ramsay MacDonald to form a government early in 1924. Some, including Baldwin, blamed the result on the hostility of Rothermere and Beaverbrook; the former had acquired the *Daily Mail* after Northcliffe's death (but had sold *The Times*) and the two men had made a business deal that gave them some interests in common.[124] Oddly enough, both were instinctive protectionists, and might have been expected to support Baldwin on this occasion. However, *The Spectator*, drawing attention to 'the noticeable commendations which have been showered by the gramophone papers on Mr. Lloyd George and Mr. Churchill', detected a Rothermere–Beaverbrook conspiracy to reconstitute the former coalition.[125]

Were there any grounds for such suspicions? Before the election, Beaverbrook had hosted a weekend party at his house which included, in addition to Churchill, Lloyd George and others, the leading former Coalitionists Lord Birkenhead and Austen Chamberlain.[126] Yet Beaverbrook reported to Rothermere that 'Conclusion of Conference was unanimous advice to Chamberlain and Birkenhead to join Baldwin's Government'—a move which would have helped restore Tory unity, not the Coalition.[127] Nevertheless, the antics on display were not attractive. Arnold Bennett, the novelist, was also on the scene. In a letter to his nephew he deplored the politicians present, perhaps a little unfairly, as 'a self-seeking crowd who were plotting and conspiring against the govt under the benign influences of Max. I never heard the welfare of the country mentioned.' Churchill became drunk and argumentative. Bennett thought the whole affair pitiable but nonetheless enjoyed himself.' "Arnold", said Max to me this morning, while I sat in his bathroom as he laved his limbs, "you've seen hell with the lid off." Well, I had.'[128]

During 1924, Churchill once more turned his hand systematically to journalism. Brendan Bracken, a young Irish adventurer who had lately caught his fancy, helped him gain a global audience for his articles, which were placed not only in American publications but in French, Indian, and Malayan ones too. The official biography asserts that the majority of the pieces were attacks on socialism, and these certainly significant; but as a matter of fact the bulk of the articles were lighter, mainly autobiographical contributions, a number of which helped lay the groundwork for *My Early Life* (1930).[129] Now that he had been without a minister's or MP's salary for over a year, and now that he had the costs of running Chartwell, this type of writing (which he referred to as 'quasi-sensational') helped pay the bills.[130] As he proudly acknowledged, 'During my whole life I have regarded the use of the pen as a means by which, whatever happened, whatever government came into power, whatever laws they passed, I would be able to succeed in earning something to support my family.'[131]

At this time, although he was moving away from Liberalism, he was not yet willing to commit himself unequivocally to the Tories, or at least was unwilling to subject himself fully to party discipline.[132] In March, with Rothermere and Beaverbrook offering him their complete backing, he stood in a by-election in the Abbey Division of Westminster as an independent anti-socialist in opposition to an official Conservative.[133] The inherent ambiguity of his position left plenty of room for newspaper speculation. Some believed that he was part of an anti-Baldwin plot, others that he was still thinking in terms of a Centre Party.[134] During the campaign, Churchill secured the backing of much of the Tory press, as well as the profound hostility of other parts of it, notably *The People* and the *Morning Post*. The battle was cast by some as one between the party machine and the 'Press Trust', a term which summoned up fears of oligopolistic power. The *Evening Standard* insistently denied that a Press Trust existed, even though, having just been acquired by Beaverbrook and Rothermere on a 51/49 per cent basis, it epitomized it itself.[135] Although Churchill was defeated by fewer than fifty votes—the news wire initially reported 'Mr. Churchill returned'—the fact that he had come so close could be presented as a moral victory over Conservative Party officialdom.[136] The Conservative *National Review* fulminated against the journalistically driven 'Churchill Boom'. 'As usual Mr. Churchill was too clever by half and over-reached himself. Though professing "Anti-Socialism"—whatever that may be—his real object as that of Lord Beaverbrook and Co., was to injure and humiliate the Conservative Party so that it should surrender to the Boomsters and sacrifice its leader.'[137]

Baldwin seems to have shared this interpretation for he soon afterwards gave an interview to *The People* in which he denounced Beaverbrook and Rothermere's 'Trust Press' and 'this Churchill plotting'.[138] When the article was published, it was 'the sensation and scandal of the week'.[139] Baldwin (very implausibly) told Churchill that 'the offensive remarks were never uttered by me'.[140] It was an interesting moment heralding a breakdown of the convention that political interviewees would be sent transcripts of their remarks for approval. But in spite of his doubts about Churchill, Baldwin knew that he remained a star turn, and that having him on board would help shore up his own 'Liberal Conservative' credentials.[141] The two men soon reached an accommodation. In an interview with the *Evening Standard* in August, Churchill affirmed that the Conservative Party's official policy was 'progressive' and 'not in any respect illiberal in the broad sense of the word'.[142] A speech he gave in Edinburgh in September was heavily trailed in advance, the *Sheffield Independent* noting that 'Even the Die-Hard Press is now hailing this as the chief event in the Tory programme for the autumn'.[143] That same month he was adopted as a 'Constitutionalist' candidate in Epping, and although he did not formally rejoin the Tory party until the following year, this was in effect the moment that he returned to the Conservative fold. The nonconformist *British Weekly* observed that 'The Liberal Press has shown commendable restraint in confining its comment upon Mr. Churchill's tergiversation to good-tempered banter.'[144]

Almost at once there was a general election, called after the Labour government was defeated on a vote of confidence. The most striking feature of the campaign was the so-called 'Zinoviev letter', a forgery cooked up by MI5 and the *Daily Mail* in an attempt to show the risk of communist subversion if Labour won. Churchill told the *Evening News* that it was 'proof of the dictatorship of the Russian Bolshevists over the British Communists'.[145] The *Daily Sketch* claimed to have exposed a 'Red Plot' to 'make things hot for Winnie' by disrupting his efforts in Epping.[146] All that happened in practice was that a deputation of unemployed who had marched from London to help the Labour candidate briefly looked in upon Churchill too: 'A member of the deputation afterwards told the *Daily Herald* that they had received nothing but evasive replies from Mr. Churchill. "He is still a tricky customer," remarked one of the men.'[147]

Returned with a majority of almost 10,000, Churchill was surprised and delighted when Baldwin, who had won a landslide, made him Chancellor of the Exchequer. That same night, he dined with Beaverbrook but declined, at first, to reveal which office he had been given. Birkenhead then arrived and promptly announced that he himself had been made Secretary of State for India—and then reproved Churchill when he found out that he would not reveal his own appointment in front of Beaverbrook, on whom he had previously relied for advice and support. At last Churchill burst out that he had been made Chancellor of the Exchequer. Beaverbrook declared that he would not make use of the scoop in the *Express* unless he heard of it from another source. But when another member of the Cabinet rang up and told him the news, he said he would publish—before finally yielding to Churchill's pleadings and keeping it under wraps. As the men parted for the evening, Beaverbrook had 'a kind of flash of intuition' and guessed that Clementine Churchill had made her husband promise that he would not disclose the secret. Churchill confessed to him: 'You are right. She drove me to the door of your house.'[148]

When the news did become public, there was 'no little surprise and some annoyance at Winston's preferment', as Leo Amery, the new Colonial Secretary, noted in his diary.[149] Strikingly, though, there was little if any genuine anger and quite a lot of praise. The *Financial Times* reported that the appointment was welcomed in the City because of the 'rigour' of Churchill's free trade principles.[150] To St Loe Strachey in *The Spectator* Churchill was a 'wise choice' to manage the national finances because 'He knows all the twists and turnings in the official labyrinth'.[151] The *Daily Telegraph* characterized the decision as 'very courageous', not because it doubted Churchill's capacity to do the job, but on account of many Conservatives' hostility towards him.[152] The *Morning Post* was sceptical, because working-class dislike of Churchill would make Baldwin's task of securing class cooperation more difficult.[153] But as the London correspondent of the *Belfast News-Letter* summarized: 'Mr. Churchill [...] has had on the whole a good Press, even some of the more virulent Radical organs commending his appointment, and predicting big things of him as Chancellor. True, the suggestion is made there, as in the Unionist Press, that he will have less scope for mischief at the Treasury than in any other Department of State. But "Winston," I take it, makes light of such reflections. The laugh is his side, and as he drove straight from the Privy Council meeting to the Treasury today he appeared to be enjoying it.'[154]

'I have gone through moments when I have really hated the press', Churchill had confessed, to laughter, at a Press Club dinner earlier in the year. 'I have taken up my trusty pen to denounce and anathematize the whole lot, but I thought better of it and waited until the wind changed.' As we have seen, he had not, in fact, always been nearly as restrained as this suggested; but now, as he turned fifty, the wind did seem to be changing once again in his favour. But the nature of the news was changing too, not least the changing relationship of the press to Parliament. In Churchill's words, instead of the press being a supplicant, 'instead of knocking upon the door of Parliament, Parliament has to go out and say "Why aren't you reporting our debates? Why don't you report all these fine things we're saying? What is the meaning of it?"'[155] This factor, combined with the rise of radio and the continuing development of cinema newsreels, meant that the news culture of British politics was becoming harder to navigate. This was a challenge with which Churchill wrestled as he moved into the second half of his career of celebrity.

5

Born to Trouble

'Most people think of Winston as still youthful', wrote the London correspondent of the Hull *Daily Mail* upon Churchill's appointment to the Treasury. 'It is a tribute to his vivid personality. Not only is Winston now 50 but, despite eyes that still hold their sparkle and zest, in face and figure he looks it. Between the slight portly, bent Chancellor of the Exchequer to-day, and Bindon Blood's slim galloper [...] Time has set his mark.'[1] Churchill's stoop, spectacles, and increasing baldness were, of course, the unavoidable product of age and worry, but they interacted with his choice of style to help create the image most people have of him today. It was during the Exchequer years that he and cigars became firmly linked in the public eye, perhaps because of their association with high finance. David Low later noted that, just as the early Churchill 'wore normal hats when the photographers were not around', so in later years 'it was noticeable to keen eyes that his public cigars were smoked never more than about one inch'.[2]

He was neither the first nor last politician to deploy an accessory; Joe Chamberlain had his monocle, Neville Chamberlain his umbrella, and Margaret Thatcher her handbag.[3] This is not to say that the cigar was pure artifice or that Churchill's private conduct was radically different from his public behaviour. Walter Citrine of the Trades Union Congress, who first met him during emergency talks to avert a coal strike, recalled that Churchill was unaffected by the crisis: 'He was fresh-faced and very much like the cartoons in the newspapers. He was smoking a long cigar all the time. I noticed that when he was in the room with Baldwin, during the negotiations, he put his tall silk hat on the table in front of him, with his gloves and walking stick alongside it. Possibly some of these actions were characteristics of his journalist days.'[4]

Churchill's initial major challenge was to devise his first Budget, which he presented in April 1925, at a time of high unemployment and continued post-war dislocation. Budget Day was not, as yet, the great media extravaganza that it would soon become, but he, Clementine, and two of their children did feature in photos on the front page of the *Daily Mirror*.[5] In the Commons, Churchill put on an enjoyable and press-friendly performance, taking a long drink of whisky and soda as he made a joke about the Excise, and making sculling motions as he described how he had battled against the stream of public expenditure. Newsworthy items in the Budget included a plan to introduce a contributory old age and widows' pension scheme, as well as the long-awaited confirmation that Britain would return to the Gold Standard.[6] Churchill held back his announcement of a 6d. cut in income tax until the final few minutes of his two-and-a-half-hour speech, at which point there was 'a concerted rush for the telegraph-office and the telephone-boxes', not least, one imagines, by financial journalists.[7]

Churchill was partially successful in his aim of appealing to Liberal opinion, insofar as the *Daily News* declared that it had been a 'Great Social Budget' that would 'receive the sympathetic consideration of every social reformer'.[8] *The Economist* backed him strongly over the gold standard, but (like the *Manchester Guardian*) regarded his reimposition of the wartime McKenna duties as an offence against the principles of free trade.[9] For its part, the *Daily Express* lambasted 'A BUDGET THAT BURDENS TRADE', and followed this the next day with 'TORY REVOLT AGAINST THE BUDGET'.[10] Beaverbrook boasted a few months later, in his book *Politicians and the Press*, that 'The *Daily Express* was the only paper which, on the very day of the Budget speech, perceived its full implications and opposed it accordingly. The rest of the critical Press only followed in its wake.' He complained that it was as if 'some malign spirit had entered into the mind of a Conservative Chancellor'; expenditure had gone up rather than down, the Pensions Bill placed new costs on manufacturers and workers, and the return to gold made British exports uncompetitive. These criticisms were likely sincere, and his attack on the gold standard was arguably far-sighted. Yet pique may have been involved too. In Beaverbrook's account, it was press support for Churchill at the Abbey by-election that had turned him once again into a force to be reckoned with and explained his emergence as Chancellor. But 'The popular Press had seen its nominee elected and he immediately turned round on all its doctrines.'[11] In other words, Churchill had had the temerity to demonstrate his independence.

For Churchill was now holding both Rothermere and Beaverbrook at arm's length. It was true that, prior to the Budget, he invited them both down to Chartwell. Rothermere went, Beaverbrook didn't. Churchill and Beaverbrook afterwards engaged in a long wrangle about whether or not the former had intended to consult the latter over his plans, something Churchill denied. The key point is that, in practice, the Chancellor did not leak anything significant to either of them. Rothermere, showing the hypersensitivity and egotism of his late brother, complained to Beaverbrook:

> I feel Winston has treated me with great incivility. To me more than any one else he owes his return to the political arena. Yet he brings in a budget taxing artificial silk without consulting me who outside the actual manufacturer knows more about this trade than possibly any-one living. When he took me down to his home at Westerham, he must have had this design in his mind and when I gave him a half promise to back his budget candour required him to get my views about such a tax.[12]

Churchill was, in fact, still careful to be civil to the press lords—but not much more than that. Indeed, he was uncharacteristically relaxed

about his treatment by the newspapers. To Clementine, he argued that
their headlines and the parts of Commons debates to which they gave
prominence were unrepresentative of public or parliamentary opinion (which was a shift from his pre-1914 view). He pointed out that
the *Daily Mail* story 'Revolt against the Pensions Bill' included the
buried admission that 'the muster of Conservatives to vote for the
Pensions Bill was the largest seen this Session and no Conservative
voted against the measure'.[13] He referred in the House of Commons
to the 'very great though superficial influence' of the popular press,
mocking the *Mail* for its continual harping on government waste and
the *Express* for its obsession with the gold standard.[14] According to
Beaverbrook, Churchill 'really had a lucky escape over his Budget
which might easily have ruined him. [...] But he is born to trouble for
like Jehovah in the hymn—"He plants his footsteps on the deep and
rides upon the storm".'[15]

Churchill, though, clearly felt secure, writing to Beaverbrook that
their relations during 1925 had been

> those of the Wolf and the Lamb. The Wolf has made repeated
> and extremely spiteful attacks upon the Lamb, and has avowedly
> compassed his destruction. The Lamb, on the other hand, conscious
> not only of his innocence but of the strength of the fold, and sus-
> tained by the sympathy of the Shepherd and the other Sheep, has
> preserved a moody silence not, however, unaccompanied by some
> complacency.[16]

Churchill, of course, was hardly lamb-like. But he was so often accused
of bad judgement, often with good reason, that it is worth pausing to
reflect on his wisdom at this time in keeping the Wolf (Beaverbrook)
at a distance. Doubtless he realized that the Shepherd (Baldwin) was
the true arbiter of his fate, and that consorting with danger would do
him no good in that quarter. In an unpublished article written at
some point in the later twenties, Beaverbrook wrote that 'Mr. Churchill
was going to be the man to embark on a policy of Tory democracy,
to protect the people against the interests, and to "shake up the old
gang" like his father. He obtained progressive, Independent and

popular support precisely on these grounds. *But he has not shaken off the old gang—he has simply joined it.*[17]

Meanwhile, Baldwin's suspicion of the press was confirmed by his edict that his ministers were not to engage in paid journalism.[18] His real target seems to have been Birkenhead's 'ceaseless outpourings' on controversial, present-day questions.[19] Churchill, in practice, managed to sidestep the rule (or, as the *Daily Telegraph* alleged, actually break it).[20] Further volumes of *The World Crisis* were serialized in *The Times*, and he published a number of other occasional writings, such as a tribute to Asquith after his death in 1928. But he was not now in general using his writings in the press to advance his political agenda. The exception, of course, was Churchill's brief but notorious editorship of the government-run newspaper, the *British Gazette.*

This affair had been brewing for a long time. As British coal exports faltered in the harsh economic climate, the mine-owners demanded that their workers accept lower wages and longer hours. The miners' leaders stood firm, using the slogan 'Not a penny off the pay, not a minute on the day'. A temporary state subsidy to the industry bought a nine-month breathing space (and also allowed the government to make emergency preparations) but when this ran out at the end of April 1926 talks between the government and the TUC proved fruitless. The unions began planning for a general strike in support of the miners. In an unpublished article written ten years later, Churchill claimed that the unions were determined to silence the press completely in the event of such a strike, lest it raise public opinion against them.

As Churchill noted, it was in Fleet Street that the final breach was triggered. Printers at the *Daily Mail* refused to put a leader on the crisis headlined 'For King and Country' into type. According to Churchill, 'This attempt to bludgeon the press into accepting the trade union censorship demonstrated finally the futility of further discussion.'[21] Union boss Ernest Bevin later claimed that Churchill 'saw red, walked into the Cabinet room with news of the *Daily Mail* business, and upset the Cabinet, with the result that the Government delivered an ultimatum whilst the trade union leaders were actually drafting peace terms'.[22] Churchill denied this allegation, which is not supported by other evidence. Whether or not the printers' action was merely a pretext for the decision to call off negotiations, the Cabinet was united in its determination to do so: it was a calculated choice, not a response to a Churchillian provocation. This was on the night of 2/3 May: then began the general strike.

Churchill quickly held a meeting at the Treasury with representatives of the Newspaper Proprietors' Association, including Lord Burnham, Lord Riddell, and Esmond Harmsworth (Rothermere's son and a Conservative MP). A significant figure on the government side was J. C. C. Davidson MP, a close friend and adviser to Baldwin who was in charge of government publicity during the strike. The meeting discussed the practicalities of producing a government paper and what its content should be. Churchill said that 'the essential thing is that we should produce a really powerful readable broadsheet not merely to contain news but to relieve the minds of the people'. It was important to prevent alarming news spreading, he went on. 'I do not contemplate violent partisanship, but fair strong encouragement to the great mass of our loyal people.'[23] The following day, according to the diary of civil servant and prime ministerial confidant Thomas Jones, Churchill came into 10 Downing Street 'and announced that he had commandeered the offices and machinery of the "Morning Post" with a view to bringing out some sort of government news sheet'.[24]

Although the Post's diehard editor, H. A. Gwynne, had been wholly antagonistic to Churchill during the war, he was not unhappy to put his newspaper in the service of the government. This was not simply a question of seeking to act in the national interest. Whereas other papers were keen to use such resources as were available to continue publishing their own editions during the strike—and to some extent they succeeded—the Morning Post was in severe financial trouble. As Stephen Koss has noted, in its adversity it 'had nothing to lose and possibly something to gain' from playing ball.[25] At Churchill's request, Beaverbrook lent some skilled operatives, and other papers helped out too. This was fortunate because the withdrawal of union labour meant that the *Post*'s editorial staff had to pitch in in the print-room to ensure that the paper could be produced.[26] The *British Gazette*, No. 1, appeared on 5 May. It contained an anonymous article by Churchill himself on 'The "British Gazette" and Its Objects'. This said that, with nearly all other papers 'silenced by violent concerted action', the country had been reduced 'to the level of African natives dependent only on the rumours which are carried from place to place'. Churchill went on to draw a lurid picture of what would happen without an official source of timely information: 'rumours would poison the air, raise panics and disorders, inflame fears and passions together, and carry us all to depths which no sane man of any Party or class would care even to contemplate.'[27]

Churchill later wrote that the days of the general strike formed 'one of the most vivid experiences of my somewhat variegated life, and were utterly different from every other episode'.[28] Notwithstanding the famous Plymouth football match between strikers and policemen—news of which Churchill actually attempted to suppress—the notion of the strike as a peaceable, friendly affair is something of a folk myth.[29] But although violence was perpetrated by both sides, Churchill was wrong to claim that it had been used to shut down the press. Sir William Acland, a partner in the newsagents W.H. Smith, lent his assistance to the *British Gazette*, and later recalled that although there were pickets they were quite friendly. However, 'just in case of trouble Winston sent me round half a dozen men with machine guns of some sort [who were] mounted on various roofs'. It was initially quite hard for people to get hold of a copy of the *Gazette*, with distribution depending upon a pool of private cars, including the Prince of Wales's Rolls Royce, driven by an equerry.[30]

The TUC produced its own newspaper, the *British Worker*, edited by Hamilton Fyfe of the *Daily Herald*, who appears to have had informants in the other camp. In the diary of events which he published soon after the strike, Fyfe suggested that Churchill admired his opponents for getting the rival paper out. 'He reads it with keen interest. He speaks well of its appearance. But he wants to get rid of it all the same.'[31] Although Churchill had said that his paper would eschew partisanship, this was far from the case. In his retrospective account, Churchill was unapologetic. 'Some captious people—more fit for a lunatic asylum than public life—complained that this Gazette was not impartial', he wrote. 'Of course it was not impartial. [...] Who, but a ninny, would pretend to be impartial between the fire and the fire brigade?'[32]

Moreover, Churchill's instinct seems to have been to monopolize information. The Cabinet agreed that 'Ministers should avoid personal interviews with the British or foreign Press, publicity of the kind being sufficiently provided for by the signed articles appearing in the "British Gazette"' and by ministerial broadcasts.[33] Churchill certainly gave the impression of great activity, but how far he was really in control of the paper is a moot point. Baldwin later claimed that putting him in charge of the *British Gazette* had been his cleverest move because 'otherwise he would have wanted to shoot someone'.[34] According to Davidson's later recollection, Baldwin promised to back him up against Churchill if the latter acted too wildly, and in fact consistently did so. 'Winston, I must say, bore no ill-will and accepted the situation, but it didn't stop him or FE [Smith, i.e. Lord Birkenhead] from telling everybody that they were running the *British Gazette*, when they weren't.' In the latter stages of the strike the *Gazette* refused to print an appeal from the Archbishop of Canterbury for negotiations to resume. For this, the *British Worker* dubbed Churchill 'Winston, the suppressor'. But the decision had actually been that of Davidson, who was very angry when Churchill relented in response to criticism in the House of Commons. Eventually, as a compromise, the appeal was printed without comment on the back page.[35]

Davidson's complaints about Churchill's difficult personality were not mere retrospective inventions. At the time he had written to Baldwin that 'The failure to some extent in the details of distribution of the British Gazette has been due entirely to the fact that the Chancellor occupied the attention of practically the whole of the staff who normally would have been thinking out the details.' Moreover: 'He thinks he is Napoleon, but curiously enough the men who have been printing all their life in the various processes happen to know more about their job than he does.'[36] Similarly, Gwynne reported to Lord Eustace Percy, the Education Minister, that Churchill had been his most frequent visitor: 'between ourselves, he has been a bit of a nuisance, for he is constantly coming in and dictating articles, some of which I have to cut out.'[37]

There was certainly a comic-opera dimension to it all. Churchill 'posted up in the Printing Office a list of the General Staff of the paper, with Winston as Commander-in-Chief, etc. etc.'[38] He was no mere figurehead, though, as his substantive contributions to the paper make evident, and, if nothing else, he had the power to wreak havoc. By commandeering a substantial portion of the paper stocks of *The Times* he actually posed a threat to the freedom of the press, as Geoffrey Dawson, its editor, complained.[39] In Cabinet, Churchill launched a tirade about 'the selfishness of *The Times* in wishing to increase its circulation at the expense of others during the crisis' which ended with him expressing 'his determination to suppress the *Daily Express*, if, as they intended, they started an evening paper in the next few days.'[40]

Newspapers were, however, only one part of the story. The British Broadcasting Company had been established in 1922 (it received a Royal Charter and became a Corporation five years later). It initially operated with a skeleton staff out of Marconi House in The Strand; its first news bulletin included a report of one of Churchill's rowdy Dundee election meetings.[41] However, the BBC did not have an independent news-gathering operation, and, in the face of a hostile press that was jealous of its potential power, it was careful to limit its news output. The strike presented an opportunity for the Company, but also risks. John Reith, of Presbyterian background and of immense height and ego, was on the one hand determined to help the government as best he could and on the other to preserve at least a nominal independence for the BBC. On 4 May he recorded in his diary his efforts to prevent it being treated 'as a kind of off-shoot' of the *British Gazette*. On the 5th he wrote that 'Things are really badly muddled and Churchill wants to commandeer the BBC.' On the 6th he attended a meeting with ministers and officials, at which the Home Secretary, Sir William Joynson-Hicks, declared that Baldwin had authorized him to say that he preferred to trust Reith and the BBC to take the right course of action. 'Winston emphatically objected, said it was monstrous not to use such an instrument to the best possible advantage.' The matter was left in abeyance. Three days later Reith had an awkward personal encounter with Churchill whom he thought 'really very stupid [...] I told him that if we put out nothing but government propaganda we should not be doing half the good that we were'. In the end there was no government takeover. As Reith noted, with remarkable frankness, 'They want to be able to say that they did not commandeer us, but they know that they can trust us not to really be impartial.'[42] Churchill, though, seems to have failed to appreciate that Reith, in spite of the somewhat greater subtlety of approach, shared his fundamental objectives. Churchill's suspicion of the BBC would persist throughout his career.

At last, on 12 May, the TUC called off the strike. In effect, it was an unconditional surrender, although the dispute in the coalfields dragged on miserably for many months more. Churchill was not quite ready to give up his toy. Geoffrey Dawson told Thomas Jones of a meeting at the Treasury at which Churchill 'harangued' newspaper owners about how long the *British Gazette* was to be continued. It was, however, 'sentenced to immediate death'.[43] Reflecting on the progress of the strike during its aftermath, Kingsley Martin (future editor of the *New Statesman*) argued: 'As the days went on the cry of "revolution" fell flat even in the columns of the *British Gazette* and was increasingly dropped. [...] No doubt if Mr. Churchill and the *Daily Mail* had had their way violence would have begun and disorder would have increased, and the revolutionary feeling they advertised might have come into being.'[44]

Whether or not Churchill can be convicted of deliberately fomenting disorder, he can certainly be found guilty of indulging his taste for melodrama at the expense of common sense.[45] As Hamilton Fyfe had noted on the first day of the strike, he was like a film producer who intended to act the hero himself: 'Thus he will first play the part of newspaper editor!'[46] Churchill was not, however, entirely lacking in self-awareness. In July 1926, during a heated debate in the Commons, he showed his capacity for self-mockery and skilful political humour. The Liberal (and later Labour) MP William Wedgwood Benn wrote in his diary:

> I made an attack on Churchill, not for producing the 'British Gazette' which was necessary in the unjustifiable Press strike, but for producing a vulgar propaganda sheet. Churchill replied in his very best style. He never tackled any of the arguments, but went off into brilliant banter which captured the House in a way rarely seen.[47]

The best moment came at the end, when Churchill responded to a Labour MP's warning that there might be another general strike in the future. Putting on a threatening attitude and wagging his finger, he said: 'Make your minds perfectly clear that if ever you let loose upon us again a general strike, we will loose upon you—another "British Gazette".'[48] Everyone dissolved into laughter at the brilliant anticlimax.

After the strike, Churchill quickly returned to the more stable demeanour that had previously characterized his Chancellorship. When Beaverbrook offered him the chance to appear in an early talking picture he declined, with uncharacteristic modesty, saying that he might not be able to do it well and that it might make him enemies.[49] He continued to give some hostages to fortune, though. In 1927 he visited Rome and met with Mussolini. It had been billed as a private visit, but according to the British Ambassador, 'The press were a perfect nuisance and simply besieged the Embassy, while photographers dogged Churchill's every step.' Churchill therefore agreed to receive the journalists (both foreign and Italian) on his last morning.[50]

At the press conference Churchill helpfully 'informed his audience that he had prepared what he, as an ex-journalist, considered the questions most likely to help them in their work, and that a typed copy of this would be given to whomsoever desired one'. Yet if this was designed to prevent him getting into hot water, it didn't quite work out. Churchill said that he had been 'charmed' by the Duce's 'gentle and simple bearing' and added that 'If I had been Italian, I am sure I should have been wholeheartedly with you from the start to finish in your triumphant struggle against the bestial appetites and passions of Leninism.'[51] True, he qualified this by saying that the British had a different way of doing things, so arguably his remarks did not truly merit the *Nottingham Evening Post* headline 'WINSTON A FASCIST'.[52]

Nevertheless, the reception of his declaration in the Italian press confirms that he was saying very much what the Fascist authorities wanted to hear. His statement was reproduced in full in all the newspapers and was commented on with enthusiasm; it was portrayed as a landmark recognition of the regime's legitimacy. An article in *Tribuna* took Churchill's words as evidence that Fascism need not worry about 'journalistic defamations' organized by 'international social democracy'. The *Corriere della Sera* drew attention to the 'great moral and political significance' of 'Mr. Churchill's admission of the international role of Fascism as an essential factor of the anti-Communist struggle'. The *Mezzogiorno* deduced that if the communist threat in England ever 'assumed the alarming proportions in which it presented itself in Italy, no doubt H.M. Government would adopt the Fascist method'. Only one paper, the *Resto del Carlino*, took any notice of the qualifications he had offered. It observed that 'Mr. Churchill had, in his review of Fascism, limited himself to its prevalent anti-subversive and anti-Communist aspect. This formed the only ground on which he could move with liberty, taking into account the opinion of his own party and of the vast majority of the country. The fascist experiment was, however, broader and richer.'[53] There is no indication that Churchill's comments caused his Conservative colleagues significant discomfort, but in left-wing or progressive circles they were to dog him for years.

In the final years of his Chancellorship, Churchill remained on good terms with Beaverbrook (although that did not mean that the Beaverbrook press was uncritical of him). Relations were more problematic with Rothermere. The latter was strongly opposed to the 1928 Representation of the People (Equal Franchise) Bill, which would finally give the vote to women on the same terms as men.[54] Churchill was also a sceptic, and was one of nearly 150 Conservative MPs who abstained on the Second Reading. But he had not actually expected a division to take place, and he distanced himself from the 'idiotic' fulminations of the *Daily Mail*, which did its best to talk up the significance of the abstentions.[55] Furthermore, Churchill came under direct fire for his plan to relieve industry and agriculture from the form of local taxation known as the rates. Rothermere preferred to see a cut in income tax, and the *Mail* labelled the scheme the 'Higher Rates Bill'. Churchill, though assuring Rothermere that he had never forgotten his support during the war, fought back against the 'astonishing untruths' in a series of telegrams, which did appear to have the effect of blunting the attack.[56] In the run-up to the general election of 1929, he did publish one piece in the *Mail* himself (on 'Socialist Quackery'), but negotiations to print another in the final stages of the campaign descended into acrimony and came to nothing.[57]

The *Mail*'s treatment of the derating scheme may well have contributed to Churchill's sense that he was not getting a fair deal from the press. This in turn stimulated his interest in broadcasting. The first occasion that a speech of his was broadcast was in June 1924.[58] In a speech at a civil service dinner in 1928 (which was itself broadcast) he hit out at the BBC's convention that political controversy should be kept from the airwaves. The press, he complained, would no longer report politicians' speeches. 'They only go about dogging your steps from place to place to see if you say something that, clipped from its context, can be made into a headline.' Yet, he argued, these same papers adopted a dog-in-the-manger attitude to political broadcasting. One hour of the radio schedule should be given up to politics each night, he said, with the time being divided up according to the strength of the parties in the Commons.[59]

In April 1928 he invited John Reith to visit him at the Treasury. Both men were keen to broadcast the Budget direct from the House of Commons, but the proposal was not approved. Instead, Churchill gave a broadcast afterwards. Reith recorded in his diary: 'Collected Winston Churchill at the House of Commons at 9.15 and took him to Savoy Hill, where he delivered a good defence of his Budget, supposed to be non-controversial but was not.'[60] The following year Churchill alleged that under a Labour government the press would be gagged. 'Broadcasting apparatus, for all we know, would be entirely monopolized by a recreant Government, or under some pretence of impartiality between those who tried to wreck the country and save it, would disseminate counsels of disaster and alarm.'[61] During the general strike, of course, he had been keen to monopolize broadcasting for the government; he was now keen to deny his opponents what he had attempted to arrogate for himself.

The result of the 1929 election was Conservative defeat and a new minority Labour government under MacDonald. The Liberals, in spite of Lloyd George's bold programme to conquer unemployment, failed to make a real breakthrough. In an article in *John Bull* magazine, Churchill blamed the outcome in part on the 'prolonged campaign of disparagement' that had been aimed against the Baldwin administration by the popular press.[62] That, undoubtedly, had been a contributory factor, but the uninspired and complacent nature of the Tory campaign was surely more significant. In the months that followed, Churchill seemed politically at a loss, increasingly out of sympathy with Baldwin and his supporters, yet without a popular cause to latch on to. He found relief in a long visit to North America, together with members of his family. When they stayed at the Chateau Frontenac in Quebec, the party could see Rothermere paper mills from their windows. Churchill commented: 'fancy cutting down those beautiful trees we saw this afternoon to make pulp for those bloody newspapers, and calling it civilization.'[63] But he continued to provide the fodder for those bloody newspapers, all the same. 'There is no mistaking him', wrote C. B. Pyper, an Ulster-born journalist, in the *Winnipeg Tribune*.

> See him on the platform of his private car, dressed in a light-grey suit, with a long cigar in his mouth, plump, round-shouldered, round-cheeked, his head thrust slightly forward, and you recognize him at once. See him on the station platform, hatted, his hands thrust into his overcoat pockets, his cigar still in his mouth, talking to policemen, talking to strangers, buying a few cigars in a drygoods store, looking inquisitively in at the lunch counter, and you recognize him again. There is the hat. It is the hat of caricature. It is an ordinary hat, but his is no ordinary head. His head would give an appearance of uniquity—pardon the word—to any hat.[64]

A man who often wore a special silk dressing gown and snakeskin slippers to receive the press, in the apparent interests of subverting expectations about British statesmen, cannot have been unaware of the impression he was creating.[65]

When visiting California, Churchill stayed for a week with the press and film magnate William Randolph Hearst. Charlie Chaplin recalled him standing 'Napoleon-like with his hand in his waistcoat', looking 'lost and out of place'.[66] Churchill found Hearst less anti-British than he had expected—the supposedly isolationist Hearst even proposed 'an Anglo-American union of cooperation'—and was impressed by the fact that Hearst's papers sold 15 million copies a day, earning him the equivalent of £1 million a year.[67] 'I got to like him—a grave simple child—with no doubt a nasty temper—playing with the most costly toys.'[68] Churchill's own finances now took a huge hit from the Wall Street crash, as he had speculated recklessly. He calculated the full extent of his losses on the voyage home, using information from the ship's ticker tape. He had already been planning to step up his journalistic activities, having secured writing deals worth almost £10,000 during the trip.[69] His financial disaster merely increased the urgency. Sometimes during the thirties he resorted to hack work, and knew it. He admitted that two articles he wrote for the American magazine *Collier's* were 'awful stuff, I fear, but it is what they like and what they pay for'.[70] Increasingly, he turned to others for assistance. Thus, for six *News of the World* articles summarizing the plots of well-known novels, he received £2,000 with a further £1,800 for syndication in the *Chicago Tribune*—pieces that had actually been written by his friend Eddie Marsh for £25 each.[71]

The years 1930–1 saw worsening unemployment, the nadir of Baldwin's fortunes, the apex of Beaverbrook and Rothermere's influence, and a continued lack of direction for Churchill. Beaverbrook's new strategy, his 'Empire Crusade', involved rebranding protectionist Tariff Reform as 'Empire Free Trade'. At a dinner at Stornoway House, his London residence, he tried to convert Churchill to the cause. 'Winston drunk but unconvinced', noted *Evening Standard* columnist Robert Bruce Lockhart. 'He gave Beaverbrook some encouragement, however.'[72] Harold Nicolson—like Lockhart, a former diplomat who had been recruited to the Beaverbrook press—was also present. 'Winston complains pitiably: "But Max, Max, you are destroying my party"'.[73] Beaverbrook, in alliance with Rothermere, now launched the United Empire Party, with a view to running candidates against Conservatives at by-elections. In March, Beaverbrook warned Rothermere that 'Winston is denouncing us violently, saying he is being bullied and dragooned'.[74] But Churchill's opposition, such as it was, was ineffective. 'No one that I know of has ever risen to the first rank in politics in so short a space', Churchill wrote to Beaverbrook, a little ruefully, that September. 'Naturally I regret that the growth of your influence should have been almost exactly proportionate to the diminution of mine.'[75] He privately denounced the *Express* and the *Mail*'s 'vilest personal attacks' on Baldwin, claiming that these two papers 'unquestionably exercised an extraordinary degree of influence on Conservative voters'.[76]

Churchill still seems to have felt the lure of Beaverbrook's personality. Even though still a member of the Shadow Cabinet, on one occasion he actually helped his friend draft a public response to Baldwin.

This was hypocritical and, to say the least, risky, as it put the journalists who witnessed it in a position to 'spring a bombshell which would ruin Winston's and Max's career'.[77] One can imagine that, had she known, Clementine would have disapproved. She observed in November that 'Mr. Baldwin is again firmly seated in the saddle and this has been brought about entirely by the exaggeration and unfairness of the attacks upon him by Lord Beaverbrook'.[78] In fact, Baldwin was not yet out of the woods. Early in 1931 he came to the brink of resignation, but then decided to fight back. In a deservedly famous speech, he denounced the press lords for seeking 'power without responsibility—the prerogative of the harlot throughout the ages'.[79] When Duff Cooper, standing as an official Conservative, defeated a candidate backed by Rothermere and Beaverbrook at a by-election in the St George's constituency, Baldwin was safe.

By this time, Churchill had resigned from the front bench. Having passed up the opportunity to resign in defence of free trade, he chose another issue: India. He had long been out of sympathy with Baldwin's bipartisan support of the MacDonald government and the Viceroy (Lord Irwin, later Lord Halifax), in their policy of reform. When Irwin released Gandhi from jail with a view to starting talks on the question of greater Indian self-government, Churchill took his chance. With Baldwin on the ropes, he may well have believed that he could seize the leadership of the Conservative Party. Rothermere, who pledged Churchill the full support of his papers, assured him that his feet were on 'the ladder that quite soon leads to the premiership'.[80]

But as Baldwin rebounded, the Tory grassroots enthusiasm displayed at Churchill's mass meetings proved of limited value. Although some commentators highlighted the 'air of expectancy' that surrounded Churchill, *The Economist* was accurate in predicting that he would plough a lonely furrow.[81] His views were highly popular with a rather narrow and reactionary section of opinion at home, but many of the white rulers in India, though themselves hostile to the forces of nationalism, regarded him as a dilettante. When he labelled Gandhi as a 'half-naked fakir', an article in the British-owned *Times of India* branded his speech as foolish, 'a triumph of oratory, rather than of logic'. Tongue-in-cheek, the author added, 'now we realise exactly why it is that Mr. Churchill feels so terribly annoyed: he has not the courage to add a Gandhi cap to his large collection of headgear'.[82]

A March 1931 newsreel of Churchill speaking about India was apparently the first in which he was recorded addressing the camera directly. He was filmed by the Movietone company sitting behind his library desk, haranguing the cinema-goers loudly on their duties as citizens of the British Empire.[83] As the transition to sound newsreels was not complete in Britain until 1932, we can see that Churchill was operating at the cutting-edge.[84] Of course, like many such films of the era it does now come across as rather stilted, for he, like a number of fellow politicians, had not adjusted from a style of speaking designed for public meetings. (Baldwin successfully cultivated a more intimate 'fireside' manner.[85]) Churchill's habit of making 'speeches into the microphone' did seem to work on radio, but he was perhaps never wholly comfortable talking straight to camera, although he was certainly not averse to being filmed in general.[86] In an article published later in the decade he affirmed the superiority of the press to film and radio as a method for delivering news. This was partly on the common-sense ground that one could read a newspaper at any time and that one was thus much less likely to miss an item, but he added that 'Under dictatorships the press is bound to languish, and the loud-speaker and the film to become ever more important.'[87]

Churchill's decision to leave the Shadow Cabinet meant that, when the Labour government collapsed in August 1931, he was excluded from the cross-party 'National Government' that replaced it. MacDonald, who was expelled from the Labour Party for his actions, remained as Prime Minister, but Baldwin, as Lord President of the Council, was the power behind the throne. An unpublished article by Churchill on the crisis is notable for its ambivalence towards the actions of these men, and for its lack of inside testimony on the events; for he was now an outsider, albeit an extremely well-connected one.[88] During the general election that followed in the autumn, he was kept off the airwaves; he had previously been prevented from broadcasting on India too. The BBC had an arrangement whereby the political parties would determine among themselves which individuals should be given the slots for election or other political broadcasts, and he did not take well to the news that he was considered *persona non grata* for these purposes.[89]

When the votes were finally counted it became clear that Labour had been smashed. Something similar happened to Churchill at the end of the year when, on a visit to New York, he stepped out in front of a car and was seriously hurt. But, unlike Churchill, the Labour Party could not write up its experiences and publish them for a large fee in a globally syndicated article.[90] The accident and its aftermath were symbolic of Churchill's tendency to inflict mishaps and injuries upon himself, of his powers of recovery, and his talent for turning adversity to advantage. He very rarely suffered from writer's block, which he referred to as 'stage-fright', but juggling his commitments to different publications was a severe challenge.[91] For example, when he inadvertently published different pieces simultaneously in the *Daily Telegraph* and the *Daily Mail* it was quickly made plain to him by the former that 'to have another paper giving an article from your pen on the same day detracts enormously from the value of our publication'.[92] Reprints were a further source of income, but these had to be weighed carefully because to reproduce a politically sensitive piece at the wrong time might backfire.[93] Work on his biography of the Duke of Marlborough—which was in due course serialized in the *Sunday Times*—added to the pressure. All this work required a growing team of secretaries and assistants. In terms of producing articles, a key figure was the journalist Adam Marshall Diston, whom Churchill used as a ghost-writer from 1934 if not earlier. On the basis of a few notes or suggestions from the ostensible author, Diston would turn out articles (including ones on international issues) that Churchill would often publish under his own name with only minor changes.[94]

Because the subject-matter of Churchill's articles was driven to a great degree by the demands of the market, it is not possible to use them as a true gauge of his political priorities. From the start of 1932 until mid-1935, much of his energy was expended opposing what became the Government of India Act, which conceded greater self-government (while stopping well short of conceding full independence). Yet he published only six pieces on the topic during that time, a fraction of his overall output. Moreover, his campaign suffered from a relative lack of press support—the main exception being the *Daily Mail* and other Rothermere papers such as the *Sunday Dispatch*. Ian St John, who has explored this issue in depth, draws attention to a number of factors that helped determine this. The *Morning Post*, still under Gwynne, did back Churchill, but it was now genuinely on its last legs, prior to its absorption by the *Daily Telegraph* in 1937. The *Telegraph* itself, which had a rising circulation, was owned by Lord Camrose (formerly William Berry) and his brother Sir Gomer Berry (later Lord Kemsley). Although Camrose had overcome his previous suspicions of Churchill to a degree, he did not share his views on India, and owed his peerage to Baldwin. Garvin of *The Observer*, in spite of his friendship with Churchill, acknowledged that he and the other opponents of the government's White Paper were 'honest and zealous', but accused them of ignoring 'the inexorable laws of practical politics'. Although the supposedly progressive *Manchester Guardian* did not actually have a very distinguished record of highlighting British abuses in India, it is unsurprising that it and other Liberal newspapers were unsupportive of Churchill. The *Times* journalist Colin Coote, moreover, judged that his paper's dislike of Churchill 'amounting to a vendetta' dated back to the India campaign. In terms of their impact on Indian opinion, Churchill's arguments were almost certainly counter-productive. When he suggested that the White Paper proposals were a 'gimcrack edifice' rather than a proper constitution, the Indian National Congress-supporting press leapt upon the notion that the reforms were a sham.[95]

Importantly, too, Churchill had failed to win over Beaverbrook, who at this point regarded him as 'a busted flush'.[96] 'He has held every view on every question', Beaverbrook wrote to Garvin in 1932.

'He has apparently been quite sincere in all his views. Perhaps he has convinced himself. But he is utterly unreliable in his mental attitude.'[97] Beaverbrook was not much interested in India, and if he had a view it was in line with Baldwin's. Moreover, he was a personal friend of Samuel Hoare, the Secretary of State for India, and refused to damage him by supporting Churchill's attacks.[98] There is also some indication that Beaverbrook suffered from envy or resentment of the man he claimed as his friend. Bruce Lockhart once noted how he ran into problems when writing his *Evening Standard* column:

> This morning I wanted to do a paragraph comparing Winston (who has had about six articles in the papers during the week-end) to Dumas who once had six serials running in the Paris papers at the same time. [Percy] Cudlipp, our editor, said: 'The idea is first-class, but I think you had better keep off it. The Chief (Max) will say that you are giving publicity to Winston. He hates paragraphs about Winston. He pulled me up the other day.'[99]

Of course, there were broader factors, beyond mere personal jealousies, working against Churchill. As far broadcasting was concerned, he saw himself as the victim of an establishment stitch-up. There was certainly a contrast between the BBC's restrictions and the freedom afforded to him on US radio. In 1932, he broadcast to the USA on international monetary policy, but the Corporation refused to transmit the programme to British listeners; some succeeded in capturing it anyway via an American relay station.[100] In 1933, he publicly poured scorn on the Corporation, and accused it of abuse of power.[101] Later that year, one hapless BBC man tried to flatter him into broadcasting on a non-political topic by telling him that the younger generation regarded him as a great war correspondent, 'and they want you to help them become war correspondents too'. 'Oh', shot back Churchill, 'They want me to start a war in order to provide them with jobs.'[102] In 1934, he was allowed to speak on the question of 'Whither Britain?' and—perhaps strategically— was sufficiently anodyne that it became hard to argue that he could not be let loose on any other topic.[103] Later that year he spoke on 'The Causes of War' and consented to have his text vetted by the Foreign Office.[104] In January 1935 he was finally permitted to broadcast on India.[105] By that point, his battle against the government's plans had in effect already been lost.

David Reynolds has rightly noted that Churchill's post-war memoirs greatly played down the Indian question, making it appear that during his wilderness years he had been almost wholly focused on the threat posed by the European dictators.[106] In order to understand the public reception of both these issues, it is important to grasp how the early stages of his struggle for rearmament unfolded concurrently with the latter phases of his India campaign. (Nor were these his only interests: one commentator even suggested that his ideas about parliamentary reform were the reason 'that Mr. Churchill's speeches get so little support or approval from the millionaire Press.'[107]) Churchill first expressed concern about the Nazis as early as October 1930. Prince Otto von Bismarck, of the German Embassy, recorded an after-dinner conversation: 'Churchill, who had apparently been following recent newspaper reports in detail and was extremely well informed [...] expressed himself in cutting terms on National Socialism.'[108] But in the year Hitler took power, a very large portion of Churchill's political efforts (and the resulting media coverage) still focused elsewhere.[109] A magazine profile that asked 'Is Mr. Churchill staking everything on one last gamble?' was referring to India.[110]

By that point, though, Churchill had already begun to make his European foreign policy anxieties public. In March 1933 he made two Commons speeches criticizing what he regarded as unrealistic proposals for international disarmament.[111] In April, he joined Austen Chamberlain in denouncing developments in Germany, and specifically mentioned the persecution of the Jews.[112] There was a sharp reaction in Berlin. The *Times* correspondent there reported that 'The Nazi Press as yet limits itself to a brief summary of the debate, with the headline "Aggressive Speeches by Churchill and Chamberlain"'.[113] In Britain the coverage tended to present Churchill as playing second fiddle to Chamberlain, who as an ex-Foreign Secretary could be seen as especially authoritative.[114] The *Daily Express* ran the headline 'Sir

Austen Chamberlain Wild With Indignation' but did not mention Churchill.[115] The *Daily Mirror* did not cover the story at all; its main headline on the day concerned dealt with a group of Britons on trial for sabotage in Moscow.[116] So Churchill, at this stage, was not presented as having taken any radical new turn in his career. Indeed, it was not until the following February that he launched a more systematic campaign warning of Britain's vulnerability to attack.[117] Nevertheless, by that point, his efforts were being presented as somewhat predictable. 'Mr. Churchill's characteristic intervention need not be taken too tragically;' stated *The Economist* from on high, 'for he is now accepted, even abroad, as our brilliant but erratic *enfant terrible*.'[118]

Churchill had a potential supporter in Rothermere, who was also concerned about Britain's weakness in this field. Rothermere was, however, a problematic ally. First, he had used the *Daily Mail* to back Oswald Mosley's British Union of Fascists. His article 'Hurrah for the Blackshirts!' remains notorious even today, as do his several visits to Hitler, with whom he conducted a mutually admiring correspondence.[119] Churchill told Clementine that he was revolted by the *Mail*'s fawning treatment of the Führer, and suggested that Rothermere 'wants us to be v[er]y strongly armed and frightfully obsequious at the same time'.[120] Yet Churchill could scarcely throw Rothermere over. He relied on him to supply free advertising for the India Defence League, and continued to publish in the *Mail* himself.[121] Of the articles he published there in 1934, most were of the anodyne variety, and only one—'How I Would Procure Peace'—dealt with foreign policy.[122] (Reginald Pound, the paper's features editor, liked it but expressed concern that it would 'knock all the others in the series a serious blow, making them look rather cheap.'[123]) Thus for the most part, Churchill did not challenge the paper's editorial line within its own pages.

Furthermore, Rothermere was difficult even where, in broad terms, the two men were in agreement. Churchill was being secretly assisted by Major Desmond Morton, head of the Committee of Imperial Defence's Industrial Intelligence Committee, who provided him with confidential information about German air strength. In July 1934, using figures from this source, Churchill asserted in the Commons that at current rates of expansion Germany would overtake Britain in terms of air power at some point in 1936.[124] Rothermere wrote to him complaining that the speech massively underestimated German plans, claimed that the Nazis would soon have 20,000 planes and asked 'Is everybody in this country blind?'[125] Churchill (whose own estimates of German strength were possibly excessive) did his best to introduce a note of reality into the discussion.[126] He also showed Rothermere's letters to Morton, who pointed out that 'it would be the gravest pity to spoil a good case by anything which might later be revealed to be gross or even ludicrous exaggeration'.[127]

Churchill continued to press the government, and succeeded in extracting admissions that German rearmament was progressing faster than previously acknowledged. By April 1935, he was reproaching Rothermere for his inconsistencies. Now that the German danger was recognized, and when the public was sure to realize that it had been let down, he heaped fulsome praise on the ministers responsible, Churchill complained. 'At the same time you continue to quote figures which are so fantastic that they simply deprive you of the enormous credit which otherwise would have been due to your foresight and vigilance.'[128] Still, the two men stayed in touch and for the while Churchill continued to write for the *Mail*. Rothermere even did him the favour of betting Randolph—now a hot-headed and very boozy journalist—hundreds of pounds to stay teetotal. Randolph won the money but soon went back to his alcoholic ways.[129]

Churchill at this time professed himself astonished at press and public indifference to the country's defence weakness.[130] In fact, he was far from friendless in Fleet Street. The loyal Brendan Bracken, an MP since 1929, was heavily involved in the business of financial journalism. He, like Rothermere, Beaverbrook and Camrose, was a member of the Other Club, the exclusive dining circle of which Churchill was a founder member and which comprised a zone of masculine political gossip.[131] This did not necessarily translate into the kind of coverage he wanted, but not all the print world was apathetic towards his message. *Strand* magazine asked him to write a piece called 'The Truth About Hitler'. Its editor, Reeves Shaw, wanted Churchill 'to be as outspoken as you possibly can in your appraisement of Hitler's personality and ambitions, and absolutely frank in your judgement of his methods'.[132] Churchill haggled about the price, but agreed.[133] Published in the November 1935 issue, it must certainly have lived up to Shaw's hopes.

Yet the article was in certain respects ambiguous, perhaps deliberately so. As *The Spectator* noted, 'it does not tell the truth; it merely asks what the truth is.'[134] Churchill himself—perhaps with tongue in cheek—afterward described it as 'a highly complimentary appeal'.[135] It presented the issue of whether or not Hitler would someday achieve true greatness as an open question: 'We cannot tell whether Hitler will be the man who will once again let loose upon the world another war in which civilization will irretrievably succumb, or whether he will go down in history as the man who restored honour and peace of mind to the great Germanic nation and brought them back serene, helpful and strong, to the European family circle.' Yet Churchill's own conclusion, although he stopped short of making it absolutely explicit, ought to have been clear to most readers. The concluding section of the article consisted of a powerful denunciation of the previous year's 'Night of the Long Knives', in which Hitler had ordered the cold-blooded killing of former associates. Churchill described it as squalid, gruesome butchery, although his final sentence did contain a hint of equivocation.

> Can we really believe that a hierarchy and society built upon such deeds can be entrusted with the possession of the most prodigious military machinery yet planned among men? Can we believe that by such powers the world may regain 'the joy, the peace and glory of mankind'? The answer, if answer there be, other than the most appalling negative, is contained in that mystery called HITLER.[136]

When the article came out, it provoked fury in Berlin. There were headlines such as 'Churchill Goes Wild', 'Unheard of Attack on the

Leader', and 'Scandalous and Provocative Attack'. The German ambassador made an official protest.[137] The magazine was banned in the Fatherland.[138] Within a few days, H. W. Thost, the London correspondent of two Nazi papers, was expelled from Britain. It was suggested at the time that this was because of his vitriolic denunciation of the article in the *Völkischer Beobachter*.[139] It seems that in fact it was a reprisal for the expulsion of a British official from Germany; Thost was also suspected of espionage.[140] The *Manchester Guardian*, which had often lambasted Thost for his distorted reports, suggested that, rather than blaming Churchill's attitude on the Jews, he would have done better for the purposes of propaganda to exploit the 'considerable admiration for Germany and for Hitler' which it believed the *Strand* piece implied.[141] It is notable that in a later article Churchill praised Hitler's 'patriotic achievement' while expressing dislike for his 'system'.[142]

Another contemporary suggestion was that the Nazis were especially angered by the article because they believed that Churchill was about to be appointed to the Cabinet and they thus thought that it signalled a newly hostile government line.[143] It is true that it had been published in America a few months previously, without arousing their ire.[144] However, there is no evidence that the Germans had been aware of this earlier version, and their outrage is easily explained by the Nazis' extreme sensitivity to any form of criticism. Churchill was publicly defiant in the face of their fulminations, but the row was such that he opted to 'soften' a follow-up piece entitled 'The Truth About Myself'.[145] The reaction may also explain why later on, having consulted the Foreign Office, he opted to bowdlerize the Hitler article by deleting the final paragraphs when he republished it in his book *Great Contemporaries*.[146] It was a pointless gesture; the Nazis banned the book anyway, and Churchill's other articles and speeches often enraged them too.[147]

In the summer of 1935, MacDonald had retired; Baldwin thus became Prime Minister for the final time. Garvin urged Churchill's inclusion in the new Cabinet, but to no avail.[148] A few months later, with Mussolini's invasion of Abyssinia dominating public debate,

Baldwin called a general election and won a big victory. 'Well, you're finished now', Beaverbrook told Churchill. 'Baldwin has so good a majority that he will be able to do without you.' Churchill was offended, but Beaverbrook had a point.[149] Churchill later recalled that there was 'much mocking in the Press' over his exclusion from the government.[150] Actually, it was not too long before the papers started speculating once more about his future. The Labour-supporting Sunday paper *Reynold's News* thought he might be aiming at the premiership: 'He is playing adroitly to Right and Left. Right with his insistence on big armaments, Left with his new-found enthusiasm for the League [of Nations] and his vehement anti-Nazism—just as vehement as his anti-Communism of hardly any time ago.'[151] Even Moscow radio proclaimed satisfaction when Churchill said that Hitler's talk of the 'Bolshevist menace' was a red herring to distract attention from Germany's internal problems.[152]

Churchill's efforts to court progressive opinion extended to praising the *Daily Herald*, which, after a joint takeover by the printing company Odhams and the TUC, had become a mainstream mass-market Labour paper. In January 1936, while on his winter holiday in the South of France, he read an article by the *Herald*'s city editor, Francis Williams, which used figures from the commodity markets to show that Germany was importing huge quantities of materials essential to weapons production. He rushed to the beach 'waving an airmail copy of the *Herald* in his hand and shouting, "This proves it, this proves it." '[153] In March, after Hitler's troops had marched into the Rhineland, Churchill referred to these revelations in the Commons and commended the paper for having never tried to shield its readers from the truth about the European situation.[154] Thereafter, Williams 'fed him with everything we were able to quarry from commodity market dealings and statistical reports'.[155] Churchill took his facts wherever they were to be found. The idealistic young journalist Shiela Grant Duff recalled meeting him at Chartwell: 'He wanted to see me simply and solely because I had lived for a year in Czechoslovakia and could perhaps give him useful information.'[156]

By November 1936, *The Spectator* judged of Churchill that 'in spite of his erratic movement about the floor of the House of Commons in the past no one is better qualified to give clarity to, and assume direction of, a popular movement that is beginning to acquire self-consciousness and gain momentum'.[157] But his recovering prestige was then dealt a new blow by his support for Edward VIII during the abdication crisis, which was triggered by the King's desire to marry Wallis Simpson, an American divorcee, against the advice of his ministers. Churchill was probably motivated mainly by personal sympathy for Edward, but others suspected him of wanting to use the imbroglio to grab the keys to No. 10 himself.[158] Leo Amery wrote in his diary of rumours 'that Winston was trying to work a big intrigue through the press' and viewed the crisis as a means of 'scuppering' Baldwin, with the help of Esmond Harmsworth and Beaverbrook; although a few days later he conceded that he might have been too harsh.[159] As events moved towards their climacteric, Churchill issued a statement to the press calling for 'time and patience'.[160] Finally, in the Commons, he overplayed his hand by again asking for delay. Geoffrey Dawson, observing from the gallery, described how 'Winston, protesting and gesticulating on the floor of the House, was practically shouted down.'[161]

In the end, the King determined to abdicate. As Beaverbrook put it to Churchill, 'Our cock won't fight.'[162] Within a few months, Baldwin retired in a blaze of glory, to be succeeded by Neville Chamberlain. James Margach, the veteran *Sunday Times* political correspondent, described Chamberlain as 'the first Prime Minister to employ news management on a grand scale'. He added that 'From the moment he entered No. 10 in 1937 he sought to manipulate the Press into supporting his policy of appeasing the dictators.'[163] This is a verdict that historians have generally endorsed, and indeed applied to newsreels and the BBC as well as newspapers.[164] Richard Cockett judges that the Chamberlain government to a great degree succeeded in muzzling the press, 'with the willing connivance of journalists, editors and newspaper proprietors'.[165] There is much evidence to support these claims, which need to be understood in the context of the *de*globalization of the European press on account of post-1914 disruption and the resultant increased insularity of British coverage. The establishment in 1931 of an International Court of Honour for Journalists at The Hague had done little to address contemporary concerns about 'false news'; according to a 1933 survey, readers were at any rate more interested in crime and gossip than in foreign affairs, although this may have changed as the threat posed by Hitler grew.[166]

Dawson at *The Times* made particularly egregious efforts to avoid offending Nazi sensibilities, and Churchill had good reason to believe that it was prejudiced against him personally. There were also plenty of other examples of pusillanimity and cravenness.[167] Nevertheless, a degree of qualification is in order. Churchill's own citation of the *Daily Herald* demonstrates that there was brave and innovative anti-Fascist journalism. And Anthony Eden, when reviewing a draft chapter of Churchill's post-war memoirs, reminded him that although the British press had been 'nearly all appeasement-minded' this had not been true across the board. Eden cited the *Manchester Guardian* and the *Yorkshire Post*: 'The latter was the only Conservative paper, you will remember, to actively oppose Chamberlain's policy.'[168] Churchill made a minor adjustment to his text to acknowledge that there had been 'honourable exceptions' to the general tendency of influential papers to reassure the public that all was well.[169]

At the time, and doubtless wisely, Churchill never did launch a substantive attack on press–government collusion. If he felt resentment at his treatment in the media it was more directed at the BBC than at the newspapers, although the Corporation itself grew increasingly unhappy at ministerial pressure to keep him off the airwaves.[170] He did allow himself the occasional jocular sideswipe at modern journalism, and he disliked the new-style 'candid' photography that captured celebrities in unflattering poses.[171] But he was sceptical of the view that the concentration of newspaper ownership in a few hands was a threat to press freedom, arguing that no paper could afford to suppress news that its rivals would print.[172] As far as can be judged, he did not believe that there were problems with the structure of the press or that his own viewpoint was not actually making it into print. There was a different reason, he thought, that he was not listened to: 'the newspapers spread such a vivid page each morning that it must be very hard for the ordinary man or woman to discern what is really going on. Every day the headlines draw their sensation, and no proportion is shown between some exciting murder or prize fight or dog race, and the tremendous events unfolding remorselessly before us.'[173] Indeed insofar as Churchill found important outlets for his opinions in the press, he had few grounds for personal complaint. From 1936, he had a fortnightly column in the *Evening Standard*, even though his views on foreign policy were in clear opposition to Beaverbrook's isolationism. 'The Beaver' put pressure on Percy Cudlipp, as editor, to get Churchill to pay more attention to domestic matters in place of his 'gloomy thunderings on foreign affairs'. It was to no avail.[174] Churchill also secured the assistance of the press agent Emery Reves, a Hungarian-born Jewish émigré who had been forced to leave Berlin in 1933. Reves secured him a wider European and global syndication as well as considerably more money.[175] In March 1938, shortly after Germany enforced its Anschluss with Austria, the *Standard*'s new editor terminated Churchill's series, on the grounds that the articles clashed with the paper's editorial policy.[176] Churchill pointed out that the divergence had been clear from the start, and that in fact it was less stark than that presented by David Low's left-wing cartoons, which also appeared in the *Standard*.[177] Happily, he was able to transfer publication to the *Daily Telegraph* at once. He wrote his articles on Sundays for publication on Thursdays; they were then released for European publication but there was scope for revision to the English version up to the last minute.[178] At the *Telegraph* he was allowed more latitude than the paper's correspondent Eric Gedye, who was sacked for publishing a book exposing 'the uncensored truth' about the Nazis.[179]

During the Sudetenland crisis of the autumn, as a consequence of which Czechoslovakia was forced to cede territory to Germany under threat of war, Churchill was frenetically anxious and busy, and yet not especially visible in the media. W. P. Crozier, the editor of the *Manchester Guardian*, informed one of his journalists on 14 September: 'I spoke tonight with Winston Churchill, who is deeply perturbed but agreed that we ought not to criticise until we had some results.'[180] As the crisis developed, Churchill did issue press statements, one of which urged a 'solemn warning' to Germany; Rothermere telegraphed his support.[181] Churchill wished Chamberlain 'God-speed' in his mission to negotiate with Hitler at Munich, but he regarded the actual outcome of the talks as a devastating defeat.[182] For the time being Chamberlain—whose arrival back at Heston aerodrome was a media milestone, captured on live TV—remained strong but doubts among journalists and editors began to grow.[183] Germany's invasion of the rump of Czechoslovakia in the spring of 1939 was something of a turning point.[184] Churchill attempts to win over the left-wing press had already been paying off—although his reputation as a warmonger caused some resistance—and now a wider newspaper movement in his favour began.[185] Moreover, as Daniel Hucker has shown, there was a movement in both the British and the French press to support a 'Grand Alliance' with the Soviet Union of the type that Churchill himself favoured.[186]

In April, the *Sunday Pictorial* (which had attempted to recruit Churchill as a contributor after Munich) proclaimed 'THE GREAT CHURCHILL SCANDAL'—the scandal being that he wasn't in the government.[187] Of the 2,400 readers who wrote in in response, only 73 were opposed to Churchill.[188] In May, the *News Chronicle* published a poll suggesting that 56 per cent of voters wanted him to join the Cabinet with 18 per cent opposing.[189] Reaching a peak early in mid-summer, a swathe of publications from across the political spectrum joined the ranks of his supporters.[190] Chamberlain was especially 'taken aback' by the conversion of the *Daily Telegraph* to Churchill's cause; he summoned Lord Camrose to explain to him why he would not budge on the matter.[191] The rabidly pro-Chamberlain *Truth* magazine declared that there was an intrigue afoot, 'backed by a blatant Press campaign, the purpose of which is to enable Mr. Winston Churchill, with his satellites holding on to his apron strings, to muscle into the Cabinet.' Moreover: 'When we find a paragraph in the *Evening Standard* urging as an argument for Mr. Churchill's inclusion in the Cabinet that it is supported by the *News Chronicle*, the *Manchester Guardian*, the *Yorkshire Post*, and the *Daily Mirror*, we realise what the game is.'[192]

Rothermere having sold his shares at the start of the decade, the *Mirror* had by now evolved into a left-wing paper.[193] In July, Churchill's *Telegraph* contract having expired, the paper was able to boast:

CHURCHILL WRITES FOR US NOW
Warns Hitler: 'No Blood will flow, UNLESS – '[194]

In fact, he was only able to complete four articles before the outbreak of hostilities put an end to the arrangement. Churchill, who hoped to ensure that Italy would remain neutral in the event of a European conflict, consulted the Foreign Office about one of these pieces. He received a detailed critique from an official, E. M. B. Ingram, who suggested that there was 'more to be gained by showing up Hitler for a villain than Mussolini for a mug'.[195]

On the eve of war, then, Churchill had substantial, though certainly not unanimous, press backing. During the later thirties the media had shown itself to be fairly pliable in the face of government pressure; but it was divided, and dissatisfaction with Chamberlain's policy was reflected in a growing volume of dissent and criticism. When Churchill returned to office in wartime, this was the dichotomy with which he would have to deal: an essentially patriotic press that would be prepared to cooperate with official censorship of *information*, provided it was sensibly organized, yet in substantial parts also determinedly vocal in the expression of critical *opinion*. In time, the criticisms were to be levelled at Churchill's own government: and this notion he did not like at all.

6

'Worse Than
The Nazis'

Upon the outbreak of war, Neville Chamberlain bowed to the inevitable and brought Churchill into his government. On 4 September 1939 the *Daily Express* headline read:

FLEET BEGINS THE BLOCKADE
WINSTON BACK
He is First Lord; Eden is the new Dominions Secretary

The first subheading is intriguing, as legend has it that the Admiralty despatched a telegram to the Fleet with the simple message 'Winston is back'. Whether or not this really happened is disputed; it was only when Churchill made the claim in the first volume of his war memoirs in 1948 that the story began to be retailed in the press. Although in 1965 three readers of the *Daily Telegraph* separately wrote that the signal had indeed been received on board the ships upon which they had respectively served, this is not supported by the log of HMS *Cornwall*, the one specific vessel that was mentioned.[1] At any rate, Churchill's appointment contradicted Hitler's view that the Western allies were too decadent to prosecute the war seriously. Albert Speer was close at hand when the Führer was told of it. 'I still remember his consternation when the news came that Churchill was going to enter the British War Cabinet as First Lord of the Admiralty. With this ill-omened press report in his hand, Goering stepped out of the door of Hitler's salon. He dropped into the nearest chair and said wearily: "Churchill in the Cabinet. That means that the war is really on. Now we shall have war with England."[2]

At home, Churchill remained a media favourite. At this stage of the war, cinema news packages often fell back on comedy segments and reconstructed sequences or 'faked news'.[3] Mass-Observation made a study of early wartime newsreels, which compared audience reactions to fifteen of these with the same number of examples from the latter half of August 1939. 'The commonest pre-war figure was Neville Chamberlain; in war time up to the end of November he never appeared as a prominent feature and only three times very briefly in passing and got no response on any occasion.' Lord Halifax, the Foreign Secretary, disappeared from screens entirely. Overall, the emphasis had shifted from politicians to the royal family, who now featured heavily and who received much applause. The Queen was now the person most frequently seen in newsreels, 'but the commonest political figure, Churchill, got the highest war time response'.[4] During the latter part of the Phoney War, he remained the most popular newsreel figure, but was applauded slightly less than before; on one occasion in Manchester the only reaction was laughter at his hat.[5] MO felt that he was presented in an uninspiring way, reflecting a general official caution and lack of imagination in the field of news management. Taking a five-minute segment shown at the Gaumont cinema in London's Haymarket in November as its example, the report noted that 'For most of the time Churchill is simply talking to the audience, but there are rapid cut-ins to the Navy, Goering, Hitler and Poland. The last two minutes are entirely Churchill's face close-up.' Specialist news theatres sometimes offered better fare, but there was 'seldom anything dramatic or any real news.'[6]

MO may have been right about the filmed broadcast, but in general Churchill's speeches were warmly received in the press and by the public. Although they were not universally liked—his use of the word 'Huns' attracted some criticism—many people found them to be a refreshing change from 'the diluted news we get on the radio'.[7]

Admiral John Godfrey later noted how in Churchill's broadcasts, 'good news was made to seem better; bad news was toned down, delayed or sometimes suppressed'. Moreover, 'no one was more conscious than Mr. Churchill of the popularity of the bringer of good tidings'.[8] Nearly all French newspapers judged his oratorical efforts to be 'so frank and clear that they need little editorial comment'.[9] Reich propaganda minister Josef Goebbels, broadcasting in reply, 'called Churchill a liar a dozen times and kept shouting: "Your impudent lies, Herr Churchill! Your infernal lies!"'[10] This was typical of the German media's thoroughly unsubtle approach; Churchill consistently served as its bogeyman.

In the early weeks of the Phoney War, A. J. Cummings (one of Churchill's journalistic sympathizers) stated in the *News Chronicle* that 'It is the view of many representatives in London of American and other foreign opinion that by the time the war has passed into the next and more decisive phase Mr. Churchill will have become Prime Minister.'[11] Some of the coverage was politically unhelpful. After Poland had been crushed, the *Daily Mirror* reported (correctly) that Churchill had helped toughen Chamberlain's line against Hitler's peace proposals. Churchill saw this as an attempt to make mischief, and assured the Prime Minister he was not the source.[12] But in general he maintained his familiar taste for publicity—and journalists around the world were ready to oblige. To Sweden's *Sydsvenska Dagbladet Snällposten* he was 'England's strong man'; to the American *Saturday Evening Post* an 'Old Man In A Hurry'.[13] A gushing profile in another US magazine, *Life*, described his pre-war routine at Chartwell in detail. It noted how the house was financed by his journalistic income, and remarked how each guest received his or her favoured newspapers on their breakfast tray. Meanwhile, 'Downstairs is Host Churchill, already talking about the morning news.'[14]

Life estimated Churchill's earnings from writing at $100,000 per year, but his accession to office had caused them to drop radically. He confessed this to Charles Eade, editor of the *Sunday Dispatch*, whom he had invited to the Admiralty late one night in order to discuss republication of his old articles. 'He seemed to me to be a little drunk', Eade recorded. 'I was struck by the pallor of his face, which seemed bloodless and very clean. Our business was quickly settled. He was very affable & friendly; gave me authority to cut his stuff & said he did not want to see proofs, asked me to be careful to see the sense of his articles were not altered.' Churchill looked forward to reviving his previous *News of the World* contract at the end of the war, 'If there is anything left then.'[15] The articles were a boon to the *Dispatch*. Churchill later expressed amazement that it had been possible to keep the series going for so long: 'He had thought it might be possible to extract a few articles from his old published writings, but had no idea it would be possible to go on for over a hundred weeks.'[16]

Of course, other forms of press coverage were of far greater concern to Churchill than these recycled pieces. Initially, the Ministry of Information was badly organized and military censorship was implemented in cack-handed fashion.[17] Churchill bore some responsibility for the contradictions and chaos, because he wanted to monopolize the supply of information. He took the view that 'it was for the Admiralty or other department to purvey to the Ministry the raw meat and vegetables and for the Ministry to cook and serve the dish to the public. If the Admiralty could have their way they would prefer a policy of complete silence'.[18] The Chief Press Censor, Rear-Admiral G. P. Thomson, recalled that 'it was seldom, if ever, that any naval news of real interest or importance was allowed to come out, unless from the lips of the Prime Minister or the First Lord of the Admiralty, until so long afterwards that all interest in the event had vanished'.[19] Churchill made the unrealistic proposal that the BBC—which he regarded as too negative in its coverage—should give news of shipping losses only once a week.[20] This was a reprise of his attitude in 1914.

Churchill should not, however, be seen as a purely conservative influence on the media's output. At this stage, although radio ownership was widespread, at roughly 73 per 100 households, the news consisted mainly of bulletins read by announcers. Over time, as the press struggled with paper shortages, the BBC used the war as an opportunity to expand its mandate and provide more exciting coverage with a range of war correspondents delivering reports from the front line.[21] It seems likely that Churchill approved of such innovations, as when at the Admiralty he took note of German broadcasts that included interviews with fighting officers and suggested that the British developed a similar method:'Why should not Captain of *Spearfish* or Captain of destroyer which sank *U-39* or *U-27* give a prearranged interview at the microphone, so far as Service requirements permit?'[22]

But what of Churchill's personal ambitions? N. J. Crowson has argued that there is 'some evidence to suggest that Churchill was encouraging newspaper criticism in order to stiffen the war effort' at this time, while conceding that 'whether these were deliberate attempts to undermine Chamberlain's position for his own benefit is less than certain'.[23] The evidence in question consists of the records of Churchill's private talks with W. P. Crozier. Churchill told him that the war effort had to be intensified: 'Take a firm line, tell them what sacrifices the Government expects of the country, and set the appeal high.'[24] This seems like a fairly unexceptional request for the *Manchester Guardian* to admonish its readers into patriotic efficiency. Although perhaps Crozier was expected to read between the lines, there are no real signs that Churchill was engaged in major press intrigue. He seems to have known that his best option was to work loyally with Chamberlain and await developments. By March 1940, a rising tide of criticism was developing without any direct encouragement from the First Lord. Beaverbrook's *Sunday Express* appeared to be the only paper that backed the government blindly.[25] At the same time, faith in the mass press itself was waning, as news-hungry readers were aware that censorship was in operation; independent newsletters, often claiming special sources of information, proliferated.[26]

The attacks intensified after Hitler's lightning invasion of Norway in April. This prompted a British counter-attack followed, within weeks, by a humiliating withdrawal. The debacle posed a threat not only to Chamberlain's position but also to that of Churchill, given the major responsibility that he bore for the fate of the naval operations. Moreover, press and public opinion developed in an atmosphere of confusion. It was inherently difficult to make sense of fast-moving events in the theatre of war, there were inevitable communication problems with London, and, to boot, 'the Admiralty still does not understand how to give out news'.[27] According to MO: 'Within 48 hours of news of the invasion, rumours began. By April 11th the press and BBC were announcing British landings and British *victories*.' People became elated and started talking of further triumphs. In the Commons, Churchill endeavoured to introduce a note of realism, while nonetheless presenting Hitler's action as a reckless gamble. 'Then, on the 12th, it began to become clear that the rumours of victories had been exaggerated, and Churchill's steadying speech of the evening before had its effect.' Optimism now declined.[28]

Churchill's speech of 11 April contained a significant hostage to fortune. 'All German ships in the Skagerrak and the Kattegat will be sunk, and by night all ships will be sunk, as opportunity serves', he declared.[29] Overlooking the last three words, the *Daily Herald*, in common with other papers, read this as a pledge to sink all such ships, which certainly did not happen; Churchill reacted angrily when, towards the end of the month, the *Herald* suggested that his 'promise' did not 'help the public towards a sense of realities'.[30] On 5 May the *Sunday Dispatch* defended him, protesting that the passage had been widely misrepresented, and warned that there might be an attempt to make Churchill the scapegoat for the Norwegian reverse. 'There is a danger that if such an attempt is made, Mr. Churchill's loyalty to his colleagues would prevent him defending himself adequately', it claimed. 'He would be unlikely to defend his position at the cost of having to criticise other members of the Government publicly.'[31] The next day, the *Daily Mail* published a letter by 'A British Politician', proposing Halifax as Prime Minister and Churchill as one of four Ministers Without Portfolio.[32] The author was in fact Sir Stafford Cripps MP, who had been expelled from the Labour Party the previous year; his aim was 'to get rid of the argument that there was no alternative'.[33]

The next day, the *Mail* printed another proposal, this time from Robert Cary MP, who advocated giving Churchill himself the keys of No. 10. Cary thus appears to have been the first Conservative to openly break the government ranks.[34]

The stage was now set for a crucial debate in the House of Commons. 'Chamberlain is to face Parliament tomorrow', noted *Daily Express* journalist Albert Hird in his diary on 6 May. 'Yesterday's Sunday newspapers criticised him up hill and down dale. The News of the World, I think, was the only Sunday paper which sat on the fence.'[35] This does not mean that Chamberlain was necessarily doomed in advance. The Gloucester *Citizen* may have taken the prize for the least prescient headline ('Political Crisis Unlikely') but the government was widely expected to survive.[36] On the first day, however, Chamberlain put in an unconvincing performance, and the government was subjected to powerful attacks by Sir Roger Keyes and Leo Amery. On the second day, there was further slashing criticism from, in particular, the 77-year-old Lloyd George, and Churchill wound up the debate, defending Chamberlain, in a rowdy atmosphere. The Labour leaders had determined to force a vote, which the government won, but with a significantly reduced majority. In the *Daily Sketch*'s view, the Commons had 'surrendered itself to an orgy of personal feeling and bitterness of expression quite unworthy of the representatives of a democratic state'.[37]

On 9 May, the newspapers anticipated big Cabinet changes. Some made clear that Chamberlain's own future was in doubt, but others thought he would live to fight another day. MO diarist P. B. Pearson noted his surprise to read in the *Evening Standard* that the Prime Minister was likely to resign, having been told by the press over the previous few days that he would pull through.[38] The *Daily Mail* called for Chamberlain to be replaced by Lloyd George, with Churchill as his vice-premier.[39] The wider world had been watching too. Chamberlain's announcement of new powers for Churchill had been welcomed in French, Dominion, and American newspapers, and the Prime Minister had received a fair amount of praise, as well as being lambasted in some quarters for complacency.[40] An analysis by Chatham House found that in the Soviet Press, 'Mr. Chamberlain's and Mr. Churchill's speeches on Norway were given at exceptional length, as were also the debates in the House of Commons, with indications that important ministerial changes were thought to be imminent.'[41]

The process by which Chamberlain realized that he must definitely resign, and by which Churchill emerged over Halifax as his successor, involved many machinations, and has been told many times. Less well known is the tale of how these events were conveyed to the public. On the morning of 10 May, the *Daily Express* carried a report that Chamberlain would stand down—Labour being unwilling to serve under him in a reconstructed government—and that Churchill would likely be the new Prime Minister.[42] By the time that the paper hit readers' breakfast tables, though, they might already have heard the 7 a.m. BBC news, in which it was reported (but not officially confirmed) that the Germans had invaded Holland, and that there had been 'air activity in the Thames Estuary'. An hour later, there was no more doubt about the invasion; it was now known that Belgium had been attacked too. In the light of the news of the German actions, Chamberlain briefly determined to hang on, but quickly bowed to the inevitable. At 6 p.m. listeners were told that the British War Cabinet had met three times and that 'French Council of Ministers is in session at this moment'. At three minutes to six, Chamberlain arrived at Buckingham Palace. Just over half an hour later, he emerged, to be followed in at once by Churchill. It was now clear to journalists that the change had been made; but the public did not yet know. At 9 p.m. Chamberlain himself made a broadcast, in which he announced his replacement by Churchill. This was reiterated in the news bulletin that followed; it was also divulged that there had been widespread air-raids over France. The American news agency United Press (UP) quickly reported that 'The change of government was being accomplished in record-breaking speed for the ordinarily slow and traditionally form-bound British parliamentary system. Only this morning it generally was believed that despite the unleashing of the German attack on the low countries and the imminent threat to the British Isles that it would be 10 days or a fortnight before a new government might be formed.'[43]

A rapidly-written Mass-Observation report recorded that the British population's first impulse on the day that Chamberlain fell was to listen to the radio attentively, as that was the first source of important news. However, the document claimed, the broadcasts were unsatisfactory because they were insufficiently vivid and did not provide positive leadership: 'Optimism was low, 8%, on May 10, went up rapidly next day as the news came through that we were taking active steps, coupled with Churchill's new Cabinet etc. But it has not increased since Saturday, May 11, being 30% that day, 30% next day, and 29% today, May 13.' On 12 May, the BBC could find so little to report that the 1 p.m. bulletin finished after just eleven minutes, and the time was filled in with a gramophone record. A special bulletin announced for 4 p.m. did not take place, on the grounds that there was nothing to report! People therefore began to turn more to the newspapers, but were sceptical of them too.[44] By the following week—the Allies having experienced a series of crushing defeats—the Ministry of Information was detecting a general problem of 'disbelief in news sources'.[45]

The authorities became greatly concerned with the spread of rumours, some of them originating with German wireless propaganda, and others simply the product of 'imaginative and excitable minds'. Some involved incredible stories of Fifth Column activity, others told of German parachutists landing in specific areas, and some others could perhaps be counted as reasonable surmise. When Churchill flew to Paris for consultations on 22 May it was said that he had done so 'to prevent the French Government from "packing up there and then"'.[46] This was not correct, but as the French government did actually pack up one month later, one cannot say that this particular rumour was inherently absurd. It is worth noting that a key part of the appeal of Churchill's speeches during this period was that they helped slake the public thirst for both information and interpretation, in the absence of which rumours flourished. He thereby took direct responsibility for determining the release of previously secret facts. 'Churchill's habit of revising his speeches up to the last possible minute sprang many surprises on the censorship', recalled G. P. Thomson. 'On several occasions he revealed an item of information which, until he spoke, had been covered by a strict "stop". I, or my deputy, had then to send a directive to editors cancelling the ban.'[47] Occasionally, too, Churchill let slip something he should not—such as the information that the House of Commons had been damaged by bombs—and the Speaker had to ask journalists not to report it.[48]

Churchill often only sent his scripts to the Ministry of Information at the final hour, thus making things hard for papers that wanted to publish them, with commentary, in the regional editions that were printed in London in the early evening.[49] He did not, of course, want for coverage. German comment on his appointment was tediously predictable. He was denounced as a warmonger heading a government controlled by the dictates of high finance. His suppression of the sinking of the *Audacious* during World War I was brought into play: 'Nowadays when one reads the denials of the British Admiralty about a lost ship, one can see that the lying Lord has not yet improved.'[50] More interesting, though, is the way in which the way Nazi propagandists drew selectively on British and world press comment in order to make their case. They also quoted international news agencies, if only to pour scorn: 'Reuter announces proudly that the Commons unanimously voted confidence in the Churchill Government by 381 votes. This vote does not in any way surprise us, for we knew that more or less all English Parliamentarians have very close ties with the plutocratic clique.'[51] German and other nations' broadcasts were, in turn, captured by the BBC's impressive monitoring operation, a significant form of open-source intelligence.[52] Churchill himself made use of material it gathered.[53]

Soviet radio, reflecting this globalized aspect of wartime news, also made use of matter from Western agencies. On 4 June, after the successful evacuation of Dunkirk, and a few days before Italy's entry into the war, Churchill made his celebrated 'fight on the beaches' speech. This included the less well remembered promise that if Britain were to be subjugated then the 'Empire beyond the seas' would carry on the war. A short-wave broadcast from Moscow, intended for domestic consumption, cited UP's Washington correspondent, who 'pointed out that Churchill's statement to the effect that Britain would not surrender, even if the British isles were conquered, constitutes a sufficient guarantee of the safety of the Western hemisphere for a long period of time'.[54] The UP man's line was indicative of American media opinion more generally. According to a Chatham House assessment of US press reactions to events in May and June, German victories initially produced defeatist sentiment, as Americans did not yet have confidence in Britain's new government. However, Dunkirk stimulated a change, and Churchill's speech was 'praised for its frank admission of military disaster and for its courage in facing the future'.[55] On the radio, CBS correspondent Ed Murrow—who together with his wife struck up a friendship with Winston and Clementine—commended its 'honesty, inspiration, and gravity'.[56]

None of this automatically meant that Americans now wished to abandon neutrality, even if many of them were sympathetic to the British cause.[57] Opposition to involvement, which remained strong, was exemplified by the *Chicago Daily Tribune*. The *Tribune*—which had serialized Churchill's memoirs in the 1930s—was published by Colonel Robert McCormick. McCormick was a World War I veteran who was opposed to American entanglement in European affairs— the doctrine labelled by its opponents as 'isolationism'. He was an admirer of Churchill, and had been influenced by *The World Crisis*, but he took the view that although the new Prime Minister might be good for Britain, America need not be lured by his wiles to act against its own best interests.[58] It was thus not inconsistent for the *Tribune* to suggest that Churchill was 'worth a quarter of a million or more soldiers to Great Britain' and at the same time to persist in its claims that the war was a battle for Empire rather than for true democratic principles.[59] The British did make major public relations efforts in order to counter such beliefs, but Churchill, although desperately eager for the US to join the war, chose not to pay too much attention to 'eddies of United States opinion'. He believed that events, rather than publicity efforts, would be the main force driving people's views.[60]

He was, however, more concerned with the domestic media. In the first days of his premiership, he asked Duff Cooper (now Minister of Information) for proposals for 'establishing a more effective control over the BBC'.[61] Cooper concluded that there was already sufficient control but there continued to be grumbles at 'the higher levels of state' that the Corporation was insufficiently responsive to government directives.[62] Churchill regarded it as the 'enemy within the gate; continually causing trouble; more harm than good'.[63] The press, for its part, was simultaneously problematic and pliable. Chamberlain and Halifax had stayed in the War Cabinet after Churchill entered Downing Street, but by early June there was growing clamour to drive them and other former appeasers from office. Chamberlain—who also remained leader of the Conservative Party—identified the *News Chronicle*, the *Daily Herald*, and the *Daily Mail* as chiefly responsible. He offered his resignation to Churchill, but his loss would have seriously destabilized a government that was still fragile. After some hard bargaining with his old adversary, Churchill undertook to squash the press campaign. This he did, putting out the message to those with editorial power that unless the attacks stopped the government would collapse.[64] The effect was immediate (although the charges were quickly renewed in the best-selling pamphlet *Guilty Men*, published under a pseudonym by three Beaverbrook journalists[65]). The War Cabinet continued to lament, though, that 'While on the whole the attitude of the Press had been helpful, it was unfortunate that there was a certain tendency to encourage inquests rather than to concentrate on the tasks ahead. It was important that steps should be taken to make the Press realise that demands for inquests could only engender a spirit of doubt as to our strength, and that such demands ought therefore to be sternly discouraged.'[66]

The start of the Battle of Britain presented a new set of problems. Euphoric pilots just back from missions had a natural tendency to claim 'possible' kills as 'definites', and verifying their statements took time. The media and public, though, were hungry for numbers, while the Germans pumped out vastly exaggerated tales of their own successes.[67] Churchill poured scorn on the idea that US journalists might be allowed to check the RAF's figures. 'There is something rather obnoxious in bringing correspondents down to air squadrons in order that they may assure the American public that the Fighter pilots are not bragging and lying about their figures.'[68] It was not easy for newsreel crews to gain access to RAF bases, and their cobbled-together coverage often drew on pre-war footage.[69] In general, news packages now contained more 'actuality' material, which made them much more exciting than previously, but also, to some viewers, disturbing. Churchill was warmly applauded by newsreel audiences in May; in August MO noted that he had 'not been seen recently but would probably get an exceptionally good reception'.[70] In contrast to the press, commentaries remained almost entirely uncritical. Churchill, a cinema fan, was a consumer of newsreels himself, as may be seen from a later complaint he made about the 'boastful and trampling manner' of the Movietone commentator Leslie Mitchell.[71]

Churchill was not too fussy about ensuring that British claims about the levels of German losses were strictly accurate, but he did not in general hold back unwelcome information from the British people. Clearly there was a great deal that needed to be kept secret on grounds of necessity (notably the Ultra secret, atomic affairs, and the details of Churchill's own movements) but there were quite a lot of grey areas. The Defence Regulations made it an offence to publish information which might be of military value to the enemy, but the censorship system was voluntary. That is to say, it was an editor's decision whether or not to submit material for a judgement on whether or not it infringed the regulations, although if he or she published without checking there was a risk of prosecution.[72] On the whole, Churchill did not interfere in these matters when it came to the release of *information*. A key exception was the German bombing of the liner

Lancastria, which led to the deaths of over three thousand men. When he heard of this in the Cabinet room—on the same day that the French requested an armistice—he forbade publication, on the grounds that the newspapers had quite enough bad news for one day. Thereafter, amid the pressure of events, he simply forgot to lift the ban.[73]

The anomalous nature of the *Lancastria* episode should not lead us to conclude that Churchill's overall attitude to the press was relaxed. Was Francis Williams's later claim that he had a 'phobia about press criticism' too extreme? He certainly did not grasp that the censorship applied only to fact, not opinion, and it does seem fair to observe that 'he had no patience with a press censorship that could not do whatever he wanted it to do'.[74] His frustrations spilled over in October 1940. By this time, the Battle of Britain had been won, and his hold on power had been consolidated by the retirement of Chamberlain, who was terminally ill, and whom he would replace as leader of the Conservatives. On the other hand, the onset of the Blitz posed a new threat to civilian morale. Moreover, the failed Free French raid on Dakar (which the British had backed) had been an embarrassment to the government, which was still said by some to contain too much Chamberlainite dead wood. It was criticisms over Dakar by the *Sunday Pictorial* that drove Churchill over the edge. In Cabinet, he drew attention to an article which had labelled the Dakar affair as 'another Blunder' and which, he said, 'had used language of an insulting character to the Government'. He suggested that the *Pic*, and also the *Daily Mirror*, were deliberately trying to undermine the government:

> In his considered judgment there was far more behind these articles than disgruntlement or frayed nerves. They stood for something most dangerous and sinister, namely, an attempt to bring about a situation in which the country would be ready for a surrender peace.

> It was not right that anyone bearing his heavy responsibilities should have to submit to attacks of this nature upon his Government. It was intolerable that any newspaper should indulge in criticism and abuse, far beyond what was tolerated in times of acute Party strife, in a time of great national peril.

The Cabinet took note of the fact that the *Pictorial* and the *Mirror* were owned by a combine with an opaque structure. 'It was believed, however, that [...] Mr. Cecil Harmsworth King was influential in the conduct of the paper.'[75] This was correct. King, a nephew of Lord Northcliffe and of anti-establishment bent, was arrogant, driven, and neurotic. A pre-war admirer of Churchill, he now believed that the war effort was being frustrated by selfish vested interests and tired old men. King had some questionable private views that at times verged on defeatism, but neither he nor the papers with which he was associated can be properly be regarded as having been subversive.[76]

Reading between the lines of the Cabinet minutes, it seems that the ministers present realized the problems that would be caused by actually suppressing newspapers, and attempted to humour Churchill with the aim of calming him down. Beaverbrook, now Minister of Aircraft Production, suggested making an approach via the Newspaper Proprietors' Association, and this was agreed.[77] The next day, Churchill publicly attacked 'certain organs' of the press for their 'vicious and malignant' tone.[78] The day after that, the Cabinet considered a memorandum by Herbert Morrison, the Labour Home Secretary, which argued that the representations to the NPA should be 'in the nature of a friendly appeal' rather than a threat of action under the Defence Regulations.[79] Churchill reacted badly: 'He was determined to put a stop to these attacks and to obtain protection for the War Cabinet. It would be quite wrong that two members of the War Cabinet should be in the position of asking favours of the Newspaper Proprietors' Association.'[80]

This determined the approach when the NPA met Beaverbrook and Clement Attlee. Attlee—the leader of the Labour Party and a member of the War Cabinet—delivered a schoolmasterly telling-off. 'He said that if criticism of the irresponsible kind [...] were to continue, the government would introduce legislation making censorship of news *and* views compulsory.' Subsequently, Attlee met with King in person. The latter recorded the encounter in his diary. He told Attlee that it was 'public opinion led by the press', rather than the House of Commons or Churchill himself, that had driven the previous government from office: 'I said I thought Churchill had no objection to our kicking out poor Chamberlain, but didn't like being hurt himself.' Reporting back to the War Cabinet, Attlee claimed that his message had had a chastening effect. King saw things differently: 'Obviously the Government will do nothing more about it, and obviously we shall pipe down for a few weeks until the course of the war alters the situation.'[81] However, the government's threat was by no means wholly idle. In January 1941, it did shut down the communist *Daily Worker* which (unlike the *Mirror* and the *Pic*) was opposed to what it claimed was an imperialist war.

Churchill continued to absorb quantities of newsprint. On one occasion, Harold Nicolson spied him in the House of Commons Smoking Room, reading the *Evening News* 'intently, as if it were the only source of information available to him'.[82] As Churchill's daughter Mary recalled, he always read the papers 'with great attention'—as did Clementine— although he had at his disposal many more facts than they contained.[83] 'Over the winter, the Prime Minister continued to complain about the 'drizzle of carping criticism' in the press.[84] The death in November of Rothermere—who as a last wish provided Churchill with the posthumous gift of large Christmas turkey—meant that Beaverbrook was now definitively the most renowned (and the most widely hated) of the press lords.[85] Beaverbrook's effectiveness at the Ministry of Aircraft Production is debatable, but at the time his crash methods were credited with having dramatically increased output. As a colleague he was highly-strung, perpetually threatening resignation. His newspapers, too, were starting to get under the Prime Minister's skin.

Churchill was annoyed when the *Daily Express* published an article by the American journalist Ralph Ingersoll, which described an interview with him. Churchill had banned Ingersoll from reporting the substance of the conversation; the colour in the piece came from remarks made by John Colville, one of Churchill's key private secretaries, who was said to have commented on his boss's 'penchant for playing general himself'.[86] An embarrassed Colville claimed that Ingersoll's account was 'largely fictitious'.[87] Churchill was also angered by cartoons by David Low that suggested that Labour members of the government were too concerned about trade union rights and not enough about efficiency.[88] He protested to Beaverbrook: 'Low is a great master of black and white, but he is a Communist of the Trotsky variety.'[89] (Low in fact held fairly moderate left-wing views.) Beaverbrook responded, truthfully, that he had no control over what Low drew. As the price of recruiting him, he had given him carte blanche, even though Low's opinions were drastically at odds with the editorial line of the *Evening Standard*, in which his cartoons appeared. Officially, moreover, Beaverbrook had given up involvement in the running of his papers for as long as he remained a minister. Insisting to Churchill that he was sticking to this policy, he also threw in an offer to resign.[90] Churchill then wrote back assuring his friend that the issue was only minor, and urged him to stay in the government.[91] In April 1941 he finally allowed him to leave MAP; Beaverbrook became in quick succession Minister of State and Minister of Supply. The negotiations were fraught. Brendan Bracken commented that Beaverbrook took up more of Churchill's time than Hitler did.[92]

It was due to Beaverbrook's influence that Churchill from time to time held meetings with groups of editors at Downing Street. According to Arthur Christiansen, editor of the *Daily Express*, there was a particular technique for bringing these about:

> The Beaver got in touch with one of his favourite editors with a message that if we pressed hard enough the PM would see us, and even suggested the subjects on which he thought the PM ought to give us his views. The plot invariably worked and about twenty of us from the national Press and the chief provincial newspapers would troop into the Cabinet Room [...]

> A flurry of secretaries, Parliamentary and private, preceded the arrival of the master, who always struck me as being in a thoroughly bad humour on these occasions. Sitting in a bigger padded chair than the rest of us, a cigar firmly clenched between his lips, he looked smaller than any of us but twice as ferocious.[93]

New Statesman editor Kingsley Martin painted a similarly vivid picture of one of these events. The specific purpose on this occasion was for Churchill to explain that information about shipping losses should not be published even months after they had occurred, as this could still be useful to the enemy: 'Churchill made his point, and in five minutes I was satisfied that Nazi sinkings were not things to talk about. But the extraordinary thing was that Winston made his explanation last for a solid forty minutes. [...] His energy and eloquence simply boiled over.'[94]

Churchill probably achieved more through his public appearances than by his group sessions with editors. Early in 1941, the mission to Britain of Harry Hopkins, President Roosevelt's personal envoy, provided a chance to impress British and US audiences with the Prime Minister's popularity. Churchill took Hopkins on a tour of the country, as far as Scotland; their rapturous reception by the public became the backdrop to a media extravaganza. Hopkins gave press conferences but succeeded in remaining enigmatic as to American intentions. He would only say that he was present 'to discuss matters of mutual interest to our two countries'. When pressed, he agreed, 'Yes, I think you can say *urgent* matters.'[95] At this point the war seemed to be going well. In February, Mass-Observation offered the jaundiced judgement: 'Civilian morale is to-day acclaimed by Admirals, Mayors, Ministers and journalists, as A1. In recent weeks there have been some significant warning notes (*News Chronicle*, *Daily Express*, *Sunday Express*, *Evening News*, and *People*), but in general an immense ballyhoo on British bravery prevails, of a sort that six months ago would have sickened us with self-consciousness (and is sickening many people now).'[96] The year 1941 also became notable for the BBC's 'V for Victory' campaign, which caught the popular imagination, and led to a new facet of the Churchill public persona—the two-fingered sign that he now gave at every opportunity.[97]

However, the disastrous British intervention in Greece in the spring, followed soon after by the loss of Crete, meant that it was not long before the newspapers again became 'cantankerous'.[98] One of the most influential war commentators in the mass press—along with *Sunday Express* editor John Gordon—was Leslie Hore-Belisha MP, who had been controversially dismissed by Chamberlain in 1940. There was bad blood between him and Churchill, and he now had a weekly full-page article in the *News of the World*, the Sunday paper with the biggest circulation of them all. In these he rehearsed the criticisms of the government that he was also making in speeches. MO saw him as someone 'with an unusual grasp of the processes of public opinion, and a distinct ability to keep in touch with the public mood'. If nobody apart from himself perceived him as an alternative Prime Minister, he nonetheless filled a niche 'not altogether unlike that filled, more fully, by Mr. Churchill during the Chamberlain period before the war'.[99] In the Commons, Churchill hit back hard against Hore-Belisha—too hard, some thought.[100] Churchill was not in any real political danger at this point, but the problem of public distrust of over-optimistic official spokesmen was again in evidence at this time.[101] Even positive developments led to concerns that false hopes were being raised by the BBC and the press. According to Home Intelligence, 'People have become afraid of believing good news.'[102]

In such an atmosphere, the arrival in Scotland of Rudolph Hess, Hitler's deputy, on a bizarre peace mission, was bound to set tongues wagging. When Churchill was told of his arrival, he flatly refused to believe that the man really was Hess. Only when the Nazis themselves announced that Hess had taken an aeroplane and disappeared did Downing Street put out a statement that he was in Britain.[103] The War Cabinet was soon expressing concern about the tone of the coverage: 'The general effect of what had been published had been almost laudatory, and there had been no reference to Hess's record, which was as bloody as that of any of the Nazi leaders.'[104] Yet the lack of an official announcement about Hess's intentions led to public suspicions that he must have friends in high places. It was known that he had attempted to contact the Duke of Hamilton, who was entirely innocent of any wrongdoing, but who was now thought by some to have been a Fifth Columnist: 'it is pointed out that, when questioned about him, the Prime Minister said that the Air Ministry would answer all questions about him as the Duke is in the Air Force, and this is taken to mean that the Prime Minister knows all about him but does not want to have anything to do with him.'[105]

When Churchill met with editors on 7 June, 'with a view to damping down their criticism', he was somewhat reticent over Hess, whom he said had 'extraordinary ideas' about British public opinion: 'He simply cannot understand how the British people can fail to see that they are already beaten and must be utterly crushed unless they give in.' Churchill was more forthcoming with respect to the intelligence he had received that the Germans were concentrating huge numbers of troops on the borders of Russia. He said that a military strike was a real possibility, although he also suggested that the Soviets might make big concessions rather than fight.[106] He was clearly therefore an important source (but certainly not the sole one) for stories such as 'GERMAN ARMIES ON STALIN'S FRONTIER'.[107] Stalin, however, refused to believe that there was a threat. Churchill had given him a direct though cryptic warning. This, coming on top of the distracting mysteries of the Hess affair, merely convinced Stalin that there was a British plot afoot to draw him into war.[108] Many British people too were 'sceptical about the news of Germans massing on the Russian frontier'. What, they wondered, was the true state of British relations with Russia, and of Russian relations with Germany?[109]

When Operation Barbarossa—the Nazi invasion of the Soviet Union—did occur, the news was transmitted to Britain with remarkable speed. It was in the small hours of 22 June that a sharp-witted Reuters translator, monitoring a German broadcast, noted a proclamation by Hitler denouncing the Russians. She deduced from this, even before the formal announcement was reached, that an invasion had taken place, and thus the agency got its scoop—by a margin of ten minutes.[110] Churchill moved that same day to assure the world that, although his opposition to communism had not diminished one whit, any country that fought the Nazis would have British support.[111] His broadcast got a good reception in the American press, although of course non-interventionists continued suspicious. The Chicago *Tribune* argued that, having accepted Stalin as an ally, Great Britain 'must accept the exponents of a bloody tyranny and a brutal political system as companions in arms'. The paper further suggested that Americans who had been demanding an immediate declaration of war had had the ground washed from under their feet (presumably on the basis that the new front rendered this unnecessary). Such people 'will take the cue Mr. Churchill has passed to them in his Sunday speech, but it will not work'.[112]

In July 1941, Duff Cooper, who had been rather indolent and ineffective as Minister of Information, was replaced by Brendan Bracken. It was an inspired appointment. MoI had just gone through a period of crisis that had descended into open Whitehall warfare.[113] Now the press had regular briefings from a man whom they knew to be a close personal friend of the Prime Minister. Things that Bracken told them were regarded as coming 'straight from the horse's mouth'. Much information that he gave was off the record, but he always dished out 'titbits' that could be published as long as articles that used them were submitted to the censor.[114] Soon after the start of the new regime, the public started praising the 'obvious improvement in news and photographs issued by the Ministry of Information'. There was special welcome for photographs of an RAF daylight attack on Cologne and the mention of the numbers of bombers employed.[115] Ian McLaine has remarked on Churchill's 'apparent inability to grasp the direct relationship between news and morale', which may be fair comment, but at least he was now delegating effectively to someone who understood it well.[116]

On Saturday 2 August H. V. Morton—a journalist and popular travel writer—obeyed a summons from Bracken to see him in London at 11 o'clock without fail. Bracken offered him a mission: to immediately leave on a three-week mission away from Britain. He could not be told where he was going or what he would see when he got there; but he would certainly witness history in the making. He would be in a battleship and would spend 'several days in or near a foreign country'. His task was to describe whatever it was he was going to see. What clothes should he pack, wondered Morton, not knowing if he was headed for the equator or the Arctic. The type he was wearing, Bracken said.

'Shall I pack a dinner jacket?'
'Most certainly, I should take a dinner jacket.'[117]

Morton had been chosen as a member of the party that was to accompany Churchill and Beaverbrook to a meeting with Roosevelt off Newfoundland, which resulted in the declaration of principles known as the Atlantic Charter. Morton was a skilled writer, admired by Churchill.[118] His selection—along with the novelist Howard Spring—tells us that although the Atlantic meeting was meant to be secret at the time, it was also designed (on the British side) to be exploited for propaganda purposes once security had ceased to be a concern. If Churchill's dreams had come true, and Roosevelt had used the meeting to announce America's intention to enter the war, the publicity would have been all the more spectacular.

In spite of the efforts at confidentiality, it proved impossible, even temporarily, to keep the conference properly under wraps. According to Home Intelligence's account of the public mood, 'As soon as there was suspicion that official secrecy was shrouding the Prime Minister's movements, he was reported to be very ill, or dead, or resigning, or on the way to Russia; President Roosevelt was said to have committed suicide, as well as to have resigned; Hitler was also said to be dead.'[119] Meanwhile, Roosevelt's absence from Washington needed to be explained: the cover story was that he was enjoying a cruise off New England aboard the presidential yacht. On 5 August, with Churchill still en voyage, the news of the meeting was broadcast on German Trans-ocean Wireless (quoting a report from Lisbon), and this was quickly echoed on Swiss radio and on a German language station in Ohio. On the same day the *Daily Mail* cited reports in Washington that a 'high British personage'—either Churchill or Beaverbrook—was expected to arrive in the USA. In spite of the leaks, FDR strongly opposed an official announcement. His motto was 'When in doubt say nothing!'[120]

Therefore, news of the summit, although not its precise location, appeared in the British press only on 14 August (and in the US press the next day), once the discussions were over. Although Churchill was still at sea at this point further efforts at secrecy were redundant. According to Albert Hird, 'Newspapermen had been led to believe that something *very* important was coming' and, although he soon revised his opinion, the Atlantic Charter initially struck him as 'a damp (or rather completely wet) squib'.[121] The impact on the public seems to have been significant, although the lack of an actual declaration of war was a disappointment.[122] An MO report on industrial life in Manchester noted: 'Political talk very much absent. Only a large headline such as "Churchill–Roosevelt Meeting" could arouse any political conversation.'[123] There were persistent rumours that Hess had been taken along to meet FDR too. Remarkably enough, Home Intelligence succeeded in tracing back one of these stories to a specific individual, 'a man in a Middlesex suburb "who remembers reading something about it" in the News Chronicle'.[124]

Ministry of Information cameramen had accompanied the British party to Newfoundland: when the Americans realized this they played catch-up by sending for some Army photographers.[125] By 16 August, film footage had been flown back to London and was exhibited by Bracken at MoI. According to Colville, 'They were not yet cut or edited and some of the effects produced—in particular the singing of "Onward Christian Soldiers" at the service on HMS Prince of Wales—were almost unbearably funny.'[126] As edited, a seven-minute segment, 'Filmed by the Newsreel Association of Great Britain with the co-operation of the Ministry of Information', showed, inter alia, Churchill stroking the ship's cat, and a sailor eating a banana gifted by the Americans. As the Prime Minister and Beaverbrook descended into a launch to transfer to the US cruiser *Augusta*, the announcer stressed that this was 'a simple meeting' of the political heads of two great democracies, 'not a pompous affair like the meetings of Hitler and his lackey Mussolini at the Brenner pass'.[127] When Colville saw the finished version, he was amazed: 'I could never have believed so good a result could be achieved from so uninspiring and amorphous a farrago of material.'[128]

During the autumn, Churchill's chief difficulties with the press concerned Beaverbrook, whom he had sent on a mission to Moscow to discuss aid to Russia. On his return, Beaverbrook was fulsome in his praise of Stalin's regime, and his papers began to advocate more British help for the Soviets. At the same time, Beaverbrook restarted his offers-cum-threats of resignation, and the press started publishing stories of Cabinet dissent over the question of a Second Front to help relieve the severe German pressure on the USSR.[129] (Yet with a surprising degree of generosity, the Soviet paper *Izvestia* lavished praise on Churchill and acknowledged that Britain was making use of the 'breathing space' created by Russian resistance 'to consolidate and to prepare her armed forces'.[130]) On the basis of information from the radical Labour MP Aneurin Bevan, who was close to Beaverbrook, Cecil King concluded that the latter's plan was to be outside the government in the event of the major political crisis he expected to develop. 'In the meantime he will use his papers to attack the Government for not fulfilling its promises to Stalin. When the big political rumpus comes, he hopes to return to the Government either as Prime Minister or as an overwhelmingly powerful figure in a reconstituted Churchill administration.'[131] Whatever the truth about Beaverbrook's ambitions at this time, he certainly showed how well he deserved his reputation as a pathological mischief-maker.

Churchill, however, continued to tolerate his friend's behaviour. On 7 December, the Prime Minister was spending an evening at Chequers with US ambassador J. G. Winant and Roosevelt's envoy Averell Harriman when he learned from the 9 o'clock news that Japan had attacked Pearl Harbor. Churchill did not immediately grasp the significance of the report and had to have it confirmed by his butler, Sawyers, who had been listening in another room.[132] Newly emboldened and optimistic, he quickly determined to visit Roosevelt. Churchill encountered resistance from officials and colleagues who, believing he should stay in London at this critical moment, regarded the idea as lunatic.[133] Yet in reality it was a masterstroke, both from the strategic and the publicity points of view. As Churchill steamed westwards in the *Duke of York*—again accompanied by Beaverbrook—the official reports and press summaries that he received led him to fear that the Americans would concentrate their military efforts against Japan, leaving Britain to deal with the Germans and Italians in the Middle East, Africa, and Europe.[134] Arriving on 22 December, he was able to use his great personal popularity in the USA to help leverage a commitment from Roosevelt and his advisers to a 'Germany First' strategy.

'The principal event of the week was the arrival of the Prime Minister in Washington', reported the British Embassy, which provided a regular round-up of American press coverage, politics, and opinion. 'Though little was generally known of his discussions with the President, his public appearances at the President's press conference and before the Senate were such an unqualified success and made so strong and favourable impression on the public at large that they alone would have afforded sufficient justification for his visit.'[135] The press conference was indeed a striking affair. Churchill's meetings with editors in Britain had been on a not-for-attribution basis, but now he was subjected to on-the-record questioning. The atmosphere was warm and friendly. Roosevelt encouraged him to stand on a chair so that the pressmen could see him better, and he did so to cheers and applause. He gave an impression of frankness and humour while avoiding giving hostages to fortune:

> Q. Mr. Minister, can you tell us when you think we may lick these boys?
>
> THE PRIME MINISTER: If we manage it well, it will only take half as long as if we manage it badly. (Laughter)[136]

On the morning of 27 December, the day after Churchill's highly successful address to Congress, Sir Charles Wilson was summoned to the White House. Wilson (later ennobled as Lord Moran), was the

Prime Minister's personal physician. Churchill told him that he had got up in the night to open a window and had experienced shortness of breath and a pain over his heart. Wilson examined him and concluded that, whether or not he had actually suffered coronary thrombosis, he certainly had the symptoms of coronary insufficiency. The standard treatment for this was six weeks or more in bed. According to Wilson's account, 'That would mean publishing to the world—and the American newspapers would see to this—that the PM was an invalid with a crippled heart and a doubtful future.' He therefore decided merely to tell his patient that he had been overdoing things.[137]

In ignorance of his own condition, Churchill spent 29–31 December in Ottawa, where he addressed the Canadian parliament. It was after this speech that the Armenian-born photographer Yousuf Karsh captured what may be the most iconic photo of Churchill ever taken. Granted a mere two minutes to snap Churchill against the backdrop of the panelling of the Speaker's Chamber, Karsh wanted a warlike expression—so whisked the cigar out of Churchill's mouth. 'By the time I got back to my camera', Karsh recollected, 'he looked so belligerent he could have devoured me. It was at that instant that I took the photograph.'[138] Clementine Churchill never liked the picture because she thought it captured 'a manufactured expression and not a natural one'.[139] The image was also artificial in the sense that Karsh worked hard in the studio, accentuating the contrast between black and white and sharpening the definition.[140] The finished product built upon and augmented Churchill's 'bulldog' image; the cartoonist Strube had first drawn him in that guise for the *Daily Express*'s edition of 8 June 1940.[141] Like Herbert Mason's celebrated photo of the dome of St Paul's during the Blitz, the 'Roaring Lion' picture was widely reproduced and circulated, both at the time and throughout subsequent decades, forming a crucial building-block of wartime cultural memory.[142] The shot brought Karsh global fame—but he had to wait until 1955 for another sitting with Churchill.

After a further two weeks back in Washington, Churchill returned to Britain in mid-January 1942. He was warmly received in the

Commons. However, his request for his parliamentary speeches to be recorded and broadcast (an idea which was popular with the public) ran into opposition from MPs and he withdrew it.[143] The proposal, in fact, had received a warm welcome in the press 'despite the fact that most Fleet Streeters regarded it as yet another attempt to blanket or rather by-pass the newspapers'.[144] That might have been an understandable wish on Churchill's part, given that press and public criticism of his government was now growing.[145] The news of his American trip had been 'specially welcomed' by the British public as 'countering the depression resulting from Japanese successes in the Far East'.[146] However, Japan's rapid progress in Malaya could not be ignored. In the late 1930s, with the naval base at Singapore nearing completion, the media had reinforced the mistaken impression—which Churchill too absorbed—that the island was a 'fortress'.[147] With the position of the British forces now increasingly desperate, it was naturally difficult for the media to secure hard facts. Violet Bonham Carter recorded a lunch with Churchill that took place during the final days of the doomed defence. 'He looked disturbed, I thought—almost tears in his eyes. His first words were "The evening papers are running the *Japanese* news in their headlines." '[148]

The garrison's unconditional surrender on 15 February was a humiliation that Churchill felt deeply (although for many of the public the embarrassing news of the escape of three German battle-cruisers through the English Channel was a greater concern).[149] In a broadcast to the public, Churchill acknowledged that the loss of Singapore was a 'British and imperial defeat'; as Cecil King noted in his diary the next day, 'The speech has had a reception in the newspapers this morning varying from hostile to chilly.'[150] In the Commons, Churchill warned MPs against 'agitated or excited recriminations', leading the *Daily Mirror* to remind him of his own pre-war remark that 'The use of recriminating about the past is to enforce effective action at the present.' Moreover, 'We beg Mr. Churchill to read comments in the American and Australian Press [...] Our own criticisms (or recriminations) pale into a sort of mild lecturing beside those angry denunciations.'[151] Many UK newspaper critiques (which found a strong echo in public opinion) focused on the relationship between Churchill and his colleagues. The *Daily Mail* spoke of 'the great anxiety felt throughout the country' about Churchill's dominance over questions of war strategy. 'It is felt that the other members of the War Cabinet are either afraid or incompetent to take their share of responsibility.'[152] Even the Gaumont newsreel commentary appeared, for the first time, mildly critical: 'When the Prime Minister says that only our follies can deprive us of victory, it is a bit shattering. When it comes to follies, we're miles ahead of Ziegfield.'[153]

The nature of some of these follies were outlined in an article in *The Times* entitled 'Why Singapore Fell', which placed the blame on the attitude of colonial officials towards the indigenous population as well as on the inefficiency of the Generals.[154] According to Albert Hird, 'It has caused something of a sensation and one paper said it was the kind of article that, in other times, would have meant the downfall of the government. Happily for the Govt., however, there is no Northcliffe in this war, and the Beaver is too tied up with Churchill to do any real criticism.' After Churchill reluctantly agreed to restructure his administration, Hird compared the episode to the 1915 Shells Scandal, exposed by the same paper: 'people in touch with political circles are saying that Churchill's hasty change in his Government, after he had announced he would make no changes, are the direct result of that article.'[155]

That seems unlikely: there is no direct evidence that Churchill was influenced by the piece, and ministerial changes were probably inevitable sooner or later, but in general pressure from the press was probably significant. The most eye-catching feature of the reshuffle was the inclusion in the War Cabinet of Stafford Cripps who, upon his return from a spell as ambassador to the Soviet Union, had emerged as a potential rival to Churchill. Also striking was the departure of Beaverbrook, who had briefly accepted the role of Minister of Production, ostensibly on grounds of exhaustion and ill-health (he suffered from asthma). 'My Darling—', Clementine had written to her husband, 'Try ridding yourself of this microbe which some people fear is in your blood—Exorcise this bottle Imp & see if the air is not clearer and purer—You will miss his drive and genius, but in Cripps you may have new accessions of strength.'[156] But the real impetus for the break came from Beaverbrook himself, who in his resignation letter highlighted policy differences over Russia, although these were not referred to in the public announcement. Some believed that he expected the government to collapse in short order, and that he was now positioning himself for the future.[157] Another consequence of the crisis was that Churchill's dislike of the press intensified yet further. He had always taken criticism personally; now, he apparently said, he 'hated the newspapers worse than the Nazis'.[158] The evidence that he said this is second-hand: but Churchill's resentment of the Fourth Estate was shortly to be proven beyond doubt.

7

'The War is not Fought to Amuse the Newspapers'

It began with a cartoon. It came from the pen of Philip Zec, a London-born Jewish socialist of Russian descent. Having worked as a much sought-after advertising illustrator, at the outbreak of World War II, when he was about to turn thirty, he was recruited by the *Daily Mirror* as a political cartoonist, even though he had no previous experience of that role. His powerful anti-Nazi cartoons were a valuable propaganda weapon, which led to the frustration of his desire to join the forces. 'I was already virtually in the RAF', he recalled. 'I waited for my damned ticket but it never turned up. I didn't get into the RAF. The Government decided I was more useful where I was.'[1] But as Churchill's relationship with the *Mirror* soured during the early months of his premiership, Zec annoyed him with a 'singularly mischievous' cartoon which portrayed Emperor Hirohito as the middle link in an evolutionary chain that started with an ape and Neanderthal man, rising through Mussolini and at last Hitler. Churchill considered it offensive, but he was not concerned with the racism so much as the risk that it might strengthen the hand of the War Party in Tokyo, at a sensitive time in Anglo-Japanese relations.[2] This, however, was merely a minor prelude to the storm that erupted over Zec's cartoon of 5 March 1942 which showed a physically-drained merchant seaman clinging to a raft, under louring skies, after his ship had been torpedoed.

The caption read: 'The Price of Petrol Has Been Increased by One Penny—Official'.

Zec's intention was to show that bringing fuel to Britain in war-time was a highly dangerous business; therefore people should be careful not to waste it. There is evidence to suggest that this is the way that the public interpreted it too.[3] Churchill and his colleagues, how-ever, read it as an accusation that the men's lives were being thrown away in the interests of oil company profits. As far as they were con-cerned, the cartoon was merely one aspect of a much broader pattern of offence, whereby the paper systematically published material calcu-lated to foment opposition to the prosecution of the war. Theoretically, at least, this was something that could lead to its suppression under Defence Regulation 2D.[4] During a lunchtime conversation with W. P. Crozier, Churchill was 'very hot and strong' about the question of the *Mirror*, and wanted to 'flatten them out', although he also com-plained about the *News Chronicle*, the *Daily Herald*, the *Daily Mail* 'and its Sunday paramour, the *Sunday Dispatch*'. Crozier asked Churchill why he was so sensitive about newspaper criticism, given that he had a great Commons majority and the backing of the country as a whole. Churchill responded that he did not think he was being treated fairly and that the prestige of the government was being injured. But Crozier discerned that the press attacks hurt him because he was simultaneously experiencing 'anguish and self-reproach' at the loss of Singapore.[5] In other words, the critics were rubbing salt into his wounds.

The *Mirror* had survived Churchill's wrath before, but the danger was arguably now more intense, on account of Labour ministers' own growing resentment at the press.[6] Ernest Bevin, as Minister of Labour, may have been angered by the *Mirror*'s support of his potential rival, Stafford Cripps.[7] It appears to have been with some sense of relish, moreover, that the Labour Home Secretary Herbert Morrison—'one of the least popular ministers at any time' according to MO—summoned the *Mirror*'s editor and chairman for a talking to.[8] Speaking with the full authority of the War Cabinet, he accused them of being unpatriotic. He also said that the Zec cartoon was worthy of Goebbels, and reminded them that he had previously shut down the *Daily Worker*. 'You might bear that in mind', he remarked. 'If you are closed it will be for a long time.'[9] Morrison followed this up with an official warning in the Commons.[10]

Meanwhile, on Fleet Street the mood was turning. The *Mirror*, with its brash, lower-class appeal, was not greatly loved by its rivals, and there was a tendency at first to think that the paper deserved anything that was coming to it. But editors suddenly woke up to the enormous powers granted to the Home Secretary under Regulation 2D. They were shaken by the thought that, without even having to go to court, he could suppress any newspaper which *in his view* hindered the war effort by the criticisms that it made. Therefore, with the exception of Lord Camrose's *Daily Telegraph*, all the capital's papers came out against the government. 'True it is that in a scrap of this kind most London newspapers prefer to defend someone better than the Mirror', noted Albert Hird, 'but they are convinced that the challenge having been issued, it must be taken up without delay.'[11]

Morrison's statement was followed by a wider Commons debate on 'Freedom of the Press' later in the month. The left-wing backbencher Aneurin Bevan brutally pointed to the critical articles that Morrison himself had written for the *Mirror* during the Phoney War period. He also suggested that for him and Churchill to talk about fighting for freedom while seeking to suppress newspapers would evoke cynicism. Another Labour MP, Frederick Bellenger, noted that Churchill clearly resented criticism of himself and his government: 'He has said so, and he has shown his resentment in this manner, that he has warned at least one newspaper proprietor that he would deal with that newspaper, and not by the methods of Regulation 2D.'[12] (Bellenger did not disclose the name of the proprietor, but promised to disclose it in person to Brendan Bracken afterwards; the truth of the matter is not clear.) Ministers seem to have been taken aback at the parliamentary reaction, and the threat to the *Mirror* receded. The Ministry of Information found that the public was somewhat ambivalent about Morrison's action but was anxious about 'this further threat to the freedom of the Press and democratic criticism'.[13] Mass-Observation found that most people disapproved of the government's heavy-handed approach. Furthermore, according to MO's research, there was no evidence that *Mirror* readers were any more depressed or demoralized than those of the *Daily Mail* or the *Daily Express*. Few of them actually paid much attention to its politics, and they tended to 'treat it purely as a sort of daily magazine centred around the unique page of strip cartoons'. Although almost half of the population disapproved of the *Mirror*, the affair actually increased the proportion who felt favourably towards it, and many people who had never read it now wanted to do so![14] Because it had a fixed paper ration, the *Mirror* could not increase its circulation, but it now sold out at 8 a.m. rather than 9 a.m.[15]

In retrospect, it might appear that whole affair was a serious misjudgement on the part of Churchill and the government. In a critique published in 1978, James Margach portrayed the episode as a symptom of Churchill's intolerance of press criticism, which in turn reflected the Prime Minister's lack of appreciation of the difficulties under which political journalists laboured. Margach also argued that Churchill handled British pressmen incompetently and aggressively, in contrast with his treatment of their US counterparts, whom he handled smoothly at his joint press conferences with Roosevelt. According to this analysis, whereas Lloyd George had preferred to 'square' the press when he could, Churchill's instinct was to 'squash' it, using 'the majesty of office to steamroller Fleet Street'.[16]

Margach's account perhaps placed insufficient weight on the severe strain that Churchill was under, and somewhat exaggerated his neglect of press contacts. Churchill did cultivate sympathetic editors, such as Robert Barrington-Ward of *The Times* (and of course Crozier). Contrary to Margach's specific claim that Churchill never met the journalists of the Parliamentary Lobby, he actually did so at this time, although he grumbled defensively about unfair press criticism.[17] However, the broader point stands, as the *Mirror* affair did reveal Churchill's 'authoritarian and repressive' streak.[18] Francis Williams, the former *Daily Herald* journalist who was now Controller of Press and Censorship at MoI, recalled that Churchill

> tended to regard any press criticism of the Government as personal and by no means confined his hatred to the *Mirror*. Criticism in Parliament was bad enough. But there he had an answer. He could demand a vote of confidence and stamp his critics into the ground. Criticism by the press was less easy to beat down. He remained absurdly sensitive to it.

Moreover, 'even when he was restrained from trying to gag the British press he insisted on trying to put a stop to the free thoughts of overseas correspondents and what he regarded as their nasty habit of cabling home anything nasty a British newspaper said about him'.[19]

Concurrent with the *Daily Mirror* imbroglio, ministers determined to tackle this problem of messages 'sent overseas by Press Correspondents in this country which were calculated to arouse ill feeling between this country and certain of the Dominions or of our Allies'.[20] The War Cabinet decided that it could no longer be assumed that material already published in the UK could be cabled abroad without further question. Moreover, tighter control would be exercised over outgoing messages, including those 'calculated to create ill-feelings' between the Allies.[21] In a message to the Australian Prime Minister, John Curtin, Churchill argued that the crackdown was necessary to tackle those journalists who decried Britain's war effort, as the criticisms echoed back and forth across the oceans. 'We cannot afford this indulgence', he wrote. 'The war is not fought to amuse the newspapers but to save the peoples.'[22]

The practical impact of the warnings to the *Mirror* and these other measures is hard to assess. The effect was not obviously dramatic but, even though the threat to close the paper never materialized, it may have had a chilling (if rather intangible) effect on the press in general, at least in the short term. On the other hand, from the government's point of view, there was perhaps more to be achieved through more subtle methods. Churchill often rang Francis Williams late at night, fulminating about some items in the next day's papers. When Williams objected that censorship applied only to facts and not views, Churchill would either berate him for talking 'like a bureaucrat' or, when in a brighter mood, would dismiss such concerns as of no importance. 'Nonsense, Mr. Williams', he would say. 'You are a man of influence. Pray use it.'[23]

Maybe Williams really did always hold firm, but he was surely not the only recipient of this type of pressure, although only occasionally can the proof be found in the archives.[24] 'A quiet word dropped in the appropriate ear must often have secured a discreet silence on issues judged to be sensitive', notes Ian McLaine in his history of MoI.[25] The late-night calls, of course, resulted in part from the fact that Churchill remained an inveterate reader of the press. At Chequers, the official prime ministerial country residence, there was a daily delivery of *The Times*, the *Daily Telegraph*, the *Daily Express*, the *Daily Mirror*, the *Daily Mail*, the *Daily Herald*, and the *News Chronicle*. On Sundays, there arrived the *Sunday Times*, *The Observer*, the *Sunday Dispatch*, the *Sunday Pictorial*, the *Graphic*, and the *News of the World*.[26] We do not have the equivalent list for 10 Downing Street, but we do know that he also liked to read the *Manchester Guardian* 'though I don't always agree with it'.[27] *The Times* was always his penultimate read, and then last the *Telegraph* 'because I know that will be all right'.[28]

During the late spring of 1942, a new source of trouble for Churchill emerged. Following his resignation from the government, Beaverbrook had determined to present himself as the champion of Russia. The Soviet Union, which was making enormous military sacrifices, was hugely popular in Britain, and a press cult had developed around its personable and intelligent ambassador, Ivan Maisky.[29] Beaverbrook skilfully exploited this atmosphere; in March he used the *Evening Standard* and the *Daily Express* to stoke up demands for British military action to relieve the USSR. The campaign for the Second Front, as it was to be known, made some strange bedfellows. A rally in Trafalgar Square attended by 40,000 people was addressed by both *Sunday Express* editor John Gordon and a communist speaker, Ted Bramley.[30] Mass-Observation noted that at a meeting arranged by the *Daily*

Express, there were no speakers against a Second Front among the whole audience: 'The nearest that there was to any opposition was from a religious fanatic, who shouted from the gallery that "you are all drinking too much intoxicating spirit." '[31]

In May, a pseudonymous writer penned a series of articles in *Tribune*. These further ramped up the Second Front fever, criticizing Churchill and the 'Churchillised Press' in the process. The author was in fact Frank Owen, who, until his recent call-up, had been editor of the *Standard* and who was writing with Beaverbrook's knowledge.[32] Churchill, for his part, believed with reason that to attempt an invasion of Europe in the near future would be desperately premature. As he needed to persuade the Americans of this, Beaverbrook's machinations were wholly unhelpful. It was rumoured that he thought Churchill's number was up and that his departure was only a matter of time.[33] Privately, Beaverbrook stressed his complete loyalty to his friend, while ominously remarking 'I hope nothing will ever force me to take a different view.' He even said that he himself might be the best man to run the war.[34]

In June, Churchill made a further journey to Washington, fuelling British and US press and radio speculation that his talks with Roosevelt concerned the Second Front. The fall of the Libyan city of Tobruk, which occurred during his trip, was a heavy blow and a shock. Churchill's military assistant Hastings Ismay recalled that the news came in a telegram which Roosevelt read and silently handed to the Prime Minister. It was the first time Ismay had seen Churchill wince. As he recalled: 'The British and American newspapers were filled with stories of our crushing defeat and criticisms of the Prime Minister. The American papers carried banner headlines. 'CHURCHILL FACES STORMY SESSION WHEN HOUSE CONVENES'; 'BRITISH IRE IS HIGH. CHURCHILL UNDER FIRE'.[35] Nevertheless, Churchill's visit was a diplomatic success, in that he secured American agreement for landings in North Africa rather than Europe. After returning home, he defeated a vote of no confidence in the Commons by an overwhelming margin. In August—the month the ban on the *Daily Worker* was lifted—he travelled to Moscow.

En route, he cabled his colleagues, arguing that damage was being done to Anglo-Soviet relations by press articles urging a Second Front. 'We cannot allow an unbridled agitation to disturb the country', he wrote. 'Cabinet should consider seriously the Beaverbrook agitation through the "Daily Express" meetings. We cannot have vehement speculation and controversy about potential forthcoming operations.'[36]

When Churchill met Stalin he had to break the unwelcome news that there would be no Second Front in Europe in 1942. The discussions were fraught, but the two men did achieve a rapport of kinds. When they discussed Operation Torch—the planned North African invasion—the following exchange occurred:

> M. Stalin hoped that nothing about it would appear in the British Press.
>
> The Prime Minister replied that he wished he could control the British press as M. Stalin controlled the Soviet press.
>
> M. Stalin said that Mr. Churchill had quite enough powers to exercise control whenever he wished to.[37]

Arguably, Stalin was right. Churchill generally lacked the ability to suppress political opinion or artistic expression—he notably failed in his efforts to halt production of *The Life and Death of Colonel Blimp*, a mildly satirical film based on David Low's pompous and reactionary cartoon character. But he did have considerable power to prevent publication of information-based stories on national security grounds.[38] Indeed, the point had been proved the month prior to his Moscow trip, after officials had invited journalists to examine and photograph new anti-aircraft equipment known as 'Z' batteries. As the Red Army was using a similar weapon, it was judged that the Nazis were already aware of the technology. However, before the information itself was actually published, the *Daily Mail* ran an article explaining that they and other papers were in possession of it and asking if it should really be disclosed. It was headlined 'But WHY Tell the Germans?'[39] Churchill read the piece, agreed, and gave an order that the matter was to be kept secret. In the *Daily Express* office there was consternation, 'all arising out of the [...] almost lunatic-asylum like atmosphere' that prevailed in the newsrooms of popular papers whenever something unusual occurred.[40] The problems were worse for the *Daily Mirror* which had already printed papers that contained the story. If a new edition was made, trains for Ireland and Scotland would be missed. The Air Ministry stepped in and the RAF flew the reprinted papers to their destinations. Churchill might have objected had he known that his nemesis, the *Mirror*, was being helped in this way, but the paper's Irish and Scottish readers got their daily fix on time the next day.[41]

In the run-up to Torch, Churchill worried about the dangers of press articles prognosticating about future operations—speculation which it was naturally very tempting to print when hard information needed to be kept secret. Admiral G. P. Thomson, as Chief Censor, asked for a letter to be sent to editors asking them not to publish such pieces. (Retired Major-General J. F. C. 'Boney' Fuller, who wrote for the *Sunday Pictorial*, told Thomson: 'For weeks and weeks I have been writing that the Allies ought to make a landing in North Africa. If I suddenly stop now, what are the Germans going to think?')[42] Churchill was particularly exercised by the telegrams of the British United Press news agency, which he appears to have read carefully. In the 1930s, BUP had been suspected of being a front for the United Press of America, but Churchill's doubts went even further.[43] 'It is very easy for the Germans to introduce traitors and agents in our midst. The British United Press personnel and control should be subjected to considerable scrutiny.'[44]

From this point in the war onwards, however, Churchill's problems with the press—although not necessarily his anxieties about it—lessened considerably. The news of his meeting with Stalin, coming on top of an earlier announcement that the British, Soviet, and American governments had reached 'full understanding' on the question of a Second Front in 1942, had taken the wind out of the sails of those campaigning for a European invasion.[45] 'The Daily Express states emphatically that Mr. Churchill's conduct of the war does not deserve criticism', declared that paper in September.[46] In the *News Chronicle* in October, A. J. Cummings noted that it seemed from Churchill's and Roosevelt's public statements that a major offensive was imminent. 'At such a moment it is futile to continue to expound the true and blessed gospel of the Second Front, as so many correspondents vehemently urge me to do.'[47] At around the same time, Cecil King recorded a discussion of future *Daily Mirror* and *Sunday Pictorial* policy, which reached the conclusion that 'criticism is now futile and merely boring. The war no longer rouses interest and therefore the only possible line— until things start moving—is great preoccupation with the young, both in services and factories'.[48]

It was military success, though, that did most to calm the press criticism that so infuriated the Prime Minister. In early November, the successful 'Torch' landings coincided with the second battle of El Alamein. News from the desert fighting played out in headlines in papers from across the spectrum:

ROMMEL IN FULL RETREAT (*Financial Times*, 5 November)

EIGHTH ARMY SWEEPS ON, BLASTS AXIS ON COAST ROAD (*Daily Worker*, 6 November)

WE TRAP 3 WOP DIVNS (*Daily Mirror*, 7 November)

'ALAMEIN A COMPLETE VICTORY' (*Daily Telegraph*, 7 November)

Simultaneously, readers could learn about the ongoing battering that the Germans were taking at Stalingrad. Churchill was now able to state publicly that he had told the Soviets in the summer that he could not promise landings in Europe before the end of the year, but that by issuing the communiqué that said that agreement on a Second Front had been reached it had been possible to fool the Germans into thinking otherwise.[49] The *Mirror* hailed this Commons speech as 'a compound of good cheer and detailed information of our recent successes'.[50] The *Manchester Guardian* described Churchill as not 'jolly' but 'blithe', and pointed out that not even former critics had scoffed when he announced that church bells were to be rung in honour of the victory.[51] In the

Daily Mail, the cartoonist Illingworth portrayed Churchill as a colossus bestriding the battlefield.[52] At the start of December, the *Yorkshire Post* gave a vivid description of Churchill on a visit to Bradford, 'in a long, blue greatcoat, muffler, and black Sandringham hat (which on one occasion he twirled gaily on the silvered head of his cane), smoking a cigar, and wearing the air of a bulldog who has cleared the field of all rivals'.[53]

Yet Churchill's press problems did not simply evaporate. The triumph at El Alamein was quickly followed by the publication of Sir William Beveridge's report into social services, a blueprint for the post-war future that was highly popular with the public. The Ministry of Information initially leapt upon it as a means of boosting home morale, aided by the press and by Beveridge's skills as a publicist.[54] The plan also had global propaganda value as evidence of British optimism and forward thinking. (It provoked interest as far away as China.[55]) On the other hand, it caused a political headache for Churchill, who feared raising 'false hopes and airy visions of Utopia and Eldorado' and who felt that discussion of reconstruction issues in general was a distraction from the war effort.[56] Subsequent efforts to clamp down on official publicity—notably by withdrawing an Army Bureau of Current Affairs pamphlet about the plan—were inevitably ineffective in the face of the huge press interest that had already been stoked up.[57] Ironically, Churchill was losing control of the domestic agenda just at the moment earlier newspaper attacks on his military leadership appeared to have been refuted by events.

This is not to say that criticism with respect to his conduct of the war had simply evaporated. After the North African landings, Churchill was immediately confronted by the problem of Admiral François Darlan, who at one stage ousted the Beveridge Report as the top question of popular discussion.[58] As the Pathé newsreel commentator put it, Darlan was 'a shifty customer who astutely somersaulted out of the pro-Axis camp and landed among his former enemies'.[59] To be more specific, he was a prominent Vichy figure who did a controversial deal with the Americans, agreeing to order a ceasefire in return for being appointed 'High Commissioner for North Africa'. Churchill went along with the bargain reluctantly, and in a secret session of the House of Commons defended the move as a temporary necessity. His old friend Violet Bonham Carter met Clementine at the wedding of Beveridge, who was marrying for the first time at the age of 63. Bonham Carter's son was in the Grenadier Guards; she told Clementine how the soldiers of the regiment had detested news pictures of Darlan saluting a march past that it had performed at Algiers.[60] Hearing this, Clementine entirely lost her temper and nearly spilled a glass of champagne.[61] She said 'the Prime Minister was sore about Darlan but resented having the whole matter kept on the boil like this: the newspapers had published pictures very unnecessarily of this march past, and "that horrid newspaper, the Sunday Pictorial" had gone too far and actually used a sentence, slightly misquoted, from an important speech in the secret debate!'[62]

Yet when Cordell Hull, the US Secretary of State, complained about the British press's criticisms of the Darlan affair, Churchill told Eden to inform him 'that, under our present Constitution and wartime procedure, we have been ceaselessly exposed to the "emotional views of little men on political matters", and to check this entirely would involve His Majesty's Government in a direct attack on the freedom of Parliament and Press'.[63] After Darlan was assassinated on Christmas Eve, and his killer rapidly executed, the whole issue was swept under the carpet. The affair did, however, give rise to rumours that Darlan's death had been orchestrated variously by a) the British, b) the Americans, c) the Germans, d) the Italians, e) the Gaullists, or f) the Russians.[64] The Chinese and the Japanese were apparently above suspicion.

In January 1943, Churchill headed for North Africa himself, and made a rendezvous with Roosevelt at Casablanca. The Prime Minister's movements were a constant source of press and public speculation. If he was away from Parliament at a time when it was thought an overseas visit might be in the offing, the journalistic telegrams might read: 'It was noted that Mr. Eden answered questions on behalf of the

Prime Minister today.' The censors kept a careful watch on this type of hint, but on this occasion the secret was well kept, in spite of a Moroccan radio station broadcasting a message that 'Cigarette and friend have arrived'.[65] On many occasions suspicions among the British public as to Churchill's whereabouts turned out to be substantially correct, but this time the rumours falsely placed him in Washington.[66]

Harry Hopkins's 21-year-old son Robert was summoned by telegram to cover the ten-day conference as a newsreel photographer with the US Army Signal Corps. (Initially, only photographers employed by the military were permitted access to the conference.[67]) When he arrived at Casablanca he knew only of a rumour that 'something big' was going on, and, having negotiated his way past security, was astonished to find his father together with the President. The following day, the younger Hopkins photographed FDR and his staff, followed by Churchill and his staff. 'The day was beautiful and clear and especially suitable for me since I was shooting all my picture in color', he wrote in an article for *Life* magazine shortly afterwards. 'The gold braid and shiny insignia blazed under the African sun.'[68] In advance of a subsequent photoshoot, Churchill remarked to Hopkins *père* that 'he wished the pictures were going to be taken later in the day, because he didn't look his best at twelve o'clock'. He added that he 'could put on a very warlike look whenever he wanted to'.[69] Meanwhile, Churchill was becoming frustrated at the shortage of information he was receiving from home, and the efforts of officials in London to 'pad out the daily news wire' failed to satisfy him with regard to speed and volume.[70]

The climax of the summit was a joint press conference by Churchill and Roosevelt. It took place on the lawn outside the latter's bungalow.[71] Around fifty war correspondents and photographers had flown down from Algiers the day before, and were stunned see the President and the Prime Minister and to learn how long they had already been in Morocco. They were also startled by the presence of the rival French generals de Gaulle and Giraud, who had been driven during the conference into an uneasy rapprochement. In his memoirs, Churchill recalled that he and Roosevelt had 'forced' the two men to shake hands in front of the reporters and cameramen.[72] Newsreel outtakes show Roosevelt obliging them to repeat the exercise for the benefit of those who missed the shot.[73] 'The picture which the photographer obtained may be stuff for the historian', wrote Lord Moran. 'He will see the long, stiff-necked de Gaulle gingerly proffering his hand, though his face is without the flicker of a smile. Behind the outstretched arms he will detect the seated President, his head thrown back in hilarious enjoyment of the moment, while Winston sits demurely on the edge of his chair.'[74] Churchill himself thought that it was impossible to look at the image without laughing.[75] The newspapermen were certainly able to deduce that relations between the two Frenchmen were not as cordial as was being made out.[76] After de Gaulle and Giraud departed, Harry Hopkins noted, 'Churchill and the President were left sitting together in the warm African sun—thousands of miles from home—to talk to the correspondents of war and the waging of war. It would be flashed around the world the moment a release date was fixed.'[77]

One notable feature of the press conference was Roosevelt's unexpected demand for the 'unconditional surrender' of the Axis forces. The two men had discussed the idea beforehand but Churchill thought that the idea of making a public announcement about it had been dropped. He was therefore angered to be caught on the hop and feared that the result of the statement might be to prolong the war. In the interests of unity, though, he made no objection; so this became the official policy of the Allies.[78] In his own remarks, Churchill acknowledged that the pressmen in North Africa had had 'a hard, provoking time' because of organizational problems in the aftermath of the invasion. He urged that they not permit 'the minor annoyances of censoring, etc.' to lead them to exaggerate the difficulties: 'To keep your sense of proportion is a patriotic duty.'[79]

Mass-Observation reported that, when the fact that the conference had occurred became public a couple of days later, there was little excitement amongst the British people, 'except for the immediate news interest'.[80] E. Robertson, a middle-aged teacher, noted in her diary how an acquaintance told her of the anticipation caused by a late-night BBC announcement urging listeners to 'Stand by for a momentous piece of news in the 12 o'clock bulletin.' However, the revelation that 'Churchill and Roosevelt had a talk at Casablanca this week' came as an anticlimax. She was glad the next day that she hadn't waited up:'Of course they will have to have conferences, but why such a hell of a fuss.'[81] Edith Lea, also a teacher, noted:'Headlines reporting the Casablanca meeting roused a spark of interest—no more. My landlady—"Where's Morocco—in Russia?" Nobody at school seemed interested, though the Head was delighted because his prophecies were fulfilled—he had been wondering for many days if Churchill was out of the country.'[82] On the other hand, there were those who considered the meeting 'momentous'.[83] G. South, a secretary, considered it 'Big News' but wondered why no Russian representative had been present and felt 'very uneasy' about the Giraud/de Gaulle position. The next day she continued to speculate anxiously: 'Accounts of the conference first item in Moscow news broadcast, but NO COMMENTS made. How inscrutable they are.'[84] The absence of Russian (and Chinese) delegates also provoked some concern in the United States, where the conference was the biggest news of the week. It provoked 'virtually no carping even from isolationists' but there was an undercurrent of disappointment about the lack of 'any obvious concrete results'.[85]

Churchill made a further tour (including visits to Turkey and Cyprus) before returning home. According to Home Intelligence, the public was delighted by the news of his travels, which boosted his popularity as well as causing concern for his safety: 'His aerial trips excite considerable anxiety.'[86] Not long after Churchill got back to the UK, he fell victim to pneumonia. With characteristic contempt for the truth, German radio claimed that his illness was a diplomatic ploy, undertaken so that he could avoid having to celebrate Red Army Day.[87]

In Britain there was widespread concern that Churchill had 'worn himself out on our behalf'.[88] Although some feared that the true seriousness of his illness was being covered up, he exercised his remarkable powers of recovery. Roosevelt, who had also been unwell, cabled him: 'Tell Mrs. Churchill that when I was laid up I was a thoroughly model patient and that I hope you will live down the reputation in our Press of having been the "world's worst patient." '[89]

For the next few months, Fleet Street was, to use Churchill's own term, quiescent.[90] There were some minor annoyances, from his point of view, such as some newspapers' tendency to pay excess tribute to the chivalry of Rommel's troops.[91] There was also, however, a more serious headache, arising from a bitter row between the Soviet Union and the Polish government-in-exile led by General Władysław Sikorski. In April, the Nazis revealed to the world their discovery in the Katyn Forest of mass graves containing the bodies of Polish officers massacred by the Soviets three years earlier. When the Poles urged an investigation by the Red Cross, Stalin broke off diplomatic links with them. Churchill claimed to Ambassador Maisky that he did not believe the German allegations, but Maisky rightly suspected him of entertaining 'mental reservations'.[92] Churchill's real concern was to prevent the affair damaging Anglo-Soviet relations, which he believed the Polish press in Britain was putting at risk. He fulminated to the Cabinet that 'no Government which had accepted our hospitality had any right to publish articles of a character which conflicted with the general policy of the United Nations and which would create difficulties for this Government'. Bracken, as Minister of Information, was delegated 'to ask the British Press not to canvass the Russo-Polish quarrel or to take sides in it', although the Soviets were unlikely to be satisfied with mere neutrality.[93]

'The Cabinet here is determined to have proper discipline in the Polish Press in Great Britain', Churchill told Stalin. 'Even miserable rags attacking Sikorski can say things which the German broadcast repeats open-mouthed to the world to our joint detriment. This must be stopped and it will be stopped.'[94] Yet in practice, it was little easier to control Polish papers than British ones. There were at least thirty-nine of the former, some of them private newsletters, and even the threat of withholding paper supplies was considered unlikely to be effective, as even in wartime paper could always be got hold of somehow. The Polish press did in fact show a degree of self-restraint, perhaps not wanting to test the limits of the government's powers.[95] Meanwhile, the *Daily Worker* presented the whole affair as a Nazi–Polish conspiracy and deplored the vague official line that the whole situation was regrettable: 'the British authorities are continuing to try to maintain just the attitude they have maintained throughout the whole period of rising Fascist, anti-Soviet, anti-Semitic agitation by the Polish Junkers here. They "regret"—but they give them the paper for a dozen periodicals to carry on the agitation.'[96] Churchill suspected Maisky had had a hand in this criticism, and suggested warning the *Daily Worker* 'that if it does not lay-off mischief-making it will be suppressed again'.[97] However, ministers concluded that this would be 'inexpedient'.[98] As usual, the Prime Minister's bark was worse than the Cabinet's bite.[99]

In May, Churchill made a further visit to America. The British Embassy noted: 'The isolationist press has joined in the general welcome of Mr. Churchill along its usual line deploring that no such patriot was in power in America.'[100] The trip, was highly successful, although among the British public it was 'outshone [...] by the North African news'.[101] People were now 'getting used' to these types of journey so there was less surprise and comment than on previous occasions.[102] As well as giving a speech to Congress and a joint press conference with Roosevelt, Churchill gave a briefing at the British Embassy to thirty Empire correspondents. Don Iddon of the *Daily Mail* provided his readers with a rapturous description of Churchill's demeanour and capacity to mesmerize. 'His manner was most gracious, without the slightest trace of arrogance. He did not talk down to us or at us, and once when a young correspondent asked a somewhat stupid question and then flushed with embarrassment, the Prime Minister, noticing his discomfiture, put him at ease by a light, easy reply.'[103] Although the actual substance of what he said was off the record, we know from the diary of Lord Halifax (who was now

Ambassador to Washington) that Churchill developed the theme of 'fraternal association' between Britain and the USA. According to Halifax, Churchill told the journalists he had had the idea in his bath that morning, 'which wasn't strictly true, because he had given it to me last night!'[104] Again, it seemed that Churchill was considerably more relaxed with journalists when abroad than he was at home.

The Allied invasion of Italy in July raised the spirits of a rather 'bored and apathetic' public that had to some degree lost interest in the progress of the war. Many people exulted at the news of the landings in Sicily: 'The war has begun at last—what a thrill!'[105] The bombing of Rome caused surprise and delight.[106] Addressing the Commons, however, Churchill was careful not to appear jubilant. 'On the contrary, he seemed at times almost lugubrious', according to A. J. Cummings, 'and he was as cautious in assessing the course of events in Italy as the newspaper photographs on the same day showed him to be in feeding a large though unaggressive-looking lion at the Zoo'.[107] Mussolini's dismissal by the Fascist Grand Council was accompanied by some minor embarrassment for Churchill, when *Tribune* ferreted out the fulsome praise of the Duce that he had offered on his 1927 visit to Italy; the *New Leader* also reproduced the comments. H. G. Wells, assuming that the remarks had been faked, wrote to warn Churchill that he was being traduced. A private secretary, John Peck, replied, confirming that the remarks were genuine, and helpfully enclosing the original clipping from *The Times* to prove it.[108]

In August, Churchill returned once more to North America, meeting Roosevelt for a strategy meeting in Quebec. On the way he made a visit to Niagara Falls. When a journalist asked if they had changed since his first visit in 1900, he replied: 'Well, the principle remains the same. The water still keeps falling over.'[109] Clementine and their daughter Mary were with him on the trip. In general, Clementine was a significant public relations asset, particularly in connection with her work as head of the Aid to Russia Fund.[110] However, this particular journey caused a certain amount of resentment at home, because it was felt that she and Mary were enjoying a vacation when ordinary people were being asked not to go on holiday.[111] Overall, the visit was warmly welcomed by the British public, qualified by 'anxiety about the seeming lack of co-operation between Russia and the other Allied Nations', as once more there was no Soviet representative.[112]

Churchill's arrival was front page news in all the Canadian papers, whether French or English language, but there were few official conference statements for the leader-writers to get their teeth into.[113] (A key decision, necessarily secret, was the setting of the target date of 1 May 1944 for Operation Overlord, the planned invasion of Northern France.) He made a triumphal public tour while the journalists tagged along in hastily hired cabs. In the words of Don Iddon, 'Here we saw Churchill—worried about the Italian invasion, preoccupied with relations with Russia—emerge as a great showman, smiling and waving to cheering French-Canadians, shaking their outstretched hands as his car stopped, ordering security agents away, putting on a bigtime performance for the people.'[114] After the conference concluded, Churchill travelled on to Washington, where on 4 September he attended a lunch organized jointly by the National Press Club, the White House Correspondents Association, the Gridiron Club, the National Women's Press Club, the Standing Press Committees of Congress, and the Overseas Writers Club. Churchill, introduced to his admiring audience as a fellow-journalist, 'did awfully well in reply to questions'. [115] The only glitch involved a microphone placed in front of him that was 'turned on during the luncheon so that only strange sounds, clearly traceable to Mr. Churchill, emanated therefrom'.[116] At a press event on the roof of the Citadel in Quebec he had seemed 'gloomy and morose', sitting 'slumped in his chair, apologising for the lack of hard news'. Now, however, he seemed like 'a giant refreshed'.[117]

Churchill also gave a speech at Harvard University at which he rehearsed his notion of 'fraternal association' between Britain and the USA, and speculated that one day the two countries might share a common citizenship.[118] In spite of a number of mishaps which diminished the coverage, including a sensational train wreck which monopolized the headlines, the speech received extensive treatment in the

American press.[119] His theme was by no means uncontroversial, as it touched on the sensitivities of isolationists, and could also be seen as an attempt to shape debate in advance of the 1944 presidential election. This probably helps explain why he took so much interest in the speech's reception, asking for 'a tabular report of all important American newspapers to my Harvard statement, showing which are for and which against'.[120] A picturesque response came from the New York *Daily News*, which portrayed Churchill's speech as a matchmaking exercise whereby Britain, cast as a poverty-stricken blue-blooded aristocrat, sought the hand of 'Miss Columbia, heiress of the Western world'. The *News*, having reflected on the British inability to make good coffee, the lack of central heating, 'and the prevalence of warm beer', advised the young lady to remain friends with Britain, 'but nothing more'.[121]

Rome radio presented the Harvard address as proposing a world based 'on domination by the Anglo-Saxon countries through a controlled, super League of Nations'.[122] This, in fact, was broadcast on the very day that Italy herself surrendered. Churchill instructed: 'Films should be taken if possible of surrender of Italian Fleet, their courteous reception by the British and kindly treatment of wounded, etc.'[123] However, hopes of a quick victory evaporated, as the Germans reacted speedily to disarm Italian troops and to prevent the Allies capitalizing; Mussolini was rescued from captivity and established as the leader of a puppet state in the north. It was against this backdrop that Churchill conferred with Roosevelt and Stalin at Tehran in November, the first meeting of the 'Big Three'. Whereas Churchill wanted to press on in the Mediterranean, even at the possible cost of delaying Overlord, the Soviets and the Americans were united in prioritizing the invasion of France. In spite of Churchill's aspirations for Anglo-American unity, Roosevelt and Stalin ganged up together to needle him. Publicly, however, Churchill's presentation to Stalin of the Sword of Stalingrad—a gift from George VI—provided the opportunity for a 'Photographic orgy'. Off camera, the sword slipped out of its scabbard and the pommel hit Marshal Voroshilov on the toe.[124]

The mere fact of the meeting was reassuring to the British public. Because people had got so used to Churchill travelling to conferences they were no longer regarded as anything out of the ordinary, but Stalin's presence led to special enthusiasm.[125] One RAF Corporal noted in his diary: 'Even discounting all the "flannel" given in the Press accounts, it does seem that the conference was a success, and that Allied unity is rather more of a reality than it was a month or two ago.'[126] Another diarist, a schoolmistress, more cynically reflected that 'it wouldn't be surprising if Stalin were reluctant to meet the rabid anti Bolshevist, Churchill, or Churchill to meet Comrade Murderer Stalin. It's amusing to find them at one on all points!'[127]

Before he returned to Britain, Churchill again fell seriously ill with pneumonia, and was obliged to spend a lengthy period of recuperation in a villa near Carthage. He was sick for five days before the public was informed.[128] On 17 December, the story spread in Washington that he had died; Harry Hopkins rang up Lord Halifax to find out if it was correct. Halifax wrote in his diary: 'I felt pretty sure that this was not likely to be true but was none the less relieved when the BBC gave a good report in the evening.'[129] American newspaper offices were swamped with enquiries about Churchill's health, and even the *Times Herald*, an 'isolationist' paper, offered a prayer for his recovery.[130]

People in Fleet Street started discussing potential successors.[131] According to Cecil King, 'The political reaction was first: "What if he dies?" and the reflection that this is the worst possible moment for a change in leadership. The second and more realistic reaction is: "Assuming he recovers from his second attack of pneumonia in ten months, it will be clear to all that his days as Prime Minister are numbered, or at least that his days as sole political and military dictator are over. Who will now share his throne?"[132] Lord Moran had initially kept out of his bulletins the fact that Churchill's heart had been troubling him but, as the patient improved, he allowed the public to know that there had been 'some irregularity of the pulse'. He saw it as his job to manage expectations of Churchill's recovery.[133] 'Widespread anxiety and sympathy followed the report of Mr. Churchill's illness, which put all other topics in the background', noted Home Intelligence. Moreover: 'Bulletins were eagerly awaited and the later news brought profound relief.'[134]

On 18 January 1944, with his convalescence complete, Churchill surprised MPs by making a dramatic reappearance in the House of Commons. At the same time, the outward harmony of the Tehran meeting was belied by the publication in *Pravda* of a rumour that the British had secretly held discussions with the Nazis about possible peace terms. This claim—also relayed by Moscow radio—was certainly untrue but the Soviets may have been seeking a stick with which to beat the British, in response to what they saw as unwarranted interference in their dispute with the Poles.[135] Churchill remonstrated over the affair with Stalin, who responded that 'there is no ground to contest the right of a newspaper to publish reports of rumours received from trustworthy newspaper correspondents. We ourselves at least have never laid claim to interference of such kind in the affairs of the British press, although we have had and still have incomparably more serious cause to do so.'[136] In fact, not long after this, Stalin did protest that the contents of one of his letters to Churchill had appeared, in distorted form, in British newspapers.[137] The British government believed that, although the Poles were responsible for some leaks, this particular one had actually come from the Soviet Embassy; the full truth of the matter is unclear.[138]

Meanwhile, Churchill's anxieties about press control were heightened by what he perceived as alarmist and defeatist reports about the Italian campaign, where the attempt to outflank the Germans by making an amphibious landing at Anzio quickly got bogged down.[139] He particularly objected to a report by NBC's Algiers correspondent, who had telegraphed 'There is no chance now to disguise the truth that in this sector (Anzio) the struggle is desperate.' In Churchill's words, 'The word "desperate" was being taken in this country as a headline and it in no way represented the truth.' But when he asked the military authorities to subject reporters in Algiers to tougher censorship, they overreacted by denying broadcasting facilities to accredited journalists at the front.[140] Complaints were raised that reports were now being censored on policy grounds rather than on the basis of security concerns; this was described by the *Daily Mail* as an intolerable interference with press freedom.[141] The radio facilities were restored but, while absolving the correspondents at the bridgehead from blame, Churchill justified his action with reference to his own experience as a journalist. To MPs' cheers, he remarked: 'I should not have been allowed in South Africa, where I was a war correspondent for some time, to say, for instance, that the position inside Ladysmith was desperate.'[142]

If he was thus influenced by a somewhat Victorian conception of government–press relations, Churchill's immediate concern may have been the impact of negative coverage on American views of the Italian campaign. This was a time, of course, when he was also worried about the possibility of security leaks in the run-up to Overlord; for the censors, 1944 was the toughest and busiest year of the war.[143] Steven Casey has noted that Dwight Eisenhower, as Supreme Commander of the Allied Expeditionary Forces in Europe, understood that there was a fine line between controlling reporters' activities and upsetting them. By contrast, 'Churchill emphasized the suppression of all information.'[144] The Prime Minister was particularly exercised by the activities of Captain Basil Liddell Hart, who wrote for the *Daily Mail* and *Sunday Express*. Before 1939, Liddell Hart had been an influential military commentator, and he and Churchill had shared an interest in civil liberties issues.[145] Liddell Hart's star had dimmed early on in the war due to his urgings of a compromise peace.[146] Nevertheless, he remained well connected, and spoke to a range of British and American military figures in the run-up to D-Day. In conversation with Churchill's son-in-law, Duncan Sandys, he revealed that he had knowledge of the details of Overlord.[147] MI5 launched an investigation but, despite opening Liddell Hart's mail and bugging his phone, could not find conclusive proof of where his information came from, although it seemed certain he knew the location of planned landing areas in Normandy. Churchill instructed that Liddell Hart be prosecuted on the grounds that this would 'induce him to take "more care", even though the proceedings ultimately are unsuccessful'. But the Director of Public Prosecutions opposed this idea, which went no further.[148] As Liddell Hart did not misuse the knowledge he had uncovered, the episode was soon forgotten, but it did show how journalistic persistence could ferret out even the deepest secrets.

By this point, the public was waiting expectantly for the launch of the Second Front. For several hours during the night of 5–6 June, the continuous sound of aeroplanes was heard. At 8 a.m. the BBC quoted German reports that the invasion had started. At 10 a.m. this was confirmed in a broadcast by General Dwight D. Eisenhower, Supreme Commander of the Allied Expeditionary Forces in Europe. People's emotions were mixed, ranging from excitement to fear for loved ones; above all, perhaps, there was tension and desire for news. In the Commons, Churchill announced both the liberation of Rome two days previously and the fact that the landings in Normandy had begun. Outside Parliament, one newspaper vendor observed: 'We'll know more about it in a week or two. Churchill only told them in there that it 'ad started. That's all 'e said.' Over the next few days, there was continued anxiety over the outcome, together with a fair amount of cautious optimism. 'It's going well—well but slowly', commented one 55-year-old man. 'Churchill's quite right when he says it won't be finished in a rush.'[149]

Morale received a setback, however, when the Germans launched flying bombs (known as V-1s) at Britain. This occurred for the first time on 12–13 June. News about the attacks had to be carefully censored, as revelations about where and when the weapons had fallen could help the Germans with range-finding. Attacks, therefore, were initially described merely as occurring in 'Southern England'. However, evacuees spread the impression that 'it's sheer hell in London'. It was not until 6 July that Churchill made a statement on the issue in the Commons, but this was effective in quelling rumours and putting the attacks in perspective.[150] As Admiral Thomson recalled, 'This speech made things much easier for the censors, for the fact that the flying bombs were landing in London was no longer banned from the newspapers.'[151] A British Pathé newsreel film, which described 'robot warfare on the Capital', showed the Prime Minister inspecting damage. The narrator intoned: 'Mr Churchill gleans first-hand information for his speech in the House, when he told the nation that the phrase "Southern England" passes out of currency. *London*, eighteen miles wide and twenty miles deep, is the target for the weapons from across the Channel.'[152]

The V-1 issue was the last great wartime crisis of morale. Churchill still, however, faced the challenge of damping popular expectations that the war was almost over. In September, there was a repeat of the previous year's Quebec conference, which to the British public now seemed almost routine.[153] Indeed, when Churchill travelled to Moscow in October there was resentment at the amount of travelling that Britain's allies seemed to expect him to do. According to MoI, there was 'comment to the effect that Mr. Churchill always has to do the running about and that it is high time "the others came here"—as the Prime Minister's many journeys involve a risk both to his health and to British prestige.'[154] The meeting saw continued wrangling over Poland. Eden sent 'Wild telegrams' back to the Foreign Office, urging the Permanent Secretary 'to damp down [the] British, *and* Polish, Press!'[155] It was also the occasion of the notorious 'percentages agreement', via which Churchill believed he had secured Stalin's consent for the division of the Balkans into British and Soviet spheres of influence. Prior to a banquet in his honour at the Kremlin, he gave an off-the-record briefing to British, American, and Russian journalists. This was fairly clearly the basis of the *Times* correspondent's report that 'Very real and sensible results were achieved in the coordination of the policy of the two Governments in the Balkan region'.[156] What, if anything, Stalin had really agreed is open to debate.[157] It is striking, though, that the Soviet press reported that the two men had reached genuine unanimity over Rumania, Bulgaria, Yugoslavia, Hungary, and Greece, and warmly welcomed the 'disappearance of the Balkan powderkeg' from the European scene.[158]

Churchill's belief that Greece now fell within the British sphere of influence affected his approach to the crisis that blew up there at the end of the year. As German troops withdrew from the country, the British occupied it, but the EAM/ELAS resistance movement, which was dominated by communists, held on to its weapons.[159] The returning government-in-exile struggled to establish control, and early in December British soldiers in Athens failed to act when ten unarmed EAM demonstrators were shot dead by Greek police. Churchill instructed the local British commander, General Sir Ronald Scobie, to 'act as if you were in a conquered city where a local rebellion is in progress'.[160] The substance of this cable rapidly found its way, probably via the US ambassador to Italy, into the hands of the American columnist Drew Pearson, who did not hesitate to publish. Churchill regarded Pearson as 'a most bitter foe' of Britain.[161] In Washington, the British Embassy's opinion summary noted that it was now open season against the UK's *realpolitik* foreign policy, which was regarded by many commentators as reactionary. According to the Chicago *Tribune*, Churchill had felt emboldened to act because 'he was authorized to do so in a deal with Stalin for the division of Europe into spheres of influence'.[162] Some papers, such as the *New York Times*, offered qualified support of Britain's position. But ironically, noted the embassy, 'Our strongest press allies have been Hearst papers which acclaim Mr. Churchill as [the] long-wanted champion of humanity against the advance of the red menace.'[163]

Churchill's actions were also highly controversial in Britain, particularly on the Left, but by no means exclusively so.[164] Indeed, with the exception of the *Daily Telegraph*, the initial press reaction was hostile across the board. A. J. Foster has commented on 'the universal assumption on the press's part of Churchill's very personal responsibility for all the major decisions over Greece', which was connected to the belief that he wanted to restore the Greek monarchy, 'swayed in part by his romantic attachment to the idea of monarchy as such'. Churchill, however, succeeded in weathering the storm; during a swift pre-Christmas visit to Athens, he conceded that the King should not yet return to Greece, pending a referendum on his future.[165] In a Commons speech in mid-January 1945, Churchill made an astute defence of his position, dwelling on atrocities committed by ELAS. He also lambasted the press, protesting at the 'melancholy exhibition' put on 'by some of our most time-honoured and responsible journals'.[166] This was a reference to *The Times*, which had been highly critical. According to the Labour MP Chuter Ede, 'His denunciation of the language and attitude of The Times evoked the longest cheer I have ever heard in the course of a speech in the Commons. There could be no doubt the Tories deeply resented the policy pursued by *The Times* on Greece.'[167]

The February meeting of the Big Three at Yalta, though its outcome provoked a minor Conservative rebellion because of the alleged sell-out of the Poles, was far less problematic in terms of the press and public response. Roosevelt, who had just won a fourth presidential term, was seriously and observably ill, but nonetheless put on a decent show for the cameras.[168] One young man noted in his diary that he couldn't help laughing at the pictures of him with the other leaders: 'Churchill, especially, with his Russian fur cap and cigar, cuts a comic figure. I said to my landlady, "They look like three music-hall comedians." She said, "That's a fact. There's nothing inspiring about them."' However, the diarist thought that their joint declaration seemed 'very promising', a view that others seem to have shared.[169] Roosevelt's death, announced in the newspapers on 13 April, came as a shock to many, some of whom regarded him almost as a personal friend.[170]

When Churchill woke on 7 May, Captain Richard Pim, the naval officer in charge of his map room, told him that the Germans had surrendered. 'For five years you've brought me bad news, sometimes worse than others', Churchill remarked. 'Now you have redeemed yourself.'[171] By this point, the public had become tired of repeated announcements, which were then contradicted, that peace was at hand. 'Churchill had said previously that he wouldn't hold up the news for a minute,' grumbled one Mass-Observer, 'and yet here were the papers with definite statements that the war in Europe was over—and articles giving the highlights of the war—and no word from him.' Such frustrations were forgotten when he broadcast at 3 p.m. the following day, VE Day. Crowds in Whitehall, listening to the speech on specially erected loudspeakers, hung on his every word. There were whoops of joy and the waving of flags and hats at the moment in his speech when he declared that the German war was at an end.[172]

In the aftermath of the European victory, Labour and the Liberals withdrew from the Coalition; Churchill formed a new caretaker government which was to run the country until the upcoming general election. On 4 June, he launched the campaign with a broadcast in which he made the notorious claim that, if elected, a Labour government would have to 'to fall back on some form of Gestapo, no doubt very humanely directed in the first instance'.[173] This, like all the other election broadcasts that year, was recorded and retransmitted at four different times the following day via short-wave, in order that overseas servicemen would have exactly the same opportunities to listen as voters at home.[174] All speakers were asked to provide the BBC with advance copies of their scripts, but the Corporation carefully checked the recordings too. 'The value of this precaution was proved when an enquiry was received from No. 10 Downing Street as to what had actually been said in a very contentious passage in the Prime Minister's speech of 30th June.'[175] This was probably a reference to Churchill's claim that socialist ministers might be obliged to disclose state secrets to the Labour Party's National Executive Committee, which he portrayed as a sinister and undemocratic body.[176]

Churchill's decision to focus on the arguably rather obscure issue of Labour's constitution may seem surprising. But he had been handed a weapon by Professor Harold Laski, a well-known socialist intellectual who happened to hold the rotating NEC chairmanship in this particular year. Out of courtesy, Churchill had extended an invitation to Attlee, as Labour leader, to attend the Potsdam meeting with Stalin and President Truman, which would begin after polling day but before the election results were announced. Laski put out a press statement which said that the Labour Party could not be committed to any decisions taken at the conference, as it would be discussing matters that the NEC and the Parliamentary Labour Party had not yet debated. Laski was much less important than he thought he was or than the Tory press professed to believe; but his action gave Churchill the chance to paint him as Attlee's puppet-master.[177] The battle was fought out to a great extent in letters between Attlee and Churchill published in the press. On one occasion Churchill released his text shortly before 11.30 p.m., apparently to ensure that his opponent's reply could not be published alongside the next day.[178]

Beaverbrook (who had returned to government in the autumn of 1943) lent his papers' full-throated support. Although he had been falsely blamed for the 'Gestapo' speech, he was indeed a major figure in the campaign, which he thought should concentrate on exploiting Churchill's personal popularity with the public.[179] Albert Hird noted: 'We at the D.E. [*Daily Express*] are apparently to take the same (or even a more prominent) part in this election as the Mail in old Rothermere's time did after the last war, for we are taking on extra reporters to cope with the work—a quite unnecessary thing if we were merely playing the part of an ordinary newspaper.'[180] Moreover: 'The Beaver is having a great time. He is stumping up and down the country and most of the opposition credits him with being the real leader of the Tory party and the evil (that's what they call it) genius behind Churchill. All of which he finds entirely to his liking.'[181]

The support of the *Daily Mail* was somewhat less ardent than that of the *Express*, but Churchill could also depend on the backing of the organs owned by Lords Camrose and Kemsley.[182] The latter had just been elevated from a mere baron to a viscount, having pledged to throw his papers' weight behind Churchill in the campaign.[183] However, in contrast to previous contests, Labour now had truly substantial press support too. The authors of the Nuffield election study gauged that pro-Labour London-based papers between them had six million readers, and Tory ones 6,800,000; *The Times*, for its part, 'was peculiarly detached about the election'.[184] Churchill, who obtained much coverage for his apparently triumphal national election tour, himself published one newspaper article during the final days of the campaign.

This was in the *News of the World*, and he sought to explode the popular notion that people could vote Labour and nonetheless somehow retain him as Prime Minister.[185] There were many factors that contributed to the election result, and this false belief may have been one of them. The most important, however, was Churchill's inability to find a compelling message to counter the themes of modernity and hope put forward by an ideologically astute and media canny Labour Party.[186] Churchill's newsreel election pitch—which may have been seen by as many as twenty million people—revealed, if nothing else, his sheer physical exhaustion.[187] Attlee's much snappier effort was no rhetorical masterpiece, but it demonstrated the no-nonsense competence of a man who had long been overshadowed by rivals within his party.[188]

The hiatus between the polling and the results was due to the need for time to count the votes of those serving abroad. Churchill and Attlee returned from Potsdam prior to the declaration of the outcome on 26 July. At 10 a.m. that day, Captain Pim brought Churchill the first results: 'I think the first ten [constituencies] were Labour. The Prime Minister was in his bath and certainly appeared surprised if not shocked. He asked me to get him a towel and in a few minutes, clad in his blue siren suit and with a cigar, he sat in his chair in the map room where he remained all day.'[189] By one o'clock it was clear that the Conservatives had lost; in fact, there was a Labour landslide. That evening, Churchill tendered his resignation to the King and issued a concession statement that was read out on the 9 o'clock news.[190] In America, the news of Churchill's defeat 'was received with a shock of astonishment that was almost reminiscent of the reactions to the Pearl Harbor bombing. Newspapers headlined it as "one of the most portentous events of our times" and the radio commentators naturally squeezed the maximum pathos and drama out of the news.'[191] Downcast though he was, Churchill seems never to have contemplated retiring, but immediately determined to lead the battle against Attlee's new government as Leader of the Opposition. Just two days after his catastrophic defeat, the *Daily Mail* ran the headline 'CHURCHILL DECIDES TO FIGHT BACK'.[192]

8

Whose Finger?

In spite of his determination to hold on to his position as leader of the Conservative Party, Churchill was undoubtedly hit hard by his defeat. A few days after the blow fell, he declined the offer of twenty thousand pounds from *Time* and *Life* magazines for four brief articles, on the grounds that he would have to pay too much tax: 'I'm not going to work when they take nineteen and six out of every pound I earn.'[1] Once some ingenious tax arrangements had been devised, involving the creation of a new trust for the benefit of his descendants, he did spend much of his Opposition period working on his memoirs, yet the new set-up did not cover newspaper articles. This may explain why, in spite of a $1.25 million bid from the *Chicago Sun*, Churchill did not attempt a serious revival of his pre-war journalistic career.[2] From now on, although his writings continued to appear in the press, serializations of the six-volume *Second World War* accounted for the vast majority of this output. Colin Coote, who had by this point left *The Times* for the *Daily Telegraph*, later noted: 'Winston always delivered his first proofs dead on time, for, though not strictly speaking a journalist, he had a journalist's awareness of the supreme importance of punctuality. But there followed only too often massive overtakes and pieces of rewriting which caused a lot of trouble.'[3]

Churchill also stayed in close contact with the *Telegraph*'s proprietor Lord Camrose, who negotiated in America to help him achieve maximum returns for his book. But although Churchill maintained a high level of activity, he also showed a growing tolerance for a slower pace. When he was on holiday in Italy in September 1945, six days passed without the arrival of any newspaper, letter, or telegram. 'If this had happened in the old days, what a terrific uproar Winston would have made!' wrote Lord Moran. 'Telegrams would have been sent off, peremptory orders flashed back, abashed officials would have read, "I will not be treated like this."' Taking solace in his painting, as he had done after Gallipoli decades before, Churchill barely seemed to register the lack of news.[4]

Although his Lake Como sojourn improved his mood, Churchill's leadership that autumn lacked dynamism; the *Sunday Times* political correspondent reported that many Conservative MPs thought that he had 'shown insufficient vigour'.[5] He preferred to leave the day-to-day tasks to Anthony Eden, while he set about reconstructing his reputation on the world stage.[6] Indeed, he was suspected of preferring the US media over the British when he permitted *Life* to print some of his paintings as well as giving it another scoop with the first publication of his wartime secret session speeches.[7] He himself had approached Walter Graebner, area director of *Time* and *Life* in Europe, with these proposals, which were more tax-efficient than writing original articles.[8] Churchill does not seem to have been guilty of purposeful pro-American favouritism, but he appears to have given more thought to money than to appearances. At the same time, though, his continued exploitation of his global celebrity was not merely vainglorious. Rather, his landmark pair of 1946 speeches—the 'iron curtain' in Fulton, Missouri, in March, and 'the United States of Europe' in Zürich in September—were partly about the about the quest for domestic advantage.[9] In other words, he wanted to seize the political initiative in the USA and on the European continent in order to make up for his exclusion from power at home. This would of course require the help of broadcasters and the press; and as usual, when it came to cultivating them, Churchill seemed most at home when he was abroad.

In mid-January 1946, Winston and Clementine arrived in New York on the *Queen Elizabeth*. At 9.30 p.m. they walked down the gangplank together. The brilliant lighting provided by the newsreel men made the scene look like a film set, with Churchill, cigar in mouth and gloves and cane in hand, as the unmistakeable star. The *New York Times* reported: 'Smiling, jovial, his adeptness at repartee much in evidence, Mr. Churchill spent half an hour talking to reporters on the upper level of Pier 90, at Fiftieth Street, immediately after the giant liner had pulled in.' It was one of the largest press conferences ever held in the city, and the session was broadcast around the world. Churchill stated that he had no intention of giving up the Conservative leadership for the time being, while holding out the possibility that he would do so as soon as the party could make 'a better arrangement'. His performance was a masterclass in saying little with maximum geniality. He sensibly refused to be drawn into attacking Attlee's socialist programme, and drew applause and laughter when he said: 'I never criticize the Government of my country abroad; I very rarely leave off criticizing at home.' Churchill closed the news conference by thanking his interviewers for their kindness, by recalling that he had been a journalist in his youth, and stressing his keenness to keep good relations with the press.[10] Given the trouble he was soon to stir up, it was a wise precaution.

Churchill immediately headed south where he was to spend several weeks vacationing at the home of a friend, Colonel Frank W. Clarke. Besieged by journalists as he descended from the train into the Miami heat, his answers this time were rather more substantive. He warned that US troops would continue to be needed in Europe, and stated his support for America's $3.75 billion loan to Britain, an issue which had divided the Conservative Party and which was still winding its way through Congress.[11] He gave a further press conference on the patio of Colonel Clarke's modest residence, and this time Clementine was questioned too. Asked what women should do as their contribution to permanent peace, she replied: 'If you are young, get married and have babies. If you are old, I don't know.' After a pause, she added:

'Keep out of the way I suppose.'[12] Throughout the couple's holiday British Information Services (BIS), an official body which promoted Britain in the USA, sent Churchill copies of BBC news bulletins and London press digests from its New York base.[13] Meanwhile, he and Clementine became the 'Top celebrities in Miami Beach'; Clementine's clothing became the focus of fashion editors, and the editors of the women's pages gave details of where and with whom she ate lunch.[14] Cartoonists showed American hands lighting Churchill's cigar; as the influential US journalist Dorothy Thompson noted, 'even the cigar becomes a promotional asset of Anglo-American relations, which are the warmer when they just exist and are not too much discussed'.[15]

There was a star-struck quality to much of the coverage; there was no doubt about Churchill's 'enormous prestige and popularity' in America.[16] There were, however, undercurrents of suspicion from some quarters. To Democratic cries of 'headline-hunting' and 'fishing expeditions', there was a demand from two Republican members of the Pearl Harbor Investigating Committee that Churchill be asked to appear as a witness. While neither made the explicit claim that he had somehow inveigled America into the war, the notion was surely lurking in the background.[17] Moreover, Churchill's visit coincided with the publication in the *Saturday Evening Post* of the diaries of Captain Harry C. Butcher, who had served as Eisenhower's naval aide from 1942 to 1945. These not only cast light on Ike's foibles but described his contacts with Churchill and other Britishers.[18] This caused only minor embarrassment to Churchill's relations with Eisenhower—who assured him that he had never complained of being kept up late—but it did give fuel to American Anglosceptics.[19] The Chicago *Tribune* used Butcher's disclosures to argue that 'the ill fated Anzio beachhead was forced on the allied commander by Churchill's insistence'. It wove this into a wider story of how Churchill's poor military judgement, which failed to match his genius as a political leader of the British Empire, had cost America lives. What was more, 'We are still paying for Mr. Churchill's influence over our leaders.'[20]

An early trail for the Fulton speech seemed likely to stoke such anxieties. 'Mr. Churchill proposes to make a strong plea for Anglo-American solidarity closer than ever before [...] said informed quarters in close touch with him', reported Reuters in mid-February.[21] At this point, the speech was being billed as a sequel to his 1943 Harvard address, with its suggestion of common citizenship, yet there was also speculation that he would propose a military alliance between the two countries, as a counter to what appeared to be a growing Soviet threat.[22] When asked directly if he had discussed Russia with President Truman, Churchill remained cagey. 'I think "no comment" is a splendid expression', he said, grinning broadly. 'I am using it again and again.' (He claimed to have got the phrase from the former Under-Secretary of State Sumner Welles during the latter's tour of Europe during the Phoney War.)[23] In early March, he travelled by train with President Truman from Washington to Missouri, where the small town where he was to speak was 'Agog and Gay for Churchill'.[24] A four-person crew from St. Louis radio station KXOK interviewed local residents.[25] On the platform at Westminster College, where he received an honorary degree, he stopped short of calling for a formal alliance, but many observers thought that his language of 'fraternal association' meant just that. In America, this was at least as controversial as his famous 'iron curtain' phrase and his reference to the 'expansive and proselytizing tendencies' of the USSR.[26]

Among radio commentators, there were those who thought that Churchill had given 'his greatest prophetic utterance', those who considered his (thinly veiled) proposal for an alliance 'shocking', and those who agreed with him on Russia but who thought that an Anglo-American alliance was the wrong answer to the question. Newspaper opinion was similarly split.[27] On the one hand, the British Empire still aroused widespread distrust, not least in the African-American press.[28] On the other, the 'special relationship' which Churchill proposed could be seen by progressive idealists as a threat to the mission of the newly formed United Nations (even though he insisted he meant to support it). The speech provoked interest and much disquiet around the world, as it was seen by some less as a proposal for avoiding war than as an announcement that a new one was imminent. Many French papers described it as the 'Churchill Bomb'.[29] Stalin was stung into responding via an interview with *Pravda*, in which he denounced Churchill's 'racial theory' which maintained 'that only nations speaking the English language are fully valuable nations, called upon to decide the destinies of the entire world'.[30]

In the face of the controversy, Truman disingenuously denied having had advance knowledge of what Churchill would say. As a matter of fact, newsreel footage showed him applauding soundly, and official approval was also suggested by the fact that 'the British Information Services in the United States had been asked by the White House to help to provide liaison with the Press over the speech'. Feeling unable to refuse, the BIS had cabled the text of the speech to the Ministry of Information in London, which had issued advance copies to British journalists.[31] Ministers, however, did not see it. This allowed the government (which broadly approved of Churchill's line, but which did not want to say so openly) to maintain an element of plausible deniability. The former *Times* journalist A. L. Kennedy deduced from internal evidence that it and other papers had seen the speech beforehand but that 'The Govt. had *not*. If so, quite explainable. WSC didn't want to make the Govt. responsible, but *did* want publicity.'[32] This analysis seems to have attributed too much agency to Churchill, but the outcome was certainly convenient for him.

The speech was broadcast live in the United States. In the UK, the first summary came on the 11 p.m. news. Churchill was said to have made 'a strong appeal for an Anglo-American alliance—with the possibility of common citizenship—to stabilise the foundations of peace. [...] Nobody knew what Soviet Russia and its communist international organisation intended to do in the immediate future. He [Churchill] declared that the prevention of another great war could only be achieved by reaching *now*, in 1946, good understanding with Russia under the authority of the United Nations.' None of Churchill's own words were directly quoted, but after the three-minute bulletin roughly seventeen minutes of recorded extracts were played. Perhaps surprisingly, the passage containing the words 'iron curtain' was omitted, and was merely glossed by the announcer as follows: 'Mr. Churchill then went on to list some of the activities of the Communist Parties in Europe and the Far East and he compared the outlook of people after the 1914–18 war with the last war.'[33]

Moreover, the words 'iron curtain' were not used by UK press headline writers either (although the *Daily Mail* did provide a small map showing how, according to Churchill's telling, Europe was divided from Stettin to Trieste, as well as a vivid cartoon by Leslie Illingworth).[34] The *Daily Express* ran with 'CHURCHILL URGES EMPIRE "ALLIANCE" WITH U.S.' and the *Daily Mirror* opted for 'Churchill's fears of Soviet: Suggests Anglo-U.S. pact.' Although the latter was on the *Mirror's* front page, the headline was not capitalized, unlike that of the main story, which was about alleged arson attacks on ships by a 'fascist gang' in Liverpool.[35] Meanwhile, the *Irish Times* 'managed to report and editorialize on this wide-ranging analysis of global politics [...] without mentioning its most resonant phrase'.[36] In fact, Churchill probably did not intend the 'iron curtain' metaphor, which had been used by others in different contexts many times before, to be the words that caught the headlines.[37] The speech's official title was 'The Sinews of Peace'.

According to Cecil King, who still maintained his influential role with the *Sunday Pictorial* and the *Daily Mirror*, the speech was generally thought disappointing. 'In broad outline it called for closer union between ourselves and the US plus a resolute attempt to come to terms with the USSR before it is too late', he wrote. 'This last part rang a little hollow as so many of the moves that seem so disquieting were at least partly sanctioned at Teheran, Yalta or Potsdam, at which meetings Churchill was one of the three plenipotentiaries. The reaction of the world's press would seem to show that the speech has done something to enhance Russia's suspicions and nothing to bring us closer to the US.'[38]

Mass-Observation diaries suggest that there was both broad interest and a wide range of opinions, with some people applauding Churchill's political comeback and others denouncing him as a warmonger. 'Churchill's speech is sure some blockbuster, as one American paper describes it', noted a female librarian, in an entry which drew attention to the differential impact of radio and the press. 'I read it first in full, and later heard extracts; and I must say that his delivery was so calm and flowing that the parts which had horrified me in print seemed perfectly innocuous as he spoke them.'[39] *Express* journalist Albert Hird believed that anti-Soviet forces were using the speech for their own ends. 'The old Daily Mail of course is in the van. They speak openly in their leaders that the time has come for a "show down" with Russia and "plain speaking" and so on—anything just short of advocating war'.[40] Some people, of course, were simply indifferent. A male accountant recorded how a clerk at an office he was auditing showed him two papers' headlines and expressed concern about Soviet reactions to what Churchill had said. 'The 67 year old secretary was not bothered, however. He had sufficient daily troubles, he said, without being worried by international difficulties.'[41]

All round, though, the Fulton speech was remarkably successful at promoting discussion, whereas with the Zürich speech a few months later Churchill did not quite pull off the same trick. This was not for want of trying. Part of his difficulty was the need to refresh a theme, the 'United States of Europe', that was already quite familiar from interwar Federalist movements, associated with the names of Aristide Briand and Richard Coudenhove-Kalergi. Churchill had himself used the phrase in newspaper articles in the 1930s.[42] The term, moreover, had occurred in *The Times* on at least 190 occasions prior to the Zürich speech, beginning in 1867.[43] Three of these uses were by Churchill himself in speeches in 1945–6, but in spite of being reported, they were plainly not considered of great news value.[44] It seems clear that Churchill wanted his remarks in Switzerland to be regarded as a major pronouncement, as he requested that they be broadcast.[45] This helped convey a message that went beyond questions of policy. 'Those who listened on the radio to Mr. Churchill's address at Zurich University yesterday must have realised two things', noted the

South Wales Echo, 'first that Winston is still as dynamically vigorous as ever and second that Britain's historic war leader is still a master of eloquence.'[46]

In addition to good publicity, timing helped this particular speech become another 'Churchill Bombshell', to quote one headline (although it seems not to have made as much impression on the public as that made at Fulton).[47] Not long before Churchill spoke, Truman's Commerce Secretary, the liberal Henry Wallace, had given a speech that was perceived as soft on Russia. The President would shortly demand his resignation, but the American attitude to the Cold War still looked uncertain.[48] Moreover, there was a striking new dimension to Churchill's message that gave it immediate relevance in this context. Indeed he openly predicted that his audience would be astonished by his claim that the first move towards the revival of European peace should be 'a partnership between France and Germany.'[49] This was indeed a remarkable suggestion, made just a few weeks before the verdicts in the Nuremburg trials were handed down. *Reynolds News* read it as a call for 'a new European alliance, headed by France and Germany, under the sponsorship of the Anglo-American alliance, and with the atomic bomb as its "shield and protection."'[50]

To some, then, he was raising 'the Russia bogey' again, as well as dropping a sizeable hint that the moment to create the United States of Europe was while the West still had a monopoly on nuclear weapons.[51] This breathing-space was not expected to last long. The *Daily Mail* concluded its approving leader by echoing Churchill's words: 'And, remember—"The time is short."'[52] Moscow radio, in a programme beamed to Europe in German, argued that 'American reactionary elements' were being joined by 'British imperialistic circles' in a campaign of nuclear intimidation. 'Winston Churchill also, in his speech in Zurich, used these methods of extortion and tried to frighten the democratic peoples. Churchill is supported by the OBSERVER, and the DAILY MAIL, and other conservative British papers. Thus it is evident that the reactionary and imperialistic circles of the Anglo-Saxon countries want to use the atom threat for their own purposes.'[53] Another Soviet broadcast, in Romanian, dismissed the United States of Europe idea as old hat: Churchill was 'pulling out of the dust bin the tattered flag of Pan-Europa'.[54] Moreover, as the Conservative MP Bob Boothby noted in a supportive article in the *News of the World*, in addition to the claim that he was trying to gang up on the Russians, Churchill also faced accusations from the French that he was 'appeasing' the Germans.[55] The *Manchester Guardian* commented that both Wallace and Churchill had had for their respective speeches 'what is called a bad press. They have been judged not on their merits as contributions to the general stock of ideas but on the use propagandists may make of them.'[56]

Much French opinion was certainly shocked, or at least embarrassed; initially Paris papers printed extracts without comment.[57] Reuters reported that even secret Pétainists were 'amazed by what they interpret as a suggestion that France should bury the hatchet before tangible guarantees have been obtained that Germany has abandoned aggressive designs.'[58] The short-lived *Cité-soir* newspaper said that there could be no question of a Franco-German rapprochement for a people whose wounds were still bleeding, and the communist *L'Humanité* said that the 'old fox' Churchill was 'trying to inflame opinion with vague generalities which cover sordid realities'.[59]

However, scepticism did not always translate into abject hostility. The semi-official *Le Monde* argued that the problem of Europe was now dominated by US–Soviet tensions rather than rivalry between France and Germany. 'Pretending to forget this situation, Mr Churchill plans the European future on the basis of a Franco-German entente, which he believes would enable a federation of the states of our continent.' Yet the conclusion was quite mild: 'circumstances can change, and Mr Churchill has perhaps spoken for the future.'[60] In Belgium, *Le Phare Dimanche* noted that in Paris and Brussels 'some newspapers' were making out that French opinion would be dismayed by Churchill's words, with some people even making the link between his policy and Vichy-style collaboration. Yet there was a great difference, it argued, between collaboration with an occupier in time of war and collaboration with a defeated Germany in time of peace.[61] Unsurprisingly, the speech went down better in Germany, given Churchill's stated concern to restore that country to the 'European family'. The Social Democrat Gerhard Kreyssig wrote in the *Süddeutsche Zeitung* that those who did not want Europe to be fatally paralysed were bound to agree with Churchill, and would not even find it 'astonishing' that he saw Franco–German cooperation as necessary for success.[62]

One striking feature of the press coverage is the degree to which British local newspapers, from the *Sheffield Telegraph* to Exeter's *Express & Echo*, felt called upon to comment on foreign policy. Even more striking is that Churchill himself was reading cuttings from such papers, or at the very least one article in particular, from the *Southern Daily Echo*. This, by Gordon Sewell, a locally renowned journalist, was 'written in haste to catch an edition' and published the day after Churchill's speech. 'The real demarcation between Europe and Asia is no chain of mountains, not natural frontier, but a system of beliefs and ideas which we call Western Civilisation', Sewell wrote. Moreover: 'Europe is a spiritual conception, but if men cease to hold that conception in their minds, cease to feel its worth in their hearts, it will die.'[63] Churchill quoted this in the article he now wrote for *Collier's*, at the behest of its publisher William Chenery.[64] He consciously intended this 'NOUVELLE BOMBE WINSTON CHURCHILL' (as *L'Humanité* described it) as an expansion or adumbration of what he had said in Zürich.[65] He was paid $25,000: of this he took $21,000 for himself (subject to income tax in the usual way) and $4,000 for a new 'British Handling Group' to promote European unity.[66] His son-in-law, Duncan Sandys, who would become a key figure in the European Movement, proposed some minor amendments to the draft. The purpose of these was to forestall both the Labour Party and its criticism that Churchill was anti-Russian, and 'Centre and Right-Wing circles in France' who suspected him of being pro-German.[67]

The *Collier's* piece shows that Churchill's European vision was quite expansive, including a 'uniform currency' as well as common passports and postage stamps; he proposed that an initial nucleus of countries might be joined by others as soon as they were willing and able.[68] There has been much debate, however, on whether he really intended Britain to be part of the United States of Europe he proposed. In Zürich he had been deliberately ambiguous, keeping the door open for possible British membership while trying to avoid being pinned down.[69] Journalists seem to have taken him at his word when he said that Britain should be one of 'the friends and sponsors of the new Europe', and thus implicitly at one remove from it.[70] Frances Josephy, a Liberal parliamentary candidate on many occasions and an enthusiast for Federalism, wrote to *The Times* in the aftermath of the speech. 'Many will join issue with Mr. Churchill on his exclusion of Great Britain from membership of the United States of Europe', she said. 'From every point of view this would be a major calamity.'[71] The *Collier's* article was also published in two parts in the *Daily Telegraph*. One reader of that paper asked what Britain's place in the new Federation was to be: 'Is she to be outside it, as the centre of another federation—the British Empire? Or is she to have, as her history shows she ought to have, a foot both in Europe and in the Empire?'[72] Certainly, nobody interpreted Churchill as saying that Britain should definitely join the organization he was mooting.

Churchill was attempting to shape the geopolitical landscape at a time when it was evolving rapidly. The harsh winter of 1947 was a moment of crisis for the Attlee government, marked by severe fuel shortages. When the British government informed the Americans they could no longer afford to keep up their military commitments in Greece and Turkey, Truman responded with a landmark speech to Congress, delivered on 12 March. The President not only pledged $400 million in assistance to the Greeks and the Turks, but also made the broad pledge 'that it must be the policy of the United States to support free peoples who are resisting attempted subjugation by armed minorities or by outside pressures'.[73] Considered by some as the moment that marked the true onset of the Cold War, this 'Truman Doctrine' spelt out a powerful commitment to combat

Soviet expansionism. An excited Churchill rang Walter Graebner of Time-Life. 'A very bold and courageous idea. I think I would like to write an article about it. Would your people be interested?' Graebner had not yet read the news and thus had no idea what he was talking about. Happily Churchill (who frequently failed to listen to others) did not notice and in due course produced the article, which was published in *Life* on 14 April.[74] While denying that Britain had ceased to be a great power, Churchill welcomed the extension of US power in the Middle East. He not only claimed vindication over the previous year's Fulton speech, but argued that British actions in 1944–5 had saved Greece from communism. Still clearly smarting a little, he dwelt too on the harsh press reaction he had received at the time in both Britain and America. 'I was depicted in many newspapers as a shocking jingo, Tory, Imperialist reactionary', he recalled.[75]

The article is less significant for its content than for the fact that it represented Churchill's effective swansong as a paid writer for periodicals. True, there were plenty of reprints and serializations to come; the final instalment of *A History of the English-Speaking Peoples* appeared in 1958, and Churchill's epilogue to the single-volume edition of *The Second World War* was published in the *Daily Telegraph* the same year. He also, of course, continued to issue statements to the press. But, save for an article for the opening issue of the European Movement newsletter *United Europe*, there were no more original articles.[76] Churchill's creative well may not have dried up, but clearly there was no further event that stimulated him sufficiently to forget his tax concerns and put pen to paper on the great issues of the day. His career as a journalist was over.

His interest in the news, however, was not. *Daily Express* editor Arthur Christiansen recalled how, late at night, the paper's own despatch riders took the first edition hot off the press to Churchill's London home. Often he came to the door himself in his dressing-gown:

> If Churchill had been speaking in the House or in his constituency at this time I invariably heard from him. 'What was your reaction to my speech?' he would ask. He knew that if I had put the speech in an

obscure place and given it only an inch or two, I would most likely improve its position in the paper, or give it extra length, if he discussed with me the importance of a particular passage. Far into the night I would then listen to his views on the issues of peace and war.[77]

Although still friendly, Beaverbrook and Churchill were no longer as intimate as they once had been. The former was prepared to back the latter's continued leadership in the face of grumbles about his effect-iveness, and the *Express* lavished praise on his war memoirs, but Beaverbrook was no enthusiast for the wider Conservative Party. As a diehard enthusiast for stronger Empire trade links, he was sceptical about Churchill's geopolitical orientation towards the United States and towards Europe.[78] There was also his traditional jealousy towards his friend. Therefore, Beaverbrook was none too pleased when Churchill's speeches received more coverage in the *Express* than their news value strictly justified. 'Did Winston call you last night?' he would ask Christiansen. 'Be careful now. Be careful of his propaganda!'[79]

Churchill sometimes complained about his coverage, whether in Beaverbrook's papers or elsewhere, if he considered it inaccurate or unfair. On one occasion he publicly attributed an alleged misrepre-sentation in a single paper, the *Sunday Pictorial*, to 'The socialist news-papers, almost without exception'.[80] He did not, in fact, argue during this period that he was being systematically mistreated by the media as a whole, but he did believe that his old bugbear, the BBC, had been penetrated by communist sympathizers.[81] Unsurprisingly, this was not how the Corporation—which combined both stuffy and progressive elements—was perceived by communists. In 1947, the *Daily Worker* drew attention to a Home Service bulletin which devoted around eight minutes to a report of a Churchill speech at Blenheim, 'read by the announcer in religious intonation, plus a long recorded passage by the orator himself'.[82] And indeed Churchill probably did benefit from rather reverent BBC treatment.

Overall, Churchill's interests were not too badly served by the media, which still operated on the maxim that 'Mr Churchill is news'.[83] The Conservative Party, for its part, could not afford to be complacent but in many ways it also benefited from the status quo. On the Left, by contrast, there was concern that too much press power was concentrated in too few hands, in a way that was politically unfavourable to the Labour movement. In 1947, the government appointed a Royal Commission on the Press, 'to inquire into the control, management and ownership of the newspaper and periodical Press and the news agencies, including the financial structure and the monopolistic tendencies in control'.[84] Due to continued paper shortages, newspapers were still restricted to four sheets. This was portrayed by *The Recorder*, a new-ish weekly favourable to and favoured by Churchill, as a restriction of press freedom and hence as a vindication of the 'Gestapo' speech.[85] The Royal Commission too was presented by Conservatives as evidence of the government's determination to introduce laws that would restrict freedom of expression.[86] Yet when the Commission reported after two years, although it found some evidence of excess partisanship and 'distortion for the sake of news value', it did not blame these failings on the industry's ownership structure or on pressures from advertisers.[87] It recommended the establishment of a General Press Council to enforce standards, a proposal which the industry continued to resist as a Government tool for the harassment and intimidation of the newspapers.[88] The idea was eventually implemented after Churchill returned to Downing Street, but, as it was based on self-regulation by the press, it did little to prevent abuses.[89]

By the end of the forties, the Tories were ahead in the opinion polls, as Labour's reputation for economic competence came more and more into question.[90] The *Manchester Guardian*, *The Times*, and *The Economist* became increasingly sceptical towards the government. This did not necessarily mean, though, that they avoided criticism of the Conservatives; indeed the *Guardian*'s tendency to sit high-mindedly above the fray was a Churchillian bugbear. The paper was particularly important to him because of its potential use in swaying the former Liberal voters whose support he was desperate to win. As a *Guardian* reader for fifty years (as he proclaimed himself), he praised the quality of its reporting but deplored its superior attitude and unwillingness to pick a side.[91]

Now Churchill was growing increasingly infirm, although not less politically aggressive. On a visit to America in the spring of 1949, he dined with the staff of the *New York Times*. He told them off the record that, if it transpired that the Soviets were making rapid progress towards building an atom bomb, Britain should force a 'show-down', to be preceded by the dropping of leaflets urging a general diplomatic settlement. 'You must take the occasion to let them know that if they exceed certain limits it is your intention to use the bomb without hesitation—if indeed that is your intention.' The journalist James 'Scotty' Reston recorded the meeting in his memoirs: 'As he [Churchill] left at a few minutes past eleven, a little shuffly and a little bent, Dr. Howard Rusk, the Times' favourite doctor, remarked, "Jesus, prop him up." '[92]

While on holiday in Monte Carlo that August, Churchill suffered a minor stroke. Moran was summoned. A press statement was issued saying that Churchill had 'caught a chill'.[93] Beaverbrook, who was present, knew the true diagnosis, but connived at its suppression. Churchill feared that when he disembarked the aircraft when he returned home journalists would observe that he could not walk straight. He—and, Moran suspected, Beaverbrook—dreamt up a plan whereby the pressmen would be sent to Northolt aerodrome while the plane landed at Biggin Hill. Moran put a stop to this. 'When, however, we arrived at Biggin Hill and he saw all the photographers with their cameras, he was certain they would notice something wrong with his gait, and he waved them away with an angry gesture.'[94]

The Conservative Party, meanwhile, was running a highly sophisticated media operation as well as showing a new-found interest in the science of public opinion.[95] Particular attention was paid to securing publicity for front-bench speakers at the weekends. Short press releases, of 100 to 150 words, focused on one point only: 'it is important to release news items on Sunday for the BBC's evening bulletins and for Monday papers which are often news-starved.'[96] Film, moreover, had long been a Tory strength.[97] The relevant party committee noted 'the difficulty of persuading leading Conservatives and, in particular, Mr. Churchill, to be recorded'.[98] When an election was called for February 1950, though, he did record a slightly halting three-minute newsreel talk, which concluded with him giving the viewers an extravagantly forced smile.[99] The slight rash of 'Churchill Must Go'-type articles of a few years before, which had revived with a poor by-election result in early 1949, had by now faded away.[100] But as leader he seemed like a somewhat archaic figurehead for a highly modernized, media-conscious party.

Churchill's physical and mental fitness for office did not become a matter of open public debate during the election. However, Labour's Nye Bevan, 'true to his flair for innuendo', noted that the Leader of the Opposition was not a young man and asked what would happen if he were elected and then run over by a bus.[101] On one occasion Churchill was forced to put out a statement denying that he had died: 'The rumour of his death was so widespread that newspaper switchboards were jammed with callers asking for information.' It seems that the story had been spread maliciously; according to one of his secretaries this type of unpleasantness had become 'a regular occurrence'.[102]

Other than demonstrating that he was still alive, Churchill's main task during the election was to counteract the common charges that he was a warmonger and that a Tory victory would cause a return to high unemployment, while simultaneously ensuring that Conservative plans did not appear merely as 'Tory Socialism'.[103] The party had in fact reviewed its policies in the wake of of its crushing 1945 defeat (albeit Churchill himself had not always been very enthusiastic about the process). The July 1949 document *The Right Road for Britain* committed it to the maintenance of full employment and the welfare state, and even the temporary retention of controls on prices and consumption. In his opening broadcast of the campaign, Churchill lambasted the government for revelling in controls for their own sake. At the same time he assured voters that the Conservatives and their National Liberal allies believed in a basic minimum standard of living below which no one should be allowed to fall.[104] The press reactions ran on predictable lines. Churchill's words won support from *The Times*, the *Daily Telegraph*, and the *Financial Times*.[105] The *Daily Mail* hailed him as 'The Voice of Britain'.[106] The *Manchester Guardian* found the broadcast 'woolly in its treatment of the facts' and suggested that in his attack on controls he had repudiated the analysis presented in *The Right Road for Britain*.[107] The left-wing *Daily Mirror* ran a front page leader about the broadcast under the headline 'The Insult'. It argued:

> The British people must apparently accept a picture of themselves as a miserable and spineless horde, the helpless slaves of a system of deadly 'controls.' They must accept a picture of the world in which every country outside the Iron Curtain except Britain is 'free,' happy and going at full speed on the road of progress, and that in Britain we are sinking under frustration and laziness. This is an insulting picture of the British people.[108]

Conservative Central Office had provided the party's local agents with forms and instructions to be distributed to investigators who were to ascertain the public's views on the broadcast. Over a thousand people who had heard it were asked their opinion.[109] Churchill's comments on housing, food, and the cost of living were approved by many, as were his remarks on full employment, opposition to regimentation, and his hope and faith in the future of the country. Additionally, his restraint was praised: '"Fair criticism"—"no vituperation"—"clean"—"fair without bitterness"—"country above Party"—"No rash promises".' Criticisms focused on Churchill's failure to give any credit to the Labour government, his reliance on 'Mere Propaganda' and 'False Promises', and his advocacy of the removals of controls. Churchill was also attacked for his lack of a constructive policy and for his suggestion that the National Health Service was in need of improvement. Labour supporters and a few Liberals noted that house-building would have to come at the expense of something else, and suggested that the government was doing the best it could on this score. According to the Conservatives' Public

Opinion Research Department, 'Most of the remaining reasons offered for dislike of the broadcast were stock socialist slogans, e.g. "Unemployment under Conservatives", "Churchill warmonger", etc. Eleven Socialists and two Doubtfuls wave the Daily Mirror's answer of Monday 23rd January.'[110]

On 14 February, Churchill addressed the 'warmonger' charge in a speech in Scotland by calling for high-level talks with the Soviet Union.[111] Beaverbrook later claimed the credit for this.[112] The proposal, according to the *New York Times* correspondent Raymond Daniell—one of a flock of American journalists who were following the election—appeared 'to have broken the spirit of the interparty truce on foreign policy'.[113] The following day, Daniell noted that the Labour Party appeared disconcerted: 'The Daily Mirror, which is supporting Labor and which is about the only source of information for many of its 4,500,000 readers, reported Mr. Churchill's Edinburgh speech in about 200 words published inconspicuously in a back page opposite the comic strips. The Daily Herald, official organ of the Labor party, published a digest of the speech in which reference to the new peace move was buried near the bottom of a column under the headline "Bonnie Prince Churchill Goes Over the Border."'[114] Alistair Cooke, the *Manchester Guardian*'s man in the USA, noted the coolness with which Churchill's idea had been received there. 'From the newspapers he has had respectful but unexcited treatment along party lines'; at a press conference, Secretary of State Dean Acheson declined to comment.[115]

The USSR had successfully tested a nuclear weapon the previous year but, as Kevin Ruane has persuasively argued, Churchill's 'summit' idea did not mean he had now abandoned the notion that the Americans should use their much greater atomic strength to secure the West's diplomatic objectives.[116] The Soviets had not dropped their suspicions of him either. On the day before polling day—well timed to torpedo Churchill's electoral chances—Moscow radio broadcast, in English, a denunciation of the summit idea.

Churchill's statement created quite a stir. The Labor leaders, who have so zealously been conducting Churchill's foreign policy, were taken aback. They tried to ridicule his proposal as an election stunt not worthy of attention. Meanwhile, the Conservative press, in an effort to improve the position of its party in the elections, began depicting Winston Churchill, Warmonger No. 1, as a peacemaker.

[...] Beyond all doubt Churchill's statement is designed to catch votes. However, it is something more than just an election trick. Unwittingly, Churchill's statement is a confirmation of the bankruptcy of that policy which he himself formulated in his ill-famed Fulton speech almost 4 years ago.

The argument was that the Fulton policy had led Britain and Western Europe to suffer from 'unbearable taxation' to support high levels of armaments, as well as rising costs of living and unemployment, when all that their citizens wished to do was to live in peace.[117] The next day, the *Daily Mail* led with:

STALIN ANSWERS CHURCHILL
'His atom peace move is more than an election trick'[118]

It was necessary to read quite far down the article in order to discover that 'more than an election trick' was actually a hostile comment which signalled the Soviets' firm rejection of Churchill's idea. As the author of that year's Nuffield election study noted, 'Such sub-editing was a certainly a queer way of clarifying the news.'[119]

For the first time, the election results were presented live on television.[120] (TV broadcasting had been suspended during the war and relaunched in 1946.) When all the votes were counted, it turned out that Labour had narrowly squeaked back with a single-figure Commons majority. The government's troubles increased when the Korean War broke out in June, leading to a heavy rearmament programme that exacerbated Labour's divisions. The Conservatives, moreover, regained the domestic initiative with a media-friendly promise to build 300,000 homes a year, albeit this pledge was actually forced through at the 1950 party conference against the leadership's better judgement.[121] In the autumn of 1951, with Attlee and his ministers exhausted, the country went to the polls once more. This time, television became a factor in the campaign itself. Churchill, however, took no part in this. 'Winston Churchill never looked at television', recalled Jock Colville, 'and he was not going to be televised himself if he could possibly help it. He hated the lights, he hated the glare, and he hated the heat.'[122]

Accordingly, then, the Tories' first TV election broadcast was left in the hands of Anthony Eden. This took the form of an 'interview'— actually a fully scripted dialogue—with the well-known presenter Leslie Mitchell. Eden dealt with a variety of soft-ball questions before concluding: 'I haven't the least doubt that Mr Churchill would endorse every single word of what I've said.'[123] Although the programme's unspontaneous nature was obvious to contemporaries, by the standards of the time it was slick stuff.[124] Eden showed a graph to illustrate the rising cost of living. The following evening, in response, Labour's Christopher Mayhew produced his own charts. Eden's presentation was not merely misleading, he said, but 'a deliberate fake'. Mayhew explicitly argued, in fact, that TV would make politics more honest in the future. [125] Churchill shared no such faith. 'I can't get excited about television', he once remarked. 'I can't make out what all the fuss is about. I have never given my mind to it as I did to the hydrogen bomb, but I feel this bloody invention will do harm to society and to the race.'[126]

One might conclude that Churchill's absence from the small screen was a sign of his increasing marginalization within his own party. It must be remembered, though, that only around 750,000 households owned a TV set at this time.[127] Churchill's sole radio broadcast of the campaign secured a much larger audience: it was heard by 43 per cent of the adult population, making him the single most popular speaker of any party. Moreover, as in 1950, the BBC's own radio and TV programming avoided all mention of the election. Therefore, the press remained highly important, though the continued shortage of newsprint meant that election stories had to compete for space with a crop of alarming international news as well as a royal tour of North

America. The support of *The Times* for the Conservatives was now explicit, and the *Manchester Guardian*, with some regret, came off the fence and backed them too.[128] Beaverbrook plugged for Churchill in his usual idiosyncratic way. 'The Express is of course "independent" that is to say they follow, broadly, the Tory line, plus a few ideas of the Beaver's own', noted Albert Hird. 'This time we are going all out on the iniquities of the Purchase Tax. It pleases the shopkeepers and the trade organisations, is certainly very popular with that section of the public that doesn't think too hard, and it also serves to show the Tories that the Beaver isn't entirely "in their pockets" and that if he supports them—or anybody else—there's got to be some *quid pro quo* somewhere.'[129]

It was Churchill's old sparring-partners at the *Daily Mirror*, though, who made the most memorable contribution to the coverage. In Iran, the nationalist government had recently moved to nationalize the operations of the Anglo-Iranian Oil Company (AIOC) and to expel British personnel. The Attlee government, lacking US support, declined to launch military action. This allowed Churchill to accuse them of 'scuttling' from their responsibilities and endangering the Empire. In turn, the *Mirror* revived charges of warmongering, allegedly in collusion with Herbert Morrison, the Labour Foreign Secretary, who plugged this same line on the platform.[130] Clearly favouring the sober and cautious Attlee, the paper posed the question: 'WHOSE FIN-GER DO YOU WANT ON THE TRIGGER?'[131] Churchill publicly responded that—given that it did not yet have the bomb—Britain did not actually have the capacity to launch a third world war.[132] But the *Mirror* later returned to the fray, repeating a report that had appeared in the American *Nation* magazine about Churchill's recent visit to Paris. 'The essence of his "policy" was to "talk to Stalin," and if this failed, to authorize all-out German rearmament. As his French listeners interpreted it, he was going to present Stalin with an ultimatum, and if Stalin did not yield, then the "free world" would have to accept the likelihood of war.'[133] Churchill denied having said the words attributed to him. On polling day, 25 October, the *Mirror* ran the huge headline 'WHOSE FINGER?' over a picture of a cocked revolver and photos of Attlee and Churchill. When shown the proofs of the front page the paper's office lawyer warned it would lead to a libel action. The editor, Silvester Bolam, relayed this to Guy Bartholomew, the paper's Chairman. 'I'll take full responsibility', said Bartholomew. 'Go ahead and publish.'[134] Churchill issued a writ forthwith.[135]

The *Mirror's* front page was not enough to swing the election for Churchill's opponents: the Conservatives were returned with a majority of seventeen, albeit Labour secured a larger share of the popular vote. But even though he had been reinstalled as Prime Minister Churchill was not prepared to let the libel action drop. The *Mirror*, for its part, was determined to defend itself. The paper planned to argue in court that the material it had published was not defamatory but that, even if it had been, the statements complained of were permissible fair comment.[136] Churchill received advice from, among others, Sir Valentine Holmes, a recently retired KC who specialized in libel. This 'Former Legal Person' (as Churchill dubbed him) judged that the famous front page was *not* defamatory—although he thought that a jury might nonetheless conclude that it *was*. Holmes also believed that other articles now included in the writ—including one insinuating that Churchill had lied about his Paris statement—were clearly defamatory. While it was not defamatory to say that Churchill's policies would make war more likely, to suggest that he did not care whether war broke out or not was defamation. 'By the use of a metaphor "Whose finger on the Trigger?" and "clever" journalistic methods, the Daily Mirror has avoided saying that Mr. Churchill would like to see the country involved in a war: but there are passages from which I think that the only possible inference to be drawn is that Mr. Churchill would make no effort to maintain peace or prevent a world war and that he is indifferent to whether the country is or is not involved in war.' No sane jury, Holmes thought, would believe that that was true.[137]

Yet although Churchill was on strong legal ground, pressing ahead involved risks. The *Mirror* was a wealthy paper which could afford to pay damages if it lost, and at the same time might benefit from the publicity and notoriety of a trial. There was also the chance that the jury might include committed Labour supporters who would damage Churchill's chances. Finally, there was the unseemly prospect of an elderly Prime Minister being grilled at length in the witness box about his past political positions dating back to the Russian civil war. In the end, then, he accepted a modest out-of-court settlement. The *Mirror*, having been advised that it would likely lose the action, agreed to pay Churchill's costs and to make a contribution to charity.[138] It also issued an apology that was less than abject. 'The statements and pictures referred to were never intended to suggest that Mr. Churchill did not dislike war and the possibility of war as much as the Defendants do themselves', it claimed, without conviction.[139]

Preparation for a court appearance would of course have been a major distraction for Churchill as he re-established himself in power. Raking up the bitterness of the election campaign would also have been at odds with the new image that he was trying to cultivate. As Kevin Theakston has commented, 'whereas as Leader of the Opposition his preferred approach was to mount thunderous, slashing and strongly worded attacks on the mistakes and failings of the Labour government, his tone on return to office was more restrained and consensual'.[140] Whether or not there was also genuine cross-party consensus in terms of policy is debatable, although there was clear continuity in terms of the persistence of a mixed economy and the maintenance of the welfare state. One radical plan known as 'Operation ROBOT', which would have introduced greater market discipline by floating the pound, was judged too economically risky and was rejected by ministers.[141] It is striking that the press never caught wind of this highly sensitive scheme, a fact which was a tribute to the persistence of wartime security-consciousness and to the power of Whitehall's culture of official secrecy.[142]

But although Churchill did not have to worry too much about his colleagues leaking, he still faced a challenging press. Throughout Churchill's time in Downing Street, the papers were brought to his bedside every morning, and they slowly cascaded from his eiderdown to the carpet, as he went through each of them in turn.[143] Yet upon his return to No. 10 he had appointed neither an official press spokesman nor a minister to coordinate government publicity, and had slimmed down the Central Office of Information. When the backbench 1922 committee pressed for a more coherent approach to dealing with Opposition attacks, he was forced to backtrack, and gave the job of coordinating information services to the ministerial veteran Lord Swinton.[144] According to James Margach, who collaborated with Swinton on his memoirs, the latter advised Churchill that he should 'Unbend' and 'Confide in the journalists'. When Churchill retorted that he had close relationships with editors and proprietors, Swinton told him that he was wasting his time and that he should chat informally with the Lobby correspondents over drinks. 'I'm too old, Philip, to learn these tricks', Churchill responded. 'I suppose it's the new American system of trying to persuade journalists they're important.' Actually, as his obsessive reading of newspapers showed, he clearly did think they were important; he just didn't want to meet them close up. He set great store by the views of Harry Boardman, the *Manchester Guardian*'s parliamentary correspondent, and sought out his views on his speeches—but always via an intermediary.[145]

Churchill, moreover, was uncooperative with the newsreel companies, even though they were sympathetic to the Conservative Party and in spite of the continued importance of their films as a source of news. Newsreels were seen by approximately thirty million people each week, more than the number that listened to the 9 o'clock news, and were effective in reaching the 17 to 25 age-group. But, as the Assistant Postmaster-General, David Gammans MP, reported to Swinton:

> This is the first Cabinet for many years which was not photographed when it came into office. The Prime Minister himself has consistently refused to be photographed by British companies [...] For instance, they could get no picture for the cinema of Mr. Churchill shaking hands with Dr. [Leopold] Figl, the Austrian Chancellor and this fact

was adversely commented on by the Austrians who deduced from it that the Chancellor's visit to England was not a success.[146]

Churchill's lack of engagement with the British media was on a par with his approach to domestic policy, where he was generally happy to preside rather than lead. He concentrated his diminishing strength on international affairs, a key priority being to improve Anglo-American relations. At the start of 1952 he travelled to the USA to visit Truman. Evelyn Shuckburgh, private secretary to Anthony Eden (who was now back at the Foreign Office), recorded his arrival in New York. 'A tremendous reception on shore with bands and flags and troops, marred by the wholly undisciplined behaviour of hundreds of cameramen who swarmed all over and all around the scene.'[147] Churchill was still a star attraction, though 'the shakiness of age in his face and in his voice' and his deafness when answering reporters' questions did not pass without comment.[148] His hats still attracted much interest. The one he wore on arrival was variously described in the papers as 'a sawed-off stovepipe', a 'tall flat crowned Derby', and a 'high crowned black homburg'. In fact, as the Hatters Information Service confirmed to the New York Times, it was actually a Cambridge, 'a variation of the bowler or Derby and a compromise with the topper made of hard felt'.[149]

There was press speculation that the Truman administration was unenthusiastic about Churchill's visit, and although it seems that the White House had not briefed in this sense, the conjecture was essentially accurate.[150] Although Churchill's address to Congress was a success, in private talks his 'emotional declarations of faith in Anglo–American cooperation' cut little ice with the President, who was all brisk business. It was obvious that Britain was now 'playing second fiddle', and, although the UK press split over whether the trip had been worthwhile, it was clear that in reality it served little concrete purpose.[151] As James Reston put it, 'Mr. Churchill has given the conversations a scope and lift that were absent in the Truman–Attlee talks a year ago, but no major decisions have been taken and the chances are that few if any will be.'[152]

Churchill fared little better even after Dwight Eisenhower was elected to the presidency as a Republican that same November. After the death of Stalin in March 1953, it seemed as though a breakthrough in the Cold War might be possible: *Pravda* even took the 'extraordinary' step of publishing the text of an Eisenhower speech calling for peace.[153] Yet the Americans were profoundly resistant to Churchill's hopes for a summit meeting with the Soviets (and indeed there was much scepticism within his own Cabinet). During a further sojourn in the USA towards the end of his premiership, Churchill was alleged to have told Congressmen that 'To jaw-jaw is always better than to war-war.'[154] *The Times* clarified a few days later that he had never used this 'unlikely phrase'; rather, he had said that talking 'jaw to jaw' was better than going to war, but had been misreported by one of his audience.[155] It is easy to guess which version stuck.

Back at home, anxieties about the press had moved on from monopoly and bias to sex and salaciousness, concerns which the Prime Minister to some degree shared.[156] But there were still considerable limits on the treatment of politicians' personal lives. On 23 June 1953 Churchill suffered a massive stroke, which left him partially paralysed although still mentally competent. Jock Colville, who was again serving as his private secretary, recalled that two days later Churchill gave him firm instructions to keep secret the fact of his incapacity and to make sure the government continued to run as though he were still fully in charge:

> I could not obey Churchill's injunction to tell nobody. The truth would undoubtedly leak to the press unless I took immediate defensive action. So I wrote urgently and in manuscript to three particular friends of Churchill, Lords Camrose, Beaverbrook and Bracken, and sent the letters to London by despatch rider. All three immediately came to Chartwell and paced the lawn in earnest conversation. They achieved the all but incredible, and in peacetime possibly unique, success of gagging Fleet Street, something they would have done for nobody but Churchill. Not a word of the Prime Minister's stroke was published until he casually mentioned it in a speech in the House of Commons a year later.[157]

Given the retrospective nature of Colville's account, and the possible tendency of those involved in the crisis to exaggerate their own roles, some caution is advisable.[158] Lord Hartwell, Camrose's son and biographer, confirms the discussion at Chartwell. However, he correctly questions Colville's claim that the story was buried completely. (Colville was right that Churchill did make a throwaway revelation, in March 1955).[159] Beaverbrook's view was that 'all Fleet Street knows what has happened and that it is foolish not to issue bulletins which approximate to the truth'.[160] Most papers played the game nonetheless, sticking to the official line that Churchill was simply exhausted by his duties and was in need of complete rest. The *Daily Mail*, for example, repeated the fib put out by Christopher Soames, Churchill's son-in-law, that 'Sir Winston is simply suffering from general fatigue— probably more mental than physical'.[161] 'Churchill has had a fine photograph of himself, looking very well, in all the papers', observed Harold Macmillan at the end of July.[162] In mid-August, though, *The Observer* noted the contradictory nature of reports about Churchill's condition: 'British and foreign friends who have visited the Prime Minister have emerged either glowingly confident that he would soon be back or have remained alarmingly reticent.'[163] By this time, the American journalist Stewart Alsop had already reported both that Churchill had suffered a stroke in the last week of June and that he had staged 'a near-miraculous recovery'.[164] Citing Alsop, and also reports in the French press, the *Daily Mirror* demanded: 'WHAT IS THE TRUTH ABOUT CHURCHILL'S ILLNESS?'[165]

Speculation about Churchill's future mounted; he survived in office partly due to his strong powers of recuperation, but also because he had been struck down at a moment when his heir apparent, Anthony Eden, was also out of action for medical reasons. From this point forward, to the frustration of many of his colleagues, and Eden in particular, Churchill was simply hanging on, hoping to pull off some sort of coup vis-à-vis the Soviets. In March 1954, Churchill made clear in the Commons that he was not prepared to urge the USA to halt its programme of hydrogen-bomb testing. The *New York*

Times reported that 'Sir Winston appeared unsure of himself and tired. This was not the Churchill of two years ago and was only a shadow of the great figure of 1940'.[166] The *Daily Mirror* used an editorial to put the boot into the Prime Minister: 'Old and tired, he mouths comfortless words in the twilight of his career. […] THIS IS THE GIANT IN DECAY.'[167] Writing a few weeks later, the *Observer*'s political columnist was more generous, but nonetheless realistic: 'If Sir Winston's physique stands up to the strain there is no reason, at least in theory, why he should not lead his party at another general election. […] All the same, no informed person really takes this possibility seriously.'[168]

Churchill was also increasingly gaffe-prone. In a speech to his constituents in November he said that, in 1945, he had telegraphed Montgomery to store the weapons of the defeated Nazi forces so that they might be re-issued to German soldiers if the Soviets refused to halt their own advance.[169] In fact, Churchill's memory was at fault, for no such telegram had ever been sent, but the tale produced a storm of criticism. The *Manchester Guardian*, though, called for understanding, arguing that although Churchill's comments had been ill-advised, 'he could hardly have foreseen that he would be denounced by the oddest of press choruses—The "Times," the "Daily Herald," the "Daily Mirror," and the "Daily Worker." Their common link seems to be the wish to force him out of office.'[170]

Churchill's eightieth birthday celebrations a few days later offered a respite; even the *Daily Mirror* produced a memorial issue and donated £1,000 to his birthday fund.[171] He was to be presented, in Westminster Hall, with a portrait of himself by Graham Sutherland. Grace Wyndham Goldie, an impressively determined and innovative BBC producer, was in charge of televising the occasion. She hoped to have a contribution to the show direct from Churchill, over and above his own speech. There were many potential obstacles to this. First, his detestation of the 'reds' at the BBC. (Although his own government had legislated for the introduction of commercial television he was not enthusiastic about that either.)[172] Second, his inexperience of and distrust of the medium—he hated the results of his one secret TV screen-test.[173]

However, things were tactfully arranged so that, after the day's events were over, he could be filmed watching the evening's tribute programme in a room at 11 Downing Street. Goldie watched nervously on her monitor as Churchill, 'looking very old and uncomprehending', sank into his chair. 'Like an ancient tortoise withdrawn into itself and unaware of its surroundings, he gazed blankly at the television set.' At last, in response to a contribution from Violet Bonham Carter praising his courage, he registered a reaction. Goldie watched 'the ancient head move slowly from side to side in a gesture of negation and tears roll down the leathery cheeks'. Then, as the programme came to its end, 'Churchill, coming suddenly to life like a statue from the stone age taking on humanity, started to speak straight to the television camera in No. 11—spontaneously, clearly and masterfully.' He had been 'entranced', he said, by the 'thrilling panorama' brought to him by the wonders of science.[174] Battling decline, he dug deep into his remaining reserves of strength to show the world the image it longed to see.

Conclusion

On 5 April 1955, civil servant and Mass-Observation diarist A. B. Holness was startled when the radio programme *Children's Hour* was interrupted by the message that an important announcement would come through in a few minutes. Was it the outbreak of World War III, she wondered, or had something happened to the Queen? No, it was simply that Churchill had finally stepped down as Prime Minister. 'That certainly is important News—& I'm very sorry to hear it,' Holness grumbled. 'But I don't see why it couldn't have been kept another half hour till the 6 o'clock bulletin.'[1] The events of the following day, when Churchill handed over to Anthony Eden, were captured by BBC TV news, as well as by conventional newsreel. 'From his home in Carlton Gardens this morning Sir Anthony came out in morning dress', narrated the BBC's political correspondent, E. R. Thompson. 'Photographers and cameramen were there to catch the Foreign Secretary's famous smile.' The *Manchester Guardian*'s critic praised the fifteen-minute sequence—which included shots from a 'roving eye' camera in Downing Street—as 'an excellent example of how up-to-the-minute important news can and should be shown on television'.[2]

Because of a strike by maintenance workers at the point that Churchill stepped down, UK national newspapers were not being printed. According to the *Süddeutsche Zeitung*, the wits said that Churchill would not resign after all 'because at the moment in London no newspapers are appearing and under no circumstances will he do without a thundering press-echo to accompany his exit from the arena'.[3] Local and regional titles were not affected, and were supplied by the Press Association with extracts from the leaders that the national titles would have published in the absence of a strike.[4] Churchill might have been 'done out of a National Press Do' but he could console himself with extensive international coverage of his retirement.[5] 'In the United States especially, it thrust aside all other news—29 columns in the Daily Herald Tribune', summarized the *Daily Telegraph* when the Fleet Street dispute was over. 'President Eisenhower made of his tribute a special ceremony, before newsreel and television cameras.'[6]

The Rome-based *Il Messaggero* had commented a few days earlier that Churchill had held the limelight for so many years 'that it is right and human that he should wish his departure to have an adequate repercussion in the press, and through this to touch the hearts of the people'.[7] But what he now wanted was some privacy. He quickly departed for a holiday in Sicily, where Jock Colville asked the press to leave the former Prime Minister in peace. 'He just wants to paint and rest', Colville said. 'That is all, except that, he also intends to revise his unpublished book on the history of the English-speaking people which he wrote before World War II.' He also asked journalists not to follow Churchill when he went out for a drive as 'it destroys the atmosphere'.[8]

They appear not to have taken much notice. A week later Reuters reported that Churchill had spent the day painting in the 'Rope-makers' grotto' of an ancient limestone quarry. 'Warmly wrapped, he sat on a chair beneath a white umbrella, shielded from the wind and curious visitors by a tent arrangement of blankets and sheets.'[9] The agency also put together a newsreel package on his extensive doings. In view of the fact that he was being chased around by the media, the title 'How To Have A Quiet Holiday' seems doubly ironic.[10] It was the start of a pattern. In Churchill's retirement, whether he was taking a cruise on Aristotle Onassis's yacht, celebrating his birthday, or receiving honorary citizenship from the United States, the media was omnipresent. 'Dealing with the press was not always easy, particularly on the occasions when WSC was in bad health', recalled Churchill's last private secretary, Anthony Montague Browne. 'Editors invariably assumed that each illness must be the last, and they despatched distinguished correspondents to be in at the kill, which is how WSC himself described it.' Churchill insisted on editing the medical bulletins himself, and when Browne gave them to the press he found himself exposed 'to a hurricane of questions from hungry and frustrated journalists around the world'.[11]

By the early 1960s, Churchill had sunk into apathy and depression. A section omitted from the published version of Lord Moran's memoirs records him asking, 'How long have I to go on like this, waiting for death?' According to Clementine, he feared that he was going mad, and was 'no longer capable of consecutive thought'.[12] He did, however, register the assassination of President Kennedy. At 7 a.m. the next day he summoned his chief bodyguard, Detective-Sergeant Edmund Murray, to his home at Hyde Park Gate. Sitting in bed eating breakfast Churchill asked, 'Have you heard about the dastardly thing that they have done?'[13] By this point he was heavily reliant on his advisers, who acted to defend his reputation against the misleading slurs that from time to time appeared in the press. In 1963, the irreverent new magazine *Private Eye* published a cartoon suggesting that 'The Greatest Dying Englishman' had devoted his life to 'smashing the workers (shooting Welsh miners, General Strike etc.)'. It was, though, Randolph Churchill, rather than Winston, who took legal action, on the basis that the cartoon also alleged that his planned official biography of his father would falsify history. He was granted perpetual injunctions preventing the *Eye*'s publishers, directors and board members from repeating the libel.[14]

On 10 January 1965, at home in London, Churchill suffered a further major stroke. When the news was made public several days later, Lord Moran 'stood in the doorway to read the first bulletin to a crowd of reporters'.[15] A few days later, press, TV, and radio journalists complied with Clementine's request that they withdraw from the adjacent cul-de-sac. Just a few pressmen remained huddled at the top of the street in the driving sleet and rain, but the media's death-watch continued.[16] At last, on 24 January, Churchill died. As he lay in state in Westminster Hall, the first TV pictures were relayed by ITN by satellite and shown on the three major US networks.[17] BBC 1 showed nightly episodes of *The Valiant Years* (a documentary based on Churchill's war memoirs) and an obituary was included in the regular schools' slot.[18] All that remained was the funeral, long-planned by Churchill himself under the title Operation Hope Not. Almost ninety cameras traced the funeral procession, the service in St Paul's Cathedral, and the journey of his coffin on a launch along the Thames.[19] In the UK alone, 25 million people watched the live coverage, and a further three million or more listened on the radio.[20] There were no media present when Churchill was laid to rest next to his parents and his brother Jack in Bladon churchyard in Oxfordshire. This was out of respect for Clementine's wishes: thus, having always tolerated rather than embraced publicity, she found some deserved private moments at the end of a fifty-six year marriage lived in the media's glare.[21]

Her husband, by contrast, although he had sometimes found the cameras to be intrusive, had in general been sustained by publicity rather than discomfited by it. If his own writing for the press had been, for him, largely the means to an end, he nonetheless excelled at it and in some ways beat the professionals at their own game. If his treatment by the press was sometimes bruising, this was the inevitable counterpart of the huge benefits he extracted from it. Churchill would surely have had a political career in any age; but it was only the late-nineteenth and twentieth century media that made possible the type of political career he wanted to have.

Yet, as we have seen throughout this book, Churchill was often oversensitive to press criticism and overbearing towards those he thought had traduced him. Influenced by the norms of Victorian military journalism, and quite willing as a politician to intrigue with the press in his own interests, he had little tolerance for those who printed facts and opinions that he regarded as inconvenient. His high-handedness was apparent before 1914, remained evident during and after the General Strike, and arguably reached its apogee during World War II. When he retired as Prime Minister, *Le Parisien Libéré* commented that 'The absolute power which he wielded during hostilities confirmed him in a sometimes rather cynical realism and the dangerous belief of the great that they can solve all from their Olympian heights.'[22] Although the claim that Churchill had wielded absolute power was a considerable exaggeration, it is certainly fair to say that he saw press criticism during wartime as a dangerous nuisance that was best dealt with in draconian fashion.

It might be objected that his repeated fulminations should not be taken too seriously. In some ways, his reactions were in line with those of other prime ministers. As we have seen, Neville Chamberlain was determined to enforce a tight grip on the press. Harold Wilson was paranoid about it, and Margaret Thatcher's approach to the media was illiberal at times. Furthermore, it might be argued, Churchill never went so far as to publicly label the press 'the enemies of the people', and wiser counsel generally prevailed once he had calmed down. There is an element of truth here, but the question is, why did others resist his worst impulses rather than seeking to indulge them? Here he deserves credit for choosing colleagues who were prepared to stand up to him, but considerable acknowledgement must be given to political institutions which defaulted to following the rule of law rather than the whims of the head of government. The refusal of the Director of Public Prosecutions to approve a legally unsound prosecution of Liddell Hart is a case in point. Some recognition should also go to the British press itself. One need not take too rosy a view of it, run as it was to a great degree by the unscrupulous 'trusts' that Churchill had denounced in his Edwardian Liberal days. But its heterogeneity was a strength, and even the *Daily Mirror*'s rivals mostly rallied round it in 1942, the moment of the greatest threat to press freedom during the war. At the same time, the frequent willingness of the press to give in, pragmatically or patriotically, to informal government pressure—just as it had done for Neville Chamberlain, in a less good cause—helped save it from the threat of more drastic measures. If we had better records of Churchill's late-night phone calls, we would likely know a lot more about the stories that he managed to get killed or altered.

To draw attention to Churchill's authoritarian reflexes towards the press is not to diminish his other achievements, nor to forget the immense stress that he was often under. It is not unknown or even unnatural for democratic politicians to have such impulses; the important thing is that they are kept in check. This does not require heroic officials, merely competent and principled ones. It does not require a wholly virtuous media, merely a diverse one with a wide and intelligent readership. These things are not too much to hope for; but once they are gone, who can say how they may be conjured back into existence?

Endnotes

INTRODUCTION

1. Edward Marsh to the editor of the *Daily Herald*, 18 June 1929, Churchill Papers, CHAR 2/164/40.
2. Parliamentary Debates, House of Commons, Fifth Series, Vol. 117, 8 July 1919, col. 1581.
3. Osbert Sitwell, *The Winstonburg Line: 3 Satires* (London: Hendersons, 1920), p. 5; Paul Addison, *Churchill: The Unexpected Hero* (Oxford: Oxford University Press, 2005), p. 105.
4. 'Mr. Churchill and "War"', *Morning Post*, 21 June 1929, Churchill Press Cuttings (henceforward CHPC), 10.
5. 'Mr. Churchill's Word Against Three Cameras', *Daily Herald*, 22 June 1929, CHPC 10.
6. Josephine Cummins to W. H. Stevenson, 22 June 1929, Churchill Papers, CHAR 2/164/40.
7. William Mellor to Winston S. Churchill [henceforward WSC], 23 June 1929, and Cummins to Mellor, 25 June 1929, Churchill Papers, CHAR 2/164/51–2.
8. 'Manners Makyth Man', *Daily Herald*, 27 June 1929, CHPC 10.
9. 'Mr. Churchill and "War"', *Morning Post*, 21 June 1929, CHPC 10.
10. Speech of 9 October 1954. Unless otherwise stated, all Churchill's speeches cited are to be found in Robert Rhodes James (ed.), *Winston S. Churchill: His Complete Speeches, 1897–1963*, 8 vols (New York: Chelsea House, 1974).
11. On the paper's increased moderation, see Huw George Richards, 'Constriction, Conformity and Control: The Taming of the Daily Herald 1921–30', PhD thesis, Open University, 1992.
12. George Orwell, 'The Freedom of the Press', *Times Literary Supplement*, 15 September 1972.
13. James Thompson, *British Political Culture and the Idea of 'Public Opinion', 1867–1914* (Cambridge: Cambridge University Press, 2013).

14. James Reston, *Deadline: A Memoir* (New York: Random House, 1991), p. 179.

15. Robin Day, *Grand Inquisitor: Memoirs* (London: Pan Books, 1990), p. 37.

16. The critic was R. A. Butler. John Colville, *The Fringes of Power: Downing Street Diaries, 1939–1955,* (London: Hodder & Stoughton, 1985), p. 122 (entry for 10 May 1940).

17. John Colville, 'Winston Spencer Churchill', *The Student*, 10 March 1931, CHPC 11.

18. James Margach, *The Abuse of Power: The War between Downing Street and the Media from Lloyd George to James Callaghan* (London: W.H. Allen, 1978), pp. 66–7; Paul Addison, *Churchill on the Home Front, 1900–1955* (London: Pimlico, 1993), p. 420.

19. Tamotsu Shibutani, *Improvised News: A Sociological Study of Rumor* (Indianapolis, IN: Bobbs-Merrill, 1966).

20. Peter Clarke, *The Last Thousand Days of the British Empire* (London: Allen Lane, 2007), p. xxiv.

21. Frederic Mullaly, 'On Writing About Churchill', *Tribune*, 28 December 1945, CHPC 23.

22. Brian Gardner showed the value of this approach in *Churchill in His Time: A Study in a Reputation 1939–1945* (London: Methuen, 1968).

23. Adrian Bingham, 'The Digitization of Newspaper Archives: Opportunities and Challenges for Historians', *Twentieth Century British History*, 21 (2010), pp. 225–31; Ian Milligan, 'Illusionary Order: Online Databases, Optical Character Recognition, and Canadian History, 1997–2010', *Canadian Historical Review*, 94 (2013), pp. 540–69; Lara Putnam, 'The Transnational and the Text-Searchable: Digitized Sources and the Shadows They Cast', *American Historical Review*, 121 (2016), pp. 377–402.

24. This book draws extensively on the Broadwater Collection (BRDW) and the Churchill Press Cuttings (CHPC), both held at the Churchill Archives Centre, Cambridge. The Clementine Churchill Papers (CSCT 8) contain cuttings from the 1951–5 period. Cuttings are also preserved in a number of different places within the Churchill Papers themselves.

25. Philip White, *Churchill's Cold War: How the Iron Curtain Speech Shaped the Post-war World* (London: Duckworth Overlook, 2012); Graham Farmelo, *Churchill's Bomb: How the United States Overtook Britain in the First Nuclear Arms Race* (London: Faber & Faber, 2013); Kevin Ruane, *Churchill and the Bomb in War and Cold War* (London: Bloomsbury, 2016); Alan Watson, *Churchill's Legacy: Two Speeches to Save the World* (London: Bloomsbury,

2016); Allen Packwood, *How Churchill Waged War: The Most Challenging Decisions of the Second World War* (Barnsley: Frontline Books, 2018).

26. The test for this is whether or not they are listed in Ronald I. Cohen, *Bibliography of the Writings of Sir Winston Churchill*, 3 vols (London: Thoemmes Continuum, 2006).

27. Penny Summerfield, 'Mass-Observation: Social Research or Social Movement?', *Journal of Contemporary History*, 20:3 (July 1985), pp. 439–52.

28. Robin Prior, *Churchill's 'World Crisis' as History* (London: Croom Helm, 1983); John Ramsden, *Man of the Century: Winston Churchill and His Legend Since 1945* (London: HarperCollins, 2002); David Reynolds, *In Command of History: Churchill Fighting and Writing the Second World War* (London: Allen Lane, 2004)

29. Frederick Woods (ed.), *Young Winston's Wars: The Original Despatches of Winston S. Churchill, War Correspondent, 1897–1900* (London: Leo Cooper, 1972); Warren Dockter (ed.), *Winston Churchill at the Telegraph* (London: Aurum Press, 2015).

30. D. J. Wenden, 'Churchill, Radio and Cinema', in Robert Blake and Wm. Roger Louis (eds), *Churchill* (Oxford: Oxford University Press, 1993), pp. 215–39; Ian St John, 'Writing to the Defence of Empire: Winston Churchill's Press Campaign against Constitutional Reform in India, 1929–35', in Chandrika Kaul (ed.), *Media and the British Empire* (Basingstoke: Macmillan, 2006), pp. 104–24; Peter Clarke, *Mr. Churchill's Profession: Statesman, Orator, Writer* (London: Bloomsbury, 2012); Jonathan Rose, *The Literary Churchill: Author, Reader, Actor* (New Haven, CT: Yale University Press, 2014); David Lough, *No More Champagne: Churchill and His Money* (New York: Picador, 2015); Simon Read, *Winston Churchill Reporting: Adventures of a Young War Correspondent* (Boston, MA: Da Capo Press, 2015).

CHAPTER I

1. *The Times*, 3 December 1874.

2. William Rees-Mogg, *Memoirs* (London: HarperPress, 2011), p. 143

3. Gustavus Ohlinger, 'Winston Spencer Churchill: A Midnight Interview', *Michigan Quarterly Review*, 5:2 (1966), pp. 75–9. Quotations at 77–8.

4. WSC, *Thoughts and Adventures* (London: Odhams Press, 1947; first published 1932), p. 32.

5. WSC to Lady Randolph, 10 January 1898, *Churchill Documents* 2, p. 856. (From 2006, the documentary companion volumes to the official

biography of Churchill by Randolph S. Churchill and Martin Gilbert have been republished by Hillsdale College Press under the title *The Churchill Documents*. Latterly the series has been extended under the editorship of Larry P. Arnn.)

6. Martin Hewitt, *The Dawn of the Cheap Press in Victorian Britain: The End of the 'Taxes on Knowledge', 1849–1869* (London: Bloomsbury, 2014). Quotation at p. 28.

7. David Brown, 'Compelling but not Controlling? Palmerston and the Press, 1846–1855', *History*, 86:281 (January 2001), pp. 41–61. Quotation at p. 41.

8. Roy Jenkins, *Gladstone* (London: PaperMac, 1996), pp. 225–8, 234.

9. WSC, *My Early Life: A Roving Commission* (London: Macmillan, 1941; first published 1930), p. 21.

10. H. C. G. Matthew, *Gladstone 1809–1898* (Oxford: Oxford University Press, 1897), pp. 295–301. Quotation at p. 300.

11. Stephen Koss, *The Rise and Fall of the Political Press in Britain*, Vol. 1: *The Nineteenth Century* (London: Hamish Hamilton, 1981), pp. 211–16.

12. Roy Foster, *Lord Randolph Churchill: A Political Life* (Oxford: Clarendon Press, 1981), p. 13; 'Vice-Chancellor's Court', *Jackson's Oxford Journal*, 19 March 1870.

13. 'Fashionable Intelligence', *Reynolds's Newspaper*, 20 March 1870.

14. Foster, *Lord Randolph Churchill*, p. 14.

15. Roland Quinault, 'Churchill, Lord Randolph Henry Spencer (1849–1895), politician', *Oxford Dictionary of National Biography* (Oxford University Press), online edn, https://doi.org/10.1093/ref:odnb/5404 [accessed 13 April 2016].

16. 'Foreign Intelligence', *Newcastle Courant*, 24 April 1874.

17. 'Fashionable Entertainments', *Morning Post*, 13 May 1874.

18. Henry W. Lucy, *Memories of Eight Parliaments* (London: William Heinemann, 1908), p. 250.

19. 'The Duke of Marlborough's Entry Into Dublin', *The Standard*, 11 January 1877.

20. WSC, *My Early Life*, p. 15.

21. For a very full account see 'Unveiling of the Statue of Lord Gough', *Belfast News-Letter*, 23 February 1880.

22. Foster, *Lord Randolph Churchill*, p. 62.

23. Lord Randolph Churchill to Sir Stafford Northcote, [25 December] 1883, quoted in Koss, *Rise and Fall*, Vol. 1, p. 251.

24. 'The Causes of Lord Randolph Churchill's Success', *Spectator*, 20 June 1885.

25. Herbert Vivian, 'Studies in Personality IV: Mr. Winston Churchill, MP', *Pall Mall Magazine*, April 1905.

26. 'The Election Contest at Woodstock', *Birmingham Daily Post*, 1 July 1885.

27. WSC, *Thoughts and Adventures*, p. 9. He had been moved to Brighton after unhappy experiences at a previous prep school.

28. '"Winnie's Schooldays"', *Tit-Bits*, 5 June 1915, Broadwater Collection.

29. 'Gossip From "The World"', *Blackburn Standard*, 10 April 1886.

30. 'Occasional Notes', *Pall Mall Gazette*, 5 October 1886. Roose's obituarist judged that 'he added nothing to the sum of knowledge, and his position in the profession scarcely accorded with that that he held in the eyes of the public'. *British Medical Journal*, 18 February 1905.

31. 'Our London Letter', *Sheffield & Rotherham Independent*, 7 October 1886.

32. 'Lord R. Churchill At Manchester', *The Times*, 1 July 1886.

33. WSC, *Lord Randolph Churchill*, Vol. II (London: Macmillan, 1906), p. 240.

34. Koss, *Rise and Fall*, Vol. 1, p. 296.

35. W. T. Stead, 'Government by Journalism', *Contemporary Review*, 49, May 1886, pp. 653–74.

36. WSC, *My Early Life*, p. 46.

37. Simon Read, *Winston Churchill Reporting: Adventures of a Young War Correspondent* (Boston, MA: Da Capo Press, 2015), pp. 8–9.

38. Brian Roberts, *Churchills in Africa* (London: Thistle Publishing, 2017), p. 17.

39. WSC to Lord Randolph Churchill, 22 July 1891, *Churchill Documents 1*, p. 260.

40. Lord Randolph Churchill to Lady Randolph Churchill, 18 September 1891, Churchill Papers, CHAR 28/11/36-38.

41. 'His Journalistic Fiasco', *Blackburn Standard and Weekly Express*, 18 July 1891.

42. Lord Randolph Churchill, *Men, Mines and Animals in South Africa* (London: Sampson, Low, Marston and Co., 1893).

43. See his posthumously published article 'The Dream', written in 1947–8, reproduced in Martin Gilbert, *Winston S. Churchill*, Vol. VIII: *'Never Despair', 1945–1965* (London: Heinemann, 1988), pp. 368–9.

44. Anthony Montague Browne, *Long Sunset: Memoirs of Winston Churchill's Last Private Secretary* (London: Cassell, 1995), p. 122.

45. WSC, *My Early Life*, p. 60.

46. Earl of Rosebery, *Lord Randolph Churchill* (London: Arthur L. Humphreys, 1906), p. 72.

47. 'Lord Randolph Churchill's Health', *Dundee Courier*, 26 December 1894.
48. 'Lord Randolph Churchill's Brilliant Son', *Daily Mail*, 16 February 1900.
49. *Eastern Morning News*, 7 December 1895, Broadwater Collection.
50. Quoted in Hal Klepak, *Churchill Comes of Age: Cuba 1895* (Stroud: Spellmount, 2015), p. 89.
51. WSC, 'The Insurrection in Cuba', *Daily Graphic*, 27 November 1895, *Churchill Documents* 1, p. 609.
52. The original articles and their illustrations can be accessed in the Broadwater Collection.
53. WSC, 'The Insurrection in Cuba', *Daily Graphic*, 24 December 1895, *Churchill Documents* 1, p. 609.
54. WSC, 'The Insurrection in Cuba', *Daily Graphic*, 27 December 1895, *Churchill Documents* 1, p. 613.
55. *St. James's Budget*, 13 December 1895, Broadwater Collection.
56. WSC to Lady Randolph Churchill, 6 December 1895, *Churchill Documents* 1, pp. 602–4.
57. *Newcastle Leader*, 7 December 1895, Broadwater Collection.
58. M. Shaw Bowers to Churchill, 10 December 1895, *Churchill Documents* 1, p. 618.
59. WSC, 'The Revolt in Cuba', *Saturday Review*, 15 February 1896.
60. Henry Drummond Wolff to Churchill, 24 February 1896, *Churchill Documents* 1, p. 665.
61. 'Una Carta de Mr. Winston Churchill', *La Epoca*, 24 February 1896.
62. *New York Herald*, 19 December 1895, *Churchill Documents* 1, pp. 621–2.
63. Andrew Griffiths, *The New Journalism, the New Imperialism and the Fiction of Empire, 1870–1900* (Basingstoke: Palgrave Macmillan, 2015), pp. 64–6; Joel H. Wiener, *The Americanization of the British Press, 1830s–1914: Speed in the Age of Transatlantic Journalism* (Basingstoke: Palgrave Macmillan, 2011), pp. 4, 15, 74, 116.
64. 'Interview With Lieut. Churchill', *Birmingham Mercury*, 28 December 1895.
65. 'The War in Cuba', *Daily Telegraph* (NZ), 5 February 1896.
66. 'The Dashing Soldier', *Daily News* (Perth), 24 January 1896; *St. James Budget*, 13 December 1895, Broadwater Collection.
67. Randolph S. Churchill, *Winston S. Churchill*, Vol. I: *Youth, 1874–1900* (London: Heinemann, 1966), pp. 248–52.
68. WSC to Lady Randolph, 18 November [1896], *Churchill Documents* 2, p. 703.

69. 'Chat and Comment', *Berrow's Worcester Journal*, 14 December 1895.

70. WSC to Lady Randolph, 18 November [1896], *Churchill Documents* 2, p. 704.

71. Notes pasted into the *Annual Register*, early 1897, *Churchill Documents* 2, pp. 763, 767.

72. WSC to Jack Churchill, 2 December 1896, *Churchill Documents* 2, p. 705.

73. 'A Cornet of Horse', 'The Royal Military Academy, Sandhurst', *Pall Mall Magazine*, December 1896, *Churchill Documents* 1, pp. 548–52.

74. Speech of 26 July 1897; *Bath Daily Chronicle*, 27 July 1897, *Churchill Documents* 2, pp. 770–4.

75. 'Military Letter', *Times of India*, 17 August 1897.

76. 'News of the World', *Cheshire Observer*, 31 July 1897; *Glasgow Herald*, 28 July 1897; 'Mr. Winston Churchill on the Primrose League', *Morning Post*, 27 July 1897.

77. H. C. G. Matthew, 'Borthwick, Algernon, Baron Glenesk (1830–1908), newspaper proprietor', *Oxford Dictionary of National Biography* (Oxford University Press), online edn, https://doi.org/10.1093/ref:odnb/31973 [consulted 6 May 2016].

78. Partly on account of Borthwick's early death, his relationship with the *Telegraph* would in fact be more enduring than that he had with the *Post*, although the two papers eventually merged in 1937. See Warren Dockter (ed.), *Winston Churchill at the Telegraph* (London: Aurum Press, 2015), and also Dockter's undated article ' "Playing Fair": Winston Churchill's Relationship with The Telegraph', www.gale.com [consulted 13 August 2018].

79. WSC, *My Early Life*, pp. 106–7, 136.

80. Bindon Blood to WSC, 22 August 1897, *Churchill Documents* 2, p. 780.

81. WSC to Lady Randolph Churchill, 5 September [1897], *Churchill Documents* 2, p. 784. The paper was founded in 1864, and Churchill lived long enough to approve the despatch of a congratulatory telegram in his name on its centenary. Anthony Montague-Browne to WSC, 2 July 1964, Churchill Papers, CHUR 2/560A/11.

82. Lady Randolph Churchill to WSC, 9 September [1897], *Churchill Documents* 2, p. 785.

83. See J. J. Matthews, 'Heralds of the Imperialistic Wars', *Military Affairs*, 19 (1955), pp. 145–55.

84. Richard Toye, ' "The Riddle of the Frontier": Winston Churchill, the Malakand Field Force and the Rhetoric of Imperial Expansion', *Historical Research*, 84 (2011), pp. 493–512.

85. WSC to Lady Randolph Churchill, [2 November] 1897, *Churchill Documents* 2, p. 813.

86. WSC to Frances, Duchess of Marlborough, 25 October 1897, *Churchill Documents* 2, p. 810.

87. See Ronald I. Cohen, *Bibliography of the Writings of Sir Winston Churchill*, Vol. II (London: Thoemmes Continuum, 2006), pp. 1283–8.

88. WSC, 'Malakand, 3 September', *Daily Telegraph*, 6 October 1897, in Frederick Woods (ed.), *Young Winston's Wars: The Original Despatches of Winston S. Churchill, War Correspondent, 1897–1900* (London: Leo Cooper, 1972), p. 6.

89. WSC to Lady Randolph Churchill, 25 October [1897], *Churchill Documents* 2, p. 811.

90. WSC, 'Khar, 6 September', *Daily Telegraph*, 7 October 1897, in Woods (ed.), *Young Winston's Wars*, p. 10.

91. WSC, 'Kotkai, 9 September', *Daily Telegraph*, 8 October 1897, in Woods (ed.), *Young Winston's Wars*, p. 11.

92. WSC, *My Early Life*, p. 157.

93. WSC, 'Inayat Kila, 18 September', *Daily Telegraph*, 15 October 1897, in Woods (ed.), *Young Winston's Wars*, p. 24.

94. WSC, *My Early Life*, p. 162.

95. WSC, 'Nowshera, 16 October', *Daily Telegraph*, 6 December 1897, in Woods (ed.), *Young Winston's Wars*, p. 66.

96. WSC to Lady Randolph Churchill, 9 December [1897], *Churchill Documents* 2, p. 836.

97. 'The Story of the Malakand Field Force', *The Graphic*, 19 March 1898.

98. 'The Riddle of the Frontier', *Times of India*, 5 May 1898; Lovat Fraser, 'Winston as War Lord', *Sunday Pictorial*, 15 April 1923.

99. Aylmer Haldane diary, 9 March 1898, Aylmer Haldane Papers, National Library of Scotland, MS 20247.

100. 'Concerning Cuba', *Morning Post*, 15 July 1898.

101. WSC, *My Early Life*, p. 182.

102. WSC to Lady Randolph, 30 July [1898], *Churchill Documents* 2, p. 953.

103. Keith Wilson, 'Young Winston's Addisonian Conceit: A Note on the "War on the Nile" Letters', in Edward M. Spiers (ed.), *Sudan: The Reconquest Reappraised* (London: Frank Cass, 1998, pp. 223–8). Quotation (from WSC to Oliver Borthwick, 10 August 1898) at 227.

104. WSC to Lady Randolph Churchill, 17 September 1898, *Churchill Documents* 2, pp. 980–2. Emphasis in original.

105. Read suggests that the reason for the conceit was that Churchill wanted 'to avoid getting on Kitchener's bad side' by maintaining

anonymity (*Winston Churchill Reporting*, p. 98.) But, as we have seen, Churchill intended the information to leak out, and indeed had given his mother instructions on how to achieve this. WSC to Lady Randolph, 10 August 1898, *Churchill Documents 2*, p. 962.

106. WSC, 'Korosko, 8 August', *Morning Post*, 31 August 1898, in Woods (ed.), *Young Winston's Wars*, p. 69.

107. WSC, 'Wadi Halfa, 10 August', *Morning Post*, 2 September 1898, Woods (ed.), *Young Winston's Wars*, p. 69.

108. WSC to Lady Randolph Churchill, 24 August 1898, *Churchill Documents 2*, p. 969.

109. WSC, 'Khartoum, 6 September', *Morning Post*, 29 September 1898, in Woods (ed.), *Young Winston's Wars*, pp. 111–12.

110. WSC, 'Camp Omdurman, 10 September', *Morning Post*, 6 October 1898, in Woods (ed.), *Young Winston's Wars*, p. 126.

111. WSC to Aylmer Haldane, 11 August [1898], *Churchill Documents 2*, p. 965.

112. Alexander MacCallum Scott diary, 14 March 1917, University of Glasgow Special Collections, MS Gen 1465/8.

113. For his career, see Roger T. Stearn, 'G. W. Steevens and the Message of Empire', *Journal of Imperial and Commonwealth History*, 17 (1989), pp. 210–31.

114. WSC, *My Early Life*, p. 227.

115. 'XXth Century Men', *Daily Mail*, 2 December 1898.

116. WSC, *My Early Life*, p. 227.

117. WSC, 'Man Overboard!', *Harmsworth Magazine*, January 1899, Michael Wolff (ed.), *The Collected Essays of Sir Winston Churchill*, 4 vols (London: Library of Imperial History, 1976), IV, pp. 3–5; WSC to Lady Randolph Churchill, 5 August 1898, *Churchill Documents 2*, p. 960.

118. S. J. Taylor, *The Great Outsiders: Northcliffe, Rothermere and the Daily Mail* (London: Weidenfeld & Nicolson, 1996), p. 32. Churchill later claimed to have attended a lunch on the day of the launch at which Harmsworth was the guest of honour, but he was likely remembering a later occasion. F. G. Prince-White, 'Mr Churchill Pays Tribute', *Daily Mail*, 4 May 1946.

119. 'Theft from Mr. Winston Churchill', *Daily Mail*, 30 May 1896.

120. Jonathan Rose, *The Literary Churchill: Author, Reader, Actor* (New Haven, CT: Yale University Press, 2014), pp. 36–7.

121. Jeffery Arnett, 'Winston Churchill, the Quintessential Sensation Seeker', *Political Psychology*, 12:4 (December 1991), pp. 609–21; Ohlinger, 'Midnight Interview', p. 78.

122. Andrew Roberts, *Salisbury: Victorian Titan* (London: Weidenfeld & Nicolson, 1999), p. 311.

123. WSC to Lady Randolph Churchill, 2 March 1899, *Churchill Documents 2*, p. 1012.

124. WSC to Alfred Harmsworth, 5 November [1898], Frederick D. Forsch Collection.

125. 'Making a Big Hit', *Daily Mail*, 1 July 1899.

126. 'Comedy of Manners', *Daily Mail*, 4 July 1899.

127. WSC to Alfred Harmsworth, 7 July 1899 (copy), Churchill Papers, CHAR 28/117/2.

128. 'In the Arena', *Oldham Daily Standard*, 28 June 1899.

129. 'Mr. Churchill and the Government', *Oldham Evening Chronicle*, 27 June 1899.

130. 'The Oldham Election', *Manchester Guardian*, 26 June 1899.

131. WSC to Lady Randolph Churchill, 18 September 1899, *Churchill Documents 2*, p. 1049.

132. WSC, *My Early Life*, p. 244.

133. WSC to Curzon, n.d. but September/October 1899, Lord Curzon Papers, MS Eur. F111/272, British Library.

134. Kenneth O. Morgan's admirable survey, to which I am indebted, gives Churchill only a brief mention: 'The Media and the Boer War (1899–1902)', *Twentieth Century British History*, 13 (2002), pp. 1–16.

135. WSC to Murray Guthrie, 4 October 1899, *Churchill Documents 2*, pp. 1050–1.

136. W. K. L. Dickson, *The Biograph in Battle* (London: T. Fisher Unwin, 1901), p. 2; Michael Eckardt, 'Pioneers in South African Film History: Thelma Gutsche's Tribute to William Kennedy Laurie Dickson, The Man Who Filmed The Boer War', *Historical Journal of Film, Radio and Television*, 25 (2005), pp. 637–646.

137. WSC, *My Early Life*, p. 250, 253.

138. WSC, 'Steaming South', *Morning Post*, 18 November 1899.

139. 'East London, 5 November', *Morning Post*, 27 November 1899, in Woods (ed.), *Young Winston's Wars*, p. 126.

140. 'Mr. Churchill's Despatches', *Morning Post*, 17 November 1899. Four of Churchill's telegrams, dated between 10 and 13 November, were published together in this edition—which also reported his capture by the Boers.

141. 'War and the Press', *New Zealand Herald*, 10 March 1900.

142. 'Cost of War Telegrams', *Northern Echo*, 5 May 1900.

143. Celia Sandys, *Churchill Wanted Dead or Alive* (London: HarperCollins, 1999), pp. 42–3.

144. John Black Atkins, *The Relief of Ladysmith* (London: Methuen, 1900), pp. 74–5.

145. His claim may have been valid. See Sandys, *Churchill Wanted*, p. 59.

146. Peter Quain in the *Natal Daily News*, reproduced in 'The Capture of Winston', *South China Morning Post*, 12 December 1948.

147. *Manchester Evening Chronicle*, 17 November 1899, Broadwater Collection.

148. See, for example, 'Severe British Losses', *Daily Mail*, 17 November 1899. For a summary of coverage see 'Our Captured Correspondent', *Morning Post*, 18 November 1899.

149. *Morning Herald*, 18 November 1899, Broadwater Collection.

150. Candice Millard, *Hero of the Empire: The Making of Winston Churchill* (London: Allen Lane, 2016).

151. WSC, *My Early Life*, p. 282.

152. *Dublin Herald*, 25 November 1899, Broadwater Collection.

153. *Freeman's Journal*, 18 November 1899, Broadwater Collection.

154. *Cheltenham Examiner*, 27 November 1899, Broadwater Collection.

155. Quoted in 'Our Captured Correspondent', *Morning Post*, 18 November 1899.

156. WSC, *My Early Life*, p. 315.

157. With the usual delay, the letters were published after Churchill's escape, so it is true that that they did not influence the sensational accounts published while he was still in captivity.

158. 'The Prisoners at Pretoria', *Financial Times*, 25 November 1899.

159. 'Foreign Opinion', *Morning Post*, 23 December 1899.

160. WSC, *My Early Life*, p. 313.

161. 'The War', *Morning Post*, 27 December 1899.

162. 'Winston Churchill Free', *Financial Times*, 23 December 1899.

163. WSC, *My Early Life*, pp. 313–16.

164. WSC to Pamela Plowden, 10 January 1900, *Churchill Documents* 2, p. 1144.

165. 'The War', *Morning Post*, 26 January 1900.

166. 'Operations in Natal', *Morning Post*, 29 January 1900.

167. 'Operations in Natal', *Morning Post*, 1 February 1900.

168. Sandys, *Churchill Wanted*, p. 168.

169. WSC to *The Natal Witness*, 29 March 1900, *Churchill Documents* 2, pp. 1163–4; WSC, *My Early Life*, pp. 344–5.

170. WSC, *The Boer War: London to Ladysmith Via Pretoria and Ian Hamilton's March* (London: Pimlico, 2002), pp. ix–x (preface to *Ian Hamilton's March*).

171. 'Mr. Churchill's War Story', *The Echo*, 15 May 1900, Broadwater Collection.

172. 'Historian Of This War', *Toronto Daily Star*, 31 March 1900.

173. 'Literary News and Books to be Read', *Navy and Army Illustrated*, 31 March 1900.

174. For which, see Simon J. Potter, 'Jingoism, Public Opinion, and the New Imperialism: Newspapers and Imperial Rivalries at the fin de siècle', *Media History*, 20 (2014), pp. 34–50.

175. A couple of examples will suffice: 'Escape of Churchill', *Daily Inter Mountain* (Butte, Montana), 27 December 1899; 'Winston Churchill's telegram to The Morning Post', *Taranaki Herald*, 14 February 1900. See also Simon J. Potter, *News and the British World: The Emergence of an Imperial Press System 1876–1922* (Oxford: Oxford University Press, 2003), pp. 46, 50.

176. Bob Nicholson, '"You Kick the Bucket; We Do the Rest!": Jokes and the Culture of Reprinting in the Transatlantic Press', *Journal of Victorian Culture*, 17 (2012), pp. 273–86.

177. WSC, *My Early Life*, p. 228.

178. 'Mr. Winston Churchill's Book', *Daily Express*, 12 May 1900, Broadwater Collection.

179. Glenn R. Wilkinson, *Depictions and Images of War in Edwardian Newspapers, 1899–1914* (Basingstoke: Palgrave Macmillan, 2003), p. xi.

180. 'Mr. Churchill's Despatches', *Morning Post*, 17 November 1899; 'Operations in Natal', *Morning Post*, 24 March 1900.

181. See Michael MacDonagh, 'Can We Rely on Our War News?', *Fortnightly Review*, 63 (1898), pp. 612–25.

CHAPTER 2

1. For the part that was published at the time, see WSC, 'Success in Journalism', *The Inlander*, February 1901, copy in Churchill Papers, CHAR 8/14.

2. Gustavus Ohlinger, 'Winston Spencer Churchill: A Midnight Interview', *Michigan Quarterly Review*, 5:2 (1966), pp. 75–9. Quotations at 77–8.

3. James Thompson, *British Political Culture and the Idea of 'Public Opinion', 1867–1914* (Cambridge: Cambridge University Press, 2013). Quotation at p. 23.

4. WSC, *My Early Life* (London: Macmillan, 1941; first published 1930), p. 371.

5. For Churchill's comments on the decline of parliamentary reporting, see *Special Report from the Select Committee on Procedure on Public Business* (London: HMSO, 1931), p. 146, and also his speech of 28 October 1952.

6. J. A. Spender, *Life, Journalism and Politics*, Vol. I (London: Cassell, 1927), p. 162.

7. Speech of 18 February 1901.

8. *The Scotsman*, 19 February 1901, quoted in *Churchill Documents* 3, p. 14.

9. John A. Hutcheson, Jr., *Leo Maxse and the National Review, 1893–1914: Right-wing Politics and Journalism in the Edwardian Era* (New York: Garland Publishing, 1989), pp. 158–61.

10. *New York Tribune*, quoted in 'Ministers of the Future', *Hawera and Normanby Star*, 22 May 1903.

11. Speech of 13 May 1901.

12. WSC, *My Early Life*, p. 383.

13. A. J. A. Morris, *Reporting the First World War: Charles Repington, The Times and the Great War, 1914–1918* (Cambridge: Cambridge University Press, 2015), pp. 19–20.

14. WSC, 'The Only Way', *Daily Mail*, 18 June 1901.

15. Charles à Court Repington, *Vestigia: Reminiscences of War and Peace* (Boston, MA: Houghton Mifflin, 1919), p. 252.

16. WSC to the editor of *The Times*, 25 June 1901 (published 28 June), *Churchill Documents* 3, pp. 74–5.

17. Churchill's involvement in the correspondence began in September 1901 and concluded in June 1902. *Churchill Documents* 3, pp. 79–81, 135–42.

18. 'Power of the Press', *Daily Mail*, 26 October 1903.

19. The essential work on this controversy is Frank Trentmann, *Free Trade Nation: Commerce, Consumption, and Civil Society in Modern Britain* (Oxford: Oxford University Press, 2008), but for the press dimension it is still necessary to consult Stephen Koss, *The Rise and Fall of the Political Press in Britain*, Vol. 2: *The Twentieth Century* (London: Hamish Hamilton, 1984). For Churchill's own thought and rhetoric on this issue, see Peter Clarke, 'Churchill's Economic Ideas, 1900–1930', in Robert Blake and Wm. Roger Louis (eds), *Churchill* (Oxford: Oxford University Press, 1993), pp. 79–95, and Richard Toye, 'Trade and Conflict in the Rhetoric of Winston Churchill', in Lucia Coppolaro and Francine McKenzie (eds), *A Global History of Trade and Conflict Since 1500* (Basingstoke: Palgrave Macmillan, 2013), pp. 124–41.

20. WSC to Rosebery, 10 October 1902, in *Churchill Documents* 3, p. 168.

21. WSC to Hubert Carr-Gomm, 5 December 1903 (copy), British Library of Political and Economic Science, Archives Division, Coll. Misc. 0472.

22. Lord Hugh Cecil to WSC, [30 May 1903], *Churchill Documents* 3, p. 189.

23. 'Interview With Mr. Winston Churchill', *Westminster Gazette*, 29 May 1903.

24. Lord Hugh Cecil to WSC, 27 October 1903, *Churchill Documents* 3, p. 244.

25. WSC to Strachey, 30 May 1903, John St Loe Strachey Papers, STR/4/10, Parliamentary Archives.

26. WSC to Strachey, 4 June 1903, Strachey Papers, STR/4/10.

27. WSC to Lord Rosebery, 17 November 1903, *Churchill Documents* 3, pp. 252–3.

28. WSC to Alfred Harmsworth, 11 September 1903 (copy), Churchill Papers, CHAR 28/117/9.

29. WSC to Harmsworth, 26 August 1903 (copy), Churchill Papers, CHAR 28/117/6.

30. J. Lee Thompson, *Northcliffe: Press Baron in Politics, 1865–1922* (London: John Murray, 2000), pp. 103–9.

31. H. W. Wilson to Harmsworth, 1 October 1903, Northcliffe Papers, Add MS 62201, f. 2.

32. WSC to Frederic Horne, 19 December 1903, *Churchill Documents* 3, p. 266.

33. Speech of 21 December 1903.

34. Horne to WSC, 12 December 1903, Churchill Papers, CHAR 2/10/16.

35. WSC to A. J. Balfour, 22 January 1904, *Churchill Documents* 3, p. 305.

36. Spender, *Life, Journalism and Politics*, Vol. I, p. 164.

37. WSC to Cecil, 14 November 1904, *Churchill Documents* 3, pp. 371–2.

38. Speech of 11 November 1904.

39. Koss, *Rise and Fall*, Vol. II, p. 40.

40. WSC to Alfred Harmsworth, 16 November 1903 (copy), Churchill Papers, CHAR 28/117/14.

41. Speech of 10 November 1904.

42. WSC to the editor of *The Times*, 21 November 1904, in *Churchill Documents* 3, p. 378.

43. WSC to the editor of *The Times*, 23 November 1904, in *Churchill Documents* 3, p. 381.

44. 'Mr. Churchill on the Press', *Daily Mail*, 11 May 1905.

45. 'More Adventures', *Manchester Daily Dispatch*, 25. November 1903, Broadwater Collection.

46. Speech of 16 January 1906.

47. It is also worth noting that Northcliffe's brother Cecil Harmsworth was a Liberal politician and that the press baron always sent him a fleet of cars to help out with his election campaigns. See Andrew Thorpe and Richard Toye (eds), *Parliament and Politics in the Age of Asquith and Lloyd George: The Diaries of Cecil Harmsworth, MP, 1909–1922* (Cambridge: Cambridge University Press for the Royal Historical Society, 2016), p. 6.

48. Charles E. Hands, '"Winston"', *Daily Mail*, 5 January 1906; Thompson, *Northcliffe*, p. 130.

49. *Illustrated London News*, 20 January 1906.

50. Several are reproduced in *My Early Life*. On the question of illustrations in books written by Churchill, see Paul K. Alkon, *Winston Churchill's Imagination* (Lewisburg, PA: Bucknell University Press, 2006), Chapter 3.

51. Churchill testified on behalf of one of these in a court case after the war: 'Mr. Churchill's Limitation', *Daily Mail*, 15 June 1901.

52. For example, 'Starting for a Reconnaissance at Estcourt', *The Graphic*, 16 December 1899, Broadwater Collection.

53. This was clearly the case with 'An Armoured Train Disabled in a Fierce Fight', *Illustrated Police News*, 25 November 1899 and, even more obviously, the cartoon-strip-like portrayal of 'The Escape of Brave Winston Churchill From Pretoria', *Illustrated Police News*, 6 January 1900. For other depictions of the armoured train, see *Daily News Weekly*, 25 November 1899, *Christian Herald*, 30 November 1899, *The Golden Penny*, 6 December 1899, *Black and White*, 16 December 1899, all in Broadwater Collection.

54. Glenn R. Wilkinson, *Depictions and Images of War in Edwardian Newspapers, 1899–1914* (Basingstoke: Palgrave Macmillan, 2003), p. 7.

55. For example, 'The Fight for North-West Manchester', *Illustrated London News*, 25 April 1908.

56. 'The Flying First Lord', *Illustrated London News*, 6 June 1914. Churchill was dressed 'in aviation kit—the familiar hat in his hand.'

57. WSC, *Thoughts and Adventures* (London: Odhams Press, 1947; first published 1932), pp. 9, 13.

58. Speech of 22 February 1906.

59. 'An Elgin Marble', *Punch*, 25 April 1906. The cartoon was used on the dust-jacket of Ronald Hyam's book *Elgin and Churchill at the Colonial Office 1905–1908: The Watershed of the Empire-Commonwealth* (London: Macmillan, 1968), which remains essential reading for this period.

60. Quoted in L. J. Maxse to the editor of the *Daily Mail*, 6 January 1906.

61. WSC, Memorandum, 30 January 1907, *Churchill Documents* 3, p. 626.

62. Simon J. Potter, *News and the British World: The Emergence of an Imperial Press System 1876–1922* (Oxford: Oxford University Press, 2003), p. 88.

63. 'Minutes of the Proceedings of the Colonial Conference, 1907', Cd. 5323, May 1907, p. 22.

64. '"A Failure and a Sham"', *Daily Mail*, 15 May 1907.

65. HC Deb, 15 May 1907, Vol. 174 cols. 953–4.

66. 'Sir Robert Bond and the Colonial Office', *Daily Mail*, 14 June 1907.

67. 'Why Ministers Have Lost their Temper', *Daily Mail*, 17 May 1907.

68. Speech of 18 May 1907.

69. See Thomas Marlowe to Northcliffe, 26 May 1907, Northcliffe Papers, Add MS 62198, f. 7.

70. Baron Herbert de Reuter to WSC, 17 May 1907, *Churchill Documents* 3, p. 658.

71. J. Castell Hopkins, *The Canadian Annual Review of Public Affairs 1907* (Toronto: Annual Review Publishing Company, 1908), p. 329.

72. Speech of 18 May 1907.

73. 'Cap Strike Settlement', *Manchester Courier*, 3 September 1907; *Daily Mail*, 5 September 1907.

74. Elgin to Crewe, [?] May 1908, *Churchill Documents* 4, p. 797.

75. '"Winston" on his Travels', *Bystander*, 23 October 1907, Broadwater Collection.

76. Lady Gwendeline Bertie to WSC, 26 November 1907, *Churchill Documents* 4, p. 709.

77. 'Christmas Cards for Celebrities', *Punch*, 1 January 1908.

78. 'Talk', *Star of East Africa*, 16 November 1907.

79. Christopher Hassall, *Edward Marsh: Patron of the Arts: A Biography* (London: Longmans, 1959), p. 133.

80. WSC to Jack Churchill, 17 November 1907, *Churchill Documents* 4, p. 701.

81. Hesketh Bell, *Glimpses of a Governor's Life* (London: Sampson, Low, Marston & Co., n.d.), p. 170 (diary entry for 25 November 1907).

82. 'Mr Churchill—Imperialist!', *The Observer*, 6 December 1908.

83. Roderick P. Neumann, 'Churchill and Roosevelt in Africa: Performing and Writing Landscapes of Race, Empire, and Nation', *Annals of the Association of American Geographers*, 103 (2013), pp. 1371–88.

84. Paul Addison, *Churchill on the Home Front, 1900–1955* (London: Pimlico, 1993), p. 59.

85. WSC to J. A. Spender 22 December 1907, J. A. Spender Papers, MS 46388, ff. 220–1.

86. Churchill's speech of 23 January 1908 did indeed cover the promised themes.
87. WSC, 'The Untrodden Field in Politics', *The Nation*, 7 March 1908.
88. 'The New Liberalism', *The Spectator*, 14 March 1908.
89. 'A Minimum Standard', *Daily Chronicle*, 9 March 1908, Broadwater Collection.
90. H. W. Massingham to WSC, 14 April 1908, Churchill Papers, CHAR 4/16/37; Massingham to WSC 31 October 1910, CHAR 12/4/46.
91. Note of a meeting between WSC and Massingham, June 1909, Churchill Papers, CHAR 2/39/71.
92. Vivian Phillipps, quoted in Trevor Wilson (ed.), *The Political Diaries of C.P. Scott 1911–1928* (London: Collins, 1970), p. 25.
93. Violet Bonham Carter, *Winston Churchill As I Knew Him* (London: Reprint Society, 1965), p. 165.
94. Alexander Fuller-Acland-Hood to Lord Stanley, [9 Apr. 1908], *Churchill Documents* 4, p. 770.
95. E. Stevenson to the editor of the *Westminster Gazette*, published 23 April 1908.
96. 'J.G.H.', '"Consistent" Mr. Churchill', *Manchester Courier*, 13 April 1908.
97. Speech of 15 April 1908; 'Mr. Churchill', *Manchester Guardian*, 16 April 1908.
98. Speech of 20 April 1908. This time Churchill was plainly justified in taking legal action. On a later occasion, however, he attempted to browbeat Aylmer Haldane into giving testimony favourable to him in an action against *Blackwood's* magazine, which had criticized his actions during his escape. As it turned out, the magazine failed to stand its ground, and Churchill won by default. Celia Sandys, *Churchill Wanted Dead or Alive* (London: HarperCollins, 1999), pp. 108–9.
99. Lord Northcliffe to WSC, 11 May 1908, *Churchill Documents* 4, p. 791.
100. WSC to Northcliffe, 14 May 1908, *Churchill Documents* 4, p. 792.
101. Koss, *Rise and Fall*, Vol. II, pp. 34–5.
102. WSC to Clementine Hozier, 27 April 1908, *Churchill Documents* 4, p. 787.
103. 'The Quick-Change Artist', *Pall Mall Gazette*, 1 May 1908; 'The March to Scotland', *Manchester Evening News*, 1 May 1908; 'Dundee', *Hull Daily Mail*, 1 May 1908; 'Bonnie Dundee', *Newcastle Evening Chronicle*, 2 May 1908; all in Broadwater Collection.
104. 'The Cabinet and the Army', *The Times*, 13 July 1908.

105. R. B. Haldane to Mary Haldane, 13 July 1908, Haldane Papers, MS 5980.

106. WSC to Haldane, 13 July 1908, Haldane Papers, MS 5908.

107. Haldane to Elizabeth Haldane, 15 July 1908, Haldane Papers, MS 6011.

108. Morris, *Reporting the First World War*, p. 8.

109. Haldane to Mary Haldane, 18 July 1908, Haldane Papers, MS 5980.

110. 'Winston Churchill as an Engaged Man', *New York Times*, 16 August 1908.

111. Venetia Stanley to Violet Asquith, 16 August 1908, in Mark Bonham Carter and Mark Pottle (eds), *Lantern Slides: The Diaries and Letters of Violet Bonham Carter 1904–1914* (London: Weidenfeld & Nicolson, 1996), pp. 162–3.

112. Michael Shelden, *Young Titan: The Making of Winston Churchill* (London: Simon & Schuster, 2013), p. 191. Late in life, she told Churchill's son Randolph that 'with infinite regret and sorrow' she had 'destroyed some of the most intimate and (politically) interesting' of Winston's letters 'which were of a strictly confidential nature'. Violet Bonham Carter to Randolph Churchill, MS Bonham Carter 294, ff. 86–7.

113. 'Mr. Winston Churchill Married to Miss Clementine Hozier At St. Margaret's, Westminster', *Daily Mirror*, 14 September 1908.

114. 'Mrs. Winston Churchill Makes Her First Speech At A Public Function In London', *Daily Mirror*, 21 October 1908.

115. Alexander MacCallum Scott diary, 28 July 1917, MS Gen 14565/8.

116. Winston and Clementine's youngest daughter recalled: 'I often remember him coming into her room, or vice versa, perhaps putting the paper on the bed, and saying "Have you seen that?"' Interview of Mary Soames by William Manchester, 1980, William Manchester Papers Box 450.

117. Lord Beveridge, *Power and Influence* (London: Hodder & Stoughton, 1953), p. 50.

118. WSC to H. H. Asquith, 12 January 1909, *Churchill Documents* 4, p. 870.

119. Speech of 13 January 1909.

120. Koss, *Rise and Fall*, Vol. II, Chapter 4.

121. Spender, *Life, Journalism and Politics*, Vol. I, p. 152

122. G. E. Buckle to WSC, 25 January 1909, *Churchill Documents* 4, p. 874.

123. Buckle to WSC, 9 March 1909, *Churchill Documents* 4, p. 879.

124. J. S. Sandars to A. J. Balfour, [16 December 1909], quoted in Koss, *Rise and Fall*, Vol. II, p. 130.

125. See Richard Toye, *Lloyd George and Churchill: Rivals for Greatness* (London: Macmillan, 2007).

126. 'A Lloyd George-Churchill Party?', *Western Mail*, 16 March 1908, Broadwater Collection.

127. WSC to H. H. Asquith, 12 January 1909, *Churchill Documents* 4, p. 872.

128. Speech of 13 January 1909.

129. Quoted in 'Friction in the Cabinet', *Manchester Courier*, 1 February 1909.

130. Massingham to WSC, apparently dated 27 January (1909), but more plausibly 21 January, Churchill Papers, CHAR 2/39/10-11. Churchill's 22 January letter quoted below reads logically as a response to this.

131. WSC to Massingham, 22 January 1909, *Churchill Documents* 4, p. 872. There are two copies of this letter in the Churchill Papers. One is type-written and is dated 22 January. The second is written in the hand of a secretary, Annette Anning, and is marked 'Not sent'. It thus seems doubtful that Massingham received it, a point which the Companion Volume does not make clear. CHAR 2/39/4-8.

132. Asquith to Margot Asquith, 21 February 1909, Margot Asquith Papers, MSS Eng c. 6690, f. 184.

133. 'Talk with Mr. Massingham', 7? July 1909, Churchill Papers, CHAR 2/39/70-1.

134. Massingham to WSC, 10 July [1909], Churchill Papers, CHAR 2/39/75.

135. H.N. [Henry Norman] to WSC, 15 July 1909, Churchill Papers, CHAR 2/39/72-4.

136. 'The Budget', *The Times*, 31 July 1909; Robert W. Smith, 'David Lloyd George's Limehouse Address', *Central States Speech Journal*, 18 (1967), pp. 169–76.

137. Speech of 2 August 1909. With respect to the *Daily Mail*, note the echo of Lord Salisbury's 'written by office boys' gibe.

138. 'A Poor Sense of Humour', *Pall Mall Gazette*, 23 October 1909, Broadwater Collection. Emphasis in original.

139. WSC, *Thoughts and Adventures* (London: Odhams Press, 1947; first published 1932), p. 20. Churchill dated the incident to 'the General Election of 1910'—in fact there were two. It seems likely that the episode occurred in December 1909, when the first of these elections had already been called. Winston and Clementine were certainly photographed on Southport beach—although his headgear does not look especially ridiculous, the facts (if not the hat) seem to fit. 'Mr. and Mrs. Winston Churchill', *Black & White*, 11 December 1909, Broadwater Collection.

140. David Low, *Low's Autobiography* (London: Michael Joseph, 1956), pp. 161–2.

141. Churchill, *Thoughts and Adventures*, p. 20.

142. Herbert Gladstone to WSC, 16 March 1910 and WSC to Gladstone, 17 March 1910, *Churchill Documents* 4, pp. 1156–7.

143. Not, *pace* Paul Addison, a piece of cod: *Churchill on the Home Front*, p. 118.

144. For some heavy-handed press satire on this, see 'W.R. Titterton Interviews', *P.I.P.: Penny Illustrated Paper*, 22 April 1911. For more details of the episode, see Richard Toye, *Lloyd George and Churchill: Rivals for Greatness* (London: Macmillan, 2007), p. 70.

145. David Lloyd George to Charles Masterman, 3 February 1911, Masterman Papers, CFGM 4/1/3/4.

146. 'The Home Secretary and the Dartmoor Shepherd', *The Times*, 27 January 1911.

147. See, for example, 'Mr. Churchill's Tormentors', *Daily Mail*, 6 February 1909.

148. Addison, *Churchill on the Home Front*, pp. 135–6, 143–4.

149. 'What Will Mr. Churchill Do Now?', *Daily Mail*, 23 November 1910.

150. Addison, *Churchill on the Home Front*, p. 127; WSC, *Thoughts and Adventures*, pp. 41–8.

151. 'London—Sidney Street Siege', 1911, Britishpathe.com [consulted 18 October 2016].

152. Hassall, *Edward Marsh*, p. 171.

153. Almeric Fitzroy diary, 9 January 1911, Almeric Fitzroy Papers, MS Add 48380*.

154. Unsurprisingly, Churchill insisted on the omission of the final sentence when the letter was published in a biography of Spender— at the point when he, Churchill, was leader of the Conservative Party. WSC to Spender, [4 January 1911], Spender Papers, Add MS 46388, f. 225; John Colville to Wilson Harris, 16 January 1945, Churchill Papers, CHAR 20/197B/181; Wilson Harris, *J.A. Spender* (London: Cassell, 1946), p. 84.

155. Northcliffe to Marlowe, 19 January 1911, Northcliffe Papers, Add MS 62198, f. 82.

156. 'Love and Politics', *Daily Mirror*, 12 September 1908.

157. Speech of 13 January 1909.

158. 'Mr. Churchill in Birmingham', *The Times*, 14 January 1909.

CHAPTER 3

1. John M. McEwen (ed.), *The Riddell Diaries, 1908–1923* (London: Athlone Press, 1986), p. 27 (entry for early November 1911).
2. McEwen, *Riddell Diaries*, p. 22 (entry for 2 November 1908).
3. Cameron Hazlehurst and Christine Woodland (eds), *A Liberal Chronicle: Journals and Papers of J.A. Pease, 1st Lord Gainford 1908–1910* (London: Historians' Press, 1994), p. 115 (entry for 27 April 1909); Stephen Koss, *The Rise and Fall of the Political Press in Britain,* Vol. 2: *The Twentieth Century* (London: Hamish Hamilton, 1984), p. 103.
4. McEwen, *Riddell Diaries*, p. 24 (entry for November 1911).
5. Andrew Thorpe and Richard Toye (eds), *Parliament and Politics in the Age of Asquith and Lloyd George: The Diaries of Cecil Harmsworth, MP, 1909–1922* (Cambridge: Cambridge University Press for the Royal Historical Society, 2016), p. 127 (entry for 12 August 1912).
6. 'German Coup in Morocco', *Daily Mail*, 3 July 1911.
7. Keith Wilson, 'The Agadir Crisis, the Mansion House Speech, and the Double-Edgedness of Agreements', *Historical Journal*, 15:3 (September 1972), pp. 513–32, at p. 521.
8. 'Mr. Lloyd George On British Prestige', *The Times*, 22 July 1911.
9. Winston S. Churchill, *The World Crisis*, Vol. I: *1911–1918* (New York: Barnes and Noble Books, 1993), p. 33.
10. McEwen, *Riddell Diaries*, p. 25 (entry for November 1908).
11. Trevor Wilson (ed.), *The Political Diaries of C. P. Scott, 1911–1928* (London: Collins, 1970), pp. 46–9 (entry for 22 July 1911).
12. 'England, France and Germany', *Manchester Guardian*, 10 October 1911; speech of 3 October 1911.
13. 'Anglo-German Relations', *The Times*, 7 October 1911.
14. Richard Toye, *Lloyd George and Churchill: Rivals for Greatness* (London: Macmillan, 2007), pp. 89–91; David Gethin Morgan-Owen, 'Cooked up in the Dinner Hour? Sir Arthur Wilson's War Plan, Reconsidered', *English Historical Review*, 130 (2015), pp. 865–906.
15. 'Mr. Churchill's New Post', *Manchester Guardian*, 25 October 1911.
16. Wilhelm Widenmann to Alfred von Tirpitz, 18 November 1911, and Wilhelm II's marginalia, quoted in Jan Rüger, *The Great Naval Game: Britain and Germany in the Age of Empire* (Cambridge: Cambridge University Press, 2007), p. 238.
17. Speech of 9 February 1912.
18. 'Mr. Churchill's Speech', *The Times*, 12 February 1912.

19. Lewis Harcourt Cabinet notes, 10 February 1912, Harcourt Papers, MS. Eng. C. 8267.

20. McEwen, *Riddell Diaries*, p. 32 (entry for 10 February 1912).

21. 'Mr. Churchill's Speech', *The Times*, 12 February 1912.

22. Lord Northcliffe to WSC, 1 March 1912, *Churchill Documents* 5, p. 1524.

23. Christopher M. Bell, *Churchill and Sea Power* (Oxford: Oxford University Press, 2013), pp. 16–17.

24. 'German Reply to Mr. Churchill', *Daily Mail*, 20 March 1912.

25. 'The Navy Estimates', *Daily Chronicle*, 13 March 1912, Broadwater Collection.

26. The Navy Estimates', *Daily News*, 13 March 1912, Broadwater Collection.

27. 'Mr. Churchill's Statement on the Navy Estimates', *The Economist*, 23 March 1912.

28. *Pall Mall Gazette*, 22 July 1912, Broadwater Collection.

29. *Daily Telegraph*, 13 March 1912, Broadwater Collection; 'An Offer to Germany', *Daily Mail*, 19 March 1912; 'Mr. Churchill and Germany', *The Times*, 21 March 1912.

30. 'Ships, Men and Money', *The Observer*, 10 March 1912.

31. 'Sea-Power in the Future', *The Observer*, 24 March 1912.

32. McEwen, *Riddell Diaries*, p. 43 (entry for 16 May 1912). Emphasis in original.

33. J. L. Garvin to WSC, 8 August 1912, *Churchill Documents* 5, p. 1622.

34. WSC to Garvin, 10 August 1912, *Churchill Documents* 5, p. 1625.

35. WSC to H. H. Asquith, *Churchill Documents* 5, pp. 1627–8.

36. Asquith to WSC, 16 August 1912, *Churchill Documents* 5, p. 1629.

37. Richard Toye, '"Phrases Make History Here": Churchill, Ireland and the Rhetoric of Empire', *Journal of Imperial and Commonwealth History*, 30 (2010), pp. 549–70.

38. Jeremiah MacVeagh, *Home Rule in a Nutshell: A Pocket Book for Speakers and Electors* (Dublin: Sealy, Bryers & Walker, 1911); Jeremiah MacVeagh to WSC, 7 October 1911, Churchill Papers, CHAR 2/53/43.

39. 'Mr. Churchill And Home Rule', *Manchester Guardian*, 8 January 1912; 'Mr. Churchill And Home Rule', *The Times*, 8 January 1912.

40. 'Winston's Bathos', *Yorkshire Herald*, 8 January 1912, Churchill Papers, CHAR/2/60/28.

41. 'Mr. Churchill on Home Rule', *Dundee Advertiser*, 8 January 1912, Churchill Papers, CHAR 2/60/26.

42. Daniel Jackson, *Popular Opposition to Irish Home Rule in Edwardian Britain* (Liverpool: Liverpool University Press, 2009), p. 55; Paul Bew, *Churchill and Ireland* (Oxford: Oxford University Press, 2016), p. 48.

43. *Belfast News-Letter*, 8 January 1912, Churchill Papers, 2/60/32.

44. 'Anti Home-Rulers in Action: The "First Lord" Mobbed', *Illustrated London News*, 17 February 1912.

45. 'Hostile Demonstration at Larne', *Irish Times*, 9 February 1912.

46. R. H. H. Baird diary, 8 February 1912, Public Record Office of Northern Ireland, D3330/B/1/12.

47. Herbert Samuel to WSC, 13 February 1912, *Churchill Documents* 5, pp. 1390–1.

48. Report of transmission of Churchill's speech at Belfast, 9 Feb. 1912, *Churchill Documents* 5, pp. 1391–2.

49. Here we see some of the roots of the developments described in David Edgerton, *Warfare State: Britain, 1920–1970* (Cambridge: Cambridge University Press, 2006).

50. Northcliffe to WSC, [? 20 April 1913], *Churchill Documents* 5, p. 1741.

51. WSC to Northcliffe, 5 June 1913, *Churchill Documents* 5, p. 1746.

52. Lord Northcliffe to WSC, 6 June 1913, *Churchill Documents* 5, p. 1747.

53. David Stafford, *Churchill and Secret Service* (London: Abacus, 2000), pp. 40–6.

54. Archibald Hurd to WSC, 4 December 1911, Churchill Papers, CHAR 13/1/43.

55. WSC to Hurd, 13 December 1911, Churchill Papers, CHAR 13/1/44.

56. Hurd to WSC, 3 January 1912, Churchill Papers, CHAR 13/8/9. See also the friendly correspondence (between 1913 and 1917) in the Archibald Hurd Papers 1/4 and 1/8.

57. 'Notes of Proceedings of Conferences held at the Admiralty on 13th August and 16th October 1912', DEFE 53/4, TNA.

58. Nicholas Wilkinson, *Secrecy and the Media: The Official History of the D-Notice Committee* (London: Routledge, 2009), pp. 58–9.

59. Northcliffe to WSC, 1 December 1911, *Churchill Documents* 4, p. 1348; Northcliffe to WSC, 7 March 1912, *Churchill Documents* 5, p. 1524.

60. Wilkinson, *Secrecy and the Media*, p. 56.

61. Rüger, *Great Naval Game*, p. 1.

62. 'The Naval Flying Accident', *Manchester Guardian*, 3 December 1913.

63. Speech of 4 March 1914.

64. 'Under His Master's Eye', *Punch*, 23 May 1913.

65. Charles C. Turner, 'Minister of the Air', *The Observer*, 16 November 1913.

66. 'The New Churchill', *The World*, 30 July 1912, Broadwater Collection.

67. 'Arms and the Nations: Mr. Lloyd George's Bold Indictment', *Daily Chronicle*, 1 January 1914; 'Mr. Churchill's Reply', *Daily Mail*, 5 January 1914.

68. James Masterton-Smith to Leo Chiozza Money, 23 January 1914, Chiozza Money Papers, Add. 9259/IV/23.

69. 'The Board of Admiralty and the Day of Reckoning', *The Economist*, 24 January 1914.

70. J. A. Spender to Herbert Worsley, 10 December 1941, quoted in Wilson Harris, *J. A. Spender* (London: Cassell, 1946), p. 82.

71. In fact, Churchill had pleaded innocent in a written note. Roy Jenkins, *Asquith* (London: Fontana, 1967), p. 339; H. H. Asquith to Venetia Stanley, 7 March 1914, in Michael and Eleanor Brock (eds), *H.H. Asquith: Letters to Venetia Stanley* (Oxford: Oxford University Press, 1982), p. 53.

72. Speech of 14 March 1914.

73. 'Matters of Moment', *Daily Express*, 16 March 1914, Broadwater Collection.

74. See, for example, 'Civil War Averted!', *Daily Mail*, 24 March 1914. See also A. J. A. Morris, *Reporting the First World War: Charles Repington, The Times and the Great War, 1914–1918* (Cambridge: Cambridge University Press, 2015), p. 154.

75. Northcliffe to WSC, 1 April 1914, Churchill Papers, CHAR 28/117/127.

76. Jackson, *Popular Opposition*, p. 222.

77. John W. Young, 'Conservative Leaders, Coalition, and Britain's Decision for War in 1914', *Diplomacy & Statecraft*, 25 (2014), pp. 214–39.

78. 'The Cabinet as a War Ministry', *The Observer*, 9 Aug. 1914.

79. Ralph Blumenfeld to WSC, 4 September 1914, Churchill Papers, CHAR 13/45/155. See also WSC to Blumenfeld, 6 September 1914, in *Churchill Documents* 6, p. 92.

80. Statement of 7 August 1914.

81. When Kitchener made this comment in Cabinet, Asquith joked that he must be thinking of Churchill, a reference to the tensions between the two men at the time of the Sudan campaign. Lewis Harcourt Cabinet notes, 31 August 1914, Harcourt Papers Ms.Eng.c.8269. Although some correspondents dodged Kitchener's ban, it persisted until May 1915, when a small number of journalists were officially accredited. Martin J. Farrar, *News From the Front: War Correspondents on the Western Front 1914–1918* (Stroud: Sutton Publishing, 1998), pp. 71–3.

82. John Campbell, *F.E. Smith: First Earl of Birkenhead* (London: Jonathan Cape, 1983), pp. 374–81.

83. See his interviews of 29 August and 21 September 1914, reproduced in the *Complete Speeches*.

84. Asquith to Venetia Stanley, 5 September 1914, in Brock and Brock, *Letters*, p. 221.

85. Martin Gilbert, *Winston S. Churchill*, Vol. III: *1914–1916* (London: Heinemann, 1971), pp. 125–9.

86. H. A. Gwynne to Lady Bathurst, 14 October 1914, Glenesk-Bathurst Papers, MS Dep. 1990/1/2290.

87. Gwynne to Lady Bathurst, 16 October 1914, Glenesk-Bathurst Papers, MS Dep. 1990/1/2289.

88. Gwynne to Bathurst, 22 October 1914, in Keith Wilson (ed.), *The Rasp of War: The Letters of H. A. Gwynne to the Countess Bathurst, 1914–1918* (London: Sidgwick & Jackson, 1988), p. 45. Emphasis in original.

89. Memorandum by Sir Stanley Buckmaster, n.d., HO 139/5, TNA. See also Wilkinson, *Secrecy and the Media*, pp. 84–5.

90. McEwen, *Riddell Diaries*, p. 94 (entry for 7 November 1914).

91. Douglas Brownrigg, *Indiscretions of the Naval Censor* (New York: George H. Doran Company, 1920), p. 27.

92. Brownrigg, *Indiscretions*, p. 46.

93. 'Topics of The Times', *New York Times*, 17 November 1914; 'Ein englischer Dreadnought vernichtet', *Berliner Tageblatt*, 24 November 1914; WSC to the Australian Navy Board, 23 March 1915, Churchill Papers, CHAR 13/71/37; 'HMS Audacious', *Manchester Guardian*, 14 November 1918.

94. *Outlook*, 5 December 1914, Broadwater Collection.

95. C. P. Scott to WSC, 26 February 1915, *Churchill Documents* 6, p. 567.

96. 'Mr. Churchill's Success', *Daily Mirror*, 31 December 1914, Broadwater Collection.

97. Christopher M. Bell, *Churchill and the Dardanelles* (Oxford: Oxford University Press, 2017), p. 159; Brownrigg, *Indiscretions*, p. 26.

98. 'The First Lord's Plight', *New York Times*, 28 April 1915.

99. McEwen, *Riddell Diaries*, p. 109 (entry for 22 April 1915).

100. 'Mr. Churchill and the Dardanelles', *Daily Sketch*, 28 April 1915 and 'The First Lord', *The Standard*, 28 April 1915, both in Broadwater Collection; 'Liberals Defend Churchill', *New York Times*, 30 April 1915.

101. A. J. A. Morris, *Reporting the First World War: Charles Repington, The Times and the Great War, 1914–1918* (Cambridge: Cambridge University Press, 2015), pp. 182–4.

102. John Pollock, *Kitchener* (London: Constable, 1998), pp. 442–4.

103. Almeric Fitzroy diary, 19 May 1915, Almeric Fitzroy Papers, MS Add 48380★.

104. Statement of 22 May 1915, quoted in 'Cabinet-Making', *Daily Mail*, 24 May 1915.

105. 'The National War Cabinet Formed', *Manchester Courier*, 26 May 1915.

106. Speech of 5 June 1915.

107. 'Matters of Moment', *Daily Express*, 7 June 1915, 'Mr. Churchill's Great Speech', *South Wales Daily News*, 7 June 1915, 'The Grand Reserve', *Liverpool Daily Courier*, 7 June 1915, 'Mr. Churchill's Speech', *Daily News and Leader*, 7 June 1915, and 'Ministers and Their Critics', *The Globe*, 7 June 1915; all in Broadwater Collection.

108. E. Ashmead-Bartlett, *The Uncensored Dardanelles* (London: Hutchinson & Co., 1920), pp. 121–32.

109. Secretary's Notes of a Meeting of the Dardanelles Committee, 12 June 1915, *Churchill Documents* 7, pp. 1008–15.

110. Ian Hamilton to Asquith, 30 September 1915, PRO 30/57/63/107, TNA.

111. C. à Court Repington, *The First World War 1914–1918*, Vol. 1 (London: Constable, 1920), pp. 46–8.

112. Wilson, *Scott Diaries*, p. 141 (entry for 1 October 1915).

113. J. B. Firth, 'Home Politics in 1915', *Daily Telegraph*, 31 December 1915.

114. 'Peeps at the Truth', *Daily Mail*, 16 November 1915.

115. Northcliffe to Thomas Marlowe, 7 December 1915, Northcliffe Papers, MS Add 62199, f. 44.

116. WSC to Clementine Spencer-Churchill (henceforward CSC), 27 November 1915, *Churchill Documents* 7, p. 1290.

117. 'Mr. Churchill', *The Observer*, 23 May 1915; J. L. Garvin to WSC, 3 June 1915, *Churchill Documents* 7, pp. 985–6.

118. CSC to WSC 24 March 1916, in Mary Soames (ed.), *Speaking for Themselves: The Personal Letters of Winston and Clementine Churchill* (London: Doubleday, 1998), p. 193.

119. T. H. Buck to Ralph David Blumenfeld, 21 November [1915], Ralph David Blumenfeld Papers, BLU/1//4/BU.1; Andrew Dewar Gibb, *With Winston Churchill at the Front: Winston in the Trenches 1916* (Barnsley: Frontline Books, 2016; first published in 1924 under the pseudonym 'Captain X'), p. 155.

120. 'Major Churchill Under Fire', *Manchester Guardian*, 6 December 1915.

121. Wilson, *Scott Diaries*, pp. 186–95 (entries for 6–8 and 22–4 March 1916).

122. WSC to CSC, 17 March 1916, *Churchill Documents* 7, p. 1456.

123. Scott to WSC, 24 March 1916, *Churchill Documents* 7, p. 1463.

124. Garvin to CSC, 28 March 1916, *Churchill Documents* 7, p. 1473.

125. WSC to CSC, 3 Apr. 1916, *Churchill Documents* 7, p. 1478; CSC to WSC, 6 April 1916, in Soames, *Speaking for Themselves*, p. 197.

126. Northcliffe to Geoffrey Robinson, 11 March 1916, *Churchill Documents* 7, p. 1447.

127. WSC to Northcliffe, 6 June 1916, *Churchill Documents* 7, p. 1512.

128. Northcliffe to WSC, 8 June 1916 and WSC to Northcliffe, 9 June 1916, *Churchill Documents* 7, pp. 1516–17.

129. Press statement by WSC, 3 June 1916, *Churchill Documents* 7, pp. 1511–12.

130. Brownrigg, *Indiscretions*, p. 68.

131. Michael and Eleanor Brock (eds), *Margot Asquith's Great War Diary 1914–1916: The View from Downing Street* (Oxford: Oxford University Press, 2014), p. 279 (entry for 29 August 1916).

132. WSC to John Churchill, 15 July 1916, *Churchill Documents* 7, p. 1530.

133. Repington, *First World War*, Vol. I, p. 287.

134. WSC, 'Antwerp: The Story of its Siege and Fall', *Sunday Pictorial*, 19 November 1916, and 'How Antwerp Saved the Channel Ports', *Sunday Pictorial*, 26 November 1916, in Michael Wolff (ed.), *The Collected Essays of Sir Winston Churchill*, 4 vols (London: Library of Imperial History, 1976), I, pp. 172–82; Leonard Raven-Hill, 'Mr. Winston Churchill (Journalist) Gives the Hun Another Shock', *Punch*, 1 January 1917

135. Wilson, *Scott Diaries*, p. 234 (entry for 20–2 November 1916).

136. Frank Owen to Thomas Blackburn, 6 August 1952, Thomas Blackburn Papers. Owen—who was writing a biography of Lloyd George—was reporting information from Frank Whittaker, who had worked with Riddell after the First World War.

137. A. J. P. Taylor (ed.), *Lloyd George: A Diary by Frances Stevenson* (New York: Harper & Row, 1971), p. 110 (entry for 28 July 1916).

138. Roy W. Howard, 'Lloyd George Says: "We Will Fight Germany to a Knockout"', 29 September 1916, UPI Archives, http://www.upi.com/Archives [consulted 6 January 2017].

139. Tom Clarke, *My Northcliffe Diary* (London: Victor Gollancz, 1931), p. 102 (entry for 12 October 1916).

140. J. M. McEwen, 'Northcliffe and Lloyd George at War, 1914–1918', *Historical Journal*, 24 (1981), pp. 651–72.

141. Andrew Thorpe and Richard Toye (eds), *Parliament and Politics in the Age of Asquith and Lloyd George: The Diaries of Cecil Harmsworth, MP, 1909–1922* (Cambridge: Cambridge University Press for the Royal Historical Society, 2016), p. 236 (entry for 5 December 1916).

142. Repington, *The First World War 1914–1918*, Vol. 1, p. 403.

143. Kenneth Young, *Churchill and Beaverbrook: A Study in Friendship and Politics* (London: Eyre & Spottiswoode, 1966), pp. 44–5.

144. 'What to Do with Churchill', *Daily Mail*, 11 December 1916; 'Mr. Churchill & the US', *Daily Mail*, 13 December 1916. Churchill later wrote of Northcliffe's 'violent hostility' to him at this time: *The World Crisis*, Vol. II, p. 1141.

145. McEwen, *Riddell Diaries*, pp. 178–9 (entries for 10 and 11 December 1916).

146. WSC, *The World Crisis*, Vol. II, p. 1170.

147. 'The Old Gang and Gallipoli', *Daily Mail*, 9 March 1917.

148. Speech of 17 April 1917.

149. Henry Nevinson diary, 26 April 1917, Henry Nevinson Papers, MS Eng. misc. e 620/2; Alfred F. Havighurst, *Radical Journalist: H. W. Massingham (1860–1924)* (Cambridge: Cambridge University Press, 1974), p. 255.

150. Wilson, *Scott Diaries*, pp. 296, 300 (entries for 9–11 and 24 August 1917).

151. Gwynne to Bathurst, 19, 20, and 27 July 1917, in Wilson, *Rasp of War*, pp. 220–2.

152. McEwen, *Riddell Diaries*, p. 193 (entry for 30 July 1917). Emphasis in original.

153. CSC to WSC, 30 March 1918, *Churchill Documents* 8, p. 288.

154. 'Munitions Triumph', *The Times*, 26 April 1918.

155. See Richard Hill, 'The Development and Use of Armoured Vehicles during the First World War, with Special Reference to the Role of Winston Churchill', PhD thesis, Exeter University, forthcoming.

156. Alexander MacCallum Scott diary, 9 April 1918, MS Gen 14565/9.

157. Young, *Churchill and Beaverbrook*, pp. 46–50.

158. WSC to Lord Beaverbrook, 23 February 1918, *Churchill Documents* 8, p. 250.

159. Record of a meeting between WSC and press representatives on the question of unrest in the munitions industry, 19 July 1918, Walter Layton Papers, 31/10.

160. 'The Sinews of War', *Civil and Military Gazette*, 30 August 1918, Broadwater Collection. The interview had been conducted on 27 June.

161. WSC to CSC, 3 April 1916, *Churchill Documents* 7, p. 1478; CSC to WSC, 6 April 1916, in Soames, *Speaking for Themselves*, p. 197.

CHAPTER 4

1. Speech of 13 November 1918. The programme/menu for the occasion is preserved in the Broadwater Collection.

2. Kenneth O. Morgan, *Consensus and Disunity: The Lloyd George Coalition Government 1918–1922* (Oxford: Clarendon Press, 1979), pp. 40–1.

3. George Ritchie to WSC, 23 October 1918, Churchill papers, CHAR 5/20/9–11; James K. Foggie to WSC, 21 November 1918, *Churchill Documents* 8, pp. 422–3. In a speech of 15 October 1918 Churchill had stated that Britain did not seek the 'unconditional surrender' of Germany or to ruin or trample its people. See 'The New American Note', *Dundee Advertiser*, 16 October 1918, Broadwater Collection.

4. WSC, *The World Crisis*, Vol. IV: *1918–1928: The Aftermath* (London: Bloomsbury, 2015; first published 1929), p. 20.

5. *Dundee Advertiser*, 5 December 1918, cited in Martin Gilbert, *Winston S. Churchill*, Vol. IV: *1917–1922* (London: Heinemann, 1975), p. 173.

6. 'A Black and White Ministry', *Morning Post*, 11 January 1919, Broadwater Collection.

7. 'Cabinet in Disfavour', *Daily Mail*, 14 January 1919.

8. John M. McEwen (ed.), *The Riddell Diaries, 1908–1923* (London: Athlone Press, 1986), p. 250 (entry for 30 November 1918).

9. Alexander MacCallum Scott diary, 11 January 1919, MacCallum Scott Papers, MS Gen. 1465/10.

10. Stephen Koss, *The Rise and Fall of the Political Press in Britain*, Vol. 2: *The Twentieth Century* (London: Hamish Hamilton, 1984), pp. 334–7.

11. WSC to Lord Northcliffe, 27 January 1919, *Churchill Documents* 8, pp. 490–2.

12. Northcliffe to WSC, 31 January 1919, *Churchill Documents* 8, p. 499.

13. Frederick Guest to David Lloyd George, 30 January 1919, *Churchill Documents* 8, p. 499.

14. J. Lee Thompson, *Northcliffe: Press Baron in Politics, 1865–1922* (London: John Murray, 2000), pp. 324–6.

15. Walter Long to Lloyd George, 15 June 1919, Lloyd George Papers, Parliamentary Archives, LG/F/33/2/54.

16. 'Britain's Foreign Policy', *Weekly Dispatch*, 22 June 1919, in Michael Wolff (ed.), *The Collected Essays of Sir Winston Churchill*, 4 vols (London: Library of Imperial History, 1976), I, pp. 214–17.

17. The only articles Churchill appears to have published between August 1917 and June 1919 were 'British Naval Supremacy', *The Post Sunday Special*, 8 December 1918, and 'The Whole World at a Standstill', *Sunday Pictorial*, 12 January 1919.

18. Neville Chamberlain to Ida Chamberlain, 24 January 1920, in Robert Self (ed.), *The Neville Chamberlain Diary Letters*, vol. I: *The Making of a Politician, 1915–20* (Aldershot: Ashgate, 2002), pp. 355–6.

19. David Thackeray, *Conservatism for the Democratic Age: Conservative Cultures and the Challenges of Mass Politics in Early Twentieth-Century England* (Manchester: Manchester University Press, 2013), pp. 154–5.

20. WSC to Lloyd George, 6 September 1919, *Churchill Documents* 9, p. 845.

21. H. W. Massingham to WSC, 16 March 1919, *Churchill Documents* 8, pp. 587–8.

22. Raymond Postgate, *The Life of George Lansbury* (London: Longmans, Green & Co., 1951), p. 194.

23. McEwen, *Riddell Diaries*, p. 284 (entry for 10 July 1919).

24. McEwen, *Riddell Diaries*, p. 284 (entry for 10 July 1919).

25. Lord Rothermere to WSC, 9 August 1919, *Churchill Documents* 9, p. 795.

26. 'War Secretary Reviews WRAFS', *Daily Mirror*, 21 August 1919; 'Britain and Russia', 30 May 1919.

27. Kenneth Young, *Churchill and Beaverbrook: A Study in Friendship and Politics* (London: Eyre & Spottiswoode, 1966), p. 55. The advice for dealing with the press 'When you can't square them, squash them' is often attributed to Lloyd George; but Churchill has a good claim. James Margach, *The Abuse of Power: The War between Downing Street and the Media from Lloyd George to James Callaghan* (London: W.H. Allen, 1978), p. 16; John Julius Norwich (ed.), *The Duff Cooper Diaries 1915–1951* (London: Weidenfeld & Nicolson, 2005), pp. 107–8 (entry for 3 September 1919).

28. 'The Archangel Scandal', *Daily Express*, 10 September 1919.

29. 'Promise and Performance', *Daily Express*, 6 September 1919.

30. Clifford Kinvig, *Churchill's Crusade: The British Invasion of Russia 1918–1920* (London: Hambledon Continuum, 2006), pp. 247–50.

31. Lord Londonderry to WSC, 6 September 1919, Churchill Papers, CHAR 2/106/81. For examples of criticism in the Northcliffe press, see 'Mr. Churchill and Russia', *The Times*, 29 July 1919, and 'What is the Truth about Russia?', *Daily Mail*, 9 September 1919.

32. Norwich, *Duff Cooper Diaries*, p. 108 (entry for 3 September 1919).

33. Norwich, *Duff Cooper Diaries*, pp. 111–12 (entry for 4 November 1919).

34. W. P. and Zelda K. Coates, *A History of Anglo-Soviet Relations* (London: Lawrence & Wishart, 1944), p. 2.

35. WSC, 'Zionism Versus Bolshevism', *Illustrated Sunday Herald*, 8 February 1920, in Wolff, *Collected Essays*, IV, pp. 26–30. See also speeches of 17 July 1919 and 3 January 1920, and WSC to Herbert Fisher, 25 January 1920, Churchill Papers, CHAR 2/110/3.

36. 'Mr. Churchill, Zionism, and the Jews', *Jewish Chronicle*, 13 February 1920.

37. Towards the end of Churchill's life, the article did receive brief comment in Leonard Stein, *The Balfour Declaration* (New York: Simon and Schuster, 1961), p. 349. For posthumous criticism see, in particular, Michael J. Cohen, *Churchill and the Jews* (2nd edn, London: Frank Cass, 2003), pp. 55–6.

38. Joseph Banister, 'A Defence of Mr. Churchill's Policy', *Saturday Review*, 7 August 1920; John Pollock, 'Russia: A Defence of Mr. Churchill's Policy', *Saturday Review*, 7 August 1920.

39. Clive Ponting, *Churchill* (London: Sinclair-Stevenson, 1994), pp. 229–30; speech of 3 January 1920.

40. Y Telynor ('The Harpist'), 'Winston Churchill', *Y Darian*, 4 September 1919.

41. 'Kaiser and Churchill in Same Boat', and 'Concerning Criminals', *Daily Herald*, 20 January 1920, CHPC 1.

42. 'Churchill's Part in the Russian Gamble', *Daily News*, 3 July 1920, CHPC 1.

43. 'The Great Exposure', *Daily Herald*, 5 July 1920, CHPC 1.

44. 'Brer Fox', *Daily Herald*, 7 July 1920, CHPC 1.

45. Parliamentary Debates, House of Commons, Fifth Series, Vol 131, 5 July 1920, col. 1006.

46. For this allegation, see Samuel Hoare to the editor of *The Times*, published 7 July 1920.

47. There was no reference to the conversation in the official collection of documents on 'The Evacuation of North Russia, 1919', Cmd. 818, London, HMSO, 1920.

48. WSC to James Baum, 5 August 1920, Churchill Papers, CHAR 2/110/67–8. Baum was the secretary of the Leicester and District Trades Council. In correspondence with Churchill (also included in CHAR 2/110, Churchill's side alone being reproduced in the relevant Companion Volume) he pursued the issue in forensic detail and published his letters in the press. (See, for example, 'Labour & Churchill', *Westminster Gazette*, 13 August 1920, CHPC1.) To his credit, Churchill welcomed the opportunity for this type of public debate. See WSC to Baum, 1 September 1920, *Churchill Documents* 9, pp. 1202–3.

49. A. J. P. Taylor (ed.), *Lloyd George: A Diary by Frances Stevenson* (New York: Harper & Row, 1971), p. 196 (entry for 17 January 1920).

50. Quoted in 'The Great Exposure', *Daily Herald*, 5 July 1920, CHPC 1. Although Gardiner was a long-time Churchill sceptic, World War II made him a convert. Stephen Koss, *Fleet Street Radical: A. G. Gardiner and the Daily News* (Hamden, CT: Archon Boots, 1973), p. 123.

51. There is an oblique and uninformative reference in a footnote to one of the Companion Volumes to the official biography: *Churchill Documents* 9, p. 1162 (see also the passing mention on p. 1175). The affair is not discussed in David Carlton, *Churchill and the Soviet Union* (Manchester: Manchester University Press, 2000), or in Kinvig, *Churchill's Crusade*.

52. WSC, 'Is Parliament Played Out?', *Illustrated Sunday Herald*, 30 May 1920, in Wolff, *Collected Essays*, II, pp. 70–4. Quotation at p. 72.

53. WSC, 'The Poison Peril From The East', *Evening News*, 28 July 1920, in Wolff, *Collected Essays*, I, pp. 234–7. For the placards see A.G.G. [A. G. Gardiner], 'The Case of Mr. Churchill', *Daily News*, 31 July 1920, CHPC 1.

54. Lord Derby to Lloyd George, 6 August 1920, *Churchill Documents* 9, p. 1163.

55. 'Le Remède de M. Churchill', *Le Temps*, 31 July 1920.

56. 'Winnie's Call to Germans', *Daily Herald*, 3 August 1920, CHPC 1.

57. 'Germany and Bolshevism', Morning Post, 3 August 1920, CHPC 1.

58. A.G.G. [A. G. Gardiner], 'The Case of Mr. Churchill', *Daily News,* 31 July 1920, CHPC 1; 'Churchill als Frondeur Gegen Lloyd George', *Deutsche Allgemeine Zeitung*, 1 August 1920; 'Englands haltung gegenüber Russland', *Berliner Tageblatt*, 3 August 1920.

59. Tom Clarke, *My Northcliffe Diary* (London: Victor Gollancz, 1931), p. 157 (entry for 26 July 1920).

60. 'An Anxious Situation', *The Times*, 29 July 1920; Ronald I. Cohen, *Bibliography of the Writings of Sir Winston Churchill*, Vol. II (London: Thoemmes Continuum, 2006), pp. 1328–9.

61. WSC to H. Wickham Steed, 2 August 1920, *Churchill Documents* 9, pp. 1155–8.

62. 'Ministers As Pressmen', *Daily Herald*, 31 July 1920, CHPC 1.

63. 'Malcontents Defeated', *Daily Express*, 3 August 1920.

64. 'Conflicting Policies on Russia', *Manchester Guardian*, 3 August 1920.

65. See George W. Egerton, 'The Lloyd George "War Memoirs": A Study in the Politics of Memory', *Journal of Modern History*, 60:1 (March 1988), pp. 55–94.

66. Northcliffe to WSC, 8 July 1920, Churchill Papers, CHAR 28/117/171.

67. J. G. A. Pocock, *The Discovery of Islands: Essays in British History* (Cambridge: Cambridge University Press, 2005), p. 29. Mo Moulton similarly makes the argument that 'the Anglo-Irish War and its related conflicts should be seen as a civil war, one that was fought in England as well as Ireland': *Ireland and the Irish in Interwar England* (Cambridge: Cambridge University Press, 2014), p. 12.

68. The *Morning Post*, cited in 'Civil War', *Irish Times*, 24 March 1920; James Dunn, 'Ireland—a Warning', *Daily Mail*, 14 August 1920; 'Feared Closing of Dublin Port', *Daily Mail*, 7 October 1920; 'Mr. Asquith and Ireland', *Irish Times*, 15 November 1920; '13 Killed, 50 Hurt in Belfast Rising', *New York Times*, 23 November 1921. Of course, what is now called the 'Irish Civil War' took place in 1922–3, following the creation of the Irish Free State.

69. WSC, 'The Murder Campaign in Ireland', *Illustrated Sunday Herald*, 13 June 1920, in Wolff, *Collected Essays*, II, pp. 75–8. Here, as in his approach to the South African question in 1906, Churchill prefigured the colonial administrators of the 1950s and 'their search for a plausible retreat from empire on terms that preserved material influence and national honour': Stuart Ward, 'The European Provenance of Decolonization', *Past & Present* 230 (2016), pp. 227–60, at p. 249.

70. ' "Thirsting for Irish Blood" ', *Freeman's Journal*, 20 July 1920, CHPC 1; 'Report on Revolutionary Organisations in the United Kingdom, No. 64', 22 July 1920, CAB 24/109/76, TNA. See Churchill's speech of 3 August 1922 for his comments on the *Freeman's Journal*, which he also applied to the *Dublin Independent*.

71. John M. Regan, *Myth and the Irish State: Historical Problems and Other Essays* (Sallins, Co. Kildare: Irish Academic Press, 2013), p. 215.

72. Jon Lawrence, 'Forging a Peaceable Kingdom: War, Violence, and Fear of Brutalization in Post–First World War Britain', *Journal of Modern History*, 75 (2003), pp. 557–89, at p. 577.

73. 'Mr. Churchill and "the Daily Mail" ', *Daily Mail*, 5 November 1920; Parliamentary Debates, House of Commons, Fifth Series, Vol. 134, 4 November 1920, col. 545.

74. McEwen, *Riddell Diaries*, p. 328 (entry for 20 November 1920).

75. 'Plotted To Kill Lloyd George' and 'Massacre, says E. De Valera', *Chattanooga News*, 22 November 1920; 'Eamonn De Valera Lands in Erin', *Butte Daily Bulletin*, 31 December 1920.

76. 'Britain's Irish Policy Making War With US Inevitable, Says Shaw', *Washington Times*, 6 December 1920.

77. Wickham Steed to WSC, 28 December 1920, Churchill Papers, CHAR 2/111/120–124.

78. Paul Bew, *Churchill and Ireland* (Oxford: Oxford University Press, 2016), p. 102.

79. 'An Alarming Rumour', *Daily News*, 28 January 1921, CHPC1. For the earlier criticism, see 'The War in Mesopotamia', *The Times*, 21 August 1920; WSC to David Caird, 23 August 1920, *Churchill Documents* 9, pp. 1176–7.

80. David Fromkin, *A Peace to End All Peace: The Fall of the Ottoman Empire and the Creation of the Modern Middle East* (New York: Henry Holt & Co., 1989), p. 25; Christopher Catherwood, *Churchill's Folly: How Winston Churchill Created Modern Iraq* (London: Constable, 2004); Warren Dockter, Churchill and the Islamic World (London: I.B. Tauris, 2015), Chapters 4 and 5; Sara Pursley, '"Lines Drawn on an Empty Map": Iraq's Borders and the Legend of the Artificial State (Part 1)', June 2015, http://www.jadaliyya.com [consulted 16 May 2017]; Mohammad Kareem, 'The Shaping of the Middle East: British Policy and the Kurdish Question, 1914–1923', PhD thesis, University of Exeter, 2017.

81. 'Mr. Churchill's Mission', *The Times*, 26 March 1921.

82. 'Mr. Churchill & the Pyramids', *Daily Mail*, 18 March 1921; 'Traveller', 'The Middle East', *The Times*, 25 July 1921.

83. *Punch*, 22 June 1921.

84. WSC, 'Painting as a Pastime', originally published in *Strand Magazine* in December 1921 and 1922 and reproduced in WSC, *Thoughts and Adventures* (London: Odhams Press, 1947: first published 1932), pp. 232–46. Quotation at p. 234.

85. Martin Francis, 'Tears, Tantrums, and Bared Teeth: The Emotional Economy of Three Conservative Prime Ministers, 1951–1963', *Journal of British Studies*, 41 (2002), pp. 354–87. Quotation at p. 377.

86. 'Successful Private Treaty', *Country Life*, 7 October 1922; and see, for example, 'Picture Gallery' *Daily Mail*, 4 September 1928.

87. CSC to WSC 17 April 1921, in Mary Soames (ed.), *Speaking for Themselves: The Personal Letters of Winston and Clementine Churchill* (London: Doubleday, 1998), p. 236.

88. 'A Disgrace to Journalism', *Morning Post*, 6 July 1921, CHPC 1.

89. 'Winston and the "Morning Post"', *Plain English*, 9 July 1921, CHPC 1.

90. E. H. Timlett to WSC, 27 August 1921, Churchill Papers, CHAR 1/38/107. Gilbert, *Winston S. Churchill*, Vol. IV, p.613, asserts that several photographers were present, but provides no source for this information.

91. Peter Hart, *Mick: The Real Michael Collins* (London: Macmillan, 2005), p. 316; Keith Middlemas (ed.), *Thomas Jones, Whitehall Diary*, Vol. III: *Ireland 1918–1925* (London: Oxford University Press, 1971), p. 147 (entry for 26 October 1921).

92. Kenneth O. Morgan, 'Lloyd George's Premiership: A Study in "Prime Ministerial Government"', *Historical Journal*, 13:1 (March 1970), pp. 130–57.

93. WSC to Lord Derby, 8 May 1922, *Churchill Documents* 10, pp. 1886–7; Telegram from Lord Rothermere to WSC, 27 March 1922, Churchill Papers, CHAR 2/121/116; Keith Middlemas (ed.), *Thomas Jones: Whitehall Diary*, Vol. I: *1916–1925* (London: Oxford University Press, 1969), p. 197 (entry for 28 March 1922).

94. For an earlier example, see Thomas Marlowe to Northcliffe, 30 May 1921, *Churchill Documents* 10, pp. 1477–8.

95. Untitled and unsigned memorandum of 9 May 1922 (author identified as Douglas Crawford from internal evidence), Northcliffe Papers Add MS 62200, f. 173.

96. McEwen, *Riddell Diaries*, p. 368 (entry for 20 May 1922).

97. WSC to CSC, 16 July 1922, *Churchill Documents* 10, p. 1932.

98. WSC to CSC, 9 August 1922, *Churchill Documents* 10, p. 1951.

99. Frances Lloyd George, *The Years that Are Past* (London: Hutchinson, 1967), p. 206.

100. Press communiqué, 16 September 1922, *Churchill Documents* 10, p. 1994.

101. W. L. Mackenzie King diary, 17 September 1922, www.bac-lac.gc.ca.

102. WSC, Press Statement, 9 November 1922, *Churchill Documents* 10, p. 2120.

103. 'Proceedings in Parliament', *Otago Daily Times*, 20 September 1922.

104. Lord Jellicoe to WSC, 29 September 1922, Churchill Papers CHAR 28/117/86; William Hughes to WSC, 30 September 1922, *Churchill Documents* 10, p. 2055; W. M. Hughes, *The Splendid Adventure: A Review of Empire Relations Within and Without the Commonwealth of Britannic Nations* (London Ernest Benn, 1929), p. 243.

105. WSC to William Hughes and William Massey, 30 September 1922, *Churchill Documents* 10, pp. 2057–8.

106. 'The Near East: Pronouncement by Mr. Bonar Law', *The Times*, 7 October 1922.

107. 'The War-Whooper as Economist', *Daily Express*, 2 November 1922; WSC, Press Statement, November 1922, *Churchill Documents* 10, p. 2100.

108. WSC, notes for his constituents, November 1922, *Churchill Documents* 10, p. 2101.

109. Young, *Churchill & Beaverbrook*, p. 63.

110. WSC to the editor of the *Manchester Guardian*, 3 November 1922 (published 4 November). Reproduced in *Churchill Documents* 10, pp. 2116–17, but without C. P. Scott's rejoinder which expressed bafflement at Churchill's indignation.

111. 'Mr. Churchill Shouted Down at Dundee', *Manchester Guardian*, 14 November 1922.
112. 'Churchill in a Temper', *Dundee Courier*, 15 November 1922.
113. 'Mr. Churchill With His Choler Up', *Dundee Courier*, 15 November 1922.
114. *Dundee Courier*, 16 November 1922.
115. 'Minutes of Evidence Taken Before the Royal Commission on the Press, Fifth Day, 29th October, 1947', Cmd. 7325 (London: HMSO, 1948), pp. 12, 15–16; 'Minutes of Evidence Taken Before the Royal Commission on the Press, Twenty-Seventh Day, 31st March 1948', Cmd. 7432 (London: HMSO, 1948), pp. 9, 18–19.
116. On the background, see Seth Alexander Thévoz, 'Winston Churchill's 1922 electoral defeat in Dundee', MA thesis, King's College, London, 2009.
117. Asquith's response to the second volume is particularly interesting, on account of his discussion of the Dardanelles. H. H. Asquith, 'The World Crisis—1915', published in the *Yorkshire Post* (in two parts) on 10 and 13 November 1923, CHPC 4.
118. 'Winston and Toryism', *Sheffield Independent*, 6 June 1923, 'Riddle of Mr. Churchill', *Westminster Gazette*, 22 June 1923 and 'Winston's Next', *Sunday Illustrated*, 23 September 1923, all in CHPC 3.
119. 'Winston's Hats', *Sunday Illustrated*, 14 October 1923, CHPC 3.
120. Speech of 22 November 1923; 'Mr. Churchill on Hats', *Manchester Guardian*, 23 November 1923.
121. 'Mr. Churchill to Lead Liberals?', *Daily Herald*, 5 November 1923, CHPC 4.
122. Lord Pethick-Lawrence, *Fate Has Been Kind* (London: Hutchinson & Co., 1943), p. 127.
123. Norman and Jeanne MacKenzie (eds), *The Diary of Beatrice Webb*, vol. III: *1905–1924: The Power to Alter Things* (London: Virago, 1984), p. 428 (entry for 19 November 1923).
124. Stanley Baldwin to Walter Long, 24 November 1923, cited in Philip Williamson and Edward Baldwin (eds), *Baldwin Papers: A Conservative Statesman, 1908–1947* (Cambridge: Cambridge University Press, 2004), pp. 32–3.
125. 'The Press and the Election', *The Spectator*, 1 December 1923.
126. Anne Chisholm and Michael Davie, *Beaverbrook: A Life* (London: Hutchinson, 1992), p. 219.
127. Lord Beaverbrook to Lord Rothermere, 14 November 1923, *Churchill Documents* 11, p. 67.

128. Arnold Bennett to Richard Bennett, 12 November 1923, in James Hepburn (ed.), *Letters of Arnold Bennett*, vol. IV: *Family Letters* (Oxford: Oxford University Press, 1986), p. 406.

129. Martin Gilbert, *Winston S. Churchill*,Vol.V (London: Heinemann, 1976), p. 26.

130. Speech of 19 March 1926.

131. Speech of 23 February 1924.

132. W. A. S. Hewins diary, 6 March 1924, Hewins Papers, Box 124 Section 183.

133. WSC to CSC, 24 February 1924, *Churchill Documents* 11, p. 112.

134. 'More Anti-Baldwin Plots', *The People*, 24 February 1924, CHPC 4; Cutting from *Outlook*, 19 March 1924, CHPC 5.

135. 'Westminster', *Evening Standard*, 21 March 1924, CHPC 4.

136. Norwich, *Duff Cooper Diaries*, p. 108 (entry for 20 March 1924). For newsreel coverage of the result see www.britishpathe.com/video/ winston-loses-by-45-votes [consulted 24 July 2017].

137. 'Episodes of the Month: Westminster By-Election', *National Review*, April 1924, CHPC 4.

138. 'Baldwin Turns and Rends His Critics', *The People*, 18 May 1924, in Williamson and Baldwin, *Baldwin Papers*, pp. 489–93.

139. Austen Chamberlain to Hilda Chamberlain, 25 May 1924, in Robert C. Self, *The Austen Chamberlain Diary Letters: The Correspondence of Sir Austen Chamberlain With His Sisters Hilda and Ida, 1916–1937* (Cambridge: Cambridge University Press, 1995), p. 251.

140. Stanley Baldwin to WSC, 20 May 1924, *Churchill Documents* 11, p. 161.

141. Philip Williamson, *Stanley Baldwin: Conservative Leadership and National Values* (Cambridge: Cambridge University Press, 1999), pp. 353–4.

142. 'United Resistance to Socialism', *Evening Standard*, 23 August 1924, CHPC 5.

143. 'Mr. Churchill's Future', *Sheffield Independent*, 9 September 1924, CHPC 5.

144. 'Things in General', *British Weekly*, 2 October 1924.

145. Mr. Churchill on "Crowning Exposure"', *Evening News*, 25 October 1924, CHPC 6.

146. 'Daily Sketch Kills a Red Plot', *Daily Sketch*, 27 October 1924, CHPC 6.

147. 'Visitors for Mr. Churchill', *Daily Herald*, 28 October 1924, CHPC 6.

148. Young, *Churchill and Beaverbrook*, pp. 71–3.

149. John Barnes and David Nicholson (eds), *The Leo Amery Diaries*, Vol. 1: *1896–1929* (London: Hutchinson, 1980), p. 390 (entry for 7 November 1924).

150. 'Mr. Churchill, Chancellor', *Financial Times*, 8 November 1924.

151. 'Mr. Baldwin and His Ministry', *The Spectator*, 15 November 1924.

152. 'The New Cabinet', *Daily Telegraph*, 7 November 1924.

153. *Morning Post*, quoted in 'Churchill as Minister', *New Zealand Herald*, 10 November 1924.

154. 'Our London Letter', *Belfast News-Letter*, 8 November 1924.

155. Speech of 23 February 1924.

CHAPTER 5

1. 'London Letter', *Hull Daily Mail*, 8 November 1924. See also 'London Town', *South China Morning Post*, 6 January 1927 and 'People & Their Doings', *Daily Mail*, 9 April 1927.

2. David Low, *Low's Autobiography* (London: Michael Joseph, 1956), p. 162.

3. Julie V. Gottlieb, 'Neville Chamberlain's Umbrella: "Object" Lessons in the History of Appeasement', *Twentieth Century British History*, 27 (2016), pp. 357–88. David Cannadine deals with Churchill's cigar in the episode of 'Prime Ministers' Props' broadcast on BBC Radio 4 on 22 August 2018.

4. Walter Citrine, *Men and Work* (Westport, CT: Greenwood Press, 1964), p. 142.

5. 'Budget Surprises', *Daily Mirror*, 29 April 1925.

6. Paul Addison, *Churchill on the Home Front, 1900–1955* (London: Pimlico, 1993), Chapter 7.

7. 'London Letter', *Devon and Exeter Daily Gazette*, 30 April 1925.

8. Quoted in 'The Churchill Budget', *North Devon Journal*, 30 April 1925.

9. Ruth Dudley Edwards, *The Pursuit of Reason: The Economist 1843–1993* (London: Hamish Hamilton, 1993), pp. 635–7; 'The Return to Gold' and 'A Fiscal Blunder', *The Economist*, 2 May 1925; 'The Budget', *Manchester Guardian*, 29 April 1925.

10. *Daily Express*, 29 and 30 April 1925.

11. Lord Beaverbook, *Politicians and the Press* (London: Hutchinson, n.d. but 1925), pp. 92–3.

12. Lord Rothermere to Beaverbrook, 22 June 1925, *Churchill Documents* 11, pp. 497–8.

13. WSC, notes dictated for the use of CSC, n.d., but 25 May 1925, *Churchill Documents* 11, p. 482.

14. Speech of 6 August 1925.

15. Beaverbrook to Robert Borden, 10 June 1925, *Churchill Documents* 11, p. 490. The (slightly inaccurate) quotation is from William Cowper's 1793 hymn 'God Moves in a Mysterious Way'.

16. WSC to Beaverbrook, 6 Nov. 1925, *Churchill Documents* 11, p. 573.

17. Lord Beaverbrook, 'Two Ways of Liberalism: Mr. Lloyd George and Mr. Churchill', n.d. [1924–9], Beaverbrook Papers, BBKG/5/10.

18. M. P. A. Hankey, 'Cabinet Ministers and the Press', 19 June 1925, CP 297 (25), TNA. See also Gary Love, 'The Periodical Press and the Intellectual Culture of Conservatism in Inter-War Britain', *Historical Journal*, 57 (2014), pp 1027–56.

19. 'Ministers and Journalism', *The Economist*, 13 June 1925.

20. 'Ministers as Journalists', *Daily Telegraph*, 13 April 1928.

21. WSC, unpublished article on the general strike, 1937, Churchill Papers CHAR 8/567/1-19. It seems to have been intended for a series Churchill contributed to the *News of the World*, and is marked 'Not pub even by N of W'.

22. 'Chancellor and a Strike Issue', *Daily Herald*, 24 April 1929, CHPC 9.

23. Notes of a meeting held at the Treasury, 3 May 1926, *Churchill Documents* 11, p. 694.

24. Keith Middlemas (ed.), *Thomas Jones, Whitehall Diary*, Vol. II: *1926–1930* (London: Oxford University Press, 1969), p. 36 (entry for 4 May 1926).

25. Stephen Koss, *The Rise and Fall of the Political Press in Britain*, Vol. 2: *The Twentieth Century* (London: Hamish Hamilton, 1984), p. 453.

26. Robert Rhodes James (ed.), *Memoirs of a Conservative: J. C. C. Davidson's Memoirs and Papers, 1910–37* (London: Weidenfeld & Nicolson, 1969), pp. 237–8

27. *British Gazette*, 5 May 1926. Churchill's draft is in *Churchill Documents* 11, pp. 703–6. Copies of the *British Gazette* can be found in Churchill Papers, CHAR 22/145.

28. WSC to H. A. Gwynne, 10 June 1927, *Churchill Documents* 11, p. 1014.

29. Addison, *Churchill on the Home Front*, p. 263; Jon Lawrence, 'Forging a Peaceable Kingdom: War, Violence, and Fear of Brutalization in Post–First World War Britain', *Journal of Modern History*, 75 (2003), pp. 557–89; Richard Charles Maguire, '"The Fascists...are...to be depended upon." The British Government, Fascists and Strikebreaking during 1925 and 1926', in Nigel Copsey and David Renton (eds), *British Fascism, the Labour Movement and the State* (London: Palgrave Macmillan, 2005), pp. 6–26; Martin Pugh, *'Hurrah for the Blackshirts!' Facsists and Fascism in Britain Between the Wars* (London: Cape, 2005), Chapter 6.

30. Charles Wilson, *First With The News: The History of W.H. Smith 1792–1972* (London: Guild Publishing, 1985), p. 294. W. F. Deedes, who joined the *Morning Post* in 1931, regarded the story of the machine-guns as a myth, but noted that it was still being retailed by his colleagues years later: *Dear Bill: W. F. Deedes Reports* (London: Macmillan, 1997), p. 14.

31. Hamilton Fyfe, *Behind the Scenes of the Great Strike* (London: Labour Publishing Company, 1926), pp. 43–4 (entry for 7 May 1926).

32. WSC, unpublished article on the general strike, 1937, Churchill Papers CHAR 8/567/1-19. The 'fire brigade' comment echoed a phrase which he had used in the House of Commons on 7 July 1926.

33. Cabinet minutes, 8 May 1926, CABINET 27 (26), CAB 23/52, TNA.

34. Addison, *Churchill on the Home Front*, pp. 264–5.

35. Rhodes James, *Memoirs of a Conservative*, pp. 239, 249; *British Worker*, 11 May 1926.

36. J. C. C. Davidson to Baldwin, 6 May 1926, *Churchill Documents* 11, pp. 708–9.

37. H. A. Gwynne to Lord Eustace Percy, 10 May 1926, quoted in Koss, *Rise and Fall*, Vol. II, p. 460.

38. Middlemas, *Whitehall Diary*, Vol. II, p. 54 (entry for 13 May 1926).

39. John Evelyn Wrench, *Geoffrey Dawson and Our Times* (London: Hutchinson, 1955), pp. 248–9; Geoffrey Dawson to Baldwin, 7 May 1926, Churchill Papers, CHAR 22/143/8-9.

40. John Barnes and David Nicholson (eds), *The Leo Amery Diaries*, Vol. 1: *1896–1929* (London: Hutchinson, 1980), p. 454 (entry for 11 May 1926).

41. Nick Robinson, *Live From Downing Street: The Inside Story of Politics, Power and the Media* (London: Transworld Publishers, 2012), p. 62.

42. Charles Stuart (ed.), *The Reith Diaries* (London: Collins, 1975), pp. 93–6 (entries for 4–11 May 1926).

43. Middlemas, *Whitehall Diary*, Vol. II, pp. 54–5 (entry for 13 May 1926).

44. Kingsley Martin, *The British Public and the General Strike* (London: Hogarth Press, 1926), p. 91.

45. On Churchill's melodramatic tendencies, see Jonathan Rose, *The Literary Churchill: Author, Reader, Actor* (New Haven, CT: Yale University Press, 2014).

46. Fyfe, *Behind the Scenes*, p. 25.

47. William Wedgwood Benn diary, 7 July 1926, Stansgate Papers, ST/66.

48. Speech of 7 July 1926. It was not quite another *British Gazette*, but as a curiosity, it is worth noting the publication in December 1926 of *The West Essex Constitutionalist*. This appears to have been a free-sheet

for distribution in Churchill's constituency. It included an article by Winston on 'The Challenge to the Constitution' and one by Clementine entitled 'An Appeal To Women'. Whether or not it ran beyond this single issue is unclear. Ronald I. Cohen noted that Churchill's article had been partially reproduced in *The Times* on 13 December 1926 but was unable to track down the original (*Bibliography of the Writings of Sir Winston Churchill*, Vol. II (London: Thoemmes Continuum, 2006), p. 1352). What may well be the only extant copy can be found in CHPC 7.

49. WSC to Beaverbrook, 20 September 1927, *Churchill Documents* 11, p. 1052.

50. Ronald Graham to Austen Chamberlain, 21 January 1927, *Churchill Documents* 11, p. 916.

51. 'Mr. Churchill On Fascism', *The Times*, 21 January 1927.

52. *Nottingham Evening Post*, 21 January 1927.

53. 'Summary of Press Comments on Mr. Churchill's Declaration to the Press in Rome', n.d. but 1927, T172/1598, TNA. On his way home from Italy, Churchill 'put a thrilling end' to his trip by taking part in a wild-boar hunt in a Normandy forest before crossing the channel by the night boat during a gale. Readers of the *Daily News* were assured that 'The world is richer to-day' for the word-picture which its Special Correspondent sent of 'the versatile Chancellor, vividly attired for his new role', joining his fellow huntsmen, after the kill, at lunch in a stone-floored inn parlour and chanting a hunting song with them. 'Mr. Churchill's Boar Hunt', *Daily News*, 31 January 1927, CHPC 7.

54. Adrian Bingham, '"Stop the Flapper Vote Folly": Lord Rothermere, the Daily Mail and the Equalization of the Franchise 1927–8', *Twentieth Century British History*, 13:1 (2002), pp. 17–37.

55. WSC to CSC, 5 April 1928, in Mary Soames (ed.), *Speaking for Themselves: The Personal Letters of Winston and Clementine Churchill* (London: Doubleday, 1998), pp. 319–20.

56. WSC to Rothermere, 2 December 1928 (three telegrams) and J. C. C. Davidson to Lord Irwin, 3 December 1928, *Churchill Documents* 11, pp. 1387–8.

57. *Daily Mail*, 8 May 1929, in Michael Wolff (ed.), *The Collected Essays of Sir Winston Churchill*, 4 vols (London: Library of Imperial History, 1976), II, pp. 160–4; and see the correspondence in CHAR 8/229. The problem arose partly from Churchill's need to ensure that he did not breach his contract with the *Daily Telegraph* which published three of his articles at this time: 'Hurricane Years of Politics' (25 April 1929), 'Day That Will Decide Empire History' (14 May), and 'Beware the Stalemate Danger' (21 May). These are not listed in Cohen's bibliography.

58. D. J. Wenden, 'Churchill, Radio and Cinema', in Robert Blake and Wm. Roger Louis (eds), *Churchill* (Oxford: Oxford University Press, 1993), pp. 215–39, at p. 215; speech of 27 June 1924.

59. Speech of 10 February 1928.

60. Stuart, *Reith Diaries*, pp. 99–100 (entries for 13 and 25 April 1928).

61. Churchill's speech of 12 February 1929, published by the Anti-Socialist and Anti-Communist Union, CHPC 9. The words quoted are not to be found in the version in the *Complete Speeches*.

62. WSC, 'Why We Lost', *John Bull*, 15 June 1929, Wolff, *Collected Essays*, II, pp. 165–7.

63. Randolph Churchill diary, 11 August 1929, *Churchill Documents* 12, p. 42.

64. *Winnipeg Tribune*, 19 August 1929, in David Dilks, *'The Great Dominion': Winston Churchill in Canada, 1900–1954* (Toronto: Thomas Allen, 2005), p. 80.

65. Phyllis Moir, *I Was Winston Churchill's Private Secretary* (New York: Walter Funk, 1941), pp. 74–6.

66. Charles Chaplin, *My Autobiography* (London: Bodley Head, 1964), pp. 363–4.

67. WSC to CSC, 19 September 1929, *Churchill Documents* 12, p. 87; 'To Maintain Peace', *Daily Telegraph*, 23 September 1929. On the complexity of Hearst's views, see Rodney Carlisle, 'The Foreign Policy Views of an Isolationist Press Lord: W.R. Hearst and the International Crisis, 1936–41', *Journal of Contemporary History*, 9 (1974), pp. 217–27. Moreover, the term 'isolationism' is itself problematic, and 'non-interventionism' or 'unilateralism' may be preferable. For this argument, see Andrew Johnstone, 'Isolationism and Internationalism in American Foreign Relations', *Journal of Transatlantic Studies*, 9 (2011), pp. 7–20.

68. WSC to CSC, 29 September 1929, *Churchill Documents* 12, p. 96.

69. David Lough, *No More Champagne: Churchill and His Money* (New York: Picador, 2015), pp. 191, 193.

70. WSC to Edward Marsh, 5 December 1932, *Churchill Documents* 12, p. 501.

71. Peter Clarke, *Mr. Churchill's Profession: Statesman, Orator, Writer* (London: Bloomsbury, 2012), p. 149.

72. Kenneth Young (ed.), *The Diaries of Sir Bruce Lockhart*, Vol. I: *1915–1938* (London: Macmillan, 1973), p. 113 (entry for 23 January 1930).

73. Nigel Nicolson (ed.), *Harold Nicolson: Diaries and Letters, 1930–1939* (London: Collins, 1966), p. 41 (entry for 23 January 1930).

74. Beaverbrook to Rothermere, 22 March 1930, *Churchill Documents* 12, p. 144.
75. WSC to Beaverbrook, 23 September 1930, *Churchill Documents* 12, p. 185.
76. Prince Otto von Bismarck memorandum, 20 October 1930, *Churchill Documents* 12, p. 198.
77. Young, *Lockhart Diaries*, Vol. I, p. 132 (entry for 22 October 1930).
78. CSC to RSC, 23 November 1930, *Churchill Documents* 12, p. 226.
79. 'A Vigorous Speech', *The Times*, 18 March 1931.
80. Rothermere to WSC, 31 January 1931, Churchill Papers, CHAR 2/180A/52-53.
81. 'Business Men and Mr Churchill', *Hull Daily Mail*, 7 February 1931; 'Mr Churchill's Lonely Furrow', *The Economist*, 7 February 1931.
82. Speech of 23 February 1931; 'Current Topics', *Times of India*, 25 February 1931.
83. 'Winston Churchill Sees Grave Crisis in India', 16 March 1931, www.movietone.com [consulted 19 July 2017]. See also 'Mr. Churchill's Talk Film', *Daily Mail*, 13 March 1931. Churchill's son Randolph was filmed at around the same time, during a US lecture tour; he spoke at a more appropriate volume and on the whole seemed to have mastered the medium better. 'Randolph Churchill Talks to America', 1931, www.movietone.com [consulted 19 July 2017].
84. Nicholas Pronay, 'British Newsreels in the 1930s 1. Audiences and Producers', *History*, 56 (1971), pp. 411–17, at p. 412.
85. Sîan Nicholas, 'The Construction of National Identity: Stanley Baldwin, "Englishness" and the Mass Media in Inter-war Britain', in Martin Francis and Ina Zweiniger-Bargielowska (eds), *The Conservatives and British Society, 1880–1990* (Cardiff: University of Wales Press, 1996), pp. 127–46, at pp. 135–6.
86. N. J. Crowson (ed.), *Fleet Street, Press Barons and Politics: The Journals of Collin Brooks, 1932–1940* (Cambridge: Cambridge University Press for the Royal Historical Society, 1998), p. 271 (entry for 29 August 1940). Lord Boothby, *Recollections of a Rebel* (London: Hutchinson, 1978), pp. 58–9.
87. WSC, 'Radio, News-Reel, or the Press', *Sunday Chronicle*, 12 January 1936, copy in Churchill Papers, CHAR 8/540/32.
88. WSC, '1931 Crisis', 1937, Churchill Papers, CHAR 8/567/57-121.
89. Ralph Glyn to WSC, 13 October 1931, *Churchill Documents* 12, pp. 364–5. Previously, he had threatened to publicly shame the BBC by announcing that he was willing to pay £100 out of his own pocket in order to

be allowed to broadcast about politics for half an hour. WSC to John Reith, 29 December 1929, CHAR 2/164/69.

90. WSC, 'My New York Misadventure' and 'I Was Conscious Through It All', *Daily Mail*, 4 and 5 January 1932, published as one essay in Wolff, *Collected Essays*, IV, pp. 88–95.

91. WSC to Reeves Shaw, 29 November 1931, *Churchill Documents* 12, p. 380.

92. Fred Lawson to WSC, 16 November 1931, *Churchill Documents* 12, p. 373.

93. WSC to Alice Head, March 1932, Churchill Papers, CHAR 8/567/14.

94. Frederick Woods, *Artillery of Words: Writings of Sir Winston Churchill* (London: Leo Cooper, 1992), pp. 163–7.

95. Ian St John, 'Writing to the Defence of Empire: Winston Churchill's Press Campaign against Constitutional Reform in India, 1929–35', in Chandrika Kaul (ed.), *Media and the British Empire* (Basingstoke: Macmillan, 2006), pp. 104–24; Lord Hartwell, *William Camrose: Giant of Fleet Street* (London: Weidenfeld & Nicolson, 1992), Chapter 15; J. L. Garvin, 'The Star of India', *The Observer*, 2 July 1933; Nicholas Owen, '"Facts Are Sacred": The Manchester Guardian and Colonial Violence, 1930–1932', *Journal of Modern History*, 84 (2012), pp. 643–78; Colin Coote, *Editorial: the Memoirs of Colin Coote* (London: Eyre & Spottiswoode, 1965), p. 162; 'Britain and India', *Manchester Guardian*, 13 May 1933; 'The Position in India', *The Observer*, 11 June 1933.

96. Reginald Pound, *The Strand Magazine 1891–1950* (London: Heinemann, 1966), p. 1.

97. Beaverbrook to J. L. Garvin, 2 January 1932, *Churchill Documents* 12, p. 389.

98. St John, 'Writing to the Defence of Empire', pp. 111–12; Young, *Churchill and Beaverbrook*, p. 122.

99. Young, *Lockhart Diaries*, Vol. I, p. 301 (entry for 6 August 1934).

100. Speech of 8 May 1932; WSC, Statement of 29 June 1932, *Churchill Documents* 12, pp. 445–6.

101. Speech of 22 February 1933.

102. Nick Smart (ed.), *The Diaries and Letters of Robert Bernays, 1932–1939* (Lewiston/Queenston/Lampeter: Edwin Mellen, 1996), p. 88 (entry for 31 October 1933).

103. Broadcast of 16 January 1934; Alan Howland, 'Mr. Churchill Airs His Views', *Saturday Review*, 20 January 1934.

104. Broadcast of 16 November 1934; Orme Sargent to WSC, 13 November 1934, *Churchill Documents* 12, p. 920.

105. Broadcast of 30 January 1935.

106. David Reynolds, *In Command of History: Churchill Fighting and Writing the Second World War* (London: Allen Lane, 2004), p. 105.

107. A.A.B., 'Mr. Churchill Hits Back', *Saturday Review*, 3 February 1934.

108. Prince Bismarck memorandum, 20 October 1930, *Churchill Documents* 12, p. 196.

109. Throughout the year, there were over twice as many articles in British newspapers that mentioned 'Churchill' and 'India' as 'Churchill' and 'Germany'. This estimate was devised using the Gale NewsVault database (which includes *The Times*, the *Daily Mail*, and a range of other papers) which gives 192 results for the 'Germany' search and 541 for the 'India' one, with the articles limited to those found in the News, Letters, and Politics and Parliament categories. Other databases, such as the *Telegraph* Historical Archive, yield similar results.

110. Robert Bernays, 'Turn Again Winston', *Nash's Pall Mall Magazine*, August 1933. Bernays was a Liberal (and later Liberal National) MP.

111. Speeches of 14 and 23 March 1933.

112. Speech of 13 April 1933.

113. 'Germany And The Debate', *The Times*, 15 April 1933.

114. See, for example, 'The Persecution of Jews', *Manchester Guardian*, 15 April 1933; 'Fierce Commons Attack on Hitlerism', *Aberdeen Press and Journal*, 14 April 1933; 'Commons Debate on Germany's Position', *Daily Mail*, 15 April 1933.

115. *Daily Express*, 15 April 1933.

116. *Daily Mirror*, 15 April 1933.

117. Speech of 7 February 1934.

118. 'Notes of the Week', *The Economist*, 10 February 1934.

119. *Daily Mail*, 15 January 1934; S. J. Taylor, *The Great Outsiders: Northcliffe, Rothermere and the Daily Mail* (London: Weidenfeld & Nicolson, 1996), pp. 294–8. See also Will Wainewright, *Reporting on Hitler: Rothay Reynolds and the British Press in Nazi Germany* (London: Biteback Publishing, 2017).

120. WSC to CSC, 22 August 1934, *Churchill Documents* 12, p. 853.

121. WSC to Rothermere, 20 November 1934, *Churchill Documents* 12, pp. 927–8.

122. *Daily Mail*, 9 July 1934, in *Wolff, Collected Essays*, I, pp. 322–5.

123. Violet Pearman to Churchill (telephone message), 4 July 1934, Churchill Papers, CHAR 8/490/21.

124. Speech of 30 July 1934.

125. Lord Rothermere to WSC, 1 August 1934, *Churchill Documents* 12, p. 836.

126. WSC to Rothermere, 6 August 1934, *Churchill Documents* 12, pp. 838–40. N. H. Gibbs, *Grand Strategy*, Vol. I: *Rearmament Policy* (London: HMSO, 1976), p. 140.

127. Desmond Morton to WSC, 17 August 1934, *Churchill Documents* 12, p. 849.

128. WSC to Rothermere, 29 April 1935, *Churchill Documents* 12, p. 1155.

129. Winston S. Churchill, *His Father's Son: The Life of Randolph Churchill* (London: Weidenfeld & Nicolson, 1996), pp. 141–2.

130. WSC to R. P. Pakenham-Walsh, 5 May 1935, *Churchill Documents* 12, p. 1166.

131. Colin R. Coote, *The Other Club* (London: Sidgwick & Jackson, 1971).

132. Reeves Shaw to WSC, 15 May 1935, *Churchill Documents* 12, p. 1175.

133. WSC to Reeves Shaw, 16 and 25 May 1935, Churchill Papers, CHAR 8/510/2-3.

134. 'A Spectator's Notebook', *Spectator*, 8 November 1935.

135. WSC, 'The Truth About Myself', *Strand Magazine*, January 1936.

136. WSC, 'The Truth About Hitler', *Strand Magazine*, November 1935. The quotation about 'the joy, etc.' comes from Alexander Pope's 'An Essay on Man: Epistle II'.

137. 'Germany and Mr. Churchill', *Daily Mail*, 1 November 1935.

138. Pound, *Strand Magazine*, p. 157.

139. 'German Expelled', *South China Morning Post*, 13 November 1935.

140. MI5 file on Hans Wilhelm Thost, KV 2/953, TNA.

141. 'Our London Correspondence', *Manchester Guardian*, 13 November1935.

142. 'Friendship With Germany', *Evening Standard*, 17 September 1937, in WSC, *Step By Step* (London: Odhams Press, 1947; first published 1939), p. 158.

143. 'London Day By Day', *Daily Telegraph*, 20 November 1935, Churchill Papers, CHAR 8/510/32.

144. WSC, 'Hitler—Monster or Hero?', *Today: An Independent Journal of Public Affairs*, 24 August 1935.

145. 'The Versailles Treaty', *Yorkshire Post*, 5 November 1935, CHPC 15; WSC to Reeves Shaw, 21 November 1935, Churchill Papers, CHAR 8/510/32.

146. Martin Gilbert, *Churchill: A Life* (London: Minerva, 1992), p. 581; Jonathan Rose, *The Literary Churchill: Author, Reader, Actor* (New Haven, CT: Yale University Press, 2014), p. 255.

147. 'Germany Bans British Book', *Sunday Times*, 6 November 1938, CHPC 17.

148. Thomas Jones to Lady Grigg, 12 May and 1 June 1935, in Thomas Jones, *A Diary with Letters, 1931–1950* (London: Oxford University Press, 1954), pp. 145, 149–50.

149. WSC, recollections, *Churchill Documents* 12, p. 1324.

150. WSC, *The Second World War*, Vol. I: *The Gathering Storm* (London: Cassell, 1948), p. 157.

151. *Reynold's News*, 10 May 1936, CHPC 15.

152. 'A Changed View', *Evening Standard*, 16 October 1936, CHPC 15.

153. Francis Williams, *Nothing So Strange: An Autobiography* (London: Cassell, 1970), p. 115.

154. Parliamentary Debates, House of Commons, Fifth Series, Vol. 309, 10 March 1936, col. 2006; 'Mr. Churchill Praises Daily Herald', 11 March 1936, *Daily Herald*, CHPC 15.

155. Williams, *Nothing So Strange*, p. 116.

156. Shiela Grant Duff, *The Parting of Ways: A Personal Account of the Thirties* (London: Peter Owen, 1982), p. 158. On Churchill's coterie of female anti-appeasers, see Julie Gottlieb, *'Guilty Women', Foreign Policy and Appeasement in Inter-war Britain* (Basingstoke: Palgrave Macmillan, 2015) , Chapter 9.

157. 'A Spectator's Notebook', *Spectator*, 20 November 1936.

158. Adrian Phillips, *The King Who Had to Go: Edward VIII, Mrs Simpson and the Hidden Politics of the Abdication Crisis* (London: Biteback Publishing, 2016), pp. 136–7.

159. John Barnes and David Nicholson (eds), *The Empire at Bay: The Leo Amery Diaries, 1929–1945* (London: Hutchinson, 1988), pp. 431–2 (entries for 4 and 7 December 1936).

160. Press Statement, 5 December 1936, *Churchill Documents* 13, p. 457.

161. Geoffrey Dawson, 'Abdication of Edward VIII: A Private Diary Covering the Period September–December 1936', Dawson Papers 55. This document was drawn up retrospectively.

162. Lord Beaverbrook, *The Abdication of King Edward VIII*, ed. A. J. P. Taylor (London: Hamish Hamilton, 1966), p. 80.

163. James Margach, *The Abuse of Power: The War between Downing Street and the Media from Lloyd George to James Callaghan* (London: W.H. Allen, 1978), p. 50.

164. Nicholas Pronay, 'British Newsreels in the 1930s 2: Their Policies and Impact', *History*, 57 (1972), pp. 63–72; Anthony Adamthwaite, 'The

British Government and the Media, 1937–1938', *Journal of Contemporary History*, 18 (1983), pp. 281–97; Guy Hodgson, 'Neville Henderson, Appeasement and the Press: Fleet Street and the build-up to the Second World War', *Journalism Studies*, 8 (2007), pp. 320–34.

165. Richard Cockett, *Twilight of Truth: Chamberlain, Appeasement and the Manipulation of the Press* (New York: St. Martin's Press, 1989), p. 2.
166. Christopher A. Casey, 'Deglobalization and the Disintegration of the European News System, 1918–34', *Journal of Contemporary History*, 53 (2018), pp. 267–91.
167. WSC to Abe Bailey, 3 June 1936, *Churchill Documents* 13, p. 183.
168. Anthony Eden to WSC, 19 August 1947, Churchill Papers, CHUR 4/141A-B/334.
169. WSC, *Gathering Storm*, p. 214.
170. Adamthwaite, 'The British Government and the Media', p. 291.
171. Speech of 26 October 1936; WSC to the editor of *The Times*, 10 November 1937, *Churchill Documents* 13, p. 836; '"Ban Candid camera shots," says Winston Churchill', *World's Press News*, 18 November 1937, CHPC 16. In 1934, a photographer sneaked into the grounds of the villa where Churchill was staying in the South of France. When he heard the shutter, Churchill, who had been painting, jumped up angrily and chased the man away. Also caught in the photograph was Doris, Lady Castlerosse, with whom (according to Jock Colville, and supported by other evidence) Churchill was having an affair. The relationship, however, was never revealed in Churchill's lifetime, a fact which may have owed something to Beaverbrook's help. 'Mr. Churchill Is Annoyed', *Daily Express*, 27 August 1934; Warren Dockter and Richard Toye, 'Who Commanded History? Sir John Colville, Churchillian Networks, and the "Castlerosse Affair" ', *Journal of Contemporary History*, 54:2 (2018), pp. 401–19.
172. WSC, 'Radio, News-Reel or the Press', *Sunday Chronicle*, 12 January 1936.
173. WSC, 'The Truth About Myself', *Strand Magazine*, January 1936.
174. Williams, *Nothing So Strange*, pp. 116–17.
175. See Martin Gilbert (ed.), *Winston Churchill and Emery Reves: Correspondence 1937–1964* (Austin, TX: University of Texas Press, 1997).
176. R. J. Thompson to WSC, 24 March 1938, Churchill Papers, CHAR 8/600/17.
177. WSC to Thompson, 11 April 1938, Churchill Papers, CHAR 8/600/22-3.

178. WSC to C. E. Thomas, 28 April 1939, Churchill Papers, CHAR 8/633/9.

179. Hartwell, *Camrose*, p. 223.

180. W. P. Crozier to F. A. Voigt, 14 September 1938, Guardian Archive, GB 133 GDN/220/143.

181. Press Statement, 26 September 1938, and Rothermere to WSC, 26 September 1938, *Churchill Documents* 13, p. 1177.

182. Press Statement, 28 September 1938, *Churchill Documents* 13, p. 1184.

183. K. R. M. Short, 'A Note on BBC Television News and the Munich Crisis, 1938', *Historical Journal of Film, Radio and Television*, 9 (1989), pp. 165–79. The BBC's TV service had launched in 1936.

184. Marianne Hicks, 'NO WAR THIS YEAR: Selkirk Panton and the Editorial Policy of the Daily Express, 1938–39', *Media History*, 14 (2008), pp. 167–83, at p. 175.

185. 'Agenda and Notes on Policy Conference', 21 January 1938, Walter Layton Papers, Box 89/8; Kingsley Martin, *Editor: A Second Volume of Autobiography 1931–45* (London: Hutchinson, 1968), pp. 248–9; 'Mr. Churchill on Democracy' (interview with Churchill by Kingsley Martin), *New Statesman and Nation*, 7 January 1939. For an example of continued left-wing hostility, see 'Candid Comment on Churchill', *Forward*, 12 November 1938, CHPC 17.

186. Daniel Hucker, 'Public Opinion, the Press and the Failed Anglo-Franco-Soviet Negotiations of 1939', *International History Review*, 40 (2018), pp. 65–85.

187. Hugh Cudlipp to WSC, 12 October 1938, Hugh Cudlipp Papers, HC3/4/1; *Sunday Pictorial*, 23 April 1939, CHPC 18.

188. Hugh Cudlipp to WSC, 26 April 1939, *Churchill Documents* 13, p. 1475.

189. 'Churchill and Cabinet', *News Chronicle*, 10 May 1939, CHPC 18.

190. Koss, *Rise and Fall*, Vol. II, pp. 587–8. Koss's listing is non-exhaustive: the weeklies *Tribune*, *Time & Tide*, and *The Spectator* also bear mention.

191. Robert Rhodes James (ed.), *'Chips': The Diaries of Sir Henry Channon* (London: Weidenfeld & Nicolson, 1993), p. 204 (entry for 9 July 1939); Neville Chamberlain to Ida Chamberlain, 8 July 1939, in Robert Self (ed.), *The Neville Chamberlain Diary Letters*, Vol. IV: *The Downing Street Years, 1934–1940* (Aldershot: Ashgate, 2005), p. 426.

192. 'Churchill and the Government', *Truth*, 7 July 1939, Broadwater Collection.

193. Martin Pugh, 'The *Daily Mirror* and the Revival of Labour 1935–1945', *Twentieth Century British History*, 9 (1998), pp. 420–38.

194. *Daily Mirror*, 13 July 1939.

195. E. M. B. Ingram to WSC, 25 July 1939, *Churchill Documents* 13, p. 1577.

CHAPTER 6

1. WSC, *The Second World War*, Vol. I: *The Gathering Storm* (London: Cassell, 1948), p. 330. Accepting Churchill's account: Martin Gilbert, *Prophet of Truth: Winston S. Churchill 1922–1939* (London: Heinemann, 1976), p. 1113, and, most recently (in addition to numerous others), Andrew Roberts, *Churchill: Walking With Destiny* (London: Allen Lane, 2018), p. 460. Casting doubt: Paul Addison, *Churchill: The Unexpected Hero* (Oxford: Oxford University Press, 2005), p. 156, and Richard M. Langworth, *Winston Churchill, Myth and Reality: What He Actually Did and Said* (Jefferson, NC: McFarland, 2017), p. 219. See 'Navy signals "Winston is back" again', *Daily Mail*, 12 December 1950, and the correspondence columns of the *Daily Telegraph*, 18 and 23 March 1965. The HMS *Cornwall* log is in ADM 53/108098, TNA.

2. Albert Speer, *Inside the Third Reich* (London: Sphere Books, 1971), p. 239.

3. 'News Reel Report (2)' (File Report 141), 27 May 1940, Mass-Observation Archive (henceforward MOA).

4. 'The Cinema in the First Three Months of War (September to November 1939)' (File Report 24), MOA.

5. 'News Reel Report (2)', 27 May 1940, MOA.

6. 'The Cinema in the First Three Months of War', MOA.

7. John Bouverie, 'Please, Mr. Churchill', *News Chronicle*, 14 November 1939, CHPC 18; Edward Stebbing, *Diary of a Decade 1939–50* (Lewes: Book Guild Ltd., 1998), p. 7 (entry for 1 October 1939).

8. 'The Naval Memoirs of Admiral J. H. Godfrey', 1965, quoted in David Reynolds, *In Command of History: Churchill Fighting and Writing the Second World War* (London: Allen Lane, 2004), p. 114.

9. 'Review of the Foreign Press. Series D: European Allies', p. 5, 27 October 1939, Chatham House Archive.

10. William L. Shirer, *Berlin Diary: The Journal of a Foreign Correspondent 1934–1941* (London: Hamish Hamilton, 1941), p. 191 (entry for 22 October 1939).

11. A. J. Cummings, 'Spotlight on the War', *News Chronicle*, 3 October 1939, CHPC 18.

12. WSC to Neville Chamberlain, 11 October 1939, *Churchill Documents 14*, p. 230.

13. Pierre Backman, 'Winston Churchill—Englands starke man', *Sydsvenska Dagbladet Snällposten*, 12 November 1939, and Vincent Sheean, 'Old Man In A Hurry—Winston Churchill', *Saturday Evening Post*, 17 November

1939, Broadwater Collection. Lord Randolph Churchill had described Gladstone as an 'old man in a hurry'.

14. 'Life Goes Calling on Duke of Marlborough's Descendant', *Life*, 18 September 1939.

15. Charles Eade diary, n.d. but describing the events of 6 October 1939, Charles Eade Papers, EADE 2/1.

16. Charles Eade diary, 19 November 1941, Eade Papers, EADE 2/1.

17. In this paragraph I am indebted to Ian McLaine, *Ministry of Morale: Home Front Morale and the Ministry of Information in World War II* (London: George Allen & Unwin, 1979), Chapter 2.

18. Note of a discussion between MoI and Admiralty, 6 September 1939, INF 1/852, quoted in McLaine, p. 36.

19. George P. Thomson, *Blue Pencil Admiral: The Inside Story of the Press Censorship* (London: Sampson, Low, Marston & Co., n.d. but 1947), p. 12.

20. Charles Stuart (ed.), *The Reith Diaries* (London: Collins, 1975), p. 238 (entry for 15 January 1940).

21. Brian P. D. Hannon, 'Creating the Correspondent: How the BBC Reached the Frontline in the Second World War', *Historical Journal of Film, Radio and Television*, 28 (2008), pp. 175–94.

22. WSC to John Godfrey, 6 October 1939, *Churchill Documents* 14, p. 216.

23. N. J. Crowson, *Facing Fascism: The Conservative Party and the European Dictators, 1935–1940* (London: Routledge, 1997), p. 186. See also Richard Cockett, *Twilight of Truth: Chamberlain, Appeasement and the Manipulation of the Press* (New York: St. Martin's Press, 1989), pp. 151–2.

24. W. P. Crozier, *Off the Record: Political Interviews 1933–1943*, ed. A. J. P. Taylor (London: Hutchinson, 1973), pp. 121–3 (entry for 18 January 1940).

25. Albert Hird diary, 18 March 1940.

26. 'Newsletters' (File Report 65A), 2 March 1940, MOA.

27. Hird diary, 10 April 1940.

28. *US*, 10 May 1940, MOA. Emphasis in original.

29. Speech of 11 April 1940.

30. Undated cutting from the *Daily Herald*, Churchill Papers, CHAR 2/393/100; Kathleen Hill to Percy Cudlipp, 27 April 1940, Cudlipp to Hill, 29 April 1940, and WSC to Cudlipp, 30 April 1940, *Churchill Documents* 14, pp. 1147, 1163–4.

31. 'Churchill: The Truth', *Sunday Dispatch*, 5 May 1940, CHPC 18.

32. 'A New Ministry?', *Daily Mail*, 6 May 1940.

33. Stafford Cripps diary, 2 May 1940, Stafford Cripps Papers; Peter Clarke, *The Cripps Version: The Life of Sir Stafford Cripps 1889–1952* (London: Allen Lane, 2002), p. 171.

34. 'Another Possible Cabinet', *Daily Mail*, 7 May 1940. See also, for example, 'No Cabinet Split over Norway', *Aberdeen Press and Journal*, 6 May 1940.

35. Hird diary, 6 May 1940.

36. *Citizen*, 6 May 1940.

37. Quoted in 'Press Demands Changes and New Blood', *Hull Daily Mail*, 9 May 1940.

38. P. B. Pearson diary, 9 May 1940 (diarist 5168), MOA.

39. 'Now For a Victory Cabinet', *Daily Mail*, 9 May 1940.

40. See summaries in 'World Reaction to Premier's Speech', *Nottingham Evening Post*, 8 May 1940, 'How World Opinion Sees Debate', *Aberdeen Press and Journal*, 8 May 1940, and 'World's View of Speech', *Daily Mail*, 8 May 1940.

41. 'Review of the Foreign Press. Series C: USSR and the Far East', 23 May 1940, p. 2, Chatham House Archive.

42. 'Chamberlain to Resign', *Daily Express*, 10 May 1940. See also Roger Hermiston, *All Behind You, Winston: Churchill's Great Coalition 1940–45* (London: Aurum Press, 2016), p. 4.

43. BBC News Bulletins, 10 May 1940 [consulted on microfilm at the British Library]; 'Chamberlain Out, Churchill Agrees to Form New British Government', UP Bulletin, 10 May 1940, https://www.upi.com/Archives [consulted 4 September 2017].

44. 'Second Report from Mass-Observation on Holland-Belgium Reactions' (File Report 103), 13 May 1940, MOA.

45. Home Intelligence Report, 21 May 1940, in Paul Addison and Jeremy A. Crang (eds), *Listening to Britain: Home Intelligence Reports on Britain's Finest Hour: May to September 1940* (London: Bodley Head, 2010), p. 18.

46. Home Intelligence Reports, 22 May 1940, in Addison and Crang, *Listening to Britain*, p. 21.

47. G. P. Thomson, 'Churchill and the Censorship', in Charles Eade (ed.), *Churchill By His Contemporaries* (London: Reprint Society, 1955; first published 1953), pp. 144–9, at pp. 144–5.

48. Thomson, *Blue Pencil Admiral*, p. 104.

49. Thomson, 'Churchill and the Censorship', p. 144.

50. Deutschlandsender longwave broadcast, 13.00 BST 13 May 1940 (in German for Germany), in Daily Digest of Foreign Broadcasts, 13–14 May 1940, BBC Written Archives.

51. Deutschlandsender longwave broadcast, 21.00 BST 13 May 1940 (in German for Germany), in Daily Digest of Foreign Broadcasts, 13–14 May 1940, BBC Written Archives.

52. Laura M. Calkins, 'Patrolling the Ether: US–UK Open Source Intelligence Cooperation and the BBC's Emergence as an Intelligence Agency, 1939–1948', *Intelligence and National Security*, 26 (2011), pp. 1–22. The foreign press was also an important source of intelligence, especially, after June 1941, for the Nazi-occupied territories of the USSR. See Ben Wheatley, *British Intelligence and Hitler's Empire in the Soviet Union, 1941–1945* (London: Bloomsbury Academic, 2017).

53. Asa Briggs, *The History of Broadcasting in the United Kingdom*, Vol. III: *The War of Words* (Oxford: Oxford University Press, 1995), p. 255.

54. Moscow shortwave broadcast, 21.30 BST 5 June 1940 (in Russian for USSR), 7 June 1940, BBC Written Archives.

55. 'United States Memoranda and Economic Notes', No. 24, 24 July 1940, Chatham House Archive.

56. Edward R. Murrow, *This Is London* (New York: Shocken Books, 1985; first published 1941), p. 125; Edward Stourton, *Auntie's War: The BBC During the Second World War* (London: Doubleday, 2017), p. 214. Churchill's daughter-in-law Pamela, estranged from her husband Randolph, pursued affairs with Murrow and other influential men, although how much the Prime Minister himself knew of this is not clear. See Frank Costigliola, 'Pamela Churchill, Wartime London, and the Making of the Special Relationship', *Diplomatic History*, 36 (2012), pp. 753–62 .

57. Steven Casey, *Cautious Crusade: Franklin D. Roosevelt, American Public Opinion, and the War Against Nazi Germany* (Oxford: Oxford University Press, 2001), p. 28.

58. Peter Clarke, *The Last Thousand Days of the British Empire* (London: Allen Lane, 2007), p. 4.

59. 'Mr. Churchill's Words and Deeds', *Chicago Daily Tribune*, 6 June 1940; 'The War for Empire', *Chicago Daily Tribune*, 24 June 1941.

60. WSC to Lord Lothian, 28 June 1940, *Churchill Documents* 15, p. 436. For the propaganda efforts, see Nicholas John Cull, *Selling War: The British Propaganda Campaign Against American 'Neutrality' in World War II* (Oxford: Oxford University Press, 1995).

61. WSC to Alfred Duff Cooper, 17 May 1940, *Churchill Documents* 15, p. 69.

62. Briggs, *War of Words*, p. 30.

63. Stuart, *Reith Diaries*, p. 270 (entry for 6 November 1940).

64. Neville Chamberlain to Ida Chamberlain, 8 June 1940, in Robert Self (ed.), *The Neville Chamberlain Diary Letters*, Vol. IV: *The Downing Street*

Years, 1934–1940 (Aldershot: Ashgate, 2005), pp. 537–8; William Armstrong (ed.), *With Malice Toward None: A War Diary by Cecil H. King* (London: Sidgwick & Jackson, 1970), p. 48 (entry for 7 June 1940).

65. 'Cato', *Guilty Men* (London: Victor Gollancz, 1940); Mervyn Jones, *Michael Foot* (London: Victor Gollancz, 1994), pp. 85–91.

66. War Cabinet minutes, WM (40) 168th Conclusions, 16 June 1940, CAB 65/7/63, TNA.

67. Garry Campion, *The Good Fight: Battle of Britain Propaganda and The Few* (Basingstoke: Palgrave, 2009), pp. 104–12.

68. WSC to Archibald Sinclair, 21 August 1940, *Churchill Documents* 15, p. 701.

69. Campion, *The Good Fight*, pp. 24–5, 163–4.

70. 'News Reel Report (2)', 27 May 1940, and 'Memo on Newsreels' (File Report 314), 8 August 1940, MOA.

71. Richard Farmer, *Cinemas and Cinemagoing in Wartime Britain, 1939–45: The Utility Dream Palace*, (Manchester: Manchester University Press, 2016), p. 64; WSC to Geoffrey Lloyd, 16 June 1945, Churchill Papers, CHAR 20/198B/182.

72. McLaine, *Ministry of Morale*, pp. 24–5.

73. WSC, *The Second World War*, Vol. II: *Their Finest Hour* (London: Cassell, 1949), pp. 168–9.

74. Francis Williams, *Nothing So Strange: An Autobiography* (London: Cassell, 1970), pp. 167–8.

75. War Cabinet Minutes, 7 October 1940, WM (40) 267th Conclusions, CAB/65/9/29, TNA.

76. Ruth Dudley Edwards, *Newspapermen: Hugh Cudlipp, Cecil Harmsworth King and the Glory Days of Fleet Street* (London: Secker & Warburg, 2003), esp. pp. 148–9.

77. War Cabinet Minutes, 7 October 1940, WM (40) 267th Conclusions, CAB/65/9/29, TNA.

78. Speech of 8 October 1940.

79. Herbert Morrison, 'Subversive Newspaper Propaganda', WP (40) 402, 8 October 1940, CAB 66 12/32, TNA.

80. War Cabinet Minutes, 9 October 1940, WM (40) 268th Conclusions, CAB 65 9/30, TNA.

81. Armstrong, *With Malice Toward None*, pp. 80–4 (entry for 12 October 1940). Emphasis in original. War Cabinet Minutes, WM (40) 272nd Conclusions, 16 October 1940, CAB 65 9/34, TNA.

82. Nigel Nicolson (ed.), *Harold Nicolson: Diaries and Letters 1939–45* (London: Collins, 1967), p. 125 (entry for 5 November 1940).

83. Interview of Mary Soames by William Manchester, 1980, William Manchester Papers Box 450.

84. WSC to Peter Fraser, 18 November 1940, *Churchill Documents* 15, p. 1102.

85. John Martin, *Downing Street: The War Years* (London: Bloomsbury, 1991), p. 37.

86. Ralph Ingersoll, ' "They Keep Trying to Hit My House", *Daily Express*, 26 November 1940.

87. John Colville, *The Fringes of Power: Downing Street Diaries, 1939–1955* (London: Hodder & Stoughton, 1985), p. 301 (entry for 28 November 1940).

88. He specifically complained about 'Butterfingers' (5 December 1940) and 'Full Speed Sideways' (13 December 1940), both published in the *Evening Standard*.

89. WSC to Lord Beaverbrook, 13 December 1940, *Churchill Documents* 15, p. 1229.

90. Beaverbrook to WSC, 14 December 1940, *Churchill Documents* 15, p. 1229 n.1.

91. WSC to Beaverbrook, 15 December 1940, *Churchill Documents* 15, pp. 1240–1.

92. Colville, *Fringes of Power*, p. 395 (entry for 5 June 1941).

93. Arthur Christiansen, *Headlines All My Life* (London: Heinemann, 1961), p. 221

94. Kingsley Martin, *Editor: A Second Volume of Autobiography 1931–45* (London: Hutchinson, 1968), p. 300.

95. Robert E. Sherwood, *The White House Papers of Harry L. Hopkins*, Vol. I: *September 1939–January 1942* (London: Eyre & Spottiswoode, 1948), p. 248. Emphasis in original.

96. 'Morale in 1941', File Report 568, 4 February 1941, MOA.

97. Briggs, *War of Words*, p. 342.

98. Colville, *Fringes of Power*, p. 395 (entry for 5 June 1941).

99. 'Second Weekly Report (New Series)', 16 June 1941, MOA.

100. Richard Toye, *The Roar of the Lion: The Untold Story of Churchill's World War II Speeches* (Oxford: Oxford University Press, 2013), pp. 99–100.

101. 'Home Intelligence Weekly Report No. 36', 4–11 June 1941, INF 1/292, TNA.

102. 'Home Intelligence Weekly Report No. 37', 11–18 June 1941, INF 1/292, TNA.

103. Thomson, *Blue Pencil Admiral*, pp. 94–5.

104. War Cabinet Minutes WM (41) 50th Conclusions, 15 May 1941, CAB 65/18/29, TNA.

105. 'Home Intelligence Weekly Report No. 34', 21–8 May 1941, INF 1/292, TNA.

106. Colville, *Fringes of Power*, p. 396 (entry for 7 June 1941); Crozier, *Off the Record*, pp. 225–6 (entry for June 1941).

107. *Daily Express*, 12 June 1941.

108. Gabriel Gorodetsky, *Grand Delusion: Stalin and the German Invasion of Russia* (New Haven, CT: Yale University Press, 1999), pp. 274, 292; Clarke, *Cripps Version*, pp. 214–18.

109. 'Second Weekly Report (New Series)', 16 June 1941, MOA.

110. Donald Read, *The Power of News: The History of Reuters* (Oxford: Oxford University Press, 1992), pp. 221–2.

111. Broadcast of 22 June 1941.

112. 'The War for Empire', *Chicago Daily Tribune*, 24 June 1941.

113. McLaine, *Ministry of Morale*, pp. 232–9.

114. Thomson, 'Churchill and the Censorship', p. 147.

115. 'Home Intelligence Weekly Report No. 46', 13–20 August 1941, INF 1/292, TNA.

116. McLaine, *Ministry of Morale*, p. 232

117. H. V. Morton, *Atlantic Meeting* (London: Methuen, 1943), p. 21.

118. WSC to H. V. Morton, 20 August 1942, *Churchill Documents* 17, p. 1101.

119. 'Home Intelligence Weekly Report No. 47', 20–7 August 1941, INF 1/292, TNA.

120. John Harvey (ed.), *The War Diaries of Oliver Harvey 1941–1945* (London: Collins, 1978), p. 27 (entries for 5 and 6 August 1941); Colville, *Fringes of Power*, p. 424 (entry for 5 August 1941); Morton, *Atlantic Meeting*, pp. 15–16; Chroniques du jour, 6 August 1941 (German), CJ-1941-08-06-DE, http://archives.swissinfo.ch/ww2/article.php?&lg=en [consulted 14 August 2018]; '"Churchill for US" Report', *Daily Mail*, 5 August 1941; Cordell Hull to Franklin D. Roosevelt, 6 August 1941, and Roosevelt to Hull, 6 August 1941, The President's Secretary's File, Series 1 Box 1, Roosevelt Papers online edition.

121. Hird diary, 15 and 17 August 1941. Emphasis in original.

122. 'Home Intelligence Weekly Report No. 46', 13–20 August 1941, INF 1/292, TNA; 'Eleventh Weekly Report (New Series)', File Report 832, 18 August 1941, MOA; A. Simons diary, 14 August 1941 (diarist 500-2-8), MOA.

123. 'Report on Manchester Industrial Atmosphere', File Report 839, 21 August 1941, MOA. The author of this report was Bill Naughton, a lorry-driver who later achieved success as the author of *Alfie*.

124. 'Home Intelligence Weekly Report No. 55', 29 September–6 October 1941, INF 1/292, TNA.

125. Elliott Roosevelt, *As He Saw It* (New York: Duell, Sloan and Pearce, 1946), p. 26.

126. Colville, *Fringes of Power*, p. 427 (entry for 16 August 1941).

127. 'President and Prime Minister—Historic Meeting', issued 22 August 1941, www.britishpathe.com [consulted 26 September 2017].

128. Colville, *Fringes of Power*, p. 427 (entry for 18 August 1941).

129. Jonathan Schneer, *Ministers at War: Winston Churchill and His War Cabinet* (London: Oneworld Books, 2014), pp. 164–5; Kenneth Young, *Churchill and Beaverbrook: A Study in Friendship and Politics* (London: Eyre & Spottiswoode, 1966), p. 214.

130. *Izvestia*, 13 November 1941, quoted in 'Praise for the Premier', *Yorkshire Post*, 14 November 1941, CHPC 19.

131. Armstrong, *With Malice Toward None*, p. 147 (entry for 31 October 1941).

132. WSC, *The Second World War*, Vol. III: *The Grand Alliance* (London: Cassell, 1950), p. 475.

133. Harvey, *War Diaries*, p. 70 (entry for 8 December 1941). See also David Dilks (ed.), *The Diaries of Sir Alexander Cadogan O.M., 1938–1945* (London: Cassell, 1971), p. 417 (entry for 8 December 1941).

134. WSC, *The Grand Alliance*, pp. 500–1.

135. Weekly Political Summary, 30 December 1941, in H. G. Nicholas (ed.), *Washington Despatches 1941–1945: Weekly Political Reports from the British Embassy* (Chicago: University of Chicago Press, 1981), p. 9.

136. Franklin D. Roosevelt: 'Joint Press Conference with Prime Minister Churchill', 23 December 1941, in Samuel I. Rosenman (ed.), *The Public Papers and Addresses of Franklin D. Roosevelt, 1941 Volume: The Call to Battle Stations* (New York: Harper & Brothers, 1950), p. 589.

137. Lord Moran, *Winston Churchill: The Struggle for Survival, 1940–1965* (London: Constable, 1966), p. 16; Wilson (who became Lord Moran in 1943) allegedly caused Churchill to become dependent on prescription drugs for a period in the late 1940s. Interview with Denis Kelly, 1979, Churchill Oral History Collection, CHOH 1/DEKE.

138. Martin Gilbert, *In Search of Churchill* (London: HarperCollins, 1994), p. 295. See also David Travis, *Karsh: Beyond the Camera* (Jaffrey, NH: David R. Godine, 2012), p. 24.

139. Clementine Churchill to David McFall, 13 December 1958, quoted in Jonathan Black, *Winston Churchill in British Art, 1900 to the Present Day: The Titan With Many Faces* (London: Bloomsbury Academic, 2017), p. 106.

140. Maria Tippett, *Portrait in Light and Shadow: The Life of Yousuf Karsh* (New Haven, CT: Yale University Press, 2007), pp. 144–6.

141. John Ramsden, *Man of the Century: Winston Churchill and His Legend Since 1945* (London: HarperCollins, 2002), pp. 55–6.

142. See Tom Allbeson, 'Visualizing Wartime Destruction and Postwar Reconstruction: Herbert Mason's Photograph of St. Paul's Reevaluated', *Journal of Modern History*, 87 (2015), pp. 532–78.

143. Tom Harrisson, '"The Big Debate: Broadcast to the Far East No. 5', File Report 1064, 29 January 1942, MOA.

144. Hird diary, 21 January 1942.

145. In February 1942, Lord Astor dismissed J. L. Garvin as editor of *The Observer*, after he published an article which Astor considered too sympathetic to Churchill. David Ayerst, *Garvin of The Observer* (London: Croom Helm, 1985), pp. 276–7.

146. 'Home Intelligence Weekly Report No. 65', 22–9 December 1941, INF 1/292.

147. 'The Manoeuvres At Singapore', *The Times*, 5 February 1937; 'Combined Manoeuvres Which Proved Singapore "Invulnerable"', *London Illustrated News*, 27 February 1937; Reynolds, *In Command of History*, p. 115.

148. Mark Pottle (ed.), *Champion Redoubtable: The Diaries and Letters of Violet Bonham Carter 1914–1945* (London: Weidenfeld & Nicolson, 1998), p. 235 (entry for 11 February 1942). Emphasis in original.

149. Robert Rhodes James (ed.), *'Chips': The Diaries of Sir Henry Channon* (London: Weidenfeld & Nicolson, 1993), p. 321 (entry for 13 February 1942); George Orwell, 'The British Crisis: London Letter to *Partisan Review*', 8 May 1942, in Sonia Orwell and Ian Angus (eds), *The Collected Essays, Journalism and Letters of George Orwell*, Vol. 2: *My Country Right or Left, 1940–1943* (Harmondsworth: Penguin, 1970; first published 1968), pp. 246–7; Henry Novy diary, 15 February 1942, in Sandra Koa Wing (ed.), *Our Longest Days: A People's History of the Second World War* (London: Profile Books, 2008; first published 2007), p. 115.

150. Broadcast of 15 February 1942; Armstrong, *With Malice Toward None*, pp. 158–9 (entry for 16 February 1942).

151. Speech of 17 February 1942; 'We're Not "Rattled"!', *Daily Mirror*, 18 February 1942; Churchill's remark about recrimination had been made in the Commons on 29 May 1936.

152. 'Cripps', *Daily Mail*, 10 February 1942.

153. Gaumont newsreel issued 23 February 1942, http://reuters.screenocean.com/record/311359 (accessed 29 September 2017); 'General Film Notes', 26 February 1942, Topic Collection 17 (1150), MOA.

154. *The Times*, 18 February 1942.

155. Hird diary, 21 and 25 February 1942.

156. Clementine Churchill to WSC, *c.*12 Feb. 1942, in Mary Soames (ed.), *Speaking for Themselves: The Personal Letters of Winston and Clementine Churchill* (London: Doubleday, 1998), p. 464.

157. Anne Chisholm and Michael Davie, *Beaverbrook: A Life* (London: Hutchinson, 1992), p. 430.

158. Armstrong, *With Malice Toward None*, p. 160 (entry for 24 February 1942).

CHAPTER 7

1. Donald Zec, *Don't Lose It Again! The Life and Wartime Cartoons of Philip Zec* (London: Political Cartoon Society, 2005), p. 21.

2. Zec, 'Completing the Chain!', *Daily Mirror*, 20 July 1940; WSC to Alfred Duff Cooper, 20 July 1940, CD 15, p. 552.

3. 'Memorandum on Warning the Daily Mirror', File Report 1173, 24 March 1942, MOA.

4. 'The Press: Report by the Lord President of the Council', WP (42) 124, 17 March 1942, CAB 66/23/4, TNA.

5. W. P. Crozier, *Off the Record: Political Interviews 1933–1943*, ed. A. J. P. Taylor (London: Hutchinson, 1973), pp. 309–13 (entry for 20 March 1942).

6. See, notably, 'Skilled Men In The Services', *The Times*, 1 October 1941.

7. William Armstrong (ed.), *With Malice Toward None: A War Diary by Cecil H. King* (London, Sidgwick & Jackson, 1970), p. 168 (entry for 21 March 1942).

8. 'Memorandum on Warning the Daily Mirror', File Report 1173, 24 March 1942, MOA.

9. 'The "Daily Mirror": Memorandum by the Home Secretary', WP (42) 131, 20 March 1942, CAB 66/23/11, TNA; Donald Zec, *Don't Lose It Again!*, p. 78.

10. Parliamentary Debates, House of Commons, Fifth Series, Vol. 378, 19 March 1942, cols. 1665–6.

11. 'An Abuse of Liberty', *Daily Telegraph*, 20 March 1942; Albert Hird diary, 20 March 1942.

12. Parliamentary Debates, House of Commons, Fifth Series, Vol. 378, 26 March 1942, cols. 2248–9, 2252, 2300.

13. 'Ministry of Information Home Intelligence Division Weekly Report No. 79', 8 April 1942, INF 1/292, TNA.

14. 'Further Report on "Daily Mirror"', File Report 1197, 2 April 1942, MOA.

15. Armstrong, *With Malice Toward None*, p. 173 (entry for 25 March 1942).

16. James Margach, *The Abuse of Power: The War between Downing Street and the Media from Lloyd George to James Callaghan* (London: W.H. Allen, 1978), pp. 64–85. Quotation at p. 64.

17. Donald McLachlan, *In the Chair: Barrington-Ward of The Times, 1927–1948* (London: Weidenfeld & Nicolson, 1971), p. 193.

18. Margach, *The Abuse of Power*, p. 64.

19. Francis Williams, *Nothing So Strange: An Autobiography* (London: Cassell, 1970), pp. 169–70.

20. Cabinet Minutes, WM (42) 32nd Conclusions, 9 March 1942, CAB 65/25/32, TNA.

21. Cabinet Minutes, WM (42) 35th Conclusions, 18 March 1942, CAB 65/25/35, TNA.

22. WSC to John Curtin, 23 March 1942, *Churchill Documents* 17, p. 436. Later in the year, Churchill insisted that Bracken prevent any repetition of comments in the *New Statesman* outside the UK until he, Bracken, had been personally consulted on the text of each individual message. WSC to Bracken, 24 October 1942, PREM 4/26/8, TNA.

23. Williams, *Nothing So Strange*, pp. 167–8.

24. For an example of such pressure being applied successfully, see Lord Lloyd to WSC, 5 October 1940, PREM 4/66/2, TNA. Churchill had complained in Cabinet about the *News Chronicle*'s coverage of Spain, which he feared would cause diplomatic problems, and asked that something to be done. Lloyd, the Colonial Secretary, then spoke to Gerald Barry, the paper's editor. Barry agreed that 'we should temporarily refrain as a newspaper from expressing certain of our views about the Spanish situation'.

25. Ian McLaine, *Ministry of Morale: Home Front Morale and the Ministry of Information in World War II* (London: George Allen & Unwin, 1979), p. 93.

26. William Bowdery to CSC, 27 July 1944, Churchill Papers, CHAR 1/385/23-4.

27. Crozier, *Off the Record*, p. 379 (entry for 22 October 1943).

28. Note by Donald McLachlan, quoting an account by Robert Barrington-Ward, *Churchill Documents* 18, p. 848.

29. Alan Foster, 'The Beaverbrook Press and Appeasement: The Second Phase', *European History Quarterly*, 21 (1991), pp. 5–38, at p. 15.

30. Anne Chisholm and Michael Davie, *Beaverbrook: A Life* (London: Hutchinson, 1992), p. 436.

31. 'Second Front Feelings', File report 1297, 1 June 1942, MOA.

32. Chisholm and Davie, *Beaverbrook*, pp. 436; Thomas Rainboro', 'Churchill and Russia', *Tribune*, 15 May 1942, CHPC 20.

33. Hird diary, 26 April and 23 May 1942.

34. Lord Halifax, 'Secret Diary', 25 March 1942, Halifax Papers A7-8-19.

35. Lord Ismay, *The Memoirs of General the Lord Ismay* (London: Heinemann, 1960), pp. 254–6. Quotation at p. 256.

36. WSC, extract from telegram of 2 August 1942, circulated to the War Cabinet 3 August, WP (42) 336, CAB 66/27/16, TNA.

37. 'Meeting at the Kremlin on Wednesday, 12th August, 1942', FO 800/300, TNA.

38. James Chapman, '"The Life and Death of Colonel Blimp" (1943) Reconsidered', *Historical Journal of Film, Radio and Television*, 15 (1995), pp. 19–54. Churchill did, however, attend the film's premiere, and appeared to be in excellent humour. 'Premier Sees "Col. Blimp"', *Daily Telegraph*, 11 June 1943.

39. *Daily Mail*, 7 July 1942.

40. Hird diary, 8 July 1942.

41. George P. Thomson, *Blue Pencil Admiral: The Inside Story of the Press Censorship* (London: Sampson, Low, Marston & Co., n.d. but 1947), pp. 119–20. Note that Thomson misdated the events to 1943.

42. Thomson, *Blue Pencil Admiral*, p. 127.

43. Siân Nicholas, 'Keeping the News British: the BBC, British United Press and Reuters in the 1930s', in Joel H. Wiener and Mark Hampton (eds), *Anglo-American Media Interactions, 1850–2000* (Basingstoke: Palgrave Macmillan, 2007), pp. 195–214.

44. WSC to Brendan Bracken and Leslie Hollis, 19 Sept. 1942, *Churchill Documents* 17, p. 1216.

45. 'Twenty-Year Treaty With Russia' and 'Guest Of The President', *The Times*, 12 June 1942; Hird diary, 22 August 1942.

46. 'Mr Churchill', *Daily Express*, 21 September 1942.

47. A. J. Cummings, 'Spotlight', *News Chronicle*, 16 October 1942, CHPC 20.

48. Armstrong, *With Malice Toward None*, p. 192 (entry for 24 September 1942).

49. Speech of 11 November 1942.

50. 'We could not land in Europe', *Daily Mirror*, 12 November 1942.

51. 'Our London Correspondence', *Manchester Guardian*, 12 November 1942.

52. *Daily Mail*, 12 November 1942.

53. 'With Mr. Churchill at Bradford', *Yorkshire Post*, 7 December 1942, CHPC 20.

54. Jose Harris, *William Beveridge: A Biography* (Oxford: Clarendon Press, 1997), p. 415.

55. Tehyun Ma, 'A Chinese Beveridge Plan: The Discourse of Social Security and the Post-War Reconstruction of China', *European Journal of East Asian Studies*, 11 (2012), pp. 329–49.

56. WSC, 'Promises about Post-War Conditions', WP (43) 18, 12 January 1943, CAB 66/33/18, TNA.

57. McLaine, *Ministry of Morale*, p. 182; Alan Bullock, *The Life and Times of Ernest Bevin*, Vol. II: *Minister of Labour 1940–1945* (London: Heinemann, 1967), p. 226.

58. 'Ministry of Information Home Intelligence Division Weekly Report No. 115', 17 December 1942, INF 1/292, TNA.

59. British Pathé newsreel, 17 December 1942, www.britishpathe.com [consulted 13 March 2018].

60. In fact, the similarity of the words was merely a coincidence, and the pictures had been handed out officially to the press—implying, of course, government approval of their use. Armstrong, *With Malice Toward None*, p. 202 (entry for 19 December 1942).

61. Mark Pottle (ed.), *Champion Redoubtable: The Diaries and Letters of Violet Bonham Carter 1914–1945* (London: Weidenfeld & Nicolson, 1998), p. 248 (entry for 15 December 1942).

62. Armstrong, *With Malice Toward None*, p. 203 (entry for 19 December 1942).

63. WSC to Anthony Eden, 2 January 1943, in *Churchill Documents* 18, p. 25. See also Cordell Hull, *The Memoirs of Cordell Hull*, Vol. II (London: Hodder & Stoughton, 1948), pp. 1203–4.

64. 'Mass-Observation Bulletin: Contents of Issue Dated 23 March 1943', File Report 1634, MOA.

65. Thomson, *Blue Pencil Admiral*, pp. 126, 129, 133.

66. 'Mass-Observation Bulletin: Contents of Issue Dated 23 March 1943', File Report 1634, MOA.

67. This is stated by the United Newsreel announcer in 'FDR and Churchill Meet in North Africa', January 1943, Steven Spielberg Film and Video Archive, US Holocaust Memorial Museum, Accession Number: 1992.259.1, RG Number: RG-60.0451, Film ID: 404, https://collections.ushmm.org [consulted 15 March 2018].

68. Robert Hopkins, 'A Corporal On The Job At Casablanca', *Life*, 8 March 1943.

69. Robert E. Sherwood, *The White House Papers of Harry L. Hopkins*, Vol. II: *January 1942–July 1945* (London: Eyre & Spottiswoode, 1949), p. 685.

70. Leslie Hollis to John Peck, 15 Jan. 1943, and WSC to Hollis, 18 January 1943, *Churchill Documents* 18, pp. 125, 153.

71. As the result of a 1921 bout of polio, Roosevelt was unable to walk or to stand without leg braces. Steps were taken to disguise this from the public: on this occasion, for example, he was carried to his chair, and was filmed seated. However, the notion that there was a 'gentleman's agreement' between the President and the press to conceal his condition is a myth. On the one hand, descriptions of his disability and his reliance on a wheelchair were in fact published. On the other, photographers who took pictures which revealed the truth were liable to have their photographic plates smashed by the Secret Service. See Matthew Pressman, 'Ambivalent Accomplices: How the Press Handled FDR's Disability and How FDR Handled the Press', *Journal of the Historical Society*, 13 (2013), pp. 325–59.

72. WSC, *The Second World War*, Vol. IV: *The Hinge of Fate* (London: Cassell, 1950), p. 555.

73. Casablanca Conference outtakes, Steven Spielberg Film and Video Archive, US Holocaust Memorial Museum Accession Number: 1992.254.1, RG Number: RG-60.0675, Film ID: 312, https://collections.ushmm.org (accessed 14 March 2018).

74. Lord Moran, *Winston Churchill: The Struggle for Survival, 1940–1965* (London: Constable, 1966), p. 82.

75. WSC, *Hinge of Fate*, p. 555 For the number of correspondents, see Press Conference, 24 January 1943, *Churchill Documents* 18, p. 215.

76. Hird diary, 29 January 1943.

77. Sherwood, *White House Papers*, Vol. II, p. 690.

78. Averell Harriman and Elie Abel, *Special Envoy to Churchill and Stalin 1941–1946* (New York: Random House, 1975), pp. 188–90.

79. Press Conference, 24 January 1943, *Churchill Documents* 18, p. 215.

80. 'News Letter for American *New Leader*', March 1943, File Report 1647, MOA.

81. E. Robertson diary (diarist 5412), 26 January 1943, MOA.

82. Edith Lea diary (diarist 5355), 27 January 1943, MOA.

83. E. M. Fisher diary (diarist 5309), 27 January 1943, MOA.

84. G. South diary (diarist 5429) 27 and 28 January 1943, MOA.

85. Weekly Political Summary, 1 February 1943, in H. G. Nicholas (ed.), *Washington Despatches 1941–1945: Weekly Political Reports from the British Embassy* (Chicago: University of Chicago Press, 1981), p. 142

86. 'Ministry of Information Home Intelligence Weekly Report No. 123', 11 February 1943, INF 1/292, TNA.

87. 'Churchill "Chill is Diplomatic Ruse"', Foreign Broadcast Information Service, Daily Report, 23 February 1943, FBIS-FRB-43-046.

88. 'Ministry of Information Home Intelligence Weekly Report No. 125', 25 February 1943, INF 1/292, TNA.

89. Franklin D. Roosevelt to WSC, 17 March 1943, in Warren F. Kimball (ed.), *Churchill and Roosevelt: The Complete Correspondence*, Vol. II: *Alliance Forged, November 1942–February 1944* (Princeton, NJ: Princeton University Press, 1984), p. 157. According to Lord Moran, the charge was unfair: *Struggle*, p. 88.

90. WSC to Randolph Churchill, 16 April 1943, *Churchill Documents* 18, p. 1020.

91. WSC to Harold Macmillan, 4 April 1943, *Churchill Documents* 18, pp. 909–10.

92. Gabriel Gorodetsky (ed.), *The Maisky Diaries: Red Ambassador to the Court of St. James's 1932–1943* (New Haven, CT: Yale University Press, 2015), pp. 505–11 (entry for 23 April 1943). Quotation at p. 510.

93. Cabinet Minutes, 27 April 1943, WM (43) 59th Conclusions, CAB 65/34/13, TNA.

94. WSC to FDR, 28 April 1943, including the text of Churchill's message to Stalin, in Kimball, *Alliance Forged*, p. 199.

95. P. M. H. Bell, 'Censorship, Propaganda and Public Opinion: The Case of the Katyn Graves, 1943', *Transactions of the Royal Historical Society*, 39 (1989), pp. 63–83, at p. 76.

96. 'Govt. "Regrets" Result of Nazi-Polish Plot', *Daily Worker*, 28 April 1943.

97. WSC to Eden, 16 May 1943, *Churchill Documents* 18, p. 1315.

98. Cabinet Minutes, 17 May 1943, WM (43) 59th Conclusions, CAB 65/34/69th, TNA.

99. However, the following year, one Polish newspaper 'which continuously attacked the Russian Government' did have its supplies of newsprint cut off. Cabinet Minutes, 14 February 1944, WM (44) 20th Conclusions, CAB 65/41/20, TNA.

100. Weekly Political Summary, 13 May 1943, in Nicholas, *Washington Despatches*, p. 190.

101. 'Ministry of Information Home Intelligence Weekly Report No. 137', 20 May 1943, INF 1/292, TNA.
102. 'Ministry of Information Home Intelligence Weekly Report No. 138', 27 May 1943, INF 1/292, TNA.
103. Don Iddon, 'Churchill Told Us Frankly...', *Daily Mail*, 26 May 1943.
104. Lord Halifax diary, 23 May 1943, Halifax Papers A7/8/12.
105. 'Ministry of Information Home Intelligence Weekly Report No. 145', 15 July 1943, INF 1/292, TNA.
106. 'Ministry of Information Home Intelligence Weekly Report No. 146', 22 July 1943, INF 1/292, TNA.
107. A. J. Cummings, 'Spotlight', *News Chronicle*, 28 July 1943, CHPC 21.
108. H. G. Wells 'to the Private Secretary of Mr Winston Churchill', 29 July 1943, H. G. Wells Papers, WC-37-2, and J. H. Peck to Wells, 14 August 1943, Wells Papers, C238-25b.
109. 'Churchill Finds Principle At Niagara Is Unchanged', *New York Times*, 13 August 1943.
110. Helen Jones, '"Let Us Go Forward Together": Clementine Churchill and the Role of the Personality in Wartime Britain', in Richard Toye and Julie Gottlieb (eds), *Making Reputations: Power, Persuasion and the Individual in Modern British Politics* (London: I.B. Tauris, 2005), pp. 109–22.
111. See, for example, R. M. Dilman diary (diarist 5301), 11 August 1943, and May C. Towler (diarist 5445), 15 August 1943, MOA.
112. 'Ministry of Information Home Intelligence Weekly Report No. 151', 26 August 1943, INF 1/292, TNA.
113. Denys Smith, 'President & Premier to Have Talks in Quebec', *Daily Telegraph*, 12 August 1943.
114. Don Iddon, 'A Month with Winston', *Daily Mail*, 7 September 1943.
115. David Dilks (ed.), *The Diaries of Sir Alexander Cadogan O.M., 1938–1945* (London: Cassell, 1971), p. 558 (entry for 4 September 1943).
116. 'Churchill Charts Activity in Pacific', *New York Times*, 5 September 1943.
117. Don Iddon, 'A month with Winston', *Daily Mail*, 7 September 1943.
118. Speech of 6 September 1943.
119. For a summary of the coverage see WSC to members of the War Cabinet, 20 September 1943, *Churchill Documents* 19, pp. 194–208.
120. WSC to Brendan Bracken, 10 September 1943, *Churchill Documents* 19, p. 113.
121. *Daily News*, 12 Sept. 1943, quoted in 'Churchill "A Poor Suitor"', *Daily Mail*, 13 September 1943.

122. 'New Versailles indicated By Churchill', 'Daily Report: Foreign Radio Broadcasts', 8 September 1943, Foreign Broadcast information Service, FBIS-FRB-43-215.

123. WSC to Lord Gort and Andrew Cunningham, 10 September 1943, *Churchill Documents* 19, p. 109.

124. Dilks, *Cadogan Diaries*, p. 580 (entry for 29 November 1943).

125. 'Notes on Public Opinion in 1943', File Report 2022, 25 February 1944, MOA.

126. Diary of Corporal Terry (first name unknown), 9 December 1943 (5210), MOA.

127. M. A. Pratt diary (diarist 5402), 6 December 1943, MOA.

128. Moran, *Struggle*, p. 152.

129. Halifax diary, 17 December 1943, Halifax Papers A7/8/13.

130. Weekly Political Summary, 20 December 1943, in Nicholas, *Washington Despatches*, p. 290.

131. Hird diary, 17 December 1943.

132. Armstrong, *With Malice Toward None*, p. 237 (entry for 18 December 1943).

133. Moran, *Struggle*, p. 153.

134. 'Ministry of Information Home Intelligence Weekly Report No. 168', 23 December 1943, INF 1/292, TNA.

135. 'Indignant British Deny Peace Rumour', *New York Times*, 18 January 1944; 'Roosevelt At Loss on Pravda's Rumor', *New York Times*, 19 January 1944.

136. WSC to Stalin 24 Jan. 1944 and Stalin to WSC, 29 January 1944, *Churchill Documents* 19, pp. 1447, 1553.

137. Stalin to WSC, 16 March 1944, *Churchill Documents* 19, p. 2100.

138. John Harvey (ed.), *The War Diaries of Oliver Harvey 1941–1945* (London: Collins, 1978), p. 336 (entry for 20 March 1944).

139. WSC to Henry Maitland Wilson, 15 February 1944, Churchill Papers, CHAR 20/157/17.

140. WSC to Wilson, 18 February 1944, Churchill Papers, CHAR 20/157/39.

141. 'Generals and Press', *Daily Mail*, 17 February 1944.

142. Parliamentary Debates, House of Commons, Fifth Series, Vol. 397, 22 February 1944, col. 651; Brian P. D. Hannon, 'The Story Behind the Stories: British and Dominion War Correspondents in the Western Theatres of the Second World War', PhD thesis, University of Edinburgh, 2015, p. 122.

143. Thomson, *Blue Pencil Admiral*, p. 185.

144. Steven Casey, *The War Beat, Europe: The American Media at War Against Nazi Germany* (New York: Oxford University Press, 2017), p. 219.

145. Chris Moores, *Civil Liberties and Human Rights in Twentieth Century Britain* (Cambridge: Cambridge University Press, 2017), p. 36.

146. Bryan Holden Reid, 'Hart, Sir Basil Henry Liddell (1895–1970), military thinker and historian', *Oxford Dictionary of National Biography*, online edn, https://doi.org/10.1093/ref:odnb/33737 [consulted 10 April 2018].

147. WSC to Hastings Ismay, 17 March 1944, *Churchill Documents* 19, pp. 2111–12.

148. E. J. P. Cussen, note of phone conversation with Ian Jacob, 23 March 1944 (and other items in the same file), KV 2/2411, TNA.

149. 'The Invasion of France', June 1944, File Report 2131, MOA.

150. 'Ministry of Information Home Intelligence Weekly Report No. 198', 20 July 1944, INF 1/292, TNA.

151. Thomson, *Blue Pencil Admiral*, p. 202.

152. 'Front Line London', 13 July 1944, www.britishpathe.com [consulted 11 April 2018]; James Goodchild, *A Most Enigmatic War: R. V. Jones and the Genesis of British Scientific Intelligence 1939–45* (Solihull: Helion and Company Ltd., 2017), p. 458.

153. 'Ministry of Information Home Intelligence Weekly Report No. 206', 28 September 1944, INF 1/292, TNA.

154. 'Ministry of Information Home Intelligence Weekly Report No. 212', 26 October 1944, INF 1/292, TNA.

155. Dilks, *Cadogan Diary*, p. 673 (entry for 19 October 1944). Emphasis in original.

156. 'Moscow Talks Ended', *The Times*, 21 October 1944.

157. See Albert Resis, 'The Churchill–Stalin Secret "Percentages" Agreement on the Balkans, Moscow, October 1944', *American Historical Review*, 83:2 (April 1978), pp. 368–87.

158. W. H. Lawrence, 'Russians Indicate Unity on Balkans', *New York Times*, 22 October 1944.

159. EAM was the acronym of the National Liberation Front (EAM); the National Popular Liberation Army (ELAS) was EAM's military wing.

160. WSC to Roland Scobie, 5 December 1944, in WSC, *The Second World War*, Vol. VI: *Triumph and Tragedy* (London: Cassell, 1954), p. 252.

161. WSC to Harold Alexander, 14 December 1944, Churchill Papers, CHAR/20/177/53-4; A. J. Foster, 'The Politicians, Public Opinion and the Press: The Storm over British Military Intervention in Greece in December 1944', *Journal of Contemporary History*, 19 (1984), pp. 453–94, at p. 468.

162. 'Mr Churchill Was Not Candid', *Chicago Daily Tribune*, 11 December 1944.

163. Weekly Political Summary, 17 December 1944, in Nicholas, *Washington Despatches*, p. 476.

164. Andrew Thorpe, '"In a Rather Emotional State"? The Labour Party and British Intervention in Greece, 1944–5', *English Historical Review*, 493 (2006), pp. 1075–105.

165. Foster, 'The Politicians, Public Opinion and the Press', pp. 456, 486.

166. Speech of 18 January 1945.

167. Jefferys, *Labour and the Wartime Coalition*, p. 204 (entry for 18 January 1945).

168. Kathleen M. Tipper diary (diarist 5443), 13 February 1945, MOA.

169. Edward Stebbing, *Diary of a Decade 1939–50* (Lewes: Book Guild Ltd., 1998), p. 300 (entry for 13 February 1945). See also C. H. Miller diary (diarist 5376), 13 February 1945, A. B. Holness diary (diarist 5338), 13 February 1945, J. Lippold diary (diarist 5132), 13 February 1945, MOA. By this point MoI had ceased producing Home Intelligence reports, and there was no specific Mass-Observation report on Yalta.

170. 'Death of Roosevelt' (File Report 2229), 13 April 1945, MOA.

171. Moran, *Struggle*, p. 250.

172. 'Report on Victory in Europe', File Report 2263, 10 June 1945 (with a handwritten note 'Written up July 1946'), MOA.

173. Broadcast of 4 June 1945. For full discussion, see Richard Toye, 'Winston Churchill's "Crazy Broadcast": Party, Nation, and the 1945 Gestapo Speech', *Journal of British Studies*, 49: 3 (July 2010), pp. 655–80.

174. R. A. Rendall, 'The Election Broadcasts of 1945: Overseas Coverage', 3 August 1945, BBC Written Archives, R44/189/1, General Election File 1.

175. 'The Election Broadcasts of 1945', 27 July 1945, BBC Written Archives, R44/189/1, General Election File 1.

176. Broadcast of 30 June 1945.

177. Isaac Kramnick and Barry Sheerman, *Harold Laski: A Life on the Left* (London: Hamish Hamilton, 1993), pp. 483–9.

178. 'Attlee tells Churchill: You Underrate the Common Man', *News Chronicle*, 4 July 1945, CHPC 22.

179. James Thomas, *Popular Newspapers, the Labour Party and British Politics* (London: Routledge, 2005), pp. 15–17.

180. Hird diary, 31 May 1945.

181. Hird diary, 13 June 1945.

182. Thomas, *Popular Newspapers*, pp. 17–19.

183. Lord Hartwell, *William Camrose: Giant of Fleet Street* (London: Weidenfeld & Nicolson, 1992), p. 319.

184. R. B. McCallum and Alison Readman, *The British General Election of 1945* (London: Oxford University Press, 1947), p. 181. For Churchill's resentment at the attitude of *The Times*, see McLachlan, *In the Chair*, p. 209.

185. WSC, 'Return National Government With Solid Majority', *News of the World*, 1 July 1945, CHPC 22.

186. For Labour's strategy, see Laura Beers, *Your Britain: Media and the Making of the Labour Party* (Cambridge, MA: Harvard University Press, 2010), Chapter 9.

187. 'The Parties Speak No. 5: The Rt. Hon. Winston Churchill: Conservative Party', 21 June 1945, www.britishpathe.com [consulted 12 April 2018]; Geoffrey Lloyd to Ralph Assheton, 29 May 1945, Churchill Papers CHAR 2/556/19.

188. 'The Parties Speak No. 4: The Rt. Hon. C. R. Attlee: Labour Party', 18 June 1945, www.britishpathe.com [consulted 12 April 2018].

189. John Potter, *Pim and Churchill's Map Room: Based on the Papers of Captain Richard Pim RNVR Supervisor of Churchill's Map Room 1939–1945* (Belfast: Northern Ireland War Memorial, 2014), p. 66.

190. Martin Gilbert, *Winston S. Churchill*, Vol. VIII: *'Never Despair', 1945–1965* (London: Heinemann, 1988), pp. 105–7.

191. Weekly Political Summary, 28 July 1945, in Nicholas, *Washington Despatches*, p. 595.

192. *Daily Mail*, 28 July 1945.

CHAPTER 8

1. Lord Moran, *Winston Churchill: The Struggle for Survival, 1940–1965* (London: Constable, 1966), p. 288.

2. David Lough, *No More Champagne: Churchill and His Money* (New York: Picador, 2015), p. 324.

3. Colin Coote, *Editorial: The Memoirs of Colin R. Coote* (London: Eyre & Spottiswoode, 1965), p. 272. The term 'over-takes' to refer to batches of corrections appears to have been coined by Churchill. See 'He Walked With Destiny', *News Review*, 7 October 1948, CHPC 28.

4. Moran, *Struggle*, p. 299.

5. 'Need Of More Vigorous Opposition', *Sunday Times*, 4 November 1945.

6. See John Ramsden, *Man of the Century: Winston Churchill and His Legend Since 1945* (London: HarperCollins, 2002).

7. '"Secret Session" Bombshell Originated from Earlier "Life" Scoop', *World's Press News*, 31 January 1946, CHPC 23. See also 'Churchill Criticized on Speech Release', *New York Times*, 29 January 1946.

8. Walter Graebner, *My Dear Mr. Churchill* (London: Michael Joseph, 1965), pp. 12–14. Churchill's choice is somewhat surprising given that, during the war, the Ministry of Information had formed 'the impression that "Time" is conducting a systematic campaign against the Prime Minister and also that it loses few opportunities for vilifying the British Empire'. A. S. Hodge to F. D. Brown, 16 October 1942, PREM 4/26/8, TNA.

9. Marco Duranti makes this point powerfully with respect to Churchill's campaign for European unity in *The Conservative Human Rights Revolution: European Identity, Transnational Politics, and the Origins of the European Convention* (Oxford: Oxford University Press, 2017). For Churchill's thinking on Europe, see also Felix Klos, *Churchill's Last Stand: The Struggle to Unite Europe* (London: I.B. Tauris, 2017).

10. 'Churchill, Here for 9-Week Stay, Says He Will Continue in Politics', *New York Times*, 15 January 1946.

11. 'Churchill to U.S.: Don't leave Europe', *Daily Mail*, 17 January 1946; Richard Toye, Churchill and Britain's 'Financial Dunkirk', *Twentieth Century British History*, 15 (2004), pp. 329–60.

12. 'Churchill Bids Us Help Police Europe', *New York Times*, 17 January 1946.

13. Ramsden, *Man of the Century*, p. 165.

14. Martha Lummus, 'Churchills Top Miami Beach's Celebrity List', *Chicago Daily Tribune*, 27 January 1946.

15. Dorothy Thompson, 'Churchill Takes U.S. For Granted—& Triumphs', *The Observer*, 20 January 1946.

16. Herbert Morrison, 'Visit to Canada and the United States, January 1946', 21 February 1946, CP (46) 77, FO 371/51632, TNA.

17. William S. White, 'Republicans Propose Churchill As Pearl Harbor Inquiry Witness', *New York Times*, 18 January 1946. At this time the notion circulated that Churchill, at the 1941 Atlantic Conference, had stiffened the attitude of the Roosevelt administration in such a way as to make inevitable an otherwise avoidable war with Japan. See 'Adventure in Failure', *Chicago Daily Tribune*, 19 January 1946.

18. Dwight D. Eisenhower to WSC, 18 December 1945, Churchill Papers, CHUR 2/226/32. Butcher's articles were subsequently published as *My Three Years with Eisenhower: The Personal Diary of Captain Harry C. Butcher, USNR* (New York: Simon and Schuster, 1946).

19. Martin Gilbert, *Winston S. Churchill*, Vol. VIII: *'Never Despair', 1945–1965* (London: Heinemann, 1988), p. 187.

20. 'Mr Churchill's Candor', *Chicago Daily Tribune*, 18 January 1946.

21. 'Churchill to Urge Union With America', *Reynolds News*, 17 February 1946, CHPC/23.

22. 'US Awaiting Big Speech By Mr. Churchill', *The Observer*, 3 March 1946; Henry B. Ryan, 'A New Look at Churchill's "Iron Curtain" Speech', *Historical Journal*, 22 (1979), pp. 895–920, at p. 908.

23. 'Churchill Flies Back to His Holiday; Declares He Likes "No Comment" Phrase', *New York Times*, 13 February 1946.

24. 'Town of 6,500 Agog and Gay for Churchill', *Chicago Daily Tribune*, 5 March 1946.

25. Philip White, *Churchill's Cold War: How the Iron Curtain Speech Shaped the Post-war World* (London: Duckworth Overlook, 2012), p. 147.

26. Speech of 5 March 1946.

27. Media summary by US Government Information Service, Division of Press Intelligence, 7 March 1946, Churchill Papers, CHUR 2/229/286–95.

28. Clive Webb, 'Reluctant Partners: African Americans and the Origins of the Special Relationship', *Journal of Transatlantic Studies*, 1 (2016), pp. 350–64.

29. 'French Press Views on the Churchill Speech', *Manchester Guardian*, 7 March 1946.

30. 'Stalin Interview With Pravda on Churchill', *New York Times*, 14 March 1946.

31. Cabinet minutes, CM (46) 23rd Conclusions, 11 March 1946, CAB 128/5; Ryan, 'A New Look', pp. 908–9, 915.

32. A. L. Kennedy diary, 9 March 1946, LKEN 1/25, CAC. Emphasis in original.

33. BBC Home Service 11 p.m. Bulletin 5 March 1946, and BBC Home Service 5 March 1946 'Excerpts From Speech By Mr. Churchill from Missouri', broadcast at 11.03 p.m. [consulted on microfilm at the British Library]. Emphasis in original.

34. Don Iddon, 'Churchill: "Ensure Peace Now—Time is Short"', and Leslie Illingworth, 'No Admittance: By Order—Joe', *Daily Mail*, 6 March 1946.

35. *Daily Express*, 6 March 1946; *Daily Mirror*, 6 March 1946.

36. Terence Brown, *The Irish Times: 150 Years of Influence* (London: Bloomsbury, London, 2015), p. 212.

37. Patrick Wright, *Iron Curtain: From Stage to Cold War* (Oxford: Oxford University Press, 2007).

38. Cecil King diary, 7 March 1946.

39. A. P. Raley diary (diarist 5403), 6 March 1946, MOA.

40. Albert Hird diary, 7 March 1946.

41. C. W. Gardner diary (diarist 5076), 13 March 1946, MOA.

42. WSC, 'The United States of Europe', *Saturday Evening Post*, 15 February 1930, and 'Why Not "The United States of Europe"?', *News of the World*, 29 May 1938.

43. 'The Peace Congress at Geneva', *The Times*, 3 September 1867.

44. 'Mr. Churchill In Brussels', *The Times*, 17 November 1945; 'Mr. Churchill At The Hague', *The Times*, 10 May 1946; 'Mr. Churchill At Leyden', *The Times*, 11 May 1946.

45. Elizabeth Gilliat to Jo Sturdee, 9 September 1946, Churchill Papers CHUR 2/247/245.

46. 'The Voice Above the Babel', *South Wales Echo & Evening Express*, 20 September 1946.

47. 'A Churchill Bombshell', *Huddersfield Daily Examiner*, 20 September 1946; A. P. Raley diary (diarist 5403), 20 September 1946, MOA. On the other hand, one newspaper argued that 'There was nothing of the Missouri bombshell about the speech delivered in Zurich University yesterday': 'Council of Europe', *Glasgow Herald*, 20 September 1946.

48. 'Pact of Silence', *Daily Telegraph*, 20 September 1946.

49. Speech of 19 September 1946.

50. 'Churchillism', *Reynolds News*, 22 September 1946, CHPC 24.

51. N.E. Underwood diary (diarist 5447), 'Friday' (20?) September 1946, MOA.

52. 'A plea to Europe', *Daily Mail*, 20 September 1946.

53. 'Atom Policy and War Hysteria', Moscow, in German to Europe, 8 October 1946, 9.00 a.m. EST, FBIS–FRB–46-202.

54. 'Masses Oppose Encirclement of USSR', Moscow, Soviet European Service in Rumanian, 6 October 1946, 2.00 p.m. EST, FBIS–FRB–46-200.

55. Robert Boothby, 'Britain Must Take Lead in Building New Europe', *News of the World*, 22 September 1946.

56. 'Mr. Bevin's Chance', *Manchester Guardian*, 23 September 1946.

57. Stephen Coulter, 'Mr. Churchill Accused of "Belligerence"', *Newcastle Journal*, 20 September 1946.

58. 'Sceptical French Comment', *Birmingham Post*, 20 September 1946.

59. 'French Criticism of Mr. Churchill', *The Scotsman*, 21 September 1946.

60. 'Les idées de M. Churchill', *Le Monde*, 21 September 1946.

61. 'Que l'Europe se lève!', *Le Phare Dimanche*, 27 September 1946.

62. Gerhard Kreyssig, 'Positive Europäer', *Süddeutsche Zeitung*, 24 September 1946.

63. Gordon Sewell, *Europe's Fate* (London: Victor Gollancz, 1947), p. 5.

64. William Chenery to WSC, 24 September 1946, Churchill Papers, CHUR 4/31/41–2.

65. *L'Humanité*, 28 Dec. 1946; WSC to Chenery 6 October 1946, Churchill Papers, CHUR 4/31/37.

66. WSC to Chenery, 6 November 1946, Churchill Papers, CHUR 4/31/30–1.

67. Duncan Sandys to WSC, 5 December 1946, Churchill Papers, CHUR 4/31/17.

68. WSC, 'The High Road of the Future', *Collier's*, 4 January 1947, in Michael Wolff (ed.), *The Collected Essays of Sir Winston Churchill*, 4 vols (London: Library of Imperial History, 1976), II, pp. 460–7.

69. Klos, *Churchill's Last Stand*, p. 83.

70. Speech of 19 September 1946. For examples of comment that hint at this interpretation, see 'United States of Europe!', *Evening News* (Portsmouth), 20 September 1946, and 'Churchill's US of Europe', *Sheffield Telegraph*, 20 September 1946.

71. *The Times*, 24 September 1946.

72. Thomas Richford to the editor of the *Daily Telegraph*, published 3 January 1947.

73. For discussion, see Denise M. Bostdorff, *Proclaiming the Truman Doctrine: The Cold War Call to Arms* (College Station, TX: Texas A & M University Press, 2008).

74. Graebner, *My Dear Mr. Churchill*, p. 15

75. 'If I Were An American', *Life*, 14 April 1947, in Wolff, *Collected Essays*, II, pp. 468–77. Quotation at p. 471.

76. The text of the article can be found in WSC, 'Europe Unite!', *The Recorder*, 6 March 1948, CHPC 26.

77. Arthur Christiansen, *Headlines All My Life* (London: Heinemann, 1961), pp. 220–1.

78. Kenneth Young, *Churchill and Beaverbrook: A Study in Friendship and Politics* (London: Eyre & Spottiswoode, 1966), Chapter 21; 'Churchill—The Only Hope', *The Recorder*, 19 April 1949, CHPC 25, William Barkley, 'How Churchill Got Things Done', *Daily Express*, 27 June 1949.

79. Christiansen, *Headlines*, p. 221.

80. 'Mr. Churchill: "I was misrepresented"', *News Chronicle*, 8 December 1947, and 'Impetuous Mr. Churchill, *Eastern Daily Press*, 10 December 1947, CHPC 26. Churchill had said that the substitution of state control for private enterprise would mean that at least a quarter of people then alive would 'have to disappear' because of lower living standards. The cause of his complaint was that the *Pictorial* had failed to quote the part that made clear that he was talking about what would happen under socialist conditions, thus making it appear as a generalized prediction. The paper defended itself by arguing that it had been obliged to condense the speech for reasons of space, and that Churchill's meaning had at any rate been clear from the overall context of its reporting. It also said that it was not a socialist paper, but rather editorially independent. Frederic Mullally, 'Mr. Churchill is too sensitive', *Sunday Pictorial*, 14 December 1947, CHPC 26.

81. Grace Wyndham Goldie, *Facing The Nation: Television and Politics 1936–76* (London: Bodley Head, 1977), pp. 105–6.

82. 'A Worker's Notebook', *Daily Worker*, 7 August 1947.

83. 'United States of Europe', *Evening Times* (Glasgow), 20 September 1946.

84. Royal Commission on the Press 1947–1949: Report', Cmd. 7700, HMSO, London, 1949, p. iii.

85. 'What Winston Churchill Said in 1945', *The Recorder*, 26 July 1947, CHPC 25; Young, *Churchill and Beaverbrook*, p. 279.

86. 'Conservatives And Industry', *The Times*, 22 September 1947.

87. Cmd. 7700, p. 176.

88. Hird diary, 28 February 1950.

89. A 1952 private member's bill, which threatened the creation of a statutory body, finally forced the industry to act itself to forestall legislation: Kevin Williams, 'Bringing Popular Journalism into Disrepute: The News of the World, the Public and Politics 1953–2011', in Laurel Brake, Chandrika Kaul, and Mark W. Turner (eds), *The News of the World and the British Press, 1843–2011* (Basingstoke: Palgrave Macmillan, 2016), pp 213–28, at p. 215.

90. Paul Addison, *Churchill on the Home Front, 1900–1955* (London: Pimlico, 1993), pp. 400–1.

91. Speech of 20 February 1950.

92. James Reston, *Deadline: A Memoir* (New York: Random House, 1991), pp. 180–1.

93. Press statement published on 26 August 1949, quoted in Gilbert, *'Never Despair'*, p. 486.

94. Moran, *Struggle*, p. 335.

95. Andrew J. Taylor, '"The Record of the 1950s is Irrelevant": The Conservative Party, Electoral Strategy and Opinion Research, 1945–64', *Contemporary British History*, 17 (2003), pp. 81–110; Laura Dumond Beers, 'Whose Opinion? Changing Attitudes Towards Opinion Polling in British Politics, 1937–1964', *Twentieth Century British History*, 17 (2006), pp. 177–205.

96. Gerald O'Brien, 'Weekend Publicity', 7 March 1949, CCO 4/2/156, CPA.

97. T. J. Hollins, 'The Conservative Party and Film Propaganda between the Wars', *English Historical Review*, 96 (1981), pp. 359–69.

98. Minutes of the Executive Committee of the Conservative and Unionist Films Association, 30 March 1949, CCO 4/2/25, CPA.

99. 'Mr. Winston Churchill—An Interview', 2 February 1950, www.movietone.com [consulted 20 July 2018].

100. John Carvel, 'Tories Blame Churchill', *Star*, 27 January 1947, '"Churchill Too Old To Lead Us Through"', *Birkenhead Advertiser*, 1 March 1947, 'Surprise "Churchill Should Go" Attack Sets a Puzzle', *Daily Mirror*, 13 March 1947, CHPC 24; Cecil King diary, 6 March 1949.

101. Raymond Moley, 'Meanwhile, Churchill Has Stolen the Show', *Los Angeles Times*, 14 February 1950.

102. 'Report of His Death False, Churchill Says', *Los Angeles Times*, 17 February 1950.

103. Public Opinion Research Department, 'Confidential Supplement to Public Opinion Summary No. 5', May 1949, CCO 4/3/249, CPA; H. G. Nicholas, *The British General Election of 1950* (London: Macmillan, 1951), p. 68.

104. Broadcast of 21 January 1950.

105. 'Mr. Churchill's Lead', *The Times*, 23 January 1950; 'Calm, Constructive Confidence', *Daily Telegraph*, 23 January 1950, 'Churchill's Challenge', *Financial Times*, 23 January 1950.

106. *Daily Mail*, 23 January 1950.

107. 'Mr. Churchill', *Manchester Guardian*, 23 January 1950.

108. *Daily Mirror*, 23 January 1950.

109. Chief Organising Officer to Agents, 19 January 1950, CCO/4/3/114, CPA.

110. Public Opinion Research Department, 'Public Reaction Report No. 4', 24 January 1950, CCO/4/3/250, CPA.

111. Speech of 14 February 1950.

112. Lord Beaverbrook to Brendan Bracken, 13 December 1950, in Richard Cockett (ed.), *My Dear Max: The letters of Brendan Bracken to Lord Beaverbrook, 1925–1958* (London: Historians' Press, 1990), p. 117.

113. Raymond Daniell, 'British Foreign Policy Unity Believed Split by Churchill', *New York Times*, 15 February 1950; Dewey L. Fleming, 'Candidates Generally Ignore US Attitude On British Vote Fleming', *Baltimore Sun*, 14 February 1950.

114. Raymond Daniell, 'Churchill Speech Disconcerts Labor', *New York Times*, 16 February 1950.

115. Alistair Cooke, 'Doubts in Washington', *Manchester Guardian*, 16 February 1950.

116. Kevin Ruane, *Churchill and the Bomb in War and Cold War* (London: Bloomsbury, 2016), p. 176

117. 'The Bankruptcy of the Fulton Policy', in English to the UK, 22 February 1950, FBIS–FRB–50–038.

118. *Daily Mail*, 23 February 1950.

119. Nicholas, *British General Election of 1950*, p. 202.

120. Goldie, *Facing The Nation*, pp. 62–7.

121. Harriet Jones, '"This is Magnificent!": 300,000 Houses a Year and the Tory Revival after 1945', *Contemporary British History*, 14 (2000), pp. 99–121.

122. Michael Cockerell, *Live from Number 10: The Inside Story of Prime Ministers and Television* (London: Faber & Faber, 1988), p. 14

123. Conservative Party Election Broadcast 16 October 1951, http://pebs. group.shef.ac.uk/sir-anthony-eden-leslie-mitchell [consulted 26 July 2018].

124. D. E. Butler, *The British General Election of 1951* (London: Macmillan, 1952), p. 77.

125. Labour Party Election Broadcast 17 October 1951, http://pebs.group. shef.ac.uk/sir-hartley-shawcross-and-christopher-mayhew.html [consulted 26 July 2018].

126. Moran, *Struggle*, p. 531.

127. *BBC Handbook 1976*, p. 302, cited at http://pebs.group.shef.ac.uk/ radio-and-television-audience-0.html [consulted 16 August 2018].

128. Butler, *British General Election of 1951*, pp. 63, 129–30.

129. Hird diary, 21 October 1951.

130. 'Daily Mirror Libel Action', 13 December 1951, Churchill Papers, CHUR 2/221/43–4.

131. 'Showdown', *Daily Mirror*, 21 September 1951.

132. Speech of 6 October 1951.

133. A.W. [Alexander Werth], 'Churchill Over France', *The Nation* (US), 13 October 1951; 'Churchill – A US Report', *Daily Mirror*, 18 October 1951.

134. 'Daily Mirror Libel Action', 13 December 1951, Churchill Papers, CHUR 2/221/43–4.

135. 'Mr. Churchill Issues a Writ', *The Times*, 26 October 1951.

136. 'Defence of the first-named Defendants Daily Mirror Newspapers Limited and the third-named Defendant Silvester Bolam', 8 February 1952, Churchill Papers, CHUR 2/221/99.

137. Valentine Holmes, 'Note', 30 November 1951, Churchill Papers, CHUR 2/221/53–7.

138. Hartley Shawcross, *Life Sentence: The Memoirs of Lord Shawcross* (London: Constable, 1995), p. 204.

139. 'Mr. Churchill and the "Daily Mirror"', *Daily Mirror*, 24 May 1952.

140. Kevin Theakston, 'The Oratory of Winston Churchill', in Richard Hayton and Andrew S. Crines (eds), *Conservative Orators from Baldwin to Cameron* (Manchester: Manchester University Press, 2015), pp. 30–46, at p. 31.

141. Jim Bulpitt and Peter Burnham, 'Operation Robot and the British Political Economy in the Early 1950s: The Politics of Market Strategies', *Contemporary British History*, 13 (1999), pp. 1–31.

142. The story first came out in detail in Andrew Shonfield, *British Economic Policy Since the War* (Harmondsworth: Penguin, 1958), pp. 216–23. See also Ian Waller, 'Official Secrets Act Challenged', *Sunday Telegraph*, 29 October 1961, and 'How Sterling Nearly Floated', *The Economist*, 11 November 1961.

143. 'The inside story of a scoop', *Yorkshire Post*, 6 April 1955, CHPC 56.

144. J. A. Cross, *Lord Swinton* (Oxford: Clarendon Press, 1982), pp. 270–1.

145. James Margach, *The Abuse of Power: The War between Downing Street and the Media from Lloyd George to James Callaghan* (London: W.H. Allen, 1978), pp. 67–9.

146. David Gammans to Lord Swinton, 27 May 1952, Thomas Fife Clark Papers, FICA 2/21.

147. Evelyn Shuckburgh, Descent to Suez: Diaries 1951–56 (London: Weidenfeld & Nicolson, 1956), p. 31 (entry for 5 January 1952).

148. 'Shakiness Marks Voice of Tired Old Warrior', *Los Angeles Times*, 6 January 1952; Alistair Cooke, 'US Welcome to Mr. Churchill', *Times of India*, 8 January 1952.

149. Clifton Daniel, 'Seldom Has One Worn So Many', *New York Times*, 8 January 1952.

150. Alistair Cooke, 'US To Hear Out Mr. Churchill', *Times of India*, 5 January 1952; Klaus Larres, *Churchill's Cold War: The Politics of Personal Diplomacy* (New Haven, CT: Yale University Press, 2002), pp. 161–73.

151. Shuckburgh, *Descent to Suez*, p. 32 (entry for 5 January 1952). See also 'Churchill "Won All Points in Washington"', *Evening News*, 11 January 1952, and 'Churchill gains nothing by trip', *Daily Herald*, 11 January 1952, both in CSCT 8/4.

152. James Reston, 'Churchill Helping To Shape Decisions on West's Defence', *New York Times*, 7 January 1952.

153. Charles E. Bohlen, *Witness to History 1929–1969* (New York: W.W. Norton, 1973), p. 371.

154. 'At Grips With Differences On S.E. Asia', *The Times*, 28 June 1954.

155. 'Prime Minister Leaves US', *The Times*, 2 July 1954.

156. Williams, 'Bringing Popular Journalism into Disrepute', p. 215; Adrian Bingham, *Family Newspapers? Sex, Private Life, and the British Popular Press 1918–1978* (Oxford: Oxford University Press, 2009), p. 184.

157. John Colville, *The Fringes of Power: Downing Street Diaries, 1939–1955* (London: Hodder & Stoughton, 1985), p. 669. Bracken had been ennobled after standing down from parliament following the general election of 1951.

158. Warren Dockter, 'Managing a Giant: Jock Colville and Winston Churchill', in Andrew Holt and Warren Dockter (eds), *Private Secretaries to the Prime Minister: Foreign Affairs from Churchill to Thatcher* (London: Routledge, 2017), pp. 8–33.

159. Lord Hartwell, *William Camrose: Giant of Fleet Street* (London: Weidenfeld & Nicolson, 1992), p. 338; Parliamentary Debates, House of Commons, Fifth Series, Vol. 537, 2 March 1955, col. 2116.

160. Moran, *Struggle*, p. 413.

161. 'That's Better! Premier up and Cheerful', *Daily Mail*, 29 June 1953.

162. Peter Catterall, *The Macmillan Diaries: The Cabinet Years, 1950–1957* (London: Macmillan, 2003), p. 246 (entry for 27 July 1953).

163. 'Sir Winston Must Soon Decide', *The Observer*, 16 August 1953.

164. Stewart Alsop, 'Sir Winston's Illness', *Washington Post*, 7 August 1953.

165. *Daily Mirror*, 17 August 1953.

166. Drew Middleton, 'Prime Minister Asks Unity', *New York Times*, 31 March 1954.

167. 'Twilight of a Giant', *Daily Mirror*, 1 April 1954.

168. 'The Labourer in the Vineyard', *The Observer*, 20 June 1954.

169. Speech of 23 November 1954.

170. 'Anecdote', *Manchester Guardian*, 26 November 1954.

171. Hugh Cudlipp, *Walking on the Water* (London: Bodley Head, 1976), p. 208.

172. Mark Pottle (ed.), *Daring to Hope: The Diaries and Letters of Violet Bonham Carter 1946–1969* (London: Weidenfeld & Nicolson, 2000), p. 127 (entry of 6 August 1953); Addison, *Churchill on the Home Front*, pp. 420–1.

173. Cockerell, *Live from Number 10*, pp. 22–4.

174. Goldie, *Facing the Nation*, pp. 169–72.

CONCLUSION

1. A. B. Holness diary (diarist 5338), 5 April 1955, MOA.

2. Michael Cockerell, *Live from Number 10: The Inside Story of Prime Ministers and Television* (London: Faber & Faber, 1988), p. 27; 'The Resignation Story', *Manchester Guardian*, 6 April 1955.

3. 'Das Streiflicht', *Süddeutsche Zeitung*, 7 April 1955, copy in Churchill Papers, CHUR 2/428/A-E/15/70.

4. 'Strike-silenced Press Pays Tribute Here', *Yorkshire Post*, 6 April 1955, CHPC 56.

5. M. C. Towler (diarist 5445), 5 April 1955, MOA.

6. Donald McLachlan, 'How Sir Winston Went', *Daily Telegraph*, 21 April 1955.

7. 'Review of the Italian Press', Rome, in Italian to Europe, 2 April 1955, 0750 GMT, FBIS-FRB-55-065.

8. 'Press Asked Not To Follow Churchill Party', *Canberra Times*, 14 April 1955.

9. 'Sir Winston Churchill', *Daily Telegraph*, 21 April 1955.

10. Issued 17 April 1955, www.britishpathe.com [consulted 20 August 2018].

11. Anthony Montague Browne, *Long Sunset: Memoirs of Winston Churchill's Last Private Secretary* (London: Cassell, 1995), pp. 225–6.

12. Lord Moran's notes on 19 and 31 December 1960 in the proofs of *Winston Churchill: The Struggle for Survival*, Moran Papers, PPCMW/K10/4 (2).

13. After consultations with Special Branch, Churchill decided not to increase his own levels of police protection. Interview with Edmund Murray, 1995, https://www.iwm.org.uk/collections/item/object/80014406 [consulted 21 August 2018].

14. 'Aesop Revisited', *Private Eye*, 8 February 1963; 'Injunctions Against "Private Eye"', *The Times*, 16 March 1963.

15. 'Sir Winston Churchill: Cerebral Thrombosis', *The Times*, 16 January 1965.
16. 'Sir Winston "At A Very Low Ebb" ', *The Times*, 21 January 1965.
17. 'ITN Apology to Lady Churchill for Error', *Daily Telegraph*, 29 January 1965.
18. 'Lying In State', *The Times*, 26 January 1965.
19. L. Marsland Gander, 'TV Rises to a Great Occasion', *Daily Telegraph*, 1 February 1965.
20. '25m Watched Churchill Funeral on TV', *Daily Telegraph*, 5 February 1965.
21. 'No British Press at Bladon', *Daily Mail*, 30 January 1965.
22. 'Press Comments on Churchill Retirement', Paris, French Home Service, 6 April 1955, 0700 GMT, FBIS-FRB-55-068.

Bibliography

Archival Collections

United Kingdom

British Library
Curzon Papers
Almeric Fitzroy Papers
Northcliffe Papers

British Library of Political and Economic Science, Archives Division
Hubert Carr-Gomm correspondence

Parliamentary Archives
Beaverbrook Papers
Stansgate Papers
John St. Loe Strachey Papers

Wellcome Library
Lord Moran Papers

Imperial War Museum
Albert Hird diary

The National Archives
Public Record Office of Northern Ireland
R. H. H. Baird diary

National Library of Scotland
Aylmer Haldane Papers
R. B. Haldane Papers

BBC Written Archives
Churchill Archives Centre, Cambridge
Broadwater Collection (BRDW)
Churchill Oral History Collection (CHOH)
Clementine Churchill Papers (CSCT)
Thomas Fife Clark Papers (FICA)
Churchill Press Cuttings (CHPC)

Archibald Hurd Papers (HURD)
A.L. Kennedy Papers (LKEN)

Cambridge University Library
Leo Chiozza Money Papers

Trinity College, Cambridge
Walter Layton Papers

Bodleian Library, Oxford
Margot Asquith Papers
Violet Bonham Carter Papers
Conservative Party Archive
Stafford Cripps Papers
Harcourt Papers
Henry Nevinson Papers

Cadbury Research Library, Birmingham University
Masterman Papers

Cardiff University Special Collections
Hugh Cudlipp Papers

Exeter University Special Collections
Thomas Blackburn Papers

Glasgow University Special Collections
Alexander MacCallum Scott diary

Leeds University Special Collections
Glenesk–Bathurst Papers

Manchester University Special Collections
Guardian Archive

Sheffield University Special Collections
W. A. S. Hewins Papers

USA
Dartmouth College
Frederick D. Forsch Collection

Howard Gotlieb Archival Research Center
Cecil King Papers

University of Illinois at Urbana-Champaign
H. G. Wells Papers

Wesleyan University
William Manchester Papers

Digital Archives
Chatham House Archive
Churchill Papers
Foreign Broadcast Information Service
Lord Halifax diary
Franklin D. Roosevelt Papers
Steven Spielberg Film and Video Archive

BOOKS

Addison, Paul, *Churchill on the Home Front, 1900–1955* (London: Pimlico, 1993).

Addison, Paul, *Churchill: The Unexpected Hero* (Oxford: Oxford University Press, 2005).

Addison, Paul, and Jeremy A. Crang (eds), *Listening to Britain: Home Intelligence Reports on Britain's Finest Hour: May to September 1940* (London: Bodley Head, 2010).

Alkon, Paul K., *Winston Churchill's Imagination* (Lewisburg, PA: Bucknell University Press, 2006).

Armstrong, William (ed.), *With Malice Toward None: A War Diary by Cecil H. King* (London: Sidgwick & Jackson, 1970).

Ashmead-Bartlett, E., *The Uncensored Dardanelles* (London: Hutchinson & Co., 1920).

Atkins, John Black, *The Relief of Ladysmith* (London: Methuen, 1900).

Ayerst, David, *Garvin of The Observer* (London: Croom Helm, 1985).

Barnes, John, and David Nicholson (eds), *The Leo Amery Diaries*, Vol. 1: *1896–1929* (London: Hutchinson, 1980).

Barnes, John, and David Nicholson (eds), *The Empire at Bay: The Leo Amery Diaries, 1929–1945* (London: Hutchinson, 1988).

Beaverbrook, Lord, *Politicians and the Press* (London: Hutchinson, n.d. but 1925).

Beaverbrook, Lord, *The Abdication of King Edward VIII*, ed. A. J. P. Taylor (London: Hamish Hamilton, 1966).

Beers, Laura, *Your Britain: Media and the Making of the Labour Party* (Cambridge, MA: Harvard University Press, 2010).

Bell, Christopher M., *Churchill and Sea Power* (Oxford: Oxford University Press, 2013).

Bell, Christopher M., *Churchill and the Dardanelles* (Oxford: Oxford University Press, 2017).

Bell, Hesketh, *Glimpses of a Governor's Life* (London: Sampson, Low, Marston & Co., n.d.).

Beveridge, Lord, *Power and Influence* (London: Hodder & Stoughton, 1953).

Bew, Paul, *Churchill and Ireland* (Oxford: Oxford University Press, 2016).

Bingham, Adrian, *Family Newspapers? Sex, Private Life, and the British Popular Press 1918–1978* (Oxford: Oxford University Press, 2009).

Black, Jonathan, *Winston Churchill in British Art, 1900 to the Present Day: The Titan With Many Faces* (London: Bloomsbury Academic, 2017).

Blake, Robert, and Wm. Roger Louis (eds), *Churchill* (Oxford: Oxford University Press, 1993).

Bohlen, Charles E., *Witness to History 1929–1969* (New York: W.W. Norton, 1973).

Bonham Carter, Mark, and Mark Pottle (eds), *Lantern Slides: The Diaries and Letters of Violet Bonham Carter 1904–1914* (London: Weidenfeld & Nicolson, 1996).

Bonham Carter, Violet, *Winston Churchill As I Knew Him* (London: Reprint Society, 1965)

Boothby, Lord, *Recollections of a Rebel* (London: Hutchinson, 1978).

Brake, Laurel, Chandrika Kaul, and Mark W. Turner (eds), *The News of the World and the British Press, 1843–2011* (Basingstoke: Palgrave Macmillan, 2016).

Briggs, Asa, *The History of Broadcasting in the United Kingdom*, Vol. III: *The War of Words* (Oxford: Oxford University Press, 1995).

Brock, Michael and Eleanor Brock (eds), *H.H. Asquith: Letters to Venetia Stanley* (Oxford: Oxford University Press, 1982).

Brock, Michael and Eleanor Brock (eds), *Margot Asquith's Great War Diary 1914–1916: The View from Downing Street* (Oxford: Oxford University Press, 2014).

Brown, Terence, *The Irish Times: 150 Years of Influence* (London: Bloomsbury, 2015).

Brownrigg, Douglas, *Indiscretions of the Naval Censor* (New York: George H. Doran Company, 1920).

Bullock, Alan, *The Life and Times of Ernest Bevin*, Vol. 2: *Minister of Labour 1940–1945* (London: Heinemann, 1967).

Butcher, Harry C., *My Three Years with Eisenhower: The Personal Diary of Captain Harry C. Butcher, USNR* (New York: Simon and Schuster, 1946).

Butler, D. E., *The British General Election of 1951* (London: Macmillan, 1952).

Campbell, John, *F.E. Smith: First Earl of Birkenhead* (London: Jonathan Cape, 1983).

Campion, Garry, *The Good Fight: Battle of Britain Propaganda and The Few* (Basingstoke: Palgrave, 2009).

Carlton, David, *Churchill and the Soviet Union* (Manchester: Manchester University Press, 2000).

Casey, Steven, *Cautious Crusade: Franklin D. Roosevelt, American Public Opinion, and the War Against Nazi Germany* (Oxford: Oxford University Press, 2001).

Casey, Steven, *The War Beat, Europe: The American Media at War Against Nazi Germany* (New York: Oxford University Press, 2017).

Catherwood, Christopher, *Churchill's Folly: How Winston Churchill Created Modern Iraq* (London: Constable, 2004).

'Cato', *Guilty Men* (London: Victor Gollancz, 1940).

Catterall, Peter, *The Macmillan Diaries: The Cabinet Years, 1950–1957* (London: Macmillan, 2003).

Chisholm, Anne, and Michael Davie, *Beaverbrook: A Life* (London: Hutchinson, 1992).

Christiansen, Arthur, *Headlines All My Life* (London: Heinemann, 1961).

Churchill, Lord Randolph, *Men, Mines and Animals in South Africa* (London: Sampson, Low, Marston and Co. 1893).

Churchill, Randolph S., *Winston S. Churchill*, Vol. I: *Youth, 1874–1900* (London: Heinemann, 1966).

Churchill, Winston S., *My Early Life: A Roving Commission* (London: Macmillan, 1941; first published 1930).

Churchill, Winston S., *Thoughts and Adventures* (London: Odhams Press, 1947; first published 1932).

Churchill, Winston S., *Step By Step* (London: Odhams Press, 1947; first published 1939).

Churchill, Winston S., *The Second World War*, 6 vols (London: Cassell, 1948–54).

Churchill, Winston S., *The World Crisis, 1911–1918* (New York: Barnes and Noble Books, 1993).

Churchill, Winston S., *The World Crisis*, Vol. IV: *1918–1928: The Aftermath* (London: Bloomsbury, 2015; first published 1929).

Churchill, Winston S., *His Father's Son: The Life of Randolph Churchill* (London: Weidenfeld & Nicolson, 1996).

Churchill, Winston S., *The Boer War: London to Ladysmith Via Pretoria and Ian Hamilton's March* (London: Pimlico, 2002).

Citrine, Walter, *Men and Work* (Westport, CT: Greenwood Press, 1964).

Clarke, Peter, *The Cripps Version: The Life of Sir Stafford Cripps 1889–1952* (London: Allen Lane, 2002).

Clarke, Peter, *The Last Thousand Days of the British Empire* (London: Allen Lane, 2007).

Clarke, Peter, *Mr. Churchill's Profession: Statesman, Orator, Writer* (London: Bloomsbury, 2012);

Clarke, Tom, *My Northcliffe Diary* (London: Victor Gollancz, 1931).

Coates, W. P. and Zelda K. Coates, *A History of Anglo-Soviet Relations* (London: Lawrence & Wishart, 1944).

Cockerell, Michael, *Live from Number 10: The Inside Story of Prime Ministers and Television* (London: Faber & Faber, 1988).

Cockett, Richard, *Twilight of Truth: Chamberlain, Appeasement and the Manipulation of the Press* (New York: St. Martin's Press, 1989).

Cockett, Richard (ed.), *My Dear Max: The letters of Brendan Bracken to Lord Beaverbrook, 1925–1958* (London: Historians' Press, 1990).

Cohen, Michael J., *Churchill and the Jews* (2nd edn, London: Frank Cass, 2003).

Cohen, Ronald I., *Bibliography of the Writings of Sir Winston Churchill*, 3 vols (London: Thoemmes Continuum, 2006).

Colville, John, *The Fringes of Power: Downing Street Diaries, 1939–1955* (London: Hodder & Stoughton, 1985).

Coote, Colin, *Editorial: the Memoirs of Colin Coote* (London: Eyre & Spottiswoode, 1965).

Coote, Colin, *The Other Club* (London: Sidgwick & Jackson, 1971).

Coppolaro, Lucia, and Francine McKenzie (eds), *A Global History of Trade and Conflict Since 1500* (Basingstoke: Palgrave Macmillan, 2013).

Copsey, Nigel, and David Renton (eds), *British Fascism, the Labour Movement and the State* (London: Palgrave Macmillan, 2005), pp. 6–26.

Cross, J. A., *Lord Swinton* (Oxford: Clarendon Press, 1982).

Crowson, N. J., *Facing Fascism: The Conservative Party and the European Dictators, 1935–1940* (London: Routledge, 1997).

Crowson, N. J. (ed.), *Fleet Street, Press Barons and Politics: The Journals of Collin Brooks, 1932–1940* (Cambridge: Cambridge University Press for the Royal Historical Society, 1998).

Crozier, W. P., *Off the Record: Political Interviews 1933–1943*, ed. A. J. P. Taylor (London: Hutchinson, 1973).

Cudlipp, Hugh, *Walking on the Water* (London: Bodley Head, 1976), p. 208.

Cull, Nicholas John, *Selling War: The British Propaganda Campaign Against American 'Neutrality' in World War II* (Oxford: Oxford University Press, 1995).

Day, Robin, *Grand Inquisitor: Memoirs* (London: Pan Books, 1990).

Deedes, W. F., *Dear Bill: W. F. Deedes Reports* (London: Macmillan, 1997).

Dickson, W. K. L., *The Biograph in Battle* (London: T. Fisher Unwin, 1901).

Dilks, David (ed.), *The Diaries of Sir Alexander Cadogan O.M., 1938–1945* (London: Cassell, 1971).

Dilks, David, *'The Great Dominion': Winston Churchill in Canada, 1900–1954* (Toronto: Thomas Allen, 2005).

Dockter, Warren, *Churchill and the Islamic World* (London: I.B. Tauris, 2015).

Dockter, Warren (ed.), *Winston Churchill at the Telegraph* (London: Aurum Press, 2015).

Dudley Edwards, Ruth, *The Pursuit of Reason: The Economist 1843–1993* (London: Hamish Hamilton, 1993).

Dudley Edwards, Ruth, *Newspapermen: Hugh Cudlipp, Cecil Harmsworth King and the Glory Days of Fleet Street* (London: Secker & Warburg, 2003).

Eade, Charles (ed.), *Churchill By His Contemporaries* (London: Reprint Society, 1955; first published 1953).

Edgerton, David, *Warfare State: Britain, 1920–1970* (Cambridge: Cambridge University Press, 2006).

Farmelo, Graham, *Churchill's Bomb: How the United States Overtook Britain in the First Nuclear Arms Race* (London: Faber & Faber, 2013).

Farmer, Richard, *Cinemas and Cinemagoing in Wartime Britain, 1939–45: The Utility Dream Palace* (Manchester: Manchester University Press, 2016).

Farrar, Martin J., *News From the Front: War Correspondents on the Western Front 1914–1918* (Stroud: Sutton Publishing, 1998).

Foster, Roy, *Lord Randolph Churchill: A Political Life* (Oxford: Clarendon Press, 1981).

Francis, Martin, and Ina Zweiniger-Bargielowska (eds), *The Conservatives and British Society, 1880–1990* (Cardiff: University of Wales Press, 1996).

Fromkin, David, *A Peace to End All Peace: The Fall of the Ottoman Empire and the Creation of the Modern Middle East* (New York: Henry Holt & Co., 1989).

Fyfe, Hamilton, *Behind the Scenes of the Great Strike* (London: Labour Publishing Company, 1926).

Gardner, Brian, *Churchill in His Time: A Study in a Reputation 1939–1945* (London: Methuen, 1968).

Gibb, Andrew Dewar, *With Winston Churchill at the Front: Winston in the Trenches 1916* (Barnsley: Frontline Books, 2016; first published in 1924 under the pseudonym 'Captain X').

Gibbs, N. H., *Grand Strategy*, Vol. I: *Rearmament Policy* (London: HMSO, 1976).

Gilbert, Martin, *Winston S. Churchill*, Vol. III: *1914–1916* (London: Heinemann, 1971).

Gilbert, Martin, *Winston S. Churchill*, Vol. IV: *1917–1922* (London: Heinemann, 1975).

Gilbert, Martin, *Winston S. Churchill*, Vol. V (London: Heinemann, 1976).

Gilbert, Martin, *Prophet of Truth: Winston S. Churchill 1922–1939* (London: Heinemann, 1976).

Gilbert, Martin, *Winston S. Churchill*, Vol. VIII: *'Never Despair', 1945–1965* (London: Heinemann, 1988).

Gilbert, Martin, *Churchill: A Life* (London: Minerva, 1992).

Gilbert, Martin, *In Search of Churchill* (London: HarperCollins, 1994).

Gilbert, Martin (ed.), *Winston Churchill and Emery Reves: Correspondence 1937–1964* (Austin, TX: University of Texas Press, 1997).

Goldie, Grace Wyndham, *Facing The Nation: Television and Politics 1936–76* (London: Bodley Head, 1977).

Goodchild, James, *A Most Enigmatic War: R. V. Jones and the Genesis of British Scientific Intelligence 1939–45* (Solihull: Helion and Company Ltd., 2017).

Gorodetsky, Gabriel, *Grand Delusion: Stalin and the German Invasion of Russia* (New Haven, CT: Yale University Press, 1999).

Gorodetsky, Gabriel (ed.), *The Maisky Diaries: Red Ambassador to the Court of St. James's 1932–1943* (New Haven, CT: Yale University Press, 2015).

Gottlieb, Julie, *'Guilty Women', Foreign Policy and Appeasement in Inter-war Britain* (Basingstoke: Palgrave Macmillan, 2015).

Graebner, Walter, *My Dear Mr. Churchill* (London: Michael Joseph, 1965).

Grant Duff, Shiela, *The Parting of Ways: A Personal Account of the Thirties* (London: Peter Owen, 1982).

Griffiths, Andrew, *The New Journalism, the New Imperialism and the Fiction of Empire, 1870–1900* (Basingstoke: Palgrave Macmillan, 2015).

Harriman, Averell, and Elie Abel, *Special Envoy to Churchill and Stalin 1941–1946* (New York: Random House, 1975).

Harris, Jose, *William Beveridge: A Biography* (Oxford: Clarendon Press, 1997).

Harris, Wilson, *J.A. Spender* (London: Cassell, 1946).

Hart, Peter, *Mick: The Real Michael Collins* (London: Macmillan, 2005).

Hartwell, Lord, *William Camrose: Giant of Fleet Street* (London: Weidenfeld & Nicolson, 1992).

Harvey, John (ed.), *The War Diaries of Oliver Harvey 1941–1945* (London: Collins, 1978).

Hassall, Christopher, *Edward Marsh: Patron of the Arts: A Biography* (London: Longmans, 1959).

Havighurst, Alfred F., *Radical Journalist: H. W. Massingham (1860–1924)* (Cambridge: Cambridge University Press, 1974).

Hayton, Richard, and Andrew S. Crines (eds), *Conservative Orators from Baldwin to Cameron* (Manchester: Manchester University Press, 2015).

Hazlehurst, Cameron, and Christine Woodland (eds), *A Liberal Chronicle: Journals and Papers of J.A. Pease, 1st Lord Gainford 1908–1910* (London: Historians' Press, 1994) .

Hepburn, James (ed.), *Letters of Arnold Bennett*, vol. IV: *Family Letters* (Oxford: Oxford University Press, 1986).

Hermiston, Roger, *All Behind You, Winston: Churchill's Great Coalition 1940–45* (London: Aurum Press, 2016).

Hewitt, Martin, *The Dawn of the Cheap Press in Victorian Britain: The End of the 'Taxes on Knowledge', 1849–1869* (London: Bloomsbury, 2014).

Holt, Andrew, and Warren Dockter (eds), *Private Secretaries to the Prime Minister: Foreign Affairs from Churchill to Thatcher* (London: Routledge, 2017).

Hughes, W. M., *The Splendid Adventure: A Review of Empire Relations Within and Without the Commonwealth of Britannic Nations* (London Ernest Benn, 1929).

Hull, Cordell, *The Memoirs of Cordell Hull*, Vol. 2 (London: Hodder & Stoughton, 1948).

Hutcheson, Jr., John A., *Leo Maxse and the National Review, 1893–1914: Right-wing Politics and Journalism in the Edwardian Era* (New York: Garland Publishing, 1989).

Hyam, Ronald, *Elgin and Churchill at the Colonial Office 1905–1908: The Watershed of the Empire-Commonwealth* (London: Macmillan, 1968).

Ismay, Lord, *The Memoirs of General the Lord Ismay* (London: Heinemann, 1960).

Jackson, Daniel, *Popular Opposition to Irish Home Rule in Edwardian Britain* (Liverpool: Liverpool University Press, 2009).

Jenkins, Roy, *Asquith* (London: Fontana, 1967).

Jenkins, Roy, *Gladstone* (London: PaperMac, 1996).

Jones, Mervyn, *Michael Foot* (London: Victor Gollancz, 1994).

Jones, Thomas, *A Diary with Letters, 1931–1950* (London: Oxford University Press, 1954).

Kaul, Chandrika (ed.), *Media and the British Empire* (Basingstoke: Macmillan, 2006).

Kimball, Warren F. (ed.), *Churchill and Roosevelt: The Complete Correspondence*, Vol. II: *Alliance Forged, November 1942–February 1944* (Princeton, NJ: Princeton University Press, 1984).

Kinvig, Clifford, *Churchill's Crusade: The British Invasion of Russia 1918–1920* (London: Hambledon Continuum, 2006).

Klepak, Hal, *Churchill Comes of Age: Cuba 1895* (Stroud: Spellmount, 2015).

Klos, Felix, *Churchill's Last Stand: The Struggle to Unite Europe* (London: I.B.Tauris, 2017).

Koss, Stephen, *Fleet Street Radical:A. G. Gardiner and the Daily News* (Hamden, CT: Archon Boots, 1973).

Koss, Stephen, *The Rise and Fall of the Political Press in Britain*, Vol. 1: *The Nineteenth Century* (London: Hamish Hamilton, 1981).

Koss, Stephen, *The Rise and Fall of the Political Press in Britain*, Vol. 2: *The Twentieth Century* (London: Hamish Hamilton, 1984).

Kramnick, Isaac, and Barry Sheerman, *Harold Laski: A Life on the Left* (London: Hamish Hamilton, 1993).

Langworth, Richard M., *Winston Churchill, Myth and Reality:What He Actually Did and Said* (Jefferson, NC: McFarland, 2017).

Larres, Klaus, *Churchill's Cold War: The Politics of Personal Diplomacy* (New Haven, CT:Yale University Press, 2002).

Lloyd George, Frances, *The Years that Are Past* (London: Hutchinson, 1967).

Lough, David, *No More Champagne: Churchill and His Money* (New York: Picador, 2015).

Low, David, *Low's Autobiography* (London: Michael Joseph, 1956).

Lucy, Henry W., *Memories of Eight Parliaments* (London:William Heinemann, 1908).

McCallum, R. B., and Alison Readman, *The British General Election of 1945* (London: Oxford University Press, 1947).

McEwen, John M. (ed.), *The Riddell Diaries, 1908–1923* (London: Athlone Press, 1986).

MacKenzie, Norman and Jeanne MacKenzie (eds), *The Diary of Beatrice Webb*, vol. III: *1905–1924:The Power to Alter Things* (London:Virago, 1984).

McLachlan, Donald, *In the Chair: Barrington-Ward of The Times, 1927–1948* (London:Weidenfeld & Nicolson, 1971).

McLaine, Ian, *Ministry of Morale: Home Front Morale and the Ministry of Information in World War II* (London: George Allen & Unwin, 1979).

MacVeagh, Jeremiah, *Home Rule in a Nutshell:A Pocket Book for Speakers and Electors* (Dublin: Sealy, Bryers & Walker, 1911).

Margach, James, *The Abuse of Power:The War between Downing Street and the Media from Lloyd George to James Callaghan* (London:W.H. Allen, 1978).

Martin, John, *Downing Street:The War Years* (London: Bloomsbury, 1991).

Martin, Kingsley, *The British Public and the General Strike* (London: Hogarth Press, 1926).

Martin, Kingsley, *Editor: A Second Volume of Autobiography 1931–45* (London: Hutchinson, 1968).

Matthew, H. C. G., *Gladstone 1809–1898* (Oxford: Oxford University Press, 1897).

Middlemas, Keith (ed.), *Thomas Jones: Whitehall Diary*, 3 vols (London: Oxford University Press, 1969–71).

Millard, Candice, *Hero of the Empire: The Making of Winston Churchill* (London: Allen Lane, 2016).

Moir, Phyllis, *I Was Winston Churchill's Private Secretary* (New York: Walter Funk, 1941).

Montague Browne, Anthony, *Long Sunset: Memoirs of Winston Churchill's Last Private Secretary* (London: Cassell, 1995).

Moores, Chris, *Civil Liberties and Human Rights in Twentieth Century Britain* (Cambridge: Cambridge University Press, 2017).

Moran, Lord, *Winston Churchill: The Struggle for Survival, 1940–1965* (London: Constable, 1966).

Morgan, Kenneth O., *Consensus and Disunity: The Lloyd George Coalition Government 1918–1922* (Oxford: Clarendon Press, 1979).

Morris, A. J. A., *Reporting the First World War: Charles Repington, The Times and the Great War, 1914–1918* (Cambridge: Cambridge University Press, 2015).

Morton, H. V., *Atlantic Meeting* (London: Methuen, 1943).

Moulton, Mo, *Ireland and the Irish in Interwar England* (Cambridge: Cambridge University Press, 2014).

Murrow, Edward R., *This Is London* (New York: Shocken Books, 1985; first published 1941).

Nicholas, H. G., *The British General Election of 1950* (London: Macmillan, 1951).

Nicholas, H. G. (ed.), *Washington Despatches 1941–1945: Weekly Political Reports from the British Embassy* (Chicago: University of Chicago Press, 1981).

Nicolson, Nigel (ed.), *Harold Nicolson: Diaries and Letters, 1930–1939* (London: Collins, 1966).

Nicolson, Nigel (ed.), *Harold Nicolson: Diaries and Letters 1939–45* (London: Collins, 1967).

Norwich, John Julius (ed.), *The Duff Cooper Diaries 1915–1951* (London: Weidenfeld & Nicolson, 2005).

Orwell, Sonia, and Ian Angus (eds), *The Collected Essays, Journalism and Letters of George Orwell*, Vol. 2: *My Country Right or Left, 1940–1943* (Harmondsworth: Penguin, 1970; first published 1968).

Packwood, Allen, *How Churchill Waged War: The Most Challenging Decisions of the Second World War* (Barnsley: Frontline Books, 2018).

Pethick-Lawrence, Lord, *Fate Has Been Kind* (London: Hutchinson & Co., 1943).

Phillips, Adrian, *The King Who Had to Go: Edward VIII, Mrs Simpson and the Hidden Politics of the Abdication Crisis* (London: Biteback Publishing, 2016).

Pocock, J. G. A. *The Discovery of Islands: Essays in British History* (Cambridge: Cambridge University Press, 2005).

Pollock, John, *Kitchener* (London: Constable, 1998).

Ponting, Clive, *Churchill* (London: Sinclair-Stevenson, 1994).

Postgate, Raymond, *The Life of George Lansbury* (London: Longmans, Green & Co., 1951).

Potter, John, *Pim and Churchill's Map Room: Based on the Papers of Captain Richard Pim RNVR Supervisor of Churchill's Map Room 1939–1945* (Belfast: Northern Ireland War Memorial, 2014).

Potter, Simon J., *News and the British World: The Emergence of an Imperial Press System 1876–1922* (Oxford: Oxford University Press, 2003).

Pottle, Mark (ed.), *Champion Redoubtable: The Diaries and Letters of Violet Bonham Carter 1914–1945* (London: Weidenfeld & Nicolson, 1998).

Pottle, Mark (ed.), *Daring to Hope: The Diaries and Letters of Violet Bonham Carter 1946–1969* (London: Weidenfeld & Nicolson, 2000).

Pound, Reginald, *The Strand Magazine 1891–1950* (London: Heinemann, 1966).

Prior, Robin, *Churchill's 'World Crisis' as History* (London: Croom Helm, 1983).

Pugh, Martin, *'Hurrah for the Blackshirts!' Facsists and Fascism in Britain Between the Wars* (London: Cape, 2005).

Ramsden, John, *Man of the Century: Winston Churchill and His Legend Since 1945* (London: HarperCollins, 2002).

Read, Donald, *The Power of News: The History of Reuters* (Oxford: Oxford University Press, 1992).

Read, Simon, *Winston Churchill Reporting: Adventures of a Young War Correspondent* (Boston, MA: Da Capo Press, 2015).

Rees-Mogg, William, *Memoirs* (London: HarperPress, 2011).

Regan, John M., *Myth and the Irish State: Historical Problems and Other Essays* (Sallins, Co. Kildare: Irish Academic Press, 2013).

Repington, Charles à Court, *Vestigia: Reminiscences of War and Peace* (Boston, MA: Houghton Mifflin, 1919).

Repington, Charles à Court, *The First World War 1914–1918*, Vol. 1 (London: Constable, 1920).

Reston, James, *Deadline: A Memoir* (New York: Random House, 1991).

Reynolds, David, *In Command of History: Churchill Fighting and Writing the Second World War* (London: Allen Lane, 2004).

Rhodes James, Robert (ed.), *Memoirs of a Conservative: J. C. C. Davidson's Memoirs and Papers, 1910–37* (London: Weidenfeld & Nicolson, 1969).

Rhodes James, Robert (ed.), *Winston S. Churchill: His Complete Speeches, 1897–1963*, 8 vols (New York: Chelsea House, 1974).

Rhodes James, Robert (ed.), *'Chips': The Diaries of Sir Henry Channon* (London: Weidenfeld & Nicolson, 1993).

Roberts, Andrew, *Salisbury: Victorian Titan* (London: Weidenfeld & Nicolson, 1999).

Roberts, Andrew, *Churchill: Walking With Destiny* (London: Allen Lane, 2018).

Roberts, Brian, *Churchills in Africa* (London: Thistle Publishing, 2017).

Robinson, Nick, *Live From Downing Street: The Inside Story of Politics, Power and the Media* (London: Transworld Publishers, 2012).

Roosevelt, Elliott, *As He Saw It* (New York: Duell, Sloan and Pearce, 1946).

Rose, Jonathan, *The Literary Churchill: Author, Reader, Actor* (New Haven, CT: Yale University Press, 2014).

Rosebery, Earl of, *Lord Randolph Churchill* (London: Arthur L. Humphreys, 1906),.

Rosenman, Samuel I. (ed.), *The Public Papers and Addresses of Franklin D. Roosevelt, 1941 Volume: The Call to Battle Stations* (New York: Harper & Brothers, 1950).

Ruane, Kevin, *Churchill and the Bomb in War and Cold War* (London: Bloomsbury, 2016).

Rüger, Jan, *The Great Naval Game: Britain and Germany in the Age of Empire* (Cambridge: Cambridge University Press, 2007).

Sandys, Celia, *Churchill Wanted Dead or Alive* (London: HarperCollins, 1999).

Schneer, Jonathan, *Ministers at War: Winston Churchill and His War Cabinet* (London: Oneworld Books, 2014).

Self, Robert, *The Austen Chamberlain Diary Letters: The Correspondence of Sir Austen Chamberlain With His Sisters Hilda and Ida, 1916–1937* (Cambridge: Cambridge University Press, 1995).

Self, Robert (ed.), *The Neville Chamberlain Diary Letters*, 4 vols (Aldershot: Ashgate, 2002–5).

Shawcross, Hartley, *Life Sentence: The Memoirs of Lord Shawcross* (London: Constable, 1995).

Shelden, Michael, *Young Titan: The Making of Winston Churchill* (London: Simon & Schuster, 2013).

Sherwood, Robert E., *The White House Papers of Harry L. Hopkins*, 2 vols (London: Eyre & Spottiswoode, 1948–9).

Shibutani, Tamotsu, *Improvised News: A Sociological Study of Rumor* (Indianapolis, IN: Bobbs-Merrill, 1966).

Shirer, William L., *Berlin Diary: The Journal of a Foreign Correspondent 1934–1941* (London: Hamish Hamilton, 1941).

Shonfield, Andrew, *British Economic Policy Since the War* (Harmondsworth: Penguin, 1958)

Sitwell, Osbert, *The Winstonburg Line: 3 Satires* (London: Hendersons, 1920).

Smart, Nick (ed.), *The Diaries and Letters of Robert Bernays, 1932–1939* (Lewiston/Queenston/Lampeter: Edwin Mellen, 1996).

Soames, Mary (ed.), *Speaking for Themselves: The Personal Letters of Winston and Clementine Churchill* (London: Doubleday, 1998).

Speer, Albert, *Inside the Third Reich* (London: Sphere Books, 1971).

Spender, J. A., *Life, Journalism and Politics*, Vol. I (London: Cassell, 1927).

Spiers, Edward M. (ed.), *Sudan: The Reconquest Reappraised* (London: Frank Cass, 1998).

Stafford, David, *Churchill and Secret Service* (London: Abacus, 2000).

Stebbing, Edward, *Diary of a Decade 1939–50* (Lewes: Book Guild Ltd., 1998).

Stein, Leonard, *The Balfour Declaration* (New York: Simon and Schuster, 1961).

Stourton, Edward, *Auntie's War: The BBC During the Second World War* (London: Doubleday, 2017).

Stuart, Charles (ed.), *The Reith Diaries* (London: Collins, 1975).

Taylor, A. J. P. (ed.), *Lloyd George: A Diary by Frances Stevenson* (New York: Harper & Row, 1971).

Taylor, S. J., *The Great Outsiders: Northcliffe, Rothermere and the Daily Mail* (London: Weidenfeld & Nicolson, 1996).

Thackeray, David, *Conservatism for the Democratic Age: Conservative Cultures and the Challenges of Mass Politics in Early Twentieth-Century England* (Manchester: Manchester University Press, 2013).

Thomas, James, *Popular Newspapers, the Labour Party and British Politics* (London: Routledge, 2005).

Thompson, James, *British Political Culture and the Idea of 'Public Opinion', 1867–1914* (Cambridge: Cambridge University Press, 2013).

Thompson, J. Lee, *Northcliffe: Press Baron in Politics, 1865–1922* (London: John Murray, 2000).

Thomson, George P., *Blue Pencil Admiral: The Inside Story of the Press Censorship* (London: Sampson, Low, Marston & Co., n.d. but 1947).

Thorpe, Andrew, and Richard Toye (eds), *Parliament and Politics in the Age of Asquith and Lloyd George: The Diaries of Cecil Harmsworth, MP, 1909–1922* (Cambridge: Cambridge University Press for the Royal Historical Society, 2016).

Tippett, Maria, *Portrait in Light and Shadow: The Life of Yousuf Karsh* (New Haven, CT: Yale University Press, 2007).

Toye, Richard, *Lloyd George and Churchill: Rivals for Greatness* (London: Macmillan, 2007).

Toye, Richard, *The Roar of the Lion: The Untold Story of Churchill's World War II Speeches* (Oxford: Oxford University Press, 2013).

Toye, Richard, and Julie Gottlieb (eds), *Making Reputations: Power, Persuasion and the Individual in Modern British Politics* (London: I.B. Tauris, 2005).

Travis, David, *Karsh: Beyond the Camera* (Jaffrey, NH: David R. Godine, 2012).

Trentmann, Frank, *Free Trade Nation: Commerce, Consumption, and Civil Society in Modern Britain* (Oxford: Oxford University Press, 2008).

Wainewright, Will, *Reporting on Hitler: Rothay Reynolds and the British Press in Nazi Germany* (London: Biteback Publishing, 2017).

Watson, Alan, *Churchill's Legacy: Two Speeches to Save the World* (London: Bloomsbury, 2016).

Wheatley, Ben, *British Intelligence and Hitler's Empire in the Soviet Union, 1941–1945* (London: Bloomsbury Academic, 2017).

White, Philip, *Churchill's Cold War: How the Iron Curtain Speech Shaped the Post-war World* (London: Duckworth Overlook, 2012).

Wiener, Joel H., *The Americanization of the British Press, 1830s-1914: Speed in the Age of Transatlantic Journalism* (Basingstoke: Palgrave Macmillan, 2011).

Wiener, Joel H., and Mark Hampton (eds), *Anglo-American Media Interactions, 1850–2000* (Basingstoke: Palgrave Macmillan, 2007).

Wilkinson, Glenn R., *Depictions and Images of War in Edwardian Newspapers, 1899–1914* (Basingstoke: Palgrave Macmillan, 2003).

Wilkinson, Nicholas, *Secrecy and the Media: The Official History of the D-Notice Committee* (London: Routledge, 2009).

Williams, Francis, *Nothing So Strange: An Autobiography* (London: Cassell, 1970).

Williamson, Philip, *Stanley Baldwin: Conservative Leadership and National Values* (Cambridge: Cambridge University Press, 1999).

Williamson, Philip, and Edward Baldwin (eds), *Baldwin Papers: A Conservative Statesman, 1908–1947* (Cambridge: Cambridge University Press, 2004).

Wilson, Charles, *First With The News: The History of W.H. Smith 1792–1972* (London: Guild Publishing, 1985).

Wilson, Keith (ed.), *The Rasp of War: The Letters of H. A. Gwynne to the Countess Bathurst, 1914–1918* (London: Sidgwick & Jackson, 1988).

Wilson, Trevor (ed.), *The Political Diaries of C.P. Scott 1911–1928* (London: Collins, 1970).

Wing, Sandra Koa (ed.), *Our Longest Days: A People's History of the Second World War* (London: Profile Books, 2008; first published 2007).

Wolff, Michael (ed.), *The Collected Essays of Sir Winston Churchill*, 4 vols (London: Library of Imperial History, 1976).

Woods, Frederick (ed.), *Young Winston's Wars: The Original Despatches of Winston S. Churchill, War Correspondent, 1897–1900* (London: Leo Cooper, 1972).

Woods, Frederick, *Artillery of Words: Writings of Sir Winston Churchill* (London: Leo Cooper, 1992).

Wrench, John Evelyn, *Geoffrey Dawson and Our Times* (London: Hutchinson, 1955).

Wright, Patrick, *Iron Curtain: From Stage to Cold War* (Oxford: Oxford University Press, 2007).

Young, Kenneth, *Churchill and Beaverbrook: A Study in Friendship and Politics* (London: Eyre & Spottiswoode, 1966).

Young, Kenneth (ed.), *The Diaries of Sir Bruce Lockhart*, Vol. I: *1915–1938* (London: Macmillan, 1973).

Zec, Donald, *Don't Lose It Again! The Life and Wartime Cartoons of Philip Zec* (London: Political Cartoon Society, 2005).

JOURNAL ARTICLES

Adamthwaite, Anthony, 'The British Government and the Media, 1937–1938', *Journal of Contemporary History*, 18 (1983), pp. 281–97.

Allbeson, Tom, 'Visualizing Wartime Destruction and Postwar Reconstruction: Herbert Mason's Photograph of St. Paul's Reevaluated', *Journal of Modern History*, 87 (2015), pp. 532–78.

Arnett, Jeffery, 'Winston Churchill, the Quintessential Sensation Seeker', *Political Psychology*, 12:4 (December 1991), pp. 609–21;

Beers, Laura Dumond, 'Whose Opinion? Changing Attitudes Towards Opinion Polling in British Politics, 1937–1964', *Twentieth Century British History*, 17 (2006), pp. 177–205.

Bell, P. M. H., 'Censorship, Propaganda and Public Opinion: The Case of the Katyn Graves, 1943', *Transactions of the Royal Historical Society*, 39 (1989), pp. 63–83.

Bingham, Adrian, '"Stop the Flapper Vote Folly": Lord Rothermere, the Daily Mail and the Equalization of the Franchise 1927–8', *Twentieth Century British History*, 13:1 (2002), pp. 17–37.

Bingham, Adrian, 'The Digitization of Newspaper Archives: Opportunities and Challenges for Historians', *Twentieth Century British History*, 21 (2010), pp. 225–31.

Brown, David, 'Compelling but not Controlling? Palmerston and the Press, 1846–1855', *History*, 86:281 (January 2001), pp. 41–61.

Bulpitt, Jim, and Peter Burnham, 'Operation Robot and the British Political Economy in the Early-1950s: The Politics of Market Strategies', *Contemporary British History*, 13 (1999), pp. 1–31.

Calkins, Laura M., 'Patrolling the Ether: US–UK Open Source Intelligence Cooperation and the BBC's Emergence as an Intelligence Agency, 1939–1948', *Intelligence and National Security*, 26 (2011), pp. 1–22.

Carlisle, Rodney, 'The Foreign Policy Views of an Isolationist Press Lord: W.R. Hearst and the International Crisis, 1936–41, *Journal of Contemporary History*, 9 (1974), pp. 217–27.

Casey, Christopher A., 'Deglobalization and the Disintegration of the European News System, 1918–34', *Journal of Contemporary History*, 53 (2018), pp. 267–91.

Chapman, James, '"The Life and Death of Colonel Blimp" (1943) Reconsidered', *Historical Journal of Film, Radio and Television*, 15 (1995).

Costigliola, Frank, 'Pamela Churchill, Wartime London, and the Making of the Special Relationship', *Diplomatic History*, 36 (2012), pp. 753–62.

Dockter, Warren, and Richard Toye, 'Who Commanded History? Sir John Colville, Churchillian Networks, and the "Castlerosse Affair"', *Journal of Contemporary History*, 54:2 (2018), pp. 401–19.

Eckardt, Michael, 'Pioneers in South African Film History: Thelma Gutsche's Tribute to William Kennedy Laurie Dickson, The Man Who Filmed The Boer War', *Historical Journal of Film, Radio and Television*, 25 (2005), pp. 637–4.

Egerton, George W., 'The Lloyd George "War Memoirs": A Study in the Politics of Memory', *Journal of Modern History*, 60:1 (March 1988), pp. 55–94.

Foster, A. J., 'The Politicians, Public Opinion and the Press: The Storm over British Military Intervention in Greece in December 1944', *Journal of Contemporary History*, 19 (1984), pp. 453–94.

Foster, Alan, 'The Beaverbrook Press and Appeasement: The Second Phase', *European History Quarterly*, 21 (1991), pp. 5–38.

Francis, Martin, 'Tears, Tantrums, and Bared Teeth: The Emotional Economy of Three Conservative Prime Ministers, 1951–1963', *Journal of British Studies*, 41 (2002), pp. 354–87.

Gottlieb, Julie V., 'Neville Chamberlain's Umbrella: "Object" Lessons in the History of Appeasement', *Twentieth Century British History*, 27 (2016), pp. 357–88.

Hannon, Brian P. D., 'Creating the Correspondent: How the BBC Reached the Frontline in the Second World War', *Historical Journal of Film, Radio and Television*, 28 (2008), pp. 175–94.

Hicks, Marianne, 'NO WAR THIS YEAR: Selkirk Panton and the Editorial Policy of the Daily Express, 1938–39', *Media History*, 14 (2008), pp. 167–83.

Hodgson, Guy, 'Neville Henderson, Appeasement and the Press: Fleet Street and the build-up to the Second World War', *Journalism Studies*, 8 (2007), pp. 320–34.

Hollins, T. J., 'The Conservative Party and Film Propaganda between the Wars', *English Historical Review*, 96 (1981), pp. 359–69.

Hucker, Daniel, 'Public Opinion, the Press and the Failed Anglo-Franco-Soviet Negotiations of 1939', *International History Review*, 40 (2018), pp. 65–85.

Johnstone, Andrew, 'Isolationism and Internationalism in American Foreign Relations', *Journal of Transatlantic Studies*, 9 (2011), pp. 7–20.

Jones, Harriet, ' "This is Magnificent!": 300,000 Houses a Year and the Tory Revival after 1945', *Contemporary British History*, 14 (2000), pp. 99–121.

Lawrence, Jon, 'Forging a Peaceable Kingdom: War, Violence, and Fear of Brutalization in Post–First World War Britain', *Journal of Modern History*, 75 (2003), pp. 557–89.

Love, Gary, 'The Periodical Press and the Intellectual Culture of Conservatism in Inter-War Britain', *Historical Journal*, 57 (2014), pp. 1027–56.

Ma, Tehyun, 'A Chinese Beveridge Plan: The Discourse of Social Security and the Post-War Reconstruction of China', *European Journal of East Asian Studies*, 11 (2012), pp. 329–49.

MacDonagh, Michael, 'Can We Rely on Our War News?', *Fortnightly Review*, 63 (1898), pp. 612–25.

McEwen, J. M., 'Northcliffe and Lloyd George at War, 1914–1918', *Historical Journal*, 24 (1981), pp. 651–72.

Matthews, J. J., 'Heralds of the Imperialistic Wars', *Military Affairs*, 19 (1955), pp. 145–55.

Milligan, Ian, 'Illusionary Order: Online Databases, Optical Character Recognition, and Canadian History, 1997–2010', *Canadian Historical Review*, 94 (2013), pp. 540–69;

Morgan, Kenneth O., 'Lloyd George's Premiership: A Study in "Prime Ministerial Government"', *Historical Journal*, 13:1 (March 1970), pp. 130–57.

Morgan, Kenneth O., 'The Media and the Boer War (1899–1902)', *Twentieth Century British History*, 13 (2002), pp. 1–16.

Morgan-Owen, David Gethin, 'Cooked up in the Dinner Hour? Sir Arthur Wilson's War Plan, Reconsidered', *English Historical Review*, 130 (2015), pp. 865–906.

Neumann, Roderick P., 'Churchill and Roosevelt in Africa: Performing and Writing Landscapes of Race, Empire, and Nation', *Annals of the Association of American Geographers*, 103 (2013), pp. 1371–88.

Nicholson, Bob, '"You Kick the Bucket; We Do the Rest!": Jokes and the Culture of Reprinting in the Transatlantic Press', *Journal of Victorian Culture*, 17 (2012), pp. 273–86.

Ohlinger, Gustavus, 'Winston Spencer Churchill: A Midnight Interview', *Michigan Quarterly Review*, 5:2 (1966), pp. 75–9.

Owen, Nicholas, '"Facts Are Sacred": The Manchester Guardian and Colonial Violence, 1930–1932', *Journal of Modern History*, 84 (2012), pp. 643–78.

Potter, Simon J., 'Jingoism, Public Opinion, and the New Imperialism: Newspapers and Imperial Rivalries at the fin de siècle', *Media History*, 20 (2014), pp. 34–50.

Pressman, Matthew, 'Ambivalent Accomplices: How the Press Handled FDR's Disability and How FDR Handled the Press', *Journal of the Historical Society*, 13 (2013), pp. 325–59.

Pronay, Nicholas, 'British Newsreels in the 1930s 1.Audiences and Producers', *History*, 56 (1971), pp. 411–17.

Pronay, Nicholas, 'British Newsreels in the 1930s 2: Their Policies and Impact', *History*, 57 (1972), pp. 63–72.

Pugh, Martin, 'The *Daily Mirror* and the Revival of Labour 1935–1945', *Twentieth Century British History*, 9 (1998), pp. 420–38.

Putnam, Lara, 'The Transnational and the Text-Searchable: Digitized Sources and the Shadows They Cast', *American Historical Review*, 121 (2016), pp. 377–402.

Resis, Albert, 'The Churchill–Stalin Secret "Percentages" Agreement on the Balkans, Moscow, October 1944', *American Historical Review*, 83:2 (April 1978), pp. 368–87.

Ryan, Henry B., 'A New Look at Churchill's "Iron Curtain" Speech', *Historical Journal*, 22 (1979), pp. 895–920.

Short, K. R. M. , 'A Note on BBC Television News and the Munich Crisis, 1938', *Historical Journal of Film, Radio and Television*, 9 (1989), pp. 165–79.

Smith, Robert W., 'David Lloyd George's Limehouse Address', *Central States Speech Journal*, 18 (1967), pp. 169–76.

Stead, W. T., 'Government by Journalism', *Contemporary Review*, 49, May 1886, pp. 653–74.

Stearn, Roger T., 'G. W. Steevens and the Message of Empire', *Journal of Imperial and Commonwealth History*, 17 (1989), pp. 210–31.

Summerfield, Penny, 'Mass-Observation: Social Research or Social Movement?', *Journal of Contemporary History*, 20: 3 (July 1985), pp. 439–52.

Taylor, Andrew J., '"The Record of the 1950s is Irrelevant":The Conservative Party, Electoral Strategy and Opinion Research, 1945–64', *Contemporary British History*, 17 (2003), pp. 81–110.

Thorpe, Andrew, '"In a Rather Emotional State"? The Labour Party and British Intervention in Greece, 1944–5', *English Historical Review*, 493 (2006), pp. 1075–105.

Toye, Richard, 'Churchill and Britain's "Financial Dunkirk"', *Twentieth Century British History*, 15 (2004), pp. 329–60.

Toye, Richard, 'Winston Churchill's "Crazy Broadcast": Party, Nation, and the 1945 Gestapo Speech', *Journal of British Studies*, 49: 3 (July 2010), pp. 655–80.

Toye, Richard, '"Phrases Make History Here": Churchill, Ireland and the Rhetoric of Empire', *Journal of Imperial and Commonwealth History*, 30 (2010), pp. 549–70.

Toye, Richard, '"The Riddle of the Frontier": Winston Churchill, the Malakand Field Force and the Rhetoric of Imperial Expansion', *Historical Research*, 84 (2011), pp. 493–512.

Ward, Stuart, 'The European Provenance of Decolonization', *Past & Present* 230 (2016), pp. 227–60.

Webb, Clive, 'Reluctant Partners: African Americans and the Origins of the Special Relationship', *Journal of Transatlantic Studies*, 1 (2016), pp. 350–64.

Wilson, Keith, 'The Agadir Crisis, the Mansion House Speech, and the Double-Edgedness of Agreements', *Historical Journal*, 15:3 (September 1972), pp. 513–32.

Young, John W., 'Conservative Leaders, Coalition, and Britain's Decision for War in 1914', *Diplomacy & Statecraft*, 25 (2014), pp. 214–39.

THESES

Hannon, Brian P. D., 'The Story Behind the Stories: British and Dominion War Correspondents in the Western Theatres of the Second World War', PhD thesis, University of Edinburgh, 2015.

Hill, Richard, 'The Development and Use of Armoured Vehicles during the First World War, with Special Reference to the Role of Winston Churchill', PhD thesis, Exeter University, forthcoming.

Kareem, Mohammad, 'The Shaping of the Middle East: British Policy and the Kurdish Question, 1914–1923', PhD thesis, University of Exeter, 2017.

Richards, Huw George, 'Constriction, Conformity and Control:The Taming of the Daily Herald 1921–30', PhD thesis, Open University, 1992.

Thévoz, Seth Alexander, 'Winston Churchill's 1922 electoral defeat in Dundee', MA thesis, King's College, London, 2009.

Index

For the benefit of digital users, indexed terms that span two pages (e.g., 52–53) may, on occasion, appear on only one of those pages.